THE DISGUISED RULER IN
SHAKESPEARE AND
HIS CONTEMPORARIES

Studies in Performance and Early Modern Drama

General Editor's Preface

Helen Ostovich, McMaster University

Performance assumes a string of creative, analytical, and collaborative acts that, in defiance of theatrical ephemerality, live on through records, manuscripts, and printed books. The monographs and essay collections in this series offer original research which addresses theatre histories and performance histories in the context of the sixteenth and seventeenth century life. Of especial interest are studies in which women's activities are a central feature of discussion as financial or technical supporters (patrons, musicians, dancers, seamstresses, wigmakers, or 'gatherers'), if not authors or performers per se. Welcome too are critiques of early modern drama that not only take into account the production values of the plays, but also speculate on how intellectual advances or popular culture affect the theatre.

The series logo, selected by my colleague Mary V. Silcox, derives from Thomas Combe's duodecimo volume, *The Theater of Fine Devices* (London, 1592), Emblem VI, sig. B. The emblem of four masks has a verse which makes claims for the increasing complexity of early modern experience, a complexity that makes interpretation difficult. Hence the corresponding perhaps uneasy rise in sophistication:

> Masks will be more hereafter in request,
> And grow more deare than they did heretofore.

No longer simply signs of performance 'in play and jest', the mask has become the 'double face' worn 'in earnest' even by 'the best' of people, in order to manipulate or profit from the world around them. The books stamped with this design attempt to understand the complications of performance produced on stage and interpreted by the audience, whose experiences outside the theatre may reflect the emblem's argument:

> Most men do use some colour'd shift
> For to conceal their craftie drift.

Centuries after their first presentations, the possible performance choices and meanings they engender still stir the imaginations of actors, audiences, and readers of early plays. The products of scholarly creativity in this series, I hope, will also stir imaginations to new ways of thinking about performance.

The Disguised Ruler in Shakespeare and His Contemporaries

KEVIN A. QUARMBY

ASHGATE

Published by
Ashgate Publishing Limited
Wey Court East
Union Road
Farnham
Surrey, GU9 7PT
England

Ashgate Publishing Company
Suite 420
101 Cherry Street
Burlington
VT 05401-4405
USA

www.ashgate.com

British Library Cataloguing in Publication Data
Quarmby, Kevin A.
  The disguised ruler in Shakespeare and his contemporaries. – (Studies in performance and early modern drama)
  1. Kings and rulers in literature. 2. Disguise in literature. 3. English drama – Early modern and Elizabethan, 1500–1600 – History and criticism. 4. Shakespeare, William, 1564–1616 – Characters – Kings and rulers. 5. Marston, John, 1575?–1634 – Characters – Kings and rulers. 6. Middleton, Thomas, d. 1627 – Characters – Kings and rulers. 7. Sharpham, Edward, 1576–1608 – Characters – Kings and rulers. 8. Literature and society – England – History – 16th century. 9. Literature and society – England – History – 17th century.
  I. Title II. Series
  822.3'09352621-dc22

Library of Congress Cataloging-in-Publication Data
Quarmby, Kevin A.
  The disguised ruler in Shakespeare and his contemporaries / by Kevin A. Quarmby.
    p. cm. — (Studies in performance and early modern drama)
  Includes bibliographical references and index.
  ISBN 978-1-4094-0159-9 (hardcover: alk. paper) — ISBN 978-1-4094-0160-5 (ebook)
  1. English drama—Early modern and Elizabethan, 1500–1600—History and criticism. 2. English drama—17th century—History and criticism. 3. Disguise in literature. 4. Kings and rulers in literature. 5. Plots (Drama, novel, etc.) 6. Great Britain—History—Elizabeth, 1558–1603. 7. Great Britain—History—James I, 1603–1625. I. Title.
  PR658.P6Q83 2012
  822'.3093581—dc23
                                                      2011035400
ISBN: 9781409401599 (hbk)
ISBN: 9781409401605 (ebk)

8 John Adam Street
London WC2N 6EZ

MIX
Paper from
responsible sources
FSC
www.fsc.org   FSC® C018575

Printed and bound in Great Britain by the
MPG Books Group, UK

For Liza

Contents

List of Figures

Preface and Acknowledgements

This book owes all to the dedication and support of colleagues and friends. Foremost among these are Gordon McMullan and Ann Thompson of the London Shakespeare Centre, King's College London, whose encouragement and advice have proved invaluable. My thanks also to Richard Proudfoot, Sonia Massai and John Stokes. Research is a lonely enterprise without the moral and practical support of fellow scholars. To Anne Gill, Fiona Ritchie, Hugh Adlington, Sarah Dustagheer, Gwilym Jones, Rebecca Calcagno and Abigail Rokison, I remain fondly indebted. Special thanks go to Lucy Munro for offering friendly advice since the project's inception. Elsewhere, I owe a debt of gratitude to Gabriel Egan, Brett Hirsch, Janelle Jenstad, Sara Jane Bailes and Matthew Dimmock, as well as to Patrick Spottiswoode and Farah Karim-Cooper of Shakespeare's Globe, London. Sheila Cavanagh from Emory University deserves special mention and thanks for her practical assistance and friendship. Elsewhere at Emory, I extend thanks to Holli Semetko of the Halle Institute, as well as Alan Cattier, Harry Rusche and Wayne H. Morse Jr. In the UK, the theatre directors Dominic Cooke (Royal Court Theatre) and Gregory Doran (Royal Shakespeare Company) offered invaluable advice, as did Stephen Unwin and Sir Peter Hall of the Rose Theatre, Kingston. Special thanks, however, must go to Sir Richard Eyre for giving me the practical experience of performing, in Shakespeare's *Hamlet* at the Royal Court and at The Royal National Theatre, London.

At Ashgate, my editor, Whitney Feininger, and publishing manager, Erika Gaffney, gave friendly advice and professional assistance throughout. I must also thank the unknown reviewer of the draft manuscript whose opinions and excellent suggestions are reflected throughout this book. My thanks also to Cambridge University Press. Chapter 4 of this book has drawn upon material from my article, 'Narrative of Negativity: Whig Historiography and the Spectre of King James in *Measure for Measure*', in Peter Holland (ed.), *Shakespeare Survey, Volume 64* (2011) © Cambridge University Press, reproduced with permission. I am grateful to the Saint Louis Art Museum for permission to reproduce the book's cover image, a painting by Francisco de Zurbarán (Spanish, 1598–1664), *St Francis Contemplating a Skull* (c. 1635), 91.4 x 30.5 cm (36 x 12 in.), oil on canvas, Museum Purchase 47:1941.

Farther afield, I extend thanks to Gary Taylor, John Lavagnino, Stephen A. Cohen, Jenny Wormald, Peter Hyland and Helen Cooper for offering their work in draft form. Similarly, thanks to Tiffany Stern, Martin Wiggins, Jonathan Bate, John Jowett, Andrew Gurr, Andrew Hadfield, Tom Healy, Neil Taylor and Michael J. Redmond for their insightful comments and advice. Equally supportive have been Emma Smith, Peter Holland, Carol Chillington Rutter, Michael Dobson, Russ McDonald, Boika Sokolova, Nicoleta Cinpoeş, Perry Mills, John Creaser and Martin Butler. Many arguments within this book developed from conferences and post-conference discussions with eminent scholars. My thanks therefore to Sukanta Chaudhuri, Raphael Lyne, Subha Mukherji, Paul Edmondson, Paul Prescott and Peter J. Smith. I am also grateful to Ròzsa Réka and Monica Gianola for their invaluable assistance in translating Guarini's sixteenth-century Italian text. Unless otherwise directed, translations are my own. All mistakes, therefore, are likewise entirely mine.

There is no debt greater than to my family, who have been constant in their support throughout this project. My wife Liza, and my children Belinda, Edward, Hannah and Sarah, as well as my stepson Christopher, have all shared in the creative process. The determination and fortitude of my sister, Lesley, remains a constant inspiration to me. It is, though, my father, Herbert 'Bert' Quarmby, who died when this book was in its infancy, to whom the greatest debt is owed. This work is in remembrance of him.

Before continuing, certain presentation choices must be noted. Throughout this book (and unless otherwise indicated), the original spelling of texts is preserved. The early modern 'v' for 'u' is retained (and vice versa), as well as uppercase 'I' for 'J'. Other amendments are indicated by square brackets, while a question mark in square brackets [?], immediately following an author or repertory name, indicates conjectural or disputed information. Long 's' has been regularized and black-letter converted to roman type. The retention of original spelling and pagination is possible because of the Chadwyck-Healey Database *Early English Books Online* (*EEBO*).[1] Original spelling has, however, created a problem of referencing. To facilitate cross-referencing, signature references for all primary text quotations are indicated, followed by act, scene and line numbers from modern critical editions (where available), as specified in the footnotes. Where no modern editions exist, signature references from the primary texts are as reproduced in *EEBO*. All Shakespeare First Folio plays are quoted from Hinman's facsimile edition using the 'Through Line Number' system (TLN).[2] In addition, modernized act, scene and line numbers are based on the *Norton Shakespeare* (unless otherwise stated).[3] Where the text is not drawn from the First Folio, as with the Shakespeare plays in Quarto, signature references are supplied as they appear in *EEBO*, a *Short-Title Catalogue* number is indicated where appropriate, as well as line numbers from modern editions as credited in the footnotes.

Kevin A. Quarmby, May 2011

---

[1]   *Early English Books Online* (*EEBO*), Chadwyck-Healey Database (Proquest) <http://eebo.chadwyck.com/home> [accessed 6 May 2011). Open access databases vital for this study include Ian Lancashire (ed.), *Lexicons of Early Modern English* (*LEME*) (2011), University of Toronto Press <http://leme.library.utoronto.ca/> [accessed 6 May 2011], and *Records of Early English Drama* (*REED*) (1979–2010) <http://www.reed.utoronto.ca/index.html> [accessed 6 May 2011], with *REED* project texts available at <http://www.archive.org/search.php?query=records%20of%20early%20english%20drama%20AND%20collection%3Atoronto> [accessed 6 May 2011].

[2]   Charlton Hinman (ed.), *The First Folio of Shakespeare* (New York, 1968).

[3]   Stephen Greenblatt (gen. ed.), Walter Cohen, Jean E. Howard and Katharine Eisaman Maus (eds), *The Norton Shakespeare*, 2nd edn (New York, 2008).

List of Abbreviations

Arber   Edward Arber (ed.), *A Transcript of the Registers of the Company of Stationers of London: 1554–1640 A.D.* (5 vols, London, 1875–79; Birmingham, 1894)

Bentley, *JCS*   Gerald E. Bentley, *The Jacobean and Caroline Stage* (7 vols, Oxford, 1941–68)

BJJ   *Ben Jonson Journal*

BL   British Library

BLO   Bodleian Library, Oxford

Chambers, *ES*   E.K. Chambers, *The Elizabethan Stage* (4 vols, Oxford, 1923)

EHR   *English Historical Review*

ELH   *English Literary History*

ELN   *English Language Notes*

ELR   *English Literary Renaissance*

HJ   *The Historical Journal*

JBS   *Journal of British Studies*

JMH   *Journal of Medieval History*

LEME   Ian Lancashire (ed.), *Lexicons of Early Modern English*, University of Toronto

MLQ   *Modern Language Quarterly*

N&Q   *Notes and Queries*

NLH   *New Literary History*

ODNB   *Oxford Dictionary of National Biography*

PBSA   *Papers of the Bibliographical Society of America*

PMLA   *Publications of the Modern Language Association*

PRO	Public Records Office, London
REED	*Records of Early English Drama,* University of Toronto
RES	*The Review of English Studies*
RN	*Renaissance News*
RQ	*Renaissance Quarterly*
ROMARD	*Research Opportunities in Medieval and Renaissance Drama*
SEL	*Studies in English Literature*
SP	*Studies in Philology*
SQ	*Shakespeare Quarterly*
SQF	Shakespeare Quartos in Collotype Facsimile (Shakespeare Quarto Facsimiles)
SS	*Shakespeare Survey*
STC	*A Short-Title Catalogue of Books Printed in England, Scotland & Ireland and of English Books Printed Abroad 1475–1640,* Alfred W. Pollard and G.R. Redgrave (eds), revised by W.A. Jackson, F.S. Ferguson and Katharine F. Pantzer (3 vols, London, 1976–91)
TNA	The National Archives of the UK
TRHS	*Transactions of the Royal Historical Society*
YES	*Yearbook of English Studies*

Introduction
The Disguised Ruler in Shakespeare and His Contemporaries

Towards the end of Marc Norman and Tom Stoppard's film, *Shakespeare in Love* (1998), Viola De Lesseps (Gwyneth Paltrow) hurriedly dresses herself in Juliet's costume for a fanciful first staging of *Romeo and Juliet*.[1] For much of the film this wealthy merchant's daughter has appeared as the boyish 'Thomas Kent'. Viola may fool the playhouse manager, but her lover 'Will Shakespeare' (Joseph Fiennes) knows the truth of her cross-gender disguise. By pretending to be the youthful Thomas, Viola circumvents the legal restriction that prevents her playing Juliet's role. Her 'realistic' female performance is a resounding success. The assembled actors receive rapturous applause as Will and Viola share an illicit onstage kiss. At the same moment, the Master of the Revels Edmund Tilney (Simon Callow) storms the playhouse with armed guards. Announcing that he acts 'In the name of her Majesty Queen Elizabeth', Tilney accuses the company of illegally employing a woman as player.[2] The screenplay then states that '*an authoritative voice interrupts him*'. The voice belongs, of course, to Judi Dench's majestic Queen Elizabeth. As she warns Tilney to 'Have a care with [her] name' lest he 'wear it out', '*QUEEN ELIZABETH herself* appears among the groundling audience, '*her hood and cloak thrown back*' to reveal '*an awesome sight*' as a '*shaft of sunlight hits her*'. Implicit in this filmic expression of disguised revelation is the theory that any ruler can travel secretly among her or his people simply with the aid of a hooded cloak. This seems somewhat ridiculous in the film's case since, in the cramped confines of the Curtain playhouse, Elizabeth has concealed the vast and glorious attire of a reigning Tudor monarch beneath its silken folds.

Judi Dench's cloaked appearance is representative of a motif whose heritage is traceable to classical antiquity, with the disguises of Achilles, Apollo and Odysseus.[3] Haroun al Raschid of *The Arabian Nights* walked the streets of Baghdad in lowly costume, and Jacob, pretending to be Esau to gain his brother's birthright, adds a biblical dimension (Genesis, 27.11–29). The disguised ruler secretly spying on his people is thus of timeless significance in world literatures. It remains recognizable in film, theatre and television culture, with 'Undercover Boss' and 'Secret Millionaire' reality TV shows spawning a raft of international versions.[4]

---

[1] *Shakespeare in Love*. Dir. John Madden. Miramax Films/Universal Pictures. 1998.

[2] Marc Norman and Tom Stoppard, *Shakespeare in Love* (London, 1999), p. 147.

[3] See Victor O. Freeburg, *Disguise Plots in Elizabethan Drama* (New York, 1915), p. 1.

[4] See Alessandra Stanley, 'Reality TV That Puts the Boss in Meek's Clothing', *The New York Times*, 10 April 2010 <http://www.nytimes.com/2010/04/11/weekinreview/11stanleywir.html?_r=1> [accessed 20 December 2010].

The popular appeal of these programmes confirms our continued fascination with authority figures secretly spying on employees, or wealthy entrepreneurs who offer munificent bounty to needy individuals after fooling them with their humble disguises. Indeed, the real-life exploits of a British prince add a topical immediacy to the disguised ruler. Like his Agincourt counterpart King Henry, who ironically refers to himself as 'Harry *le roi*' (*Henry V*, 4.1.50), so Prince Harry was known simply as 'Lt. Harry Wales' for his secret deployment in Helmand Province, Afghanistan, 2007–2008. All too aware of his military nickname, 'the bullet magnet', and the threat he posed to his colleagues, this twenty-first-century prince adopted his 'Harry Wales' persona to serve in a war zone.[5] The success of Prince Harry's ploy only adds to the mythology of royal disguise.

With the world now dominated by instantaneous mass communication, it is not surprising that the voluntary news blackout that accompanied Prince Harry's secret deployment should eventually fail. In the aftermath of its exposure, many complained about the wisdom of sending a prince into combat. Journalists who first ran the story were likewise condemned for their reckless disregard for Harry's safety. At no stage, however, did the prince's disguise appear particularly unusual; neither was its efficacy, on a local level, ever doubted. Prince Harry's Afghan subterfuge appeared as conventional and timeless as the threat to his person was real. The timeless appeal of the 'Harry Wales' incident would certainly resonate with Shakespeare and his contemporaries, as Henry V's Agincourt disguise confirms. Indeed, sixteenth and seventeenth-century playwrights regularly adopted and adapted the motif, recognizing the romantic and/or political potential of royal disguise. So popular did it become that, in the opening decade of the seventeenth century, Londoners saw a number of plays performed that portrayed disguised rulers as principal protagonists travelling unknown among their subjects. These men observed, encouraged and commented upon the political, social and sexual desires of those who, to use Frank Whigham's words, filled the 'opportunity-vacuum' their absence created.[6] The resulting 'climate of surveillance' also allowed these disguised rulers to reap and purvey personal and collective benefits by exposing wrongdoers to public justice.[7] This book takes as its starting point the seventeenth-century disguised ruler plays that have themselves become a commonplace of academic study.

---

[5]   See 'Prince Harry on Afghan Front Line', *BBC News*, 28 February 2008 <http://news.bbc.co.uk/go/pr/fr/-/1/hi/world/7269743.stm> [accessed 15 January 2011].

[6]   Frank Whigham, 'Flattering Courtly Desire: John Marston's *The Fawn*', in David L. Smith, Richard Strier and David Bevington (eds), *The Theatrical City* (Cambridge, 1995), pp. 137–56 (p. 139).

[7]   Ibid., p. 139.

Fig. I.1   Prince Harry 'disguised' as 'Lt. Harry Wales', on active service in Afghanistan, 2008

The Disguised Ruler Tradition

The disguised ruler plays that attract the most frequent critical attention are Shakespeare's *Measure for Measure* (performance recorded 1604; published 1623), John Marston's *The Malcontent* (published 1604) and *The Fawn* (published 1606), Thomas Middleton's *The Phoenix* (published 1607), and Edward Sharpham's *The Fleer* (published 1607).[8] The traditional dating of these plays, which at first glance appear to follow hard on the accession of James I, ensures that many critics view them as active responses to the particular 'occasion' (as opposed simply to being broadly 'topical') of this historical event.[9] An occasionalist reading, for example, informs Mark Eccles's 1980 description of *Measure for Measure* as 'most likely' written in 1604, because of the cluster of disguise plays that apparently

---

[8]   George K. Hunter, 'English Folly and Italian Vice: The Moral Landscape of John Marston', in John Russell Brown and Bernard Harris (eds), *Jacobean Theatre* (London, 1960), p. 101n.

[9]   Whigham, 'Flattering', p. 139; Jonathan Goldberg, *James I and the Politics of Literature* (Baltimore, 1983), pp. 231–9; T.F. Wharton, 'Sexual Politics in Marston's *The Malcontent*', in T.F. Wharton (ed.), *The Drama of John Marston: Critical Re-Visions* (Cambridge, 2000), pp. 181–93 (p. 183).

accompanied it.[10] Occasionality and political expediency explain the historical significance of these plays' appearance, written 'to appeal especially to the interests of King James'.[11] Eccles's cluster theory relies, however, on a construct, described by Thomas Postlewait as 'an irresolvable paradox', which remains evident in much analysis of early modern drama: historical periodization or the division of an object of study into chronological periods.[12] The titles of respective historical studies by E.K. Chambers and Gerald Eades Bentley perpetuate the concept of drama performed on the Elizabethan, Jacobean and Caroline stages.[13] Historical periodization thus assists in the individuation and isolation of those disguised ruler plays that fit comfortably into a Jacobean political timeframe, while rejecting those that do not.

Described subsequently by Gary Taylor and John Jowett as 'unimpressive', Eccles's cluster theory for dating *Measure for Measure* to 1604 was, nonetheless, fully accepted by another 1980s critic.[14] In *Power on Display*, Leonard Tennenhouse argues that the 'sudden' appearance of the disguised ruler plays demonstrates how several playwrights make a 'remarkable show of theatrical solidarity' when writing in support of the nation's new king.[15] Years of rule by an English queen professing marriage to her nation required James to find a 'new strategy' for authorizing his monarchy, and a means of reaffirming the 'patriarchal principle' that legitimized his reign.[16] A response to this 'new strategy' was thus formulated during an enforced period of plague closure.[17] Following Elizabeth's death on 24 March 1603, the playhouses did not officially reopen again until April 1604.[18] During this period, so Tennenhouse argued, 'all the major playwrights' developed a 'new form of comedy' that revised Elizabethan romantic comedy 'so drastically as to render [it] all but obsolete'.[19] The product of this 'new form' was a 'rash' of disguised ruler plays that became a commonplace for James's 'first theatrical season'.[20] This 'rash'

---

[10]   Mark Eccles (ed.), *Measure for Measure*, New Variorum Edition (New York, 1980), pp. 300–301.

[11]   Ibid., p. 301.

[12]   Thomas Postlewait, *The Cambridge Companion to Theatre Historiography* (Cambridge, 2009), p. 195.

[13]   E.K. Chambers, *The Elizabethan Stage* (4 vols, Oxford, 1923); Gerald Eades Bentley, *The Jacobean and Caroline Stage* (7 vols, Oxford, 1941–1968).

[14]   Gary Taylor and John Jowett, *Shakespeare Reshaped, 1606–1623* (Oxford, 1993), pp. 175–6.

[15]   Leonard Tennenhouse, *Power on Display* (London, 1986), pp. 153–4.

[16]   Ibid., p. 159.

[17]   See Leeds Barroll, *Politics, Plague, and Shakespeare's Theater* (Ithaca, 1991), pp. 70–116.

[18]   Chambers, *ES* 1, p. 302.

[19]   Tennenhouse, *Power*, p. 153–5.

[20]   Ibid., p. 153.

enjoyed a 'sudden and brief reign upon the London stage'.[21] Eccles's cluster theory is transformed into Tennenhouse's uncomfortable sounding 'rash'.

Although the first critic to isolate the 'Jacobean disguised ruler plays' as an active part of a new strategy for authorizing James's rule, Tennenhouse was not the first to discuss this dramatic motif in detail. Seventy years earlier, Victor O. Freeburg demonstrated a far broader heritage for disguised rulers than their Jacobean print or performance histories might suggest.[22] Tracing the stratagem from classical antiquity, Freeburg described how conventional the disguised ruler had become by the early seventeenth century. Each play served to 'advertise the other until spying in disguise became a well established tradition' on the English stage.[23] The writers of these 'spying in disguise' plays 'drew on their predecessors, not necessarily because of poverty stricken imagination, but because of shrewd recognition of theatrical success'.[24] Freeburg thus recognized two significant features that have a direct bearing on this book. Firstly, that there existed a commercial imperative for the conventionalization of the 'spying in disguise' motif, and secondly, that disguised rulers appeared in drama written many years before James's accession.

Despite Freeburg's detailed discussion to the contrary, Tennenhouse's subsequent claim – that the disguised ruler plays represent a sudden synchronic outburst of political comment – has entered our contemporary critical vocabulary largely imperceptibly. In consequence, Tennenhouse's description of the plays as indices of a 'remarkable moment … when all the major playwrights imagined the state in a manner resembling some bureaucratic mechanism overseen by deputies, impostors, or usurpers', now represents the conventional historicist view.[25] This is not surprising, since Tennenhouse's argument appeared at the vanguard of what was to become the influential critical practice, new historicism. As a concept, the 'New Historicism' was introduced into Renaissance studies by Michael McCanles in 1980.[26] It was originally (and still remains) strongly influenced by the French social scientist, anthropologist and historian, Michel Foucault, whose 1975 study, *Surveiller et punir* (*Discipline and Punish*), confirmed punishment and surveillance as a 'technique of power'.[27] Literary scholars subsequently embraced the 'New Historicism', most notably Stephen Greenblatt, whose 1982 special edition of the journal *Genre* effectively announced the critical practice's arrival.[28] One contributor

---

[21] Ibid., p. 154.

[22] Freeburg, *Disguise*, pp. 1–4.

[23] Ibid., p. 175.

[24] Ibid., p. 176.

[25] Tennenhouse, *Power*, p. 155. See Taylor and Jowett, *Reshaped*, pp. 175–6.

[26] See Michael McCanles, 'The Authentic Discourse of the Renaissance', *Diacritics*, 10 (1980): 77–87.

[27] Michel Foucault, *Discipline and Punish*, trans. Alan Sheridan (Harmondsworth, 1977), p. 23.

[28] Stephen Greenblatt, 'The Forms of Power and the Power of Forms in the Renaissance', *Genre*, 15 (1982): 3–6.

was Tennenhouse, who rehearsed his disguised ruler argument for the hegemonic/ subversive relevance of *Measure for Measure*.[29] A product of new historicism's fascination with the Foucauldian power model (*Power on Display* openly acknowledges Foucault's influence), Tennenhouse's study therefore effectively invented the narrowly-defined group of 'Jacobean disguised ruler plays', a generic construct that can be dated most specifically to 1982.[30] This same construct was unknown to writers, publishers or audiences at any time prior to the 1980s.

Although Tennenhouse's argument does not dominate recent Shakespeare criticism, whenever mention is made of a disguised ruler in scholarly discourse, a footnote invariably refers back to *Power on Display*. For academic and student alike, an unquestioned acceptance of Tennenhouse's 'solidarity' construct remains. Twenty-first-century studies of *Measure for Measure* take for granted that it belongs in this definable generic group.[31] The result is a critical imbalance caused by too restrictive a concentration on the 'Jacobean disguised ruler plays' to the exclusion of other disguised ruler dramas. This book redresses this critical imbalance by considering the disguised ruler plays as individual exemplars, not as a 1980s generic whole. Rather than as products of synchronic occasionalism written specifically in reaction to James's accession, the disguised ruler plays are instead read as part of a diachronic process of development and adaptation that owes much to preceding generations of playwrights, poets, balladeers and storytellers.

The reconsideration of this critical imbalance does not deny James's accession as a significant political event for contemporary drama. During this period of political renewal, when the security of the nation was uppermost in people's minds, dramatic interest in the disguised ruler undoubtedly increased among some of London's playwrights. Most likely fuelling this interest was public awareness of James's self-professed patriarchal principle, as gleaned from his 1599 advice-book addressed to his eldest son Prince Henry, *Basilikon Doron* ('Royal Gift').[32] Almost immediately published for general consumption in Edinburgh, *Basilikon Doron* became a bestseller on its London republication in 1603, providing James's new subjects with an insight into this '*lawfull good King*', who '*acknowledgeth himself ordeined for his people ... as their naturall father and kindly maister*'.[33] In his *The True Lawe of Free Monarchies* (1598), James had already advocated government by a king whose 'fatherly duty is bound to care for the nourishing, education and uertuous gouernment of ... his subjects'.[34] Written five years before the death of Elizabeth at a time when discussion about the future succession

---

[29]   Leonard Tennenhouse, 'Representing Power: *Measure for Measure* in its Time', *Genre*, 15 (1982): 139–56.

[30]   Tennenhouse, *Power*, pp. 13–14.

[31]   Stanley Wells, *Shakespeare & Co.* (London, 2006), pp. 172 & 190.

[32]   King James, VI & I, *Basilikon Doron* (Edinburgh, 1599).

[33]   King James, VI & I, *Basilikon Doron* (London, 1603), fols E2^v–E3^r.

[34]   King James, VI & I, *The True Lawe of Free Monarchies* (Edinburgh, 1598), fol. B4^v.

was politically sensitive, James's *True Lawe* argues that monarchy is divinely ordained, that hereditary right is indefeasible, that kings are accountable to God alone and that non-resistance and passive obedience to a monarch are the direct commandments of God.[35] For James, the allegorical links between the concepts of 'king', 'God' and 'father' confirm the divine-right strategy of his subsequent regime.[36] The 'Jacobean disguised ruler play' would seem the perfect vehicle for such a strategy. Its depiction of 'disorder' following the 'loss of the monarch's presence' might, as Jonathan Goldberg argues, signify the calling forth of 'new and distinctively Jacobean strategies of representing the orderly state' under the absolutist, divine and lawful rule of James.[37] Nevertheless, to rely solely on such a simplistic politicizing model undervalues the wider influence of sixteenth-century English and European literary and dramatic experimentation and innovation.

The ease with which a 'distinctively Jacobean' model can be applied to several disguised ruler plays is no doubt linked to the obvious fact that they *did* appear in the opening years of the seventeenth century, at least in printed form, though not necessarily on the stage. They likewise *do* share a common plot motif, with several of the plays presenting it as the dominant characteristic of their principal protagonists. It is because of these obvious similarities that the 'Jacobean disguised ruler plays' have been elevated to a distinctive critical grouping that reflects the collective response of playwrights to an historical occasion. This grouping denies the possibility, first suggested by Freeburg, that the plays represent a collective response by playwright, publisher and playhouse manager, not to a political event, but to the financial benefits of promoting an easily identifiable commodity. Dramatic and literary success in the performance and publishing marketplace appears of far greater importance. The disguised ruler as identifiable commodity also accords with Andrew Gurr's and Peter Hyland's respective arguments about the Admiral's Men, for which the oft-repeated disguise plot was a recognizable feature of the company's wares.[38] Identifiability also implies a prior heritage for a motif that alters according to prevailing fashion in order to attract knowing responses from audience and reader alike. Without a discernible heritage, the subversion or adaptation of a motif within a play's narrative, and thus its commercial worth in a novelty-driven theatrical marketplace, would be indistinguishable to its public consumers.

If an audience was indeed experiencing self-congratulatory superiority at recognizing the subversion of a theatrical motif, how might this impact on our appreciation of a less political, more economic and/or cultural response to the

---

[35]   Bernard Bourdin, 'James VI and I – Divine Right, the Doctrine of the Two Kingdoms and the Legitimising of Royal Power', in Jean-Christophe Mayer (ed.), *The Struggle for the Succession in Late Elizabethan England* (Montpellier, 2004), pp. 120–41.

[36]   Goldberg, *James*, pp. 55–112.

[37]   Tennenhouse, *Power*, p. 156.

[38]   Andrew Gurr, *Shakespeare's Opposites: The Admiral's Company 1594–1625* (Cambridge, 2009), pp. 53–4; Peter Hyland, *Disguise on the Early Modern English Stage* (Aldershot, 2011), Introduction, pp. 1–14, published while this book was under revision.

disguised ruler on the early modern stage? Significantly, the overall focus of Gurr's study offers the greatest insight into disguised rulers and the wider heritage from which they stemmed. Gurr's book engages with a critical approach pioneered in the late 1980s by Roslyn L. Knutson – repertory studies.[39] Taking as its organizing principle the company repertory, repertory studies encourages a textual and contextual specificity for its analysis of plays performed by the same company.[40] This approach does not deny the agency of the playwright, but it counters traditional author-centred analysis, which often disregards plays of unknown or 'anonymous' authorship, by focusing on the dramatic output of the individual playhouse companies. Collaboration among playwrights, playhouse managers, actors, sharers, publishers, audiences and play-purchasers thus become interrelated factors in the commercial development of the dramatic text.

When considered according to their repertory status, the 'Jacobean disguised ruler plays' are noticeably performed by only three companies: the Children of the Chapel/Queen's Revels, the Children of Paul's and the King's Men at the Globe. This contradicts the argument that *all* the nation's playwrights acted in political harmony. Likewise, prior to the seventeenth century, three adult companies – Lord Strange's and (later) the Admiral's Men at the Rose/Fortune and the Chamberlain's Men (later renamed the King's Men) at the Theatre/Curtain/Globe – appear regularly to have staged disguised rulers. These clandestine wanderings of far earlier disguised rulers provided the same disconcerting dramatic irony as their more famous Jacobean equivalents.

Repertory studies not only offers an alternative critical approach to the disguised ruler in early modern drama, but also an alternative comparative focus: that of formal or generic difference.[41] Lucy Munro's *Children of the Queen's Revels*, for instance, takes as its organizing principle the company's comedies, tragicomedies and tragedies.[42] Munro states that such formal differentiation 'provides … a historically grounded perspective on the collaborative production of plays and an interpretative link between their production and reception'.[43] Munro's reengagement with the historicity of form is associated with the work of critics such as Jean E. Howard, Douglas Bruster and Mark David Rasmussen.[44]

---

[39]   Roslyn L. Knutson, *The Repertory of Shakespeare's Company* (Fayetteville, 1991); Knutson, *Playing Companies and Commerce in Shakespeare's Time* (New York, 2001).

[40]   See Scott McMillin and Sally-Beth MacLean, *The Queen's Men and their Plays* (Cambridge, 1998); Mary Bly, *Queer Virgins and Virgin Queans* (Oxford, 2000).

[41]   Douglas Bruster, 'The Materiality of Shakespearean Form', in Stephen A. Cohen (ed.), *Shakespeare and Historical Formalism* (Aldershot, 2007), pp. 31–48.

[42]   Lucy Munro, *Children of the Queen's Revels* (Cambridge, 2005).

[43]   Ibid., p. 5.

[44]   Jean E. Howard, 'Shakespeare and Genre', in David Scott Kastan (ed.), *A Companion to Shakespeare* (Oxford, 2000), pp. 297–310; Douglas Bruster, 'Shakespeare and the Composite Text', in Mark David Rasmussen (ed.), *Renaissance Literature and Its Formal Engagements* (Basingstoke, 2002), pp. 43–66.

Our renewed interest in form, so Stephen A. Cohen argues, stems from critical 'frustration with the decades-long hegemony of New Historicism's insistence on the political and ideological implication of literature'.[45] After a promising beginning in which form was recognized as worthy of critical study (Tennenhouse's analysis of disguised rulers in the journal *Genre* is an early example), new historicism effectively entrenched itself in the 'dyadic and historically static hegemony/subversion model' that obscured the historicity of form.[46] This book returns to the 'historically grounded perspective' of form, so countering the new historicist model that has dominated recent study of the disguised ruler.

Alternative historic, economic and generic forces become evident when the 'Jacobean disguised ruler plays' are considered as individual exemplars of form. Unfortunately, a difficulty immediately arises when discussing the generic identity of the two most famous disguised ruler plays, *Measure for Measure* and *The Malcontent*. Both plays appear to belong to that most enigmatic of forms – tragicomedy. As tragicomedies, they engage with a form that, in Gordon McMullan and Jonathan Hope's words, has never 'acquired anything akin to a fixed meaning', either in recent criticism or on the early modern stage.[47] Tragicomedy is even absent from Shakespeare's First Folio generic list. Critics of *Measure for Measure*, however, regularly view this as Shakespeare's early or 'failed experiment' in the tragicomic form.[48] Jean E. Howard argues that *Measure for Measure* represents Shakespeare's conscious attempt to subvert the conventions of an emergent form. Howard thus contradicts Verna A. Foster, who sees the same 'flaws' in *Measure for Measure* as 'part of tragicomedy's inherent aesthetic' of instability.[49] If tragicomedy still represents an elusive and flexible generic concept for Shakespeareans, how might these disguised ruler plays have been perceived by early modern playgoers and readers who encountered the dramas for the first time?

Such a question presupposes that a recognizable and coherent Renaissance genre-system, consisting of tragedy, comedy and tragicomedy, was evident to the early modern consumer.[50] Although Derridean theories about the ever-changing nature of genres replaced the concept of a recognizable Renaissance genre-system,

---

[45] Cohen, *Formalism*, p. 2.

[46] Ibid., pp. 14–15.

[47] Gordon McMullan and Jonathan Hope (eds), *The Politics of Tragicomedy* (London, 1992), p. 1.

[48] Jean E. Howard, 'The Difficulties of Closure: An Approach to the Problematic in Shakespearean Comedy', in A.R. Braunmuller and J.C. Bulman (eds), *Comedy from Shakespeare to Sheridan* (Newark, 1986), pp. 113–28. For an overview of this argument, see Stephen Cohen, 'From Mistress to Master: Political Transition and Formal Conflict in *Measure for Measure*', *Criticism*, 41 (1999): 431–64 (p. 431n.).

[49] Verna A. Foster, *The Name and Nature of Tragicomedy* (Aldershot, 2004), p. 64.

[50] See Rosalie L. Colie, *The Resources of Kind*, ed. Barbara K. Lewalski (Berkeley, 1973), pp. 1–31.

a seventeenth-century representation of the same is discernible in the title-page to Ben Jonson's Folio *Workes* of 1616.[51]

Jonson's title-page shows the composite figure of '*Tragicomoedia*' adorning an ornate classical edifice, flanked by personifications of comedy and tragedy who stare defiantly at each other.[52] Dressed in the tunic and sock of comedy, while bearing the crown and sceptre of tragedy, '*Tragicomoedia*' proudly gazes straight at the reader. She is flanked by two lesser figures, a 'Satyr' with panpipes and stave and a 'Pastor' with shepherd's crook and pipe, which demonstrate tragicomedy's historical roots in Italian pastoral drama. The 'Satyr' is also indicative, however, of a peculiarly English etymological confusion between the licentious satyr of pastoral comedy and the dramatic mode of 'satire', which originated in the Roman 'medley' poems and satiric dramas that ridiculed vice, immorality or folly in an individual or society.[53] Early modern writers and publishers used the spelling 'satyre' to denote both the creature and the mode. In England, the two words eventually became synonymous, with the woodland 'Satyr' of pastoral drama metamorphosing into a railing satirical character, at home in both the rural and urban environment. Jonson's 1616 title-page suggests a primacy for the tragicomic form that recognizes these English and Italian associations with both the satiric and pastoral modes.

The superior position of tragicomedy on Jonson's title-page belies the fact that the form's legitimacy was strongly contested and much debated. Nowhere was this debate stronger, nor more virulent, than in the absolutist ducal courts of northern Italy during the Italian Cinquecento.[54] The Dukedom of Ferrara, for instance, was the birthplace of Italian vernacular comedy, notably Ariosto's *La cassaria* (1508) and *I suppositi* (1509) and Tasso's pastoral comedy *Aminta* (performed in 1573). Ferrara also patronized the development of a specifically Italian form of tragicomedy in the pastoral mode by the courtier, diplomat, playwright and professor of rhetoric, Giovanni Battista Guarini. Between 1580 and 1585, Guarini wrote his '*tragicomedia pastorale*', *Il pastor fido*, a play heavily influenced by *Aminta*.[55] Published in Venice in 1590, it remained unperformed until its 1596 staging at the Court of Mantua. The radical form of *Il pastor fido* prompted attacks from Guarini's peers and rivals, forcing (or perhaps facilitating) his publication

[51]   Jacques Derrida, 'The Law of Genre', trans. Avital Ronell, *Critical Inquiry*, 7 (1980): 55–81.

[52]   Benjamin Jonson, *The Workes* (London, 1616).

[53]   Lee Bliss, 'Pastiche, Burlesque and Tragicomedy', in A.R. Braunmuller and Michael Hattaway (eds), *Cambridge Companion to English Renaissance Drama* (Cambridge, 1990), pp. 237–61 (p. 245).

[54]   Robert Henke, *Pastoral Transformations* (Newark, 1997), pp. 19–24.

[55]   Giovanni Battista Guarini, *Il pastor fido* (Venice, 1590).

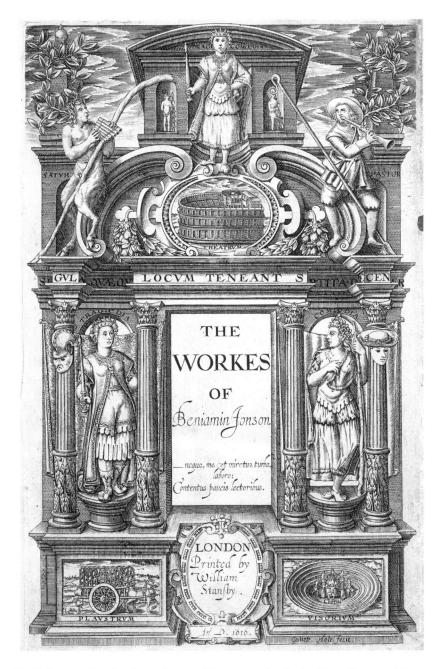

Fig. I.2   The dominant figure of Tragicomedy, flanked by a Satyr and Pastor, on the title-page of Ben Jonson's *Workes* (1616)

of a manifesto for the genre tragicomedy, *Compendio della poesia tragicomica* (1601), which also contained a reprint of *Il pastor fido*.[56]

Guarini's *Compendio* responds to criticism of *Il pastor fido* by attempting to define its elusive form:

> [T]ragicomedy is not made up of two entire plots, one of which is a perfect tragedy and the other a perfect comedy ... [nor is it] a tragic story vitiated with the lowliness of comedy or a comic fable contaminated with the deaths of tragedy. ('Compendium', 507)

Instead, as Guarini explains, tragicomedy conflates the most suitable parts of tragedy and comedy, to create a 'third thing that [is] perfect of its kind'.[57] Guarini takes from tragedy, 'its danger but not its death', and 'from comedy', its 'laughter ... modest amusement, feigned difficulty [and] happy reversal'.[58] In answer to the Renaissance critic's complaint about the mixing of 'high rank' and 'low station', Guarini claims that Aristotle 'alluded' to this lack of decorum in his *Poetics*.[59] Indeed, for the Renaissance dramatist, the mixing of rank had a classical precedent in the portrayal of gods, kings and slaves in Plautus's *Amphitrvo [Amphitryon]* (190–185 BCE), a Roman adaptation of a (lost) Greek New Comedy.[60] In the Prologue to *Amphitrvo*, Mercury twice calls the play a '*tragicomoedia*', a term apparently coined by Plautus to describe its farcical nature and combination of regal personages and slaves.[61] *Tragicomoedia* appears on Jonson's title-page, and describes Marston's *The Malcontent* when it was entered in the *Stationers' Register*, 5 July 1604.[62] Whether '*tragicomoedia*' represents Marston's own explanation, or the opinion of playhouse, publisher or Stationers' scribe, its use suggests recognition of *The Malcontent* as a tragicomedy based on a Guarinian and/or Plautine model.

Guarini's insistence that his new genre takes from tragedy 'its danger but not its death' is significant when considering both *Measure for Measure* and *The Malcontent*.[63] For Guarini, a tragicomedy brings many characters close to their deaths, but it is 'connected in no way with tragedy'.[64] The playwright's desire to distance himself from tragedy possibly reflects the religious climate of

---

[56]   Guarini, 'The Compendium of Tragicomic Poetry', in Allan H. Gilbert (ed.), *Literary Criticism: Plato to Dryden* (Detroit, 1962), pp. 505–33.

[57]   Ibid., p. 507.

[58]   Ibid., p. 511.

[59]   Ibid., p. 508.

[60]   Colie, *Resources*, pp. 22–3; Heather Dubrow, *Genre* (London, 1982), p. 59; Madeleine Doran, *Endeavors of Art* (Madison, 1954), pp. 192–4.

[61]   Titus Maccius Plautus, *Amphitrvo*, ed. David Christenson (Cambridge, 2000), p. 85 (59 & 63ff.).

[62]   Arber 3, pp. 266 & 268.

[63]   J.W. Lever (ed.), *Measure for Measure* (London, 1965), pp. lx–lxii.

[64]   Guarini, 'Compendium', pp. 521–2.

Italy's courts. The Catholic Church's suspicion of tragedy as a pagan dramatic form influenced those playwrights who could appreciate its narrative potential while seeking to shield their work from accusations of heretical paganism.[65] Guarini's choice of pastoral tragicomedy for *Il pastor fido* reflects the fashion of the time: '*Et si come l'età si mutano, cosi i costumi si cangiano*' ('And just as the age changes, habits change').[66] For critics of *Measure for Measure* and *The Malcontent*, Shakespeare or Marston were only able to assimilate Guarinian theory or dialogue after the 1602 publication of an English translation of *Il pastor fido*, attributed enigmatically to a kinsman of 'Dymock'.[67] As we will see in Chapter 2, the Englished version of Guarini's play does not represent the sole catalyst for tragicomic expression on the Jacobean stage. Rather, it is indicative of a long-held interest in Italian culture in general, and in tragicomedy in particular, among the English literary and dramatic cognoscenti.

That tragicomedy was a contentious issue in England long before the Englished *Il Pastor Fido* of 1602 is evident from Sir Philip Sidney's attack in *The Defence of Poesie* (1595) (also published as *An Apologie for Poetrie*).[68] Written in 1583 (nearly twenty years before translation of Guarini's groundbreaking tragicomedy), Sidney's *Defence* defines these 'grosse absurdities' as

> Playes [that] bee neither right Tragedies, nor right Comedies, mingling Kinges and Clownes, … [which] thrust in the Clowne by head and shoulders to play a part in majesticall matters. ('Defence', *Prose Works* 3, 39)

For Sidney, the most offensive aspect of this 'mongrell Tragicomedie' is the onstage mingling of 'Kinges and Clownes', in contravention of the precepts of the classical unities.[69] Sidney's comments demonstrate an animosity, shared by English and Italian critic alike, towards this hybrid dramatic form.

Sidney's disgust at those who create their 'mongrell Tragicomedie' confirms that, by the mid-1590s, several English dramatists were experimenting with this subversive form. Richard Edwards, for example, in his 'excellent Comedie' (A1[r]) *Damon and Pythias* (originally staged *c.* 1564–1565; published 1571), defends the avant-garde nature of '*this newe Tragicall Commedie*' (*Damon*, A2[v]; Prologue 46).[70] In print as early as 1571 (two years before Tasso's *Aminta* was performed at Ferrara), *Damon and Pythias* exemplifies Sidnean 'mongrell Tragicomedie'. It is not surprising, therefore, that by the late 1590s, Shakespeare should similarly

---

[65] Henke, *Pastoral*, p. 20.

[66] Guarini, *Compendio*, fol. B4[v]; translation Gilbert, *Literary Criticism*.

[67] Brian Gibbons (ed.), *Measure for Measure* (Cambridge, 1991), p. 19.

[68] Sir Philip Sidney, *The Defence of Poesie* (London, 1595). Page numbers from Albert Feuillerat (ed.), *The Prose Works of Sir Philip Sidney* (4 vols, Cambridge, 1962), vol. 3, pp. 3–46.

[69] Ibid., p. 39.

[70] Richard Edwards, *Damon and Pithias* (London, 1571), fol. A1[r]. Line numbers from Arthur Brown (ed.), *Damon and Pythias* (Oxford, 1957).

evoke Guarinian pastoralism in *As You Like It* (1598), with the name of Guarini's shepherd Silvio echoed in the 'faithful shepheard' Silvius (F, TLN.2488; 5.2.71). *As You Like It*'s proto-tragicomic study of disguise, ducal usurpation and malcontentedness makes it a fitting precursor to Marston's *The Malcontent*. The extent to which generic experimentation had entered the collective consciousness of English dramatist and audience alike is confirmed by Q1 *Hamlet* (1603), when Corambis (from Q2 onwards Polonius) announces the tragedians' bizarre catalogue of plays: 'The best Actors in Christendome, / Either for Comedy, Tragedy, Historie, Pastorall, / Pastorall, Historicall, Historicall, Comicall, / Comicall historicall, Pastorall, Tragedy historicall' (Q1 *Hamlet*, E3^r–E3^v; 7.295–8).[71] By satirizing the generic complexity of the age, Corambis/Polonius highlights the popularity of emerging forms like tragicomedy among English dramatists.

The overarching 'problem' of defining what is actually meant by tragicomedy has kept plays like *The Malcontent* and *Measure for Measure* consigned to a problematic generic status within the early modern canon. *Measure for Measure* even gained a new critical designation as one of Shakespeare's 'problem plays'. This label, itself an anachronistic Victorian construct, was adapted from contemporary commentary on Henrik Ibsen's Norwegian plays in translation by the Shakespeare critic Frederick S. Boas.[72] The apparent social realism of Shakespeare's corrupt Viennese state supported Boas's relabelling of it as a 'problem play'. Social realism also accounts for George Bernard Shaw's 1898 comment that Shakespeare was, with *Measure for Measure*, 'ready and willing to start at the twentieth century if the seventeenth would only let him'.[73] Less contentious seems the labelling of Brian Gibbons. His 1980s study, *Jacobean City Comedy*, assisted in re-categorizing *Measure for Measure* as an early example of this subgeneric form, written in an urban/satiric mode.[74] The London-centrism of Jacobean city comedy replaced the Ibsenite concern for social realism, thus relieving the perceived 'problem' of *Measure for Measure*.

A pernicious 'problem' still remains, however: the new historicist generic construct offered by Tennenhouse. This alternative model for *Measure for Measure* analysis pays little attention to its formal structure, preferring instead to see it as a hegemonic representation or subversion of Jacobean political ideology. As the principal protagonist in a purely political play, the Duke of *Measure for Measure* is thus paradigmatic of similar disguised rulers in *The Malcontent*, *The Phoenix*, *The Fawn* and *The Fleer*. Tragicomedy. Problem play. City comedy. All these labels remain, to a greater or lesser extent, attached to the plays most closely associated with *Measure for Measure*. The individuality of their disguised

---

[71]   Line numbers from Ann Thompson and Neil Taylor (eds), *Hamlet: The Texts of 1603 and 1623* (London, 2006).

[72]   Frederick S. Boas, *Shakspere and his Predecessors* (London, 1896), p. 345.

[73]   George Bernard Shaw, *Plays: Pleasant and Unpleasant* (2 vols, London, 1898), vol. 1, p. xxxi.

[74]   Brian Gibbons, *Jacobean City Comedy*, 2nd edn (London, 1980), p. 1.

ruler narratives, plots and formal structures remains subsumed, however, under that dominant critical label – the 'Jacobean disguised ruler plays'. This category, associated primarily with *Measure for Measure*, is also applied to a play that for many years was the focus of alternative critical study, *The Malcontent*.

'Jacobean Disguised Ruler Plays': A Marstonian Perspective

Although critical studies of the disguised ruler plays focused primarily on *Measure for Measure*, Marston's *The Malcontent* had already attracted equally author-centred interest. Since the mid-nineteenth century, commentators had argued that Marston's characters – Duke Altofronto/Malevole of *The Malcontent* and Duke Gonzago of *The Fawn* – represented barely-disguised satirical portraits of King James.[75] This notion lost its appeal when critics like G.K. Hunter began considering *The Malcontent* not as a direct satire of Marston's king, but as a more general 'rejection of corporate values' associated with court and national vice.[76] For Hunter, Marston's Malevole represented the 'prototype' for all subsequent disguised rulers, with Shakespeare's Duke a response to Marston's innovation.[77] The world-weary Jaques or the antic disposition of Hamlet might have influenced Malevole's malcontentedness, but it was Marston, not Shakespeare, that engendered the Jacobean disguised ruler phenomenon.

Hunter's argument that *The Malcontent* represents a 'rejection' of Jacobean 'corporate values' is contemporaneous with Anthony Caputi's suggestion that Marston's plays were an attempt to 'produce dramatic equivalents' for his scurrilous verse satires, *Pygmalion's Image* (1598) and *The Scourge of Villanie* (1598 and 1599).[78] The 'structural tactic' of disguise was nothing new, since Marston had already employed it in *What You Will* (*c.* 1601, Paul's[?]; published 1607), a play written perhaps two years before the Stuart succession.[79] For Caputi, *The Malcontent* was merely the product of theatrical exigency, with Marston developing a motif he had already employed with commercial success in both drama and verse satire.[80] A far earlier heritage for Marston's Malevole was detected in David J. Houser's 1974 source study, which suggested a direct link between *The Malcontent* and the anonymous *A Knack to Know a Knave* (*c.* 1592,

---

[75]   Robert Cartwright, *Shakspere and Jonson* (London, 1864), p. 118n.; A.H. Bullen (ed.), *Works of John Marston* (3 vols, London, 1887), vol. 1, p. xliii; Albert W. Upton, 'Allusions to James I and His Court in Marston's *The Fawn* and Beaumont's *Woman Hater*', *PMLA*, 44 (1929): 1048–65.

[76]   Hunter, 'English Folly', p. 101.

[77]   Ibid., pp. 101–2.

[78]   Anthony Caputi, *John Marston, Satirist* (Ithaca, 1961), p. 180.

[79]   Ibid., p. 215.

[80]   Ibid., pp. 170–71.

Strange's; published 1594).[81] Houser admits that *Knack to Know a Knave* had long been considered of interest because of a single scene in which King Edgar asks if he is '*not* [so] *well disguised*' that no man could '*discerne*' him by his '*lookes to be the King*[?]' (*Knave*, C4ʳ–C4ᵛ; 6.750–51).[82] By concentrating on Edgar's overt expression of disguise, so Houser argues, critics had failed to recognize the similarity between the sub-plot character Honesty (the play's principal disguised authority figure) and Marston's Malevole.[83]

Despite all the possible sources for Marston's 'prototype' disguised ruler – Honesty, Jaques, Hamlet, Marston's own verse satires – a distinction was drawn between the 'self-interested or insignificant disguiser' of Elizabethan drama and his Jacobean voyeuristic counterpart.[84] Even so, this change, from self-interest and insignificance to political and moral voyeurism, is already evident in the anonymous proverb-play, *The Weakest Goeth to the Wall* (*c.* mid-1590s, Oxford's; published 1600).[85] In *Weakest*, Duke Lodwick of Bullen (Boulogne) disguises himself as a church sexton to avoid his detractors.

Lodwick's sexton disguise, whose appearance prefigures the Gravedigger in *Hamlet*, aids the duke's eventual return to the French court, where he regains power and exacts his revenge. Personal safety and the restoration of authority are the motives for this disguised duke's political voyeurism, enacted in a play published three years before Elizabeth's death. Not mentioned by Tennenhouse, *Weakest* remains unnoticed by new historicist critics who see Marston, Shakespeare or Middleton as disguised ruler innovators. As long as such analysis stays firmly entrenched in a Jacobean political and/or social agenda, plays like *Weakest* will remain largely neglected. To appreciate fully the reason for this neglect, and to remedy its outcome, it is necessary to interrogate new historicist analysis of the disguised ruler plays. Fortunately, the hegemonic effect of new historicist practice on disguised ruler criticism is sufficiently recent to be traced in surprising detail.

The New Historicists and Disguised Ruler Criticism

Prior to Tennenhouse, source studies isolated the disguised ruler as an age-old motif, with both *Measure for Measure* and *The Malcontent* considered as paradigms that account for its subsequent commonplace appearance. Few agreed which play came first, although both plays served as didactic responses to England's new king and court. Following Tennenhouse's isolation of the 'Jacobean disguised ruler

---

[81]   David J. Houser, 'Purging the Commonwealth: Marston's Disguised Dukes and *A Knack to Know a Knave*', *PMLA*, 89 (1974): 993–1006; Anonymous, *A Knacke to Knowe a Knave* (London, 1594).

[82]   Line numbers from Richard Proudfoot (ed.), *A Knack to Know a Knave* (Oxford, 1963).

[83]   Houser, 'Purging', pp. 993–4.

[84]   Rosalind Miles, *The Problem of 'Measure for Measure'* (London, 1976), p. 136.

[85]   Anonymous, *The Weakest Goeth to the Wall* (London, 1600), fol. E4ᵛ.

Fig. I.3   The costume of an Elizabethan sexton, from a portrait of Robert Scarlett, gravedigger at Peterborough Cathedral, Cambridgeshire (died 1591)

plays', evidence that the first three years of James's reign now represented the exclusive timeframe for disguised ruler activity appears in Thomas A. Pendleton's 1987 study, which seeks to place the plays in order of composition.[86] Rather than *The Malcontent*, Pendleton favours Middleton's *The Phoenix* as the earliest example of what he calls this 'theatrical vogue'.[87] Culminating in *Measure for Measure*, this 'vogue' began with Middleton, who offered his disguised Prince as a 'textbook figure of sagacious majesty' and a conscious attempt to flatter James's 'self-pronounced concern for wise kingship'.[88] James's accession, combined with contemporary interest in Italian tragicomedy and Marston's foreshadowing of Malevole's 'duality as both secret revenger and social critic' in *Antonio's Revenge* (*c*. 1600), provide Pendleton with firm reasons why the 'vogue' suddenly appeared in 1603.[89]

For Steven Mullaney, the 'stage as place' for the dissemination of an iconography of state was less important than the political stage itself.[90] Mullaney argues that public displays of draconian justice and staged leniency, enacted during James I's slow progress south from Edinburgh to London in 1603, resulted in the 'specter of Jacobean rule' appearing as 'a sort of *psychotyranni*' to the awaiting London populace.[91] By the time James reached London, Mullaney claims, his new nation was in an induced state of anxiety and apprehension that helped reinvent the patriarchal imperative for his rule. Shakespeare responded to this manipulation of public anxiety with *Measure for Measure*, not as 'political allegory', but as a play 'intimately engaged with the transition of power that had recently been enacted on the stage of history'.[92] Mullaney's argument consciously develops Foucault's 'juridico-political' expression of royal authority.[93] Accordingly, it illustrates the speed with which new historicist practice and Foucauldian power modelling had established the 'Jacobean disguised ruler play' as a commonplace in Shakespeare studies in the 1980s.

Foucauldian anxiety also influences Albert H. Tricomi's 'anticourt' analysis of the disguised ruler plays.[94] In Tricomi's opinion, however, James suffers the anxiety, not his people. Focusing specifically on the 'Italianate' disguised ruler plays (*Malcontent*, *Phoenix*, *Fawn*, *Fleer* and *Measure for Measure*), Tricomi

---

[86]   Thomas A. Pendleton, 'Shakespeare's Disguised Duke Play: Middleton, Marston, and the Sources of *Measure for Measure*', in John W. Mahon and Pendleton (eds), *'Fanned and Winnowed Opinions': Shakespearean Essays Presented to Harold Jenkins* (London, 1987), pp. 79–98.

[87]   Ibid., p. 80.

[88]   Ibid., pp. 80–82.

[89]   Ibid., pp. 82–3.

[90]   Steven Mullaney, *The Place of the Stage* (Chicago, 1988), pp. 104–107.

[91]   Ibid., p. 106.

[92]   Ibid., p. 107.

[93]   Foucault, *Discipline*, p. 48.

[94]   Albert H. Tricomi, *Anticourt Drama in England 1603–1642* (Charlottesville, 1989).

claims this 'voguish form' offers an active warning for the new king that reflects a 'widespread disrespect, even contempt', for James and his court.[95] For Tricomi, Marston originated this Italianate subgenre singlehandedly:

> By 1604, when *Malcontent* was published, Marston surely knew that he had … engendered a triumphantly successful species of drama. (Tricomi, *Anticourt*, 14)

Tricomi's comment demonstrates his conviction that the disguised ruler plays represent specific attacks against James and his court, with *The Malcontent* serving as a reforming 'burlesque' that lampoons the 'ideology of self-advancement' which motivated James's courtiers.[96] With the exception of the 'anomalous' *Measure for Measure* (anomalous because set in Vienna rather than Italy), Tricomi considers the Italianateness of the 'successful species' of Jacobean disguised ruler plays as a significant factor in their collective identification.[97] The belief that *Measure for Measure* is indeed anomalous, not because of its Italianate mode but because of its Italian locus, prompted Gary Taylor and John Jowett to suggest the play's existence in a lost original form.[98] The original locus of *Measure for Measure*, according to Taylor, might thus be Italy's Ferrara, not Austria's Vienna.[99] This argument accompanies Taylor and Jowett's championing of Middleton as the interpolator and adaptor of *Measure for Measure*, which in turn, so they argue, points to its revision in the early 1620s.[100]

The Italianate disguised ruler plays now represent a definitive grouping in twenty-first-century critical studies. Michael J. Redmond, for example, argues that Shakespeare displays his 'dramatic superiority' over Marston by locating *Measure for Measure* in Vienna, while still engaging with contemporary debates over perceived political disorder and misrule in the Italian ducal states of the early 1600s.[101] Elsewhere, Redmond focuses on parodies of the Italianate disguised ruler plays, which provide insights into the intertextual reception of the motif by dramatist and theatregoer alike.[102] Despite Redmond's acknowledgement that such parodies would benefit from further research by repertory studies analysts,

---

[95] Ibid., pp. 13 & 24.

[96] Ibid., p. 19.

[97] Ibid., pp. 13–14.

[98] Taylor and Jowett, *Reshaped*, pp. 107–236.

[99] Gary Taylor, 'Shakespeare's Mediterranean *Measure for Measure*', in Tom Clayton, Susan Brock and Vicente Forés (eds), *Shakespeare and the Mediterranean* (Newark, 2004), pp. 243–69 (pp. 252–7).

[100] See John Jowett, '*Measure for Measure*: A Genetic Text', in Gary Taylor and John Lavagnino (eds), *Thomas Middleton: The Collected Works* (Oxford, 2007), pp. 1542–6 (p. 1544); hereafter *Oxford Middleton*.

[101] Michael J. Redmond, '*Measure for Measure* and the Politics of the Italianate Disguised Duke Play', in Michele Marrapodi (ed.), *Shakespeare and Intertextuality* (Rome, 2000), pp. 193–214 (p. 212).

[102] Michael J. Redmond, *Shakespeare, Politics, and Italy* (Aldershot, 2009), pp. 121–68.

he still considers them dramatic responses to a specifically Jacobean group of occasionalist plays, led by the paradigmatic *Measure for Measure*. For Redmond, the Italianate disguised ruler arrived suddenly with James's accession, the motif having no bearing on drama that had gone before. The occasionalist focus of Redmond's study is indicative of much disguised ruler analysis from the opening decade of the twenty-first century.

The Disguised Ruler: An Alternative View

Literary studies from the 1980s, influenced by the Foucauldian power model, commonly brought a resolutely occasionalist bias to 'Jacobean disguised ruler play' analysis. Such unremitting occasionalism led to a critical imbalance, with strictly 'Jacobean' examples of these plays eclipsing other disguised ruler drama. In redressing this skewed critical perspective, *The Disguised Ruler in Shakespeare and his Contemporaries* resituates the motif in the early modern canon as a whole. It also foregrounds the disguised ruler's constantly evolving dramatic status within the playhouse repertories.

   To illustrate and explain this evolutionary, non-occasionalist process, Chapter 1, 'The Disguised Ruler on the Elizabethan Stage', traces the disguised ruler's heritage in sixteenth-century drama. Many 'comical history' plays of the 1580s and 1590s portrayed libidinous rulers embarking on romantic wooing adventures, often dressed in fool's motley and encountering the Lincoln green clad outlaw, Robin Hood. Royal figures from England's historical past are thus the principal protagonists of *Friar Bacon and Friar Bungay*, *George a Greene* and *Edward I*, with Robin Hood's verdant presence evident in all. These 'comical histories' relied most specifically on the medieval chronicles, those pseudo-historical constructs that incorporated myth and folklore within narratives glorifying England's royal past. The medieval chronicles were influenced by ballads and folktales that regularly invoked the 'king and subject' theme of disguised ruler trickery and Robin Hood roguery. So prevalent was the disguised ruler/Robin Hood myth that, by the 1590s, it was already a commonplace of popular culture. The 'comical histories' reflect this commonality. The medieval chronicles that fuelled the fanciful adventures of the 'comical histories' were themselves superseded in historical importance by the Tudor Chronicles. These offered a chronological rather than mythical progression of historical facts. Tudor Chronicles provided the material for alternative 'Chronicle History' drama (the theatrical counterparts to the 'comical histories'), of which Shakespeare's 'Histories' are significant examples. Plays written in these two forms – either as 'comical histories' or 'Chronicle Histories' – appeared side by side in the Elizabethan repertories.

   As Chapter 1 also demonstrates, by the late 1590s, royal 'comical history' disguise episodes derived from the medieval chronicles become subtly conflated with 'Chronicle History' fact-based narratives from the Tudor Chronicles, resulting in a far darker expression of disguised ruler intent. Royal subterfuge was now tainted by a less sympathetic expression of social unease. This blending of intrigue, observation and infiltration, evident in *Richard III* and echoed in the physical and personality disguises of Prince Hal in *Henry IV, Parts 1 & 2* and the Heywood-attributed *1 Edward IV*, finds its fullest expression in the disguised ruler stratagem of *Henry V*. As Henry wanders among his troops on the eve of Agincourt, his disguise appears as medieval in theme as it does politically immediate in anxiety-inducing effect. The fullest expression of this medieval theme is evident in the Quarto text of *Henry V*. Some intriguing inconsistencies regarding Erpingham's disguising cloak indicate a subtle shift in theatrical focus between the Quarto and Folio texts that accord with the conventionality of Henry's disguised appearance on the Elizabethan stage. Finally, Chapter 1 discusses the importance of two contemporary plays, *1 Sir John Oldcastle* and *When You See Me You Know Me*, which each return to the medieval Robin Hood roots of Henry V's thieving character, while building on Shakespeare's factual 'Chronicle History' narrative.

Chapter 2, '*The Malcontent*: A Play in Two Forms', discusses the disguised ruler play that most obviously predates Shakespeare's *Measure for Measure*. The unusual print history of *The Malcontent* offers an alternative chronology to traditional 'Jacobean disguised ruler play' criticism. Written and produced for two repertory companies at two different times and appearing in two distinctive generic forms, *The Malcontent* represents its playwright's experimentation with that contentious new form, Italian tragicomedy. The satirical focus of Marston's drama, traceable to his earlier verse satires and re-deployed in *The Malcontent*, had already found expression in his '*Antonio*' plays. In *Antonio's Revenge*, a disguised ruler strategically dresses himself in motley to infiltrate his enemy's court and exact revenge.

Not only is Marston's malcontented disguised ruler traced to his earlier '*Antonio*' dramas, but Chapter 2 also interrogates the unfaltering belief that Marston's sole engagement with Italian culture was through the mediated text of an Englished tragicomedy. On the contrary, Marston is shown to have engaged with Guarini's play in its original Italian form. Finally, the chapter questions the traditional view that the 'adult' Globe version of *The Malcontent* represents an ultimate expression of Marston's authorial intent and anti-court wit. In consequence, John Webster is shown to be of far greater significance in altering the generic focus of Marston's children's company play. Webster introduces the very localized topicality that subsequent critics view as subversively anti-court. It is Webster who facilitates an occasionalist reading of *The Malcontent*, his revisions imposing their own uniquely Jacobean contexts on Marston's earlier play. Hence the necessity to consider not *The Malcontent*, but the '*Malcontents*'.

For Chapter 3, '*Measure for Measure*: Conventionality in Disguise', we return to Shakespeare's famous disguised ruler play. In the context of the 'comical history' royal disguises described in Chapter 1, Duke Vincentio's own subterfuge now appears decidedly conventional. Indeed, the Duke's reaction to a suggestion that his disguise might have an illicit romantic motive only serves to highlight the very convention from which he seeks to distance himself. This pivotal expression of 'comical history' expectation leads to discussion of the anonymous Elizabethan drama, *Fair Em*. Predating *Measure for Measure* by some years, *Fair Em* subtly evokes several of this Jacobean play's themes and motifs.

A prior heritage for *Measure for Measure* sits uncomfortably with traditional criticism that considers the Duke to be Shakespeare's specific, albeit unsubtle portrait of King James. Chapter 3 also demonstrates that the 'Duke as James' analogy relies heavily on partisan representations of the Stuart king by Whig historiographers, whose 'findings' were embraced by literary commentators of *Measure for Measure*. The ease with which eighteenth-century Whiggish partisanship forged a narrative of negativity about James is highlighted by the continued acceptance among many Shakespeare scholars that 'Duke as James' theorizing represents historical fact. A reluctance to incorporate revisionist historical research into literary studies of *Measure for Measure* serves to confirm the continued influence of Whig historiography, which in turn adds an anachronistically negative bias to occasionalist disguised ruler criticism. Finally, Chapter 3 considers *Measure for Measure* as a proto-tragicomic construct. Since tragicomedy is notably absent from Shakespeare's Folio, its formal relationship to *Measure for Measure* offers continued scope for debate and conjecture, as well as an alternative heritage for the play's disguised ruler subterfuge.

The overriding instability of traditional 'Duke as James' theorizing leads to Chapter 4, '*The Phoenix* and *The Fawn*: Law, Morality and the Medievalism of Disguise'. The ghostly presence of James yet again haunts traditional analysis of both plays, whether in the name of the disguised Prince/Phoenix, or the character of *The Fawn*'s duped Duke Gonzago. Analogous 'Phoenix as James' or 'Gonzago as James' readings seem inappropriate for two plays whose disguised rulers appear far more medieval than topical in their deceit. It is the inherent medievalism of *The Phoenix* and *The Fawn* – their reliance on morality themes and figures subtly altered to suit their Italianate modes – that underpins the reforming narratives of both plays. To assist their didactic narratives, these plays also evoke the sixteenth-century humanist advice-book as an aid to reform. *The Fawn* even introduces an internationally famous late-medieval trope, the 'Ship of Fools', which becomes a tangible offstage feature of the play.

The underlying late-medieval and sixteenth-century didacticism of *The Phoenix* and *The Fawn* might be reconstituted to provide moralizing critiques of contemporary Jacobean society, but the overriding topical feature of these plays is the abuse of English law by corrupt legal professionals. This dominant feature accords with another children's company play, *Law Tricks*, whose incidental disguised ruler and prodigal son intrigue suggests a far wider intertextuality than traditional 'disguised ruler play' criticism allows. *Law Tricks*, like *The Phoenix* and *The Fawn*, is specifically critical of legal chicanery. As Chapter 4 demonstrates, these plays might all introduce disguised rulers to a greater or lesser degree, but they also share the common concern for the gulling of unsuspecting citizens by a section of society privileged by an education in law. In addition, they also reflect the predisposition of playwrights who, like so many who attended the children's playhouses, were themselves trained in law, and who used this training to entertain and rebuke in equal measure.

The last of the so-called 'Jacobean disguised ruler plays', *The Fleer*, is the subject of Chapter 5, 'Disguised Ruler Afterlives: The Spectre of Terrorism'. Often viewed as an insignificant disguised ruler parody, *The Fleer* is initially compared with another parodic play, Beaumont and Fletcher's *The Woman Hater*. *The Fleer*'s clumsy disguise narrative, with its prodigal child plot of sex-trade exploitation, appears within the context of an equally real, though far more dangerous occasionalist event than the 1603 accession of James. *The Fleer* is staged in the aftermath of the attempt to assassinate the entire Stuart dynasty. The Gunpowder Plot, an act of political terrorism that threatened the security of the English and Scottish nations, tends to receive less attention from literary scholars than it does from historians. In consequence, Chapter 5 argues that the Gunpowder Plot is of far greater significance in the decline of the disguised ruler than traditional commentary would suggest.

Successfully downplayed by England's aristocracy at the time, and subsequently relegated to a quaintly archaic firework celebration, the Gunpowder Plot influenced yet another disguised ruler comedy, Jonson's *Bartholomew Fair*. Returning in that age-old costume worn by royal wooing philanderers – the fool's motley – Justice Overdo evokes his own political specificity. Jonson parodies the actions not of his king, but of a civic dignitary whose power and reforming zeal made him infamous among London's trade and criminal fraternity. Terrorism and the penal regime at Bridewell are the true topicalities of this disguised ruler, whose foolish appearance accompanies his futile attempt to reform London's horse-trading fair.

Finally, an Afterword, 'The Sting in *The Wasp*'s Tail', considers what might be the last disguised ruler to strut the London stage before the closure of the playhouses in the 1640s. Like his romantic wooing forebears, Baron Gilbert of the enigmatic manuscript *The Wasp* disguises himself in motley, thus evoking a conventional theatrical motif that spans two centuries of artistic endeavour. The disguised ruler in *The Wasp* also confirms that our continued focus on a restrictively 'Jacobean' canon of plays appears inadequate when considered alongside the motif's obvious conventionality. *The Disguised Ruler in Shakespeare and his Contemporaries* offers an alternative reading for these unique and individual plays. Unencumbered by the ghostly spectre of King James, the disguised ruler is freed from the constraints of occasionality, allowing him metaphorically to wander through the early modern dramatic canon with clandestine ease.

Chapter 1
The Disguised Ruler on the Elizabethan Stage

Shakespeare's *Measure for Measure*, Marston's *The Malcontent* and Middleton's *The Phoenix* are often presented as the ultimate expressions of disguised ruler drama. From this perspective, Duke Vincentio, Duke Altofronto and the Prince/Phoenix are archetypal disguised rulers, written specifically for a Jacobean playgoing audience. As playwrights, Shakespeare, Marston and Middleton thus become the principal exponents of very overt political commentary on the nation's new Scottish monarch. This argument results in an occasionalist focus on James's accession as the sole catalyst for subsequent disguised ruler play activity. Such a reading effectively denies the importance of another, earlier Shakespearean disguised ruler – King Henry in *Henry V* – who travels among his Agincourt troops on the eve of battle gleaning personal insight and knowledge. Because *Henry V* resides within Shakespeare's Elizabethan canon, and does not fit an anxiety-inducing model of Jacobean surveillance, its disguised ruler is ignored or dismissed by new historicist critics as an inconvenient aberration.[1] This myopia is unfortunate, since Henry's exploit echoes similar episodes in plays from the 1580s and 1590s that dramatize kings and princes disguising themselves for personal or political ends. Many of these plays engage with a folktale narrative popularized in ballads, pamphlets and provincial revelries the nation over: the legend of Robin Hood.[2]

Henry V is likewise significant because it combines two distinctive subgenres of history-based drama. These generic categories – the 'comical histories' and the 'Chronicle Histories' – are differentiated by their respective source material, the first medieval and mythical, the second more recent in its historicized Tudor bias. The subgenre to which *Henry V* most obviously belongs is the 'Chronicle Histories', a grouping more highly regarded because of its generic association with Shakespeare's First Folio. The 'Chronicle Histories' based their narratives on sixteenth-century historiography disseminated in the Tudor Chronicles of writers

---

[1]   For an alternative view, see Eleanor Rycroft, 'Facial Hair and the Performance of Adult Masculinity on the Early Modern English Stage', in Helen Ostovich, Holger Schott Syme and Andrew Griffin (eds), *Locating the Queen's Men, 1583–1603* (Aldershot, 2009), pp. 218–28 (p. 223).

[2]   See Anne Barton, 'The King Disguised: Shakespeare's *Henry V* and the Comical History', in Joseph G. Price (ed.), *The Triple Bond* (University Park, 1975), pp. 92–117.

such as Edward Hall, Richard Grafton, Raphael Holinshed and John Stow.[3] These chroniclers periodized the reigns of the English monarchs, celebrating certain historical 'facts' and, in the process, legitimizing the dynastic pretensions of their royal patrons. When repeated in Shakespearean drama, these Chronicle 'facts' helped create a collective cultural awareness and English national consciousness. As Peter Saccio states, this process 'etched upon the common memory' a selective, Tudor-biased sense of medieval history that remains with us today.[4] The Tudor Chronicles therefore influenced the anonymous *Famous Victories of Henry the Fifth* (*c.* mid-1580s) and *Troublesome Reign of John, King of England* (*c.* 1589), the anonymous manuscript (possibly Shakespeare's, possibly Samuel Rowley's) *Thomas of Woodstock* (*c.* 1592), Christopher Marlowe's *Edward II* (*c.* 1592), the Shakespeare collaboration *King Edward III* (*c.* 1592–1593), Shakespeare's First and Second Tetralogies (*c.* 1590–1599), *King John* (*c.* 1596), and (later) Shakespeare and Fletcher's *Henry VIII* (*c.* 1613).[5]

The 'Chronicle Histories' developed alongside the 'comical histories'. These 'comical histories', which incorporate their historical protagonists into fantastic comedy narratives based on medieval myth and legend, include Robert Greene's *Friar Bacon and Friar Bungay* (*c.* 1589), Greene's *George a Greene* (*c.* 1590) and George Peele's *Edward I* (*c.* 1591). Unlike the 'Chronicle Histories', which derived their historicized narratives from the Tudor Chronicles, the 'comical histories' owed their fanciful adventures to the medieval chronicle tradition. Ivo Kamps thus describes the 'comical history' plays as less concerned with the 'transient stream of human incidents' underlying the Tudor dynastic past, and more with quasi-historical or mythical events designed as lessons about the present.[6] The medieval chronicles often foregrounded instances of localized and secularized social unrest within a framework of royal romance and wooing adventurism. Eventually superseded by the Tudor Chronicles, these folkloric medieval chronicles influenced English drama from the 1560s until the decline

---

[3]   Edward Hall, *The Union of the Noble and Illustre Fameleies of Lancastre & York* [*Hall's Chronicle*] (London, 1542; reprinted 1548; 2nd edn 1550); Richard Grafton, *An Abridgement of the Chronicles of England* (London, 1563); Raphael Holinshed, *Chronicles of England, Scotlande, and Irelande* (London, 1577); John Stow, *Summarie of Englyshe Chronicles* (London, 1565); Stow, *Annales, or a Generale Chronicle of England* (London, 1580).

[4]   Peter Saccio, *Shakespeare's English Kings,* 2nd edn (Oxford, 2000), p. 4.

[5]   See Giorgio Melchiori (ed.), *King Edward III* (Cambridge, 1998), pp. 19–36. For *Thomas of Woodstock*'s attribution to Shakespeare, see Michael Egan (ed.), *'The Tragedy of Richard II, Part One': A Newly Authenticated Play by William Shakespeare* (Lampeter, 2006); to Rowley, see MacDonald P. Jackson, 'The Date and Authorship of Thomas of Woodstock: Evidence and its Interpretation', *ROMARD*, 46 (2007): 67–100.

[6]   Ivo Kamps, *Historiography and Ideology in Early Stuart Drama* (Cambridge, 1996), p. 33.

of the history plays in the late 1620s.[7] Thus, *Henry V*'s appearance in 1599 marks a generic crossroads between the 'Chronicle Histories' and 'comical histories', when several history plays present disguised rulers as romantic and mythical individuals, who are also pragmatically political in their illicit actions.

Both the 'comical histories' and the 'Chronicle Histories' rely on a shared English consciousness to supply 'real' royal characters and events. The 'comical histories' were, as their wooing narratives suggest, best suited to the representation of romantic adventures and themes based on medieval mythology. One relevant recurring theme, dating back to twelfth-century balladry, is often associated with Arthurian romance and with Robin Hood: the 'king and subject' meeting of a disguised ruler with his lowly countryman.[8] Although generally arising from some chance encounter or prior disagreement, this meeting's inevitable resolution guarantees recognition of the king's flexibility and the subject's deep-seated loyalty.[9] This 'king and subject' theme perpetuates the myth of an unmediated line of communication between a monarch and his people. It thus confirms the hegemonic predominance of an accessible, all-seeing royal authority. Conversely, it also highlights underlying tensions among the nation's aggrieved though silent masses.[10]

An early example of the 'king and subject' theme appears in *A Lytell Geste of Robyn Hode* (traceable to *c.* 1450, although possibly of twelfth-century origin).[11] Published repeatedly throughout the sixteenth century, the *Geste* cycle was particularly popular in the latter years of Elizabeth's reign. In the 'Copland' edition of *A Mery Geste of Robyn Hoode* (*c.* 1560), the 'king and subject' meeting and resolution occurs when the King borrows 'monkes wede' for himself and five of his best knights (1467–9ff.).[12] Disguised as a wealthy abbot, the King and his retinue, thus 'clothed in gray' (as 'Grey-Friars' of the English Franciscan Order), ride into Nottingham Forest to entice Robin Hood out of hiding (1485–90ff.). This late-medieval disguised ruler immediately suggests similar monk's and friar's costumes worn by later stage monarchs. Robin Hood's popularity in ballads and pamphlets ensured that the mythical heritage of such disguises was easily

---

[7]   D.R. Woolf, 'The Shapes of History', in Kastan (ed.), *Companion*, pp. 186–205 (pp. 196–9).

[8]   E.K. Chambers, *English Literature at the Close of the Middle Ages* (Oxford, 1945), pp. 128–9; Elizabeth Walsh, 'The King in Disguise', *Folklore*, 86 (1975): 3–24.

[9]   Stephen Knight and Thomas H. Ohlgren (eds), *Robin Hood and Other Outlaw Tales* (Kalamazoo, 1997), p. 84.

[10]   Rachel Snell, 'The Undercover King', in Judith Weiss, Jennifer Fellows and Morgan Dickson (eds), *Medieval Insular Romance: Translation and Innovation* (Cambridge, 2000), pp. 133–54 (pp. 150–51); David Wiles, *The Early Plays of Robin Hood* (Cambridge, 1981), p. 20.

[11]   Francis James Child (ed.), *The English and Scottish Popular Ballads* (5 vols, Mineola, 2003), vol. 5, p. 69. Line numbers from this edition.

[12]   *A Mery Geste of Robyn Hoode* [Copland] (London, *c.* 1560), BL C.21.c.63, fols F4ʳ–F4ᵛ.

recognizable to early modern audiences. The *Geste* cycle also confirms this long folkloric tradition, with the Robin Hood legend illustrating the benefit (for a king if not necessarily his subjects) of royal disguise.

Analysis of the wealth of incidental evidence in English parish records, made available through the *REED* project, confirms the enduring interest in Robin Hood throughout the Elizabethan era.[13] These documents also highlight widespread social problems associated with secular pageants and community fairs. Parish records indicate, for example, that raucous behaviour and other trouble regularly accompanied local 'theatrical' re-enactments of the Robin Hood stories.[14] Since these lowly, localized community revelries are inevitably ephemeral, few formal accounts remain. These same records nonetheless link Robin Hood with varied rural pursuits, including festivities and drunken riotousness. The Robin Hood legend, as Peter Happé argues, was thus 'etched upon the common memory' of English society.[15]

In dramatic form, the outlaw's adventures provide a commonplace focus for two lost plays, the anonymous *Robin Hood and Little John* (1594) and William Haughton's *Robin Hood's Penn'orths* (1600), as well as the anonymous (possibly Anthony Wadeson's) *Look About You* (1600).[16] Likewise, Robin Hood is central to Anthony Munday's tragic play, *The Downfall of Robert Earl of Huntingdon* (*c.* 1598), its Munday/Henry Chettle sequel, *The Death of Robert Earl of Huntingdon* (both published 1601), and numerous other sixteenth-century plays.[17] Indeed, the legend is even discernible in a play written perhaps a decade before Henry's Agincourt adventure – *Friar Bacon and Friar Bungay*. With its 'comical history' narrative, *Friar Bacon and Friar Bungay* stresses the value of disguise and secretly acquired knowledge, while presenting royal subterfuge that features the Lincoln green costume of England's favourite subversive character.

Friar Bacon and Friar Bungay: Royal Disguise and Fool's Motley

Robert Greene's *Friar Bacon and Friar Bungay* (*c.* 1589, Strange's[?], published 1594), a fanciful tale based in thirteenth-century England, features Edward, Prince of Wales, the future Edward I and son of Henry III.[18] Reprinted almost every decade up to 1700, the play has a complicated and vague early history. It was originally performed sometime between 1589 and 1591, possibly by Strange's Men at the

---

[13]   See Peter Happé, *English Drama Before Shakespeare* (Harlow, 1999), pp. 167–71.

[14]   Ibid., p. 169.

[15]   Saccio, *Kings*, p. 4.

[16]   W.W. Greg, *Look About You* (Oxford, 1913), p. v.

[17]   Jeffrey L. Singman, 'Munday's Unruly Earl', in Lois Potter (ed.), *Playing Robin Hood* (Newark, 1998), pp. 63–76 (p. 63).

[18]   Robert Greene, *The Honorable Historie of Frier Bacon, and Frier Bungay* (London, 1594).

A mery geſte of

Robyn Hoode and of hys lyſe. wyth
an newe playe for to be played
in Maye games very ple∙
ſaunte and full of paſtyme∙

Fig. 1.1   Robin Hood and Little John depicted on the title-page of *A Mery Geste of Robyn Hoode*, published *c.* 1560

Rose, or by the Queen's Men at the Theatre in Shoreditch.[19] It appeared again in 1593, this time definitely performed by Strange's Men at the Rose, and was revived by the Queen's company in 1594 in collaboration with Sussex's Men, again at the Rose.[20] Two years after their transfer to the newly-built Fortune, the Admiral's Men revived the play for a December 1602 performance at court, with an additional (lost) Prologue and Epilogue by Middleton (presumably written sometime before *The Phoenix*).[21] Despite the vagueness of *Friar Bacon*'s early performance history, this catalogue of revival and revision demonstrates its continued dramatic appeal. The play's longevity appears linked to its use of English moral and mythical themes that suited the nationalistic fervour (and national unease) that followed the failed Spanish Armada invasion of 1588.[22] Jingoistic patriotism was at its height and *Friar Bacon* became reassuringly topical for a nation uncomfortably aware of its queen's age, her lack of a natural successor and the threat from foreign forces.[23] National pride and medieval myth combined to make *Friar Bacon* a mainstay of the early modern canon.

In Greene's 'comical history', Prince Edward seeks assistance from the infamous Oxford cleric and magician, Friar Bacon. This friar invents magical devices, including a talking 'brazen head', whose prognostications aim to raise an impenetrable defence around England's coastal shore (*Bacon*, B1[v]; 2.25). Alongside this, Bacon also invents a 'glasse prospectiue' for secretly observing people's actions over impossibly vast distances (*Bacon*, C4[r]; 5.105). Greene's magical narrative was based on a mid-sixteenth-century chapbook prose tale, *The Famous Historie of Fryer Bacon* (*c.* 1555), which describes the thirteenth-century monk and scientist, Roger Bacon, whose *De nullitate magiæ* (*c.* 1240–60) led to popular accusations of sorcery.[24] *Friar Bacon* perpetuates this sorcerer's reputation as a necromancing friar by showing him conjuring devils and demons with Faustian ease. Prince Edward's adventure, moreover, introduces not one, but two instances of royal disguise. Both of these influence the moral regeneration of the play's princely protagonist, but only after the complications of Edward's yearning for the Suffolk maiden, Margaret. These lustful interludes threaten Edward's authority and the security of the nation. The prince's attempts to seduce the humble maiden provide fitting contexts for his eventual reformation. This can

---

[19]   J.A. Lavin (ed.), *Friar Bacon* (London, 1969), p. xiii; McMillin and MacLean, *Queen's*, p. 90.

[20]   R.A. Foakes and R.T. Rickert (eds), *Henslowe's Diary*, 2nd edn (Cambridge, 2002), pp. 19–20.

[21]   Ibid., p. 207.

[22]   Deanne Williams, '*Friar Bacon and Friar Bungay* and the Rhetoric of Temporality', in Gordon McMullan and David Matthews (eds), *Reading the Medieval in Early Modern England* (Cambridge, 2007), pp. 31–48.

[23]   Happé, *Drama*, p. 228.

[24]   *The Famous Historie of Fryer Bacon* (London, 1627).

only occur, however, after Prince Edward puts on a very distinctive though oft-repeated disguise.

Prince Edward is advised to adopt a disguise by his father's court fool, Rafe Simnell. Trying to relieve the young prince's melancholic infatuation, Rafe tells Edward to swap his princely finery and sword for a fool's cap, coat and dagger. Disguised as Rafe's 'foole', Edward can then 'deceiue loue' (personified as that 'proud scab' Cupid), who is only attracted by the outward trappings of wealth (*Bacon*, A3ᵛ; 1.27–35).[25] The prince happily accepts Rafe's advice, instigating an image of inversion – the prince, king or duke in fool's motley – that becomes a mainstay of disguised ruler drama.

Edward travels to Oxford, therefore, as the 'maister foole', while Rafe pretends to be the aristocratic Prince of Wales (*Bacon*, C3ʳ; 5.47–8). Predictably, their exchange is far from successful. It confirms instead the commonplace notion that fine clothes can never elevate a fool to the aristocracy, even if a prince can easily pretend to be a fool. The comic pomposity of Rafe's 'countenance like a Prince' (*Bacon*, C2ᵛ; 5.17) largely fails to impress the Oxford citizens they meet on their journey, with one notable exception. Asking directions to Brasenose College from Friar Bacon's foolish assistant Miles, Rafe refers Miles to his princely 'reparrell' (*Bacon*, C3ʳ; 5.46). This exchange confirms the fool's belief that a costume alone should guarantee his successful disguise. Although Miles is indeed duped, Rafe's deceit is no match for the Oxford Friar. Bacon's magical 'skill' ensures that no 'foole disguisd' in princely attire, nor prince in fool's motley, can 'conceale' their true identities (*Bacon*, C3ᵛ; 5.70–72). Friar Bacon immediately recognizes and acknowledges the motley-attired 'fool' before him as his royal prince. That Edward remains in motley throughout his sojourn in Oxford is suggested by Rafe's later drunken adventure, dressed still in the royal 'apparrell' of the 'great prince of Walis' (*Bacon*, D3ᵛ–D4ʳ; 7.65–6). Thus attired, Rafe fails to fool three Oxford scholars, whose anger at the deceit is only assuaged when they learn that Rafe's disguise is intended to shield Edward's secret visit to Friar Bacon (*Bacon*, D4ᵛ; 7.105–6). This politicized explanation allows Rafe to maintain his farcical persona. It also confirms that Prince Edward remains in his fool's motley for most of the remainder of the play.

Edward's motley disguise is not the only mention of royal disguising in *Friar Bacon*. Indeed, following his initial decision to exchange clothes with Rafe, Edward informs his courtiers that he has previously worn a disguise to travel among his people. Recounting the circumstances of this escapade, Edward describes his earlier meeting with the rural maiden, Margaret of Fressingfield, daughter of the royal gamekeeper. Edward prides himself on being 'vnknowne' and 'not taken for the Prince' by the simple Suffolk countryfolk. They deemed him one of several 'frolicke Courtiers' that 'reuell[ed] thus among [the king's] game' (*Bacon*, B1ʳ; 1.130–32). The unsuspecting Margaret even accepted the

---

[25]   Line numbers from Daniel Seltzer (ed.), *Friar Bacon and Friar Bungay* (London, 1964).

Fig. 1.2   Prince Edward disguised in fool's motley for a 2006 Toronto
                  performance of *Friar Bacon and Friar Bungay*

disguised Edward into her father's home. His passion excited by this earlier
(unseen) episode, Edward now explains how he has 'deuised a pollicie' to gain
the young innocent's sexual favours (*Bacon*, B1ʳ; 1.133). He commands his friend
Lacy, earl of Lincoln, to embark on a wooing embassy to Fressingfield, where he
should 'Haunt [himself] disguisd among the countrie swaines' in the lowly rags of
a 'farmers sonne' (*Bacon*, B1ʳ; 1.139–40). Once Lacy has gained their confidence,
he must confide in the beautiful Margaret 'that the Courtier tyred all in greene,
/ That helpt her handsomly to run her cheese, / And fild her fathers lodge with
venison', now commends himself to her (*Bacon*, B1ʳ; 1.143–6). Lacy's task is to
observe Margaret's reaction to this news. If she becomes pale, the embassy is lost;
if she blushes, the green courtier's overtures are obviously acceptable to the maid.
     Edward's 'greene' disguise and his ambassador's identity as earl of Lincoln
evoke a familiar folktale image from the English ballad tradition – that of Robin
Hood. This same 'greene' disguise (that also punningly suggests the playwright's
name) recurs throughout the play as a symbolic reference point for the prince's
wayward predatory intent. Thus, when Lacy, '*disguised in countrie apparell*'
(*Bacon*, B4ʳ; 3.1.0.SD), introduces himself to Margaret, he describes Edward as
the visitor 'Tyred in greene' (*Bacon*, B4ᵛ; 3.42–5). Friar Bungay also confirms
Lacy's identity and notes his mission to 'procure' Margaret's love for the royal
prince disguised 'in greene' (*Bacon*, C4ᵛ; 6.22–4). Finally, Margaret's demand
of Lacy – 'Woo you still for the courtier all in greene[?]' (*Bacon*, D1ʳ; 6.75) –

confirms Edward's distinctive attire, not seen onstage, but alluded to by the prince and all who recall meeting him. This recurring green imagery continually evokes the peculiarly English Robin Hood tradition.

Unlike the subversive disguised outlaw of Robin Hood legend, Edward has adopted his green attire merely for the self-serving seduction of an innocent country maiden. As Margaret quickly realises, the 'lure' or trap that the prince 'in green' has laid for her 'is but for lust' (*Bacon*, C4^v; 6.23–5). *Friar Bacon* thus incorporates a moral imperative into its wooing adventure, whereby disguise by a 'ruler' must benefit the nation as a whole, not simply the libidinous urges of an individual aristocrat. Edward recognizes the threat his libido poses when alluding to Margaret as '*Lucrece*' and to himself as '*Tarquine*', who might 'hazard Roome and all / To win the louely mayd of Fresingfield' (*Bacon*, A4^r; 1.85–7). Unless Edward curbs his lust, he is unfit to marry the Princess Eleanor, daughter of the King of Castile, in a union promising peace between the warring nations of England and Spain. In a dénouement that complements the play's post-Armada jingoism, Edward finally overcomes his lustful infatuation. Morally transformed, he finds contentment in the arranged political marriage with his Spanish princess.

A similar message emerges in the incomplete sequel to *Friar Bacon* (attributed likewise to Greene), *John of Bordeaux* (c. 1590–1594, Strange's[?]).[26] *John of Bordeaux* presents Friar Bacon travelling in Germany, and meeting the ruthless Prince Ferdinand at his father's imperial court. Ferdinand, like his royal counterpart Edward in *Friar Bacon*, lusts after the fair Rossalin. Unfortunately, Rossalin (unlike Margaret) is already married. Her husband, John of Bordeaux, commands the emperor's armies against the Turks. Because Rossalin refuses the prince's advances, Ferdinand ensures she is falsely accused of adultery, made homeless and forced to beg for survival. Ironically, Rossalin's son Rossacler puts on the 'disguised arraye' of a beggar and comes to his mother's aid (*Bordeaux*, 9[31]^a; TLN.839). Ferdinand's own despicable conduct requires no such disguising ploy. Although Ferdinand's behaviour in *John of Bordeaux* is far more sadistic than his princely counterpart's in *Friar Bacon*, it still mirrors Edward's blind infatuation for Margaret, while illustrating the political danger of such obsession. For *Friar Bacon*, however, the overriding image remains that of a wooing prince in disguise who has adopted the green attire of a Robin Hood outlaw for his dangerously playful sexual encounter, before returning in fool's motley.

Robin Hood, Regal Wooers and 'Comical History' Disguise

The verdant ghost of Robin Hood haunts *Friar Bacon* without ever appearing in the play. By contrast, the mythical outlaw becomes a tangible figure in several subsequent 'comical histories' from the 1590s, which each present disguised

---

[26] *John of Bordeaux*, Alnwick Castle MS.507. Through line numbers from W.L. Renwick and W.W. Greg (eds.), *John of Bordeaux, or The Second Part of Friar Bacon* (Oxford, 1936).

kings travelling to meet Robin Hood, or characters assuming his famous identity. Like the prince in *Friar Bacon*, these disguised rulers invariably bear the name 'Edward', though not all are identified specifically as Edward I. One who certainly is Edward I (thus figuring *Friar Bacon*'s prince now crowned king) appears in George Peele's 'comical history' *Edward I* (*c.* 1591, Queen's[?]; published 1593), a near-contemporary to *Friar Bacon* most likely performed at the Theatre in Shoreditch.[27] King Edward, famously nicknamed Longshanks because of his imposing height, disguises himself as a 'Gentleman' to spy on the Welsh rebel, Lluellen (*Edward I*, H1ᵛ; 11.1792).

Lluellen has entrenched himself in a forest with his outlawed retinue. The rebel recognizes the folktale heritage of this forest lair, and suggests to his followers that they acquire the 'booke of *Robin Hood*' to learn how best to play their respective mythical characters (*Edward I*, E4ʳ; 7.1176–7). The outlaws are apportioned their roles as 'little *Iohn*', 'Frier *Tucke*' and 'Maide marion', with Lluellen himself representing '*Robin Hood*' (*Edward I*, E4ʳ; 7.1183–6). Lluellen even proposes selling his precious 'chaine' to fund the purchase of clothing to dress his followers 'all in greene' (*Edward I*, E4ʳ; 7.1203). The disguised King Edward, accompanied by Lluellen's duplicitous brother, David, enters the renegade's forest. Edward confronts the Welshman who, as 'Robin Hood of the great mountaines', has been stealing from the poor country folk (*Edward I*, H2ᵛ; 11.1853–4). The king announces his true identity and wins the subsequent fight, but is forced to refrain from killing the rebel by David's treacherous intervention. Although they are still sworn enemies, Lluellen acknowledges Edward's 'courage', thus permitting him to admit that, were it not for them contesting the throne, he might 'loue and honor the man for his valour' (*Edward I*, H3ᵛ; 12.1917–19). This oblique association of Edward with the Robin Hood myth is significant because the king in *Edward I* and the prince in *Friar Bacon* are one and the same. Even *Edward I*'s 'Friar Tuck', the disguised Friar Hugh, evokes the trope of princely disguise when he comments, 'Nor can an Asses hide disguise / A Lion if he ramps and rise' (*Edward I*, F1ʳ; 8.1270–71). A mythical intertextuality therefore exists between these two 'comical histories', one that would be recognizable to early modern playgoers steeped in the Robin Hood tradition.[28]

Mythical intertextuality also permeates *George a Greene* (*c.* 1590, Sussex's[?]; published 1599), a play likewise attributed to Robert Greene. George a Greene, himself a popular folktale figure, features alongside Robin Hood in the medieval ballad *Robin Hood and the Pinner of Wakefield*.[29] In *George a Greene*, not one

---

[27]   George Peele, *The Famous Chronicle of King Edward the First* (London, 1593). Scene and line numbers from Frank S. Hook (ed.), *Edward I*, in Charles Tyler Prouty (gen. ed.), *Dramatic Works of George Peele* (3 vols, New Haven, 1952–70), vol. 2 (1961).

[28]   See Julian M. Luxford, 'An English Chronicle Entry on Robin Hood', *JMH*, 35 (2009): 70–76.

[29]   See Jeffrey L. Singman, *Robin Hood: The Shaping of the Legend* (Westport, 1998), p. 122; Benjamin Griffin, 'Moving Tales: Narrative Drift in Oral Culture and Scripted Theater', *NLH*, 37 (2006): 725–38 (pp. 734–5).

but two kings, Edward of England and James of Scotland (the latter only recently defeated after aiding an English rebellion), decide to 'disguise' themselves 'secretly' and 'make a merrie iourney for a moneth' to see the famous Pinner (*George*, E2ᵛ; TLN.917–9).[30] The patriotic fervour of George a Greene, a self-avowed '[t]rue liegeman' to King Edward (*George*, A4ʳ; TLN.104), has already been proved by his defeat and capture of the traitorous earl of Kendal. The earl, however, claims to rebel not 'against King Edward, / But for the poore that is opprest by [his] wrong' (*George*, C4ʳ; TLN.567–8). Kendal's reference to fighting for the impoverished and downtrodden, so similar to the Robin Hood myth, achieves even greater significance through the location of the rebel's earldom. Possibly again an allusion to the playwright's name (if Greene is indeed the play's author), the place-name 'Kendal' resonates with verdant imagery.[31] The name Kendal is associated with Robin Hood and royal disguise in *Hall's Chronicle*, when the recently crowned Henry VIII and his retinue are described as surprising Queen Katherine by storming her apartments, '*all appareled in shorte cotes, of kentishe kendal, with hodes on their heddes … like out lawes, or Robyn Hodes men*'.[32] Kendal likewise appears in *The Playe of Robyn Hoode*, a verse playlet appended to the 1560s 'Copland' version of *A Mery Geste*.[33] Describing Robin Hood's arrival with his unkempt men, Friar Tuck exclaims, 'Here be a sorte of ragged knaves come in, / Clothed all in Kendale grene' (97–8ff.). For Tuck, the Westmorland woad-based cloth colour, 'Kendal Green', best describes the outlaws' torn Lincoln green attire. In *George a Greene*, the earldom of Kendal likewise represents a recognizable reference to the Robin Hood myth, incorporated into a narrative of social unrest quelled by the patriotic figure, George.

Subtle and punning imagery aside, Robin Hood is himself a character in *George a Greene*, cajoled by his nagging partner, Maid Marion, into travelling to Yorkshire to fight the Pinner. She is outraged at the Pinner's popularity and his famed skill with a quarterstaff, as well as the reported beauty of George's rural love. The subsequent confrontation is staged not in Wakefield, but in nearby Bradford, a town patrolled by combative shoemakers. George's defeat of Robin Hood in combat gains the outlaw's respect and admiration. Subsequently united as comrades in arms, George and Robin then encounter the royal travellers. Edward and James have arrived in Bradford, believing that, 'Thus disguised', 'none … will take [them] to be kings' (*George*, F2ʳ; TLN.1109–10). The disguised kings are obviously clothed in simple attire, since George initially describes them as 'pesants / Trickt in yeomans weedes' (*George*, F2ᵛ; TLN.1142–3). Only later does a stage direction describe the '*bringing out* [of] *the Kings garments*' (*George*, F3ᵛ; TLN.1191.SD), thus restoring Edward and James to their true regal status.

---

[30] Robert Greene[?], *A Pleasant Conceyted Comedie of George a Greene* (London, 1599). Through line numbers from W.W. Greg (ed.), *The Comedy of George a Green* (Oxford, 1911).

[31] Happé, *English Drama*, p. 169.

[32] *Hall's Chronicle*, 'Henry VIII', Year 1 [1509–1510], fol. viᵛ (fol. 3A6ᵛ).

[33] Child, *Ballads*, vol. 5, p. 424.

Prior to this revelation, George and Robin confront the two 'pesants' and angrily denounce the strangers' behaviour. Edward and James have, in deference to a local custom imposed by the irascible Bradford shoemakers, submissively trailed their staves behind them in order to pass without argument through the town. George and Robin demand that the unknown travellers cease their humiliating display. Edward's gracious refusal disquiets the volatile George. The disguised king's measured response, spoken 'like an honest quiet fellow' (*George*, F3^r; TLN.1162), does little to appease the Yorkshireman's appetite for physical violence. Threatening the strangers should they continue to pander to the shoemakers' degrading demand, George forces Edward to yield to his request. He then pulverizes the shoemakers, at the same time swearing allegiance to 'good King Edwards selfe' (*George*, F3^v; TLN.1187). The irony of this patriotic outburst is not lost on Edward, who reveals his true identity. George declines Edward's offer of a knighthood, accepting instead his king's assistance in brokering the Pinner's marriage. Yet again, the medieval tradition of the Robin Hood 'king and subject' theme of disguised confrontation and resolution is evoked in a play that ends in mutual respect and enhanced authority for England's king. Although *George a Greene* later confirms a prevailing belief in King Edward's less honourable intentions towards the lonely wives of his subjects, the play still promotes its message of political security from, and solidarity for, rulers who wear disguises to travel in secret among their people.

Pilgrim, Shepherd and Hermit Disguises

Friar Bacon, *Edward I* and *George a Greene* recreate a mythical life for the real King Edward at various stages in his career. They also demonstrate the continued relevance of Robin Hood in late sixteenth-century disguised ruler drama. All three plays rely on audience recognition of the familiar medieval 'king and subject' theme. Rulers might have a propensity to embark on wooing adventures, but ultimately they must accept responsibility (and command respect) when national security demands it. These were not, however, the only 'comical histories' from the early 1590s to portray the romantic wooing adventures of disguised rulers. The anonymous *Fair Em* (*c*. 1590, Strange's; published 1631) presents King William travelling in disguise to the Danish court to woo the Princess Blanch. His journey culminates in a plot device that not only leads to political stability and national security, but later is also echoed in the bed trick of *Measure for Measure*. Similarly, the anonymous *The True Chronicle History of King Leir* (*c*. 1590, Queen's[?]; published 1605) portrays the Gallian King entering England 'disguisde in Palmers [pilgrim's] weeds', secretly to choose the worthiest of Leir's daughters as his bride (*Leir*, B3^r; TLN.380).[34] Falling in love with Cordella, the disguised French king pretends to woo on behalf of his monarch. His overtures are rejected by Leir's

---

[34]   Anonymous, *The True Chronicle History of King Leir* (London, 1605). Through line numbers from W.W. Greg (ed.), *The History of King Leir* (Oxford, 1907).

daughter, who expresses love for the 'pilgrim' ambassador himself. The Gallian King reveals his true identity and, now united, the pair return to France. There, Cordella and her husband travel among their subjects disguised as '*Countrey folke*' (*Leir*, H1ᵛ; TLN.2091–2.SD), until Cordella is finally reunited with Leir who has fled from England to escape capture (*Leir*, H3ʳ–H4ᵛ; TLN.2218–336). Again, the outcome is one of reconciliation and ultimate peace as Leir is reinstated as England's king with his French son-in-law's military assistance.

Yet another wooing disguised ruler appears in the anonymous *Mucedorus* (*c.* 1590, Chamberlain's[?]; published 1598).[35] In this play, Prince Mucedorus of Valencia, like the Gallian King in *Leir*, embarks on a quest to marry the worthiest daughter of the King of Aragon. Disguised initially as a shepherd (possibly an allusion to the pastoral disguise of Paris on Mount Ida) and then in the friar's habit of a 'hermite' (*Mucedorus*, D4ᵛ; 4.2.15–16), Mucedorus proves his valour by defeating first a bear, then a marauding forest dweller, to gain the love of Princess Amadine. Only after these battles does Amadine discover Mucedorus's true identity. The habit worn by Mucedorus's 'hermite' echoes the King's Grey-Friars' disguise in the *Geste* cycle. Visually, the hermit's costume and the friar's or monk's habit would, in a theatrical setting, appear exactly the same.

The hermit disguise also recalls Raymond Mounchensey's 'holy habit' in the anonymous *The Merry Devil of Edmonton* (*c.* 1599–1603, Chamberlain's/King's Men; published 1608), which was used secretly to woo the nun, Millicent (*Merry Devil*, D4ʳ; 3.2.128).[36] Raymond's 'knauery', perpetrated 'under [his] cowle' (*Merry Devil*, E4ᵛ; 5.1.28), and explicitly associated with the 'great magician' Friar Bacon who is 'about the Vniuersity' (*Merry Devil*, F1ᵛ; 5.1.91–2), prefigures the Duke's disguise in *Measure for Measure*. A play that remained popular throughout the seventeenth century (Middleton mentions it in his *Blacke Book* of 1604, and Samuel Pepys records seeing a production 10 August 1661), *Merry Devil* represents a fitting partner to *Mucedorus*, which was itself revived for the Globe in 1604.[37] *Mucedorus* and *Merry Devil*, most likely performed when *Measure for Measure* and *The Malcontent* were playing in the same repertory, demonstrate the continued importance of romantic disguise that relies on the materiality of the hermit's 'habit'.

Mucedorus was not, however, the last 'comical history' to represent the hermit's 'habit' onstage. George Chapman's complex disguise drama, *The Blind Beggar of Alexandria* (*c.* 1595, Admiral's; published 1598), star vehicle of the Admiral's Men's leading actor Edward Alleyn, relied on the same costume for the play's

[35] Anonymous, *Mucedorus* (London, 1598). Line numbers from James Winny (ed.), *Three Elizabethan Plays: Edward III, Mucedorus, Midas* (London, 1959).

[36] Anonymous, *The Merry Deuill of Edmonton* (London, 1608). Line numbers from Nicola Bennett (ed.), *The Merry Devil of Edmonton* (London, 2000).

[37] R. Thornberry, 'A Seventeenth-Century Revival of *Mucedorus* Before 1610', *SQ*, 28 (1977): 362–4. For *The Blacke Book* reference, see G.B. Shand (ed.), *The Black Book*, in *Oxford Middleton*, p. 216.

Fig. 1.3   Engraving from *La Danse Macabre* (1486), showing (right) 'Death and the Hermit' dancing together. The Hermit's habit is indistinguishable from any friar's or monk's costume of the period

apparent duke in disguise.[38] 'Apparent' because, as Duke Cleanthes admits when he describes the 'strange disguise' adopted for each of his duplicitous, bigamous and predatory alter-egos (*Blind*, E3ᵛ; TLN.1304), just one costume defines his true heritage. This is not the 'veluet gowne', pistol and eye patch of his mad-brained Count Hermes (*Blind*, E3ᵛ; TLN.1305), nor the false 'great nose' of his Leon the Usurer (*Blind*, C2ᵛ; TLN.628), but his hermit's disguise as 'blind *Irus*' (*Blind*, A3ᵛ; TLN.115). Cleanthes may have reinvented himself as a 'warlicke Duke' (*Blind*, E3ʳ; TLN.1249), the successful military commander of the Egyptian King Ptolemy's troops. He may in this guise suffer the dangerous attentions of the king's wife, Queen Aegiale, who, to gain his love, has cold-bloodedly 'made away with his Dutches' (*Blind*, A2ᵛ; TLN.44). He may likewise admit to a long-term Machiavellian 'pollicie' to 'claime [Egypt's] crowne' from the helpless Ptolemy (*Blind*, A3ᵛ; TLN.128–31), the ultimate success of which invites comparison with later disguised rulers who suffer usurpation and restoration of legitimate power. It is, however, his blind hermit's disguise that best suits a man who, as Cleanthes admits at the outset, was originally no more than 'a shepherdes sonne at *Memphis* borne' (*Blind*, A3ᵛ; TLN.118).

---

[38]   George Chapman, *The Blinde Begger of Alexandria* (London, 1598). Line numbers from W.W. Greg (ed.), *The Blind Beggar of Alexandria* (Oxford, 1929).

Fig. 1.4   Woodcut of a shepherd in traditional rustic clothing, as worn by Colin Clout in Edmund Spenser's *The Shepherd's Calendar* (1597)

This wooing trickster and military tactician, like the Tamburlaine he so closely resembles, has no aristocratic roots.[39] Instead, Cleanthes comes from lowly stock, his 'Father' a mere 'fortune teller', from whom Cleanthes 'learnt [the] art' of 'palmestrie' (*Blind*, A3ᵛ; TLN.119–21). Andrew Gurr's description of the actor Alleyn comically wearing multiple disguises, with which to 'send up his own fustian roles' as Tamburlaine or Barabas in Christopher Marlowe's *Tamburlaine the Great, Parts 1 and 2* (1586–87, Admiral's; published 1590) and *The Jew of Malta* (1589, Admiral's; published 1633), demonstrates the popular appeal of such 'comical history' shape-shifting.[40] It also demonstrates the ubiquity of the friar-like 'hermit' disguise in Elizabethan drama.

The catalogue of 'comical histories' from the years immediately following the 1588 Armada threat confirms the popularity of plays that often portray romantic rulers wearing disguises to woo their love interests. These disguises rely on imagery derived from medieval ballads that glorified the benefit of royal subterfuge as a means to learn of the nation's distress and its deep-seated patriotism. Jingoistic as many appear, these romantic adventures moralize on a monarch's ultimate duty, while highlighting contemporary social discord. They do so within narratives that underplay the darker potential of such disguised deceit. The relative innocence of such adventures is lost, however, when plays appear in the late 1590s that combine 'comical history' romance plots with the factuality of the 'Chronicle Histories', as popularized by Shakespeare. This conflation of history play forms fundamentally alters future representations of disguised rulers.

---

[39]   Hyland, *Disguise*, p. 18.
[40]   Gurr, *Opposites*, pp. 22–3.

'Hal' and *1 Edward IV*: The Conflation of Historical Subgenres

In Shakespeare's Q1 *1 Henry IV*, the earliest version of the play published in 1598 (a decade after the Armada threat), Poins plots with Prince Hal to trick the roguish Falstaff/Oldcastle as the knight robs travellers at Gadshill. Poins specifies the disguise Hal and he must adopt when stealing the stolen money from their unsuspecting compatriots: 'our vizards wee wil change after wee leaue them: and sirrha, I haue cases of Buckrom for the nonce, to immaske our noted outward garments' (Q1 *1 Henry IV*, 1.2.199–201).[41] Their 'noted outward garments' duly covered, Poins and Hal succeed in robbing the robbers, much to the cowardly chagrin of Falstaff. Later, Falstaff acknowledges the medieval heritage of this outrageous event when describing the 'three misbegotten knaues in Kendall greene [who] came at [his] backe' (Q1 *1 Henry IV*, 2.4.245–6). Echoing the verdant allusion to the disguised Henry VIII in *Hall's Chronicle*, as well as Tuck's description on first meeting the outlaws in *The Playe of Robyn Hoode*, Falstaff's colour-specific reference to the highwaymen's clothing clearly cites the medieval image of Robin Hood's outlaw band.

This incidental disguise episode in a Shakespeare 'Chronicle History' is a re-enactment of a similar robbery in the anonymous *Famous Victories of Henry the Fifth* (*c.* mid-1580s, Queen's, Bull Inn[?]; published 1598).[42] *Famous Victories* is described by the 1960 Arden 2 editor, Arthur Humphreys, as a 'chaotic' play, whose narrative 'is like going through [Shakespeare's] *Henry IV–Henry V* sequence in a bad dream'.[43] McMillin and MacLean are more sympathetic when describing *Famous Victories* as offering its 'narrative overdetermination' in accord with the 'medley' style of other Queen's Men drama.[44] Janet Clare sees this socially 'levelling play', with its 'mingling' of kings and clowns and 'plebeian emphasis', as a strong and persuasive forebear of Shakespeare's Second Tetralogy, while Richard Dutton specifically claims Q *Henry V* is directly indebted to *Famous Victories*.[45] Whether 'chaotic', 'medley' or 'levelling', *Famous Victories* presents Prince Henry, in league with Sir John 'Jockey' Oldcastle, robbing his father's tax collectors as they travel to London across Gads Hill. Despite his own wrongdoing, Henry is nevertheless scornful of another '*base-minded rascal*', who is robbing not the rich, but the poor in the neighbourhood (*Famous*, A2ᵛ; 1.22–6). Both *Famous*

---

[41]   Q1 *1 Henry IV*, STC 22280. Line numbers from Charlton Hinman (ed.), *Henry the Fourth, Part I, 1599*, SQF, 14 (Oxford, 1966).

[42]   Anonymous, *The Famous Victories of Henry the fifth* (London, 1598). For the play's possible performance at the Bull in Bishopsgate, it thus being the earliest 'extant' history play, see McMillin and MacLean, *Queen's*, pp. 89–90.

[43]   Arthur Humphreys (ed.), *King Henry IV, Part 1*, Arden 2 (London, 1960), p. xxxii.

[44]   McMillin and MacLean, *Queen's*, p. 135.

[45]   Janet Clare, 'Medley History: *The Famous Victories of Henry the Fifth* to *Henry V*', *SS*, 63 (2010): 102–13 (p. 113); Richard Dutton, '"Methinks the Truth Should Live from Age to Age": The Dating and Contexts of *Henry V*', *Huntingdon Quarterly*, 68 (2005): 173–204.

Victories and *1 Henry IV* make reference to Henry as a royal trickster, based on the description of the prince in *Hall's Chronicle* as one who had '*passed his young age*' in '*wanton pastime & riotous misorder*', but who had turned '*insolencie and wildness into grauitie and soberness, and wauerying vice into constant vertue*'.[46] Shakespeare's adaptation of the disguised adventure on Gadshill, like his addition of Hal's 'drawer' disguise in *2 Henry IV* (Q1, TLN.1127–90; 2.4.209.0.SD), calls on this Tudor Chronicle tradition.[47]

That Hal will fulfil his destiny for '*grauitie and soberness*', according to Hall's *Chronicle* prescription, is confirmed by his pragmatic self-fashioning when Poins leaves the stage. In a moment of introspective analysis, Hal describes his intention to 'vphold / The vnyokt humour' of his compatriots' 'idlenes', at the same time shielding his own princely potential from view:[48]

> PRINCE HENRY: Yet herein wil I imitate the sunne,
> Who doth permit the base contagious clouds
> To smother vp his beautie from the world,
> That when he please againe to be himselfe,
> Being wanted he may be more wondred at
> By breaking through the foule and ougly mists
> Of vapours that did seeme to strangle him. (Q1 *1 Henry IV*, 1.2.220–26)

The robbery highlights Hal's intention to 'imitate' the sun, whereby his regal integrity is merely hidden behind the 'base contagious clouds' of his wanton behaviour and wayward friends. Hal is waiting to shine forth and dispel the 'ougly mists' of his dissolute past. Although his behaviour and the company he keeps are metaphorical 'vapours' that 'strangle' his good name, Hal recognizes that his subjects' perception of him as a reprobate will make his transformation into a dutiful ruler that much more surprising and welcome. Hal's pragmatic, almost Machiavellian, description of his misdemeanours pre-empts his admission of deceptive outward 'seeming' in *2 Henry IV* (Q1, TLN.2699), which likewise precedes his glorious militarism in *Henry V*. The 'Chronicle Histories' of *1* and *2 Henry IV* rely on 'comical history' disguisings to emphasize Hal's metamorphosis into a worthy monarch. Though firmly rooted in the Tudor Chronicles, these plays also hark back to a medieval tradition of romantic disguise, now tinged with the cold political pragmatism of a calculating future ruler.

Hal's public misdemeanours and private introspection are indicative of a general conflation of history play subgenres. The disguised prince/king of the 'comical histories', whose trickster exploits are more comedic and less quixotic,

---

[46]   *Hall's Chronicle*, fol. F1ʳ.

[47]   Q *2 Henry IV*, STC 22288. Through line numbers from John Pitcher (ed.), *The Second Part of King Henry the Fourth* (Oxford, 1990).

[48]   Vickie B. Sullivan, 'Princes to Act: Henry V as the Machiavellian Prince of Appearance', in Joseph Alulis and Vickie B. Sullivan (eds), *Shakespeare's Political Pageant* (London, 1996), pp. 125–52.

combine with the 'Chronicle History' ruler, whose pragmatic and well-meaning manipulation of his people guarantees future success as a leader. This combination of 'comical history' royal trickster and 'Chronicle History' character disguise, which Hal's thieving adventure and reformation broadly evoke, is also evident in far darker portrayals of disguised ruler adventurism and immorality in late sixteenth-century historical drama. A significant example of this more sinister disguised ruler appears in *1 Edward IV* (*c.* 1599, Derby's; published 1599), attributed to Thomas Heywood and written contemporaneously to *Henry V*.[49] *1 Edward IV* combines the romantic adventures of a disguised 'comical history' king with the locus and events of a tragic episode in corrupt 'Chronicle History' misrule. With a wooing narrative that echoes similar disguised ruler episodes from the early 1590s, *1 Edward IV* presents the king putting on a disguising cloak to seduce the City of London goldsmith's wife, Jane Shore.

Long before his attempted seduction of the beautiful Jane, Edward embarks on a hunting trip disguised as one of his courtiers. In his courtier's attire, and having become separated from his companions, Edward meets Hobs, the Tanner of Tamworth. Although topically apposite, with the Tanner's profession reflecting contemporary unrest among London's over-regulated leather tradesmen, this 'king and subject' confrontation is based on a far older narrative tradition.[50] Mirroring George a Greene's mythical encounter with his king, Edward's chance meeting is traceable to a medieval ballad, recorded in a 1564 *Stationers' Register* entry that describes 'The Story of Kynge Edward the IIIJ[th] and the Tanner of Tamowthe'.[51] Unlike the overarching respect for the monarchy evident in *George a Greene*, *1 Edward IV*'s message is uncomfortable and potentially subversive. Edward learns troubling truths about his kingship from a subject whose loyalty, while never in doubt, is still based on pragmatic allegiance to whichever political regime best serves his needs. Like so many prior encounters, the 'king and subject' meeting between Edward and Hobs allows the expression of national grievances direct to a reigning monarch without the intervention of court intermediaries.

The visual description of this meeting guarantees audience recognition of the Robin Hood myth. On first seeing the 'king disguisde' (*1 Edward IV*, E4[r]; 11.79.0.SD), Hobs believes that Edward is nothing more than a common '*theefe*' out to steal his meagre earnings. To Hobs, Edward resembles those annoying '*roysters* [that] *swarme in the countrie*', claiming attachment to the royal party (*1 Edward IV*, E3[v]–E4[r]; 11.79–80). Edward is directly likened, however, to certain '*Courtnoles*' (Hobs's rural lexis for 'courtiers'), with whom the Tanner had spoken earlier in the scene (*1 Edward IV*, E4[r]; 11.81–2). Hobs's passing comment confirms the indistinguishability of Edward's costume from those of his courtiers,

---

[49]   Thomas Heywood, *The First and Second Partes of King Edward the Fourth* (London, 1599). Line numbers from Richard Rowland (ed.), *The First and Second Parts of King Edward IV* (Manchester, 2005).

[50]   Rowland, *Edward IV*, pp. 26–30.

[51]   Arber 1, p. 264.

who had, as the accompanying stage direction pointedly specifies, already entered dressed 'in Greene' (*1 Edward IV*, E3ᵛ; 11.52.0.SD). Obviously likewise attired in green, Edward is wearing a disguise that makes his Robin Hood appearance unmistakable.

Hobs is, understandably, cautious of this latest green-attired '*Courtnole*'. It is, however, Edward's intrusive questioning that prompts the Tanner's explicit invocation of Robin Hood when appraising the disguised stranger:

> EDWARD: *Holla my friend, good fellow pre thee stay.*
> HOBS: *No such matter, I haue more haste of my way.*
> EDWARD: *If thou be a good fellow, let me borrow a word.*
> HOBS: *My purse thou meanest, I am no good fellow, and I*
> *pray God thou beest not one.*
> EDWARD: *Why? dost thou not loue a good fellow?*
> HOBS: *No, good fellowes be theeues.* (*1 Edward IV*, E4ʳ; 11.83–90)

Edward's seemingly innocuous reference to Hobs as a '*good fellow*' alludes to a title regularly applied to Robin Hood and his men in medieval balladry.[52] The expression 'good fellow' also evokes the mythical Robin Goodfellow, that mischievous Pan-like imp, sometimes called Puck, who was immortalized in Shakespeare's *A Midsummer Night's Dream*. It is unclear which character influenced the other in medieval folklore, since both were known to be a scourge of forest travellers and masters of disguise. By the sixteenth century, however, the woodland fairy Robin Goodfellow had become synonymous with the greenwood Robin Hood and vice versa.[53]

Edward's greeting is understandable in the context of Hobs's trade as Tanner, the same salutation appearing in the Epistle 'To all good Fellowes' (A3ʳ) in Thomas Dekker's *The Shoemaker's Holiday* (1599, Admiral's; published 1600).[54] In *Shoemaker's Holiday*, Rowland Lacy, a 'nere kinsman' to 'Sir *Hugh Lacie* Earle of Lincolne' (*Shoemaker's*, A3ʳ; Epistle 7–9), and thus ancestor of Lacy in *Friar Bacon*, rebels against his father's attempts to send him to war by adopting the lowly costume of London's '*Gentle Craft*' (*Shoemaker's*, C2ʳ; 3.4). Thus '*disguisde*' as the '*Dutch Shooe-maker*' Hans, he is able to woo and wed his illicit love, Rose (*Shoemaker's*, C2ʳ; 3.5). As Dekker's Epistle and Lacy's 'Hans' disguise confirm, the Robin Hood/Goodfellow association with tanners was adopted by London's 'Gentle Craft' cordwainers, a factor reflected in the humiliating defeat of the pugilistic *George a Greene* shoemakers. The Robin Hood myth also accounts for 'good fellow' becoming a slang term for a pursetaker, as demonstrated by Honesty's comment in *A Knack to Know a Knave* that '*good fellowes be purse-*

---

[52] Edwin Davenport, 'The Representation of Robin Hood in Elizabethan Drama: *George a Green* and *Edward I*', in Potter (ed.), *Playing*, pp. 45–62 (p. 46).

[53] Stephen Knight, *Robin Hood: A Mythic Biography* (Ithaca, 2003), pp. 202–204.

[54] Thomas Dekker, *The Shomakers Holiday* (London, 1600). Line numbers from R.L. Smallwood and Stanley Wells (eds), *The Shoemaker's Holiday* (Manchester, 1979).

takers now a daies' (*Knave*, A3ʳ; 1.96). A similar remark is made in *King Leir*, when the faithful Perillus warns of his fear that 'a couple of those they call good fellowes, / Should step out of a hedge, and set vpon' Leir and his party (*Leir*, F1ʳ; TLN.10).[55] Likewise, in Peele's *Edward I*, when Lluellen describes his 'handsome Common-wealth' of Robin Hood outlaws as a 'handful of goodfellowes' (*Edward I*, E4ʳ; 7.1172–3). Hobs's negative response to being called a '*good fellow*', and his hope that the particular '*royster*' before him '*beest not one*', is understandable in this thieving context. For the audience to *1 Edward IV*, the green of the courtier's costume and Hobs's mention of the thieving '*good fellow*' conjure images of Robin Hood's band of robbers, thus accounting for the Tanner's indignant reply, '*good fellowes be theeues*'.

Despite initial fears that the stranger will rob him, Hobs engages in conversation with the '*Courtnole*', whose question – '*what say* [the poor] *of the king?*' (*1 Edward IV*, F1ʳ; 13.15) – betrays Edward's voyeuristic interest, and the dramatic irony of Hobs's fear that this stranger might betrayingly '*blab*' to the authorities (*1 Edward IV*, F1ʳ; 13.16). Even so, Hobs replies candidly that the poor '*feare* [they] *shalbe troubled to lend* [Edward] *money*' for his military exploits (*1 Edward IV*, F1ᵛ; 13.33). For Hobs, such 'lending' is no more than a euphemism for higher taxes, an observation compounded by his complaint '*that one subject should haue in his hand that* [which] *might do good to many through the land*' (*1 Edward IV*, F2ʳ; 13.82–3). This proto-communist comment against the hoarding of goods by corrupt engrossers would appear particularly topical following the disastrous harvests of 1594–97, and the continuing dearth and expense of corn. However, Hobs's remark that he is, like the '*Sutton Wind-mill*', able to '*grinde which way so ere the wind blows*' (*1 Edward IV*, F1ᵛ; 13.45–6), demonstrates his pragmatic support of whichever ruler holds power.

Hobs's pragmatism alerts the Plantagenet Edward to the potential for rural unrest. This factor is made more dangerous by the presence of Edward's Tudor rival, the future Henry VII, exiled in Brittany and awaiting the opportunity to seize England's crown. Edward listens to the Tanner's complaints, and accepts his invitation to stay overnight at his simple home. Having bade his host farewell (thus allowing the Tanner time to prepare for his guest), Edward contemplates the secretly acquired knowledge that his exploit has revealed:

> EDWARD: *I see plaine men by obseruation,*
> Of thinges that alter in the chaunge of times,
> Do gather knowledge, and the meanest life,
> Proportiond with content sufficiencie,
> *Is merier then the mighty state of kings.* (*1 Edward IV,* F2ᵛ; 13.97–102)

Edward claims that the humblest subject, observing events as they unfold over time, appreciates the mutability of human politics far more than those at the centre of power. With crass insensitivity to the hardships of poverty, Edward adds that

---

[55]   H. Dugdale Sykes, 'The Authorship of *A Knack to Know a Knave*', *N&Q*, 146 (1924): 389–91.

contentment with the sufficiency of life – adequate food and shelter – allows the poor to enjoy a merrier existence than that of the nation's ruler. The 'mighty state' of kingship is incompatible with a ruler's untroubled life, his lot being instead one of struggle and discontent. The hegemonic 'hardship of rule' trope, which Edward patronizingly employs, is traditionally viewed as a commonplace of Shakespearean drama, appearing in *3 Henry VI*, *2 Henry IV* and *Henry V*. Noticeably, this same trope is absent from the Quarto versions of these plays, its 'commonplace' status based solely on their 1623 Folio manifestations. Nonetheless, *1 Edward IV* provides an early evocation of this 'hardship of rule' trope, residing not within a 'Chronicle History', but rather in a 'comical history'. This same 'comical history' stages the meeting of Hobs and his disguised king, while mirroring the medieval 'king and subject' theme of Robin Hood folklore. The disguised Edward encounters his subject and, in the process, learns how he is perceived by his nation through the flexible, pragmatic patriotism of the unsuspecting Tanner.

Although Edward's encounter implies a simple evocation of the 'king and subject' theme within a 'comical history' context, the political consequence of this meeting is more far-reaching than at first appears. Edward's allusion to first-hand 'observation' as the finest arbiter of truth is significant in heralding a generic shift in contemporary drama, away from romantic 'comical history' rulers with their lustful wooing adventures, leading instead towards the historically specific 'Chronicle' kings of Shakespeare's 'Histories'. This subtle shift in motive for royal disguise, moving from romantic adventure to political voyeurism, results in a discomforting sense of social paranoia within the play. Shielded from his people behind palace walls, the king in *1 Edward IV*, like *Friar Bacon*'s prince, can only acquire knowledge and political security through direct observation. The difference between Edward's political espionage and that of earlier 'comical history' rulers is the effect it has on those subjects who identify the king's secretive adventures as acts designed to counter civil disobedience and subversive behaviour.

Later in *1 Edward IV*, the anxiety caused by this new voyeuristic disguised ruler surfaces when the London goldsmith, Matthew Shore, knowingly comments on the discomfort that Edward's exploits induce in the people. Shore is aware that the king, cloaked and '*muffled like a common Servingman*' (*1 Edward IV*, K1ʳ; 20.34), has been wooing his wife. Edward's illicit actions are a prelude to far more tragic consequences in *2 Edward IV* (published in the same 1599 quarto). For the moment, Matthew's comments to London's Lord Mayor reflect his anxiety's political dimension: '*When kings themselues so narrowly do prie | Into the world, men feare, and why not I?*' (*1 Edward IV*, K1ᵛ; 20.54–5). Of course, the regularity with which past 'comical history' kings used disguises to woo unsuspecting maids, wives and princesses, cannot help but unnerve Jane's wary husband. Matthew's comments are, however, far broader in their anxious complaint; it is all 'men' – England's common-weal – who should 'fear' when 'kings themselves' (as opposed to their paid intelligencers or spies) 'narrowly' prie into their realms.

This evocative expression of social anxiety in *1 Edward IV* demonstrates how far the disguised ruler had developed in the ten years since the defeat of the Spanish Armada. The short-lived jingoistic euphoria that followed the 1588 victory was followed by national dismay at the failed military campaigns in France in support of the Protestant Huguenots, while disastrous crop failures at home brought famine to many rural communities.[56] By 1599, insecurity about the childless queen's succession, troubles in Ireland, and a general sense of unease about open expressions of dissent or dissatisfaction colour the tone of Shore's comment. Secret 'observation' by a disguised ruler no longer leads to virtuous self-knowledge and secure government. It is now feared as much as admired, with the wooing adventure of the play's 'comical history' roots supplanted by an anxiety that highlights the immediacy and topicality of its alternative, tragic narrative. *1 Edward IV* combines its 'comical history' romantic plot with a far darker evocation of monarchy, packaged within the Tudor bias of a 'Chronicle History'. Although, with the death of Elizabeth, the fashion for 'Chronicle Histories' inevitably waned (only to be resurrected with Shakespeare and Fletcher's *Henry VIII*), *1 Edward IV* celebrates its final flowering on the late sixteenth-century stage. *1 Edward IV* also acknowledges the 'comical history' heritage of a motif which, though still used for wooing adventures and 'king and subject' confrontations, is reminiscent less of the disguised ruler of Robin Hood folktale, and more of observation, surveillance and intrigue in an uncertain political state.

Medieval Myth and Chronicle History in *Henry V*

The catalogue of disguised rulers on the late sixteenth-century stage demonstrates the pervasiveness of the motif and its association with the medieval ballad and folktale imagery of Robin Hood. The two subgenres of history play – the 'comical histories' and the 'Chronicle Histories' – had, by 1599, become intertwined sufficiently that medieval adventures by kings in disguise reside comfortably within more fact-based Chronicle drama founded on Tudor historiography. The hegemonic imperative driving such Chronicle drama was subsumed under an overarching anxiety about Elizabeth's age and uncertain succession. It is in the context of this political uncertainty that Shakespeare introduces the medieval plot motif of a disguised ruler into *Henry V*, a play whose significance as precursor to the early seventeenth-century disguised rulers is underplayed in traditional criticism.[57] An awareness of *Henry V*'s medieval heritage, and the precarious state of England's politics, allows its consideration as both radical and hegemonic in the portrayal of kingly disguise, and thus a fitting antecedent to the disguised ruler plays that followed.

A famous moment in Shakespeare's *Henry V* presents the king travelling incognito among his troops on the eve before the Battle of Agincourt, where Henry learns uncomfortable truths about his men and his nation. Significant as

---

[56]   Leah Marcus, *Puzzling Shakespeare* (Berkeley, 1988), pp. 76–80.

[57]   See Tennenhouse, *Power*, p. 155; Stephen Greenblatt, *Shakespearean Negotiations* (Oxford, 1988).

his actions are, Henry V was not the first Shakespearean character to travel in disguise. King Henry in Q *3 Henry VI* (*c.* 1591; published 1595), when newly arrived 'from *Scotland*', is likewise 'disguisde to greet [his] natiue land' in an act of political self-preservation (Q *3 Henry VI*, C5ᵛ; 3.1.13–14). Similarly, the newly-made Duke of Gloucester adds 'colours to the Camelion' when changing 'shapes with *Protheus*' for secret advantage (Q *3 Henry VI*, C8ᵛ; 3.2.191–2).[58] These Shakespearean instances of incidental political disguise from the early 1590s predate Henry V's Agincourt wandering. More intriguingly, Henry V also stages the very act of political eavesdropping to which King Richard alludes before the Battle of Bosworth Field in Q1 *Richard III* (*c.* 1591, Chamberlain's; published 1597).[59] Troubled by the ghosts of those he has murdered, and having awoken from his 'fearefull dreame' on the eve of battle (Q1 *Richard III*, M1ʳ; 5.3.212; F, TLN.3672; 5.5.166), Richard calls on his henchman Ratcliffe to accompany him as he travels among his fractious troops: 'come, go with me, / Vnder our tents Ile plaie the ease dropper, / To see if any meane to shrinke from me' (Q1 *Richard III*, M1ʳ ; 5.3.220–222; F, TLN.3681–3; 5.5.174–6). Richard's passing comment, which hints at gaining vital knowledge through secret surveillance, is eventually manifested in the disguised subterfuge of *Henry V*.

Like Richard's reference to spying on his troops in Q1 *Richard III*, the earliest mention of Henry's disguised adventure appears likewise in the Q1 version of *Henry V*.[60] Published in 1600, Q1 *Henry V* appeared soon after the play's 1599 debut at the newly-erected Globe. There is no record of *Henry V* in performance, however, until its court presentation for King James on 7 January 1605, twelve days after the first (and only) documented performance of *Measure for Measure*.[61] That two plays with such prominent disguise characters should appear in the same Christmas Revels season is, in itself, worthy of note. Certainly, this demonstrates that an established and popular six-year-old play and a radical new play were both perceived as politically apposite and/or innocuous enough to appeal to their royal audience. *Henry V* and *Measure for Measure* were both staged during the last Christmas Revels James would enjoy without fear of gunpowder plotters intent on his assassination. At the very least, the court presentations of *Henry V* and *Measure for Measure* within a fortnight of each other suggest that their respective disguised rulers would be compared by the plays' royal spectators.

Common critical insistence that *Henry V*'s disguise episode is unique and isolated from its later disguised ruler counterparts is supported by a generally held belief that the Folio text represents an earlier version of the play, published, so

---

[58]   Line numbers from W.W. Greg (ed.), *The True Tragedy of Richard Duke of York (Henry the Sixth, Part III)* 1595, SQF, 11 (Oxford, 1958).

[59]   Q1 *Richard III*, STC 22314. Line numbers from W.W. Greg (ed), *Richard the Third, 1597*, SQF, 12 (Oxford, 1959).

[60]   Q1 *Henry V*, STC 22289. Line numbers from Andrew Gurr (ed.), *The First Quarto of 'Henry V'* (Cambridge, 2000).

[61]   Chambers, *ES* 4, p. 172.

Gary Taylor concludes, from Shakespeare's 'own foul papers'.[62] Q1 *Henry V* thus represents 'a later stage of the text', derived from 'reported or memorial' material gleaned from (or for) a provincial touring production.[63] Influenced by nearly a century of bibliographic conjecture, Taylor's argument participates in the theory of the 'pirated' quarto text, whereby thieving actors make poor-quality 'memorial reconstructions' that are subsequently printed by unscrupulous publishers.[64] The lack of attention paid by twentieth-century editors to the so-called Shakespearean 'bad' quartos is, however, a cause of concern for Taylor.[65] This is not in itself surprising, since he makes radical use of Q1 when introducing the Duke of Bourbon into 2.4 and 3.5 of his Oxford edition, thus 'accepting Q's version of Agincourt'.[66] Whatever his feelings about the 'bad' quarto controversy, Taylor remains convinced that the 'superior' Folio text predates its Q1 manifestation.[67]

Taylor's argument for the 'superior' Folio *Henry V* stems in part from the apparent and unusually overt (for Shakespeare) reference in the Folio Chorus to the 'Generall of our gracious Empresse', who is 'from Ireland comming, / Bringing Rebellion broached on his Sword' (F *Henry V*, TLN.2880–82; 5.0.30–32). This 'Generall' is traditionally identified as Robert Devereux, second earl of Essex, whose hoped-for success in crushing the Irish rebellion of March to June 1599 provides the earliest dating for the play.[68] Richard Dutton, however, suggests that the 'Generall' might refer instead to Charles Blount, Lord Mountjoy, who, during the Christmas of 1601, enjoyed a far more successful campaign against the Irish uprising as victor of the Battle of Kinsale.[69] The Folio Chorus might thus refer to 'Generall' Mountjoy on his being recalled and honoured at James's accession. Whomsoever the 'Generall' actually is, his presence in the Folio Chorus has led to the designation of the 1623 text as an authentic instance of late Elizabethan (as opposed to early Jacobean) propaganda.

In line with Taylor's opinion that the corrupted Q1 *Henry V* preserves 'many of Shakespeare's own improvements on the text printed in F', Jonathan Bate and Eric Rasmussen relegate Q1 to the role of useful tool with which First Folio compositors could compare and correct errors in their far longer 'original' version.[70] This prioritization of the Folio text, either as 'superior' and/or 'original',

---

[62]   Gary Taylor (ed.), *Henry V* (Oxford, 1982), p. 18.

[63]   Ibid., pp. 22–3.

[64]   See Paul Werstine, 'A Century of "Bad" Shakespeare Quartos', *SQ*, 50 (1999): 310–33.

[65]   Taylor, *Henry V*, p. 23.

[66]   Ibid., p. 25.

[67]   Stanley Wells and Gary Taylor (eds), *Oxford Shakespeare* (Oxford, 1988), p. 567.

[68]   Taylor, *Henry V*, pp. 4–5.

[69]   Richard Dutton, '*The Famous Victories* and the 1600 Quarto of *Henry V*', in Ostovich, Syme and Griffin (eds), *Locating*, pp. 135–44 (p. 137).

[70]   Taylor, *Henry V*, p. 26; Jonathan Bate and Eric Rasmussen (eds), *RSC Shakespeare* (Houndmills, 2007), p. 1031.

has been called into question by Dutton's claim that F *Henry V* contains '*additions ... not restored excisions*' from the Quarto.[71] Dutton's argument can be considered alongside Tiffany Stern's comment about the 'dangerous ground' travelled by those who seek to date plays by their 'prologue, epilogue and, by extension, some choruses or interim entertainments'.[72] As Stern warns, it might be possible tentatively to date specific textual material, such as the Folio's *Henry V* Chorus, but certainly 'not the play it flanks'.[73] Stern's caution highlights the possibility that the Chorus, like many other early modern augmentations, might be specific to a single or later performance, and thus unrelated to the play's typical appearance on the Elizabethan or Jacobean stage.

Popular as the prioritization of the Folio text remains, it has also engendered considerable debate among those who consider the Folio's performability in comparison to Q *Henry V*. In relation to early modern acting technique and to audience or reader response, Lukas Erne argues that Q *Henry V* represents a performance text, whose obvious shortcomings are less significant than the information it offers about its oral/aural transmission and reception.[74] Erne's argument is strongly contested by Duncan Salkeld, who counterclaims that certain omissions in the shorter Quarto suggest subsequently-written authorial 'foul papers', created on separate detached sheets, that eventually find their way back into the 1623 Folio.[75] Any traces of performance in Q *Henry V*, according to Salkeld, are indicative of a 'filtered, multistage process' of text formation, with inaccuracies of 'memory, reporting, reading, hearing, transcription and composition', all combining to create an inferior quarto text.[76] Salkeld's 'multistage' list may accord with Taylor's 'reported or memorial' Q1 theory, but it also invents a spuriously specific explanation for these omissions suddenly reappearing in the Folio.[77] Regardless of which critical response is favoured – Taylor's, Erne's or Salkeld's – all maintain the integrity of Folio *Henry V* (not least because it includes famous Shakespearean dialogue), with Erne merely questioning the performance status of this 'long, literary' text, 'chiefly of value for readers and not for spectators'.[78]

The primacy of the Folio as a 'superior' performance text is likewise questioned by David Scott Kastan, who considers Q *Henry V* as 'entirely coherent, its deficiencies largely a function of its inadequate stage directions'.[79] As Kastan

---

[71]   Dutton, '*Famous Victories*', p. 136.

[72]   Tiffany Stern, *Documents of Performance in Early Modern England* (Cambridge, 2009), p. 118.

[73]   Ibid., p. 118.

[74]   Lukas Erne, *Shakespeare as Literary Dramatist* (Cambridge, 2003), p. 220.

[75]   Duncan Salkeld, 'The Texts of *Henry V*', *Shakespeare*, 3 (2007): 161–82 (pp. 169 & 175).

[76]   Ibid., p. 179.

[77]   Taylor, *Henry V*, p. 23.

[78]   Erne, *Literary*, p. 225.

[79]   David Scott Kastan, *Shakespeare and the Book* (Cambridge, 2001), p. 75.

stresses, it is wrong to ignore the quartos entirely, especially as they 'are all we have': 'In the absence of any holograph manuscripts ... the early printed texts are usually as close as we can get to Shakespeare's writing'.[80] Commendable as Kastan's observation is, it is this quest for 'Shakespeare's writing' – for a single original authorial text – that has overwhelmed Shakespeare studies in general, and consideration of *Henry V* in particular. Twenty-first-century Shakespeare editions are gradually confronting this conundrum by printing Quarto and Folio versions separately, thus pointing to comparison rather than conflation as the new editorial practice.[81] Comparative study, moreover, proves particularly fruitful when analysing the disguised ruler episode and how this differs between the Quarto and Folio versions. Differences between Quarto and Folio representations of disguise are of fundamental importance for our understanding of the shift from 'comical history' disguised rulers, influenced by medieval folktale and balladry, to the 'Chronicle History' King Henry V of the Second Tetralogy, able to travel secretly among his troops in an historically specific moment of national pride.

In Folio *Henry V*, Henry justifies his strange request for Erpingham's cloak: 'I and my Bosome must debate a while, / And then I would no other company' (F *Henry V*, TLN.1877–8; 4.1.32–3). This desire for untroubled introspection, facilitated by the anonymity of disguise, introduces Henry's later soliloquy on the responsibility and obligation of kingship (F *Henry V*, TLN.2079–2134; 4.1.212–66). By contrast, in Q *Henry V* (whether Q1 of 1600, Q2 of 1602, or the so-called 'Pavier Quarto' Q3 of 1619), Henry's 'hardship of rule' self-analysis, that commonplace trope evident in *1 Edward IV* (and repeated in the Folio's *3 Henry VI* and *2 Henry IV*), does not appear. Even the Folio's playful description of the 'little touch of *Harry* in the Night' (F *Henry V*, TLN.1836; 4.0.47), and his borrowing of Erpingham's disguising 'Cloake' (F *Henry V*, TLN.1869; 4.1.24), are completely missing from the Quarto texts. What possible reasons might there be, other than as proof for the 'corrupt' state of Quarto, for such omissions? Arguments about the performability of the Quarto versus Folio texts – that Q *Henry V* is a 'performance' text while Folio represents a literary expansion constructed specifically with a 'readership' in mind, or that Folio represents the 'complete' original text and Quarto a 'pirated' or 'memorially reconstructed' inferior – remain tentative. They do offer, however, an alternative theory based on what a 'pirated' or 'reconstructed' text implies about the people pirating and/or reconstructing it. Whether or not Q *Henry V* is nearer to the play as performed in 1600 or not, the absence of this specific dialogue negates the need for Erpingham's famous 'cloak' to be listed as a stage costume. The Quarto play's consumers, whether in the playhouse or at the booksellers, were expected to visualize the disguised ruler and recognize the 'comical history' heritage of his actions without need for further explanation or comment.

---

[80]   Ibid., p. 121.
[81]   Ann Thompson and Neil Taylor (eds), *Hamlet*, Arden 3 (London, 2006), pp. 91–4. Published in conjunction with Thompson and Taylor (eds), *Hamlet: The Texts of 1603 and 1623* (London, 2006), these account for all three *Hamlet* texts.

Fig. 1.5   Laurence Olivier as King Henry wearing Erpingham's disguising cloak in a posed publicity still for the 1944 film, *Henry V*

For the multistage creators of Q *Henry V*, the only indication necessary for Henry's subterfuge is a stage direction stating: '*Enter the King disguised, to him Pistoll*' (Q *Henry V*, D3ᵛ; 11.0.SD). Henry enters immediately after Bourbon and the Constable are informed of the close proximity of the English to their French camp (Q *Henry V*, D3ʳ; 10.44–5: F *Henry V*, TLN.1753–4; 3.7.113–14). Presuming the disguised Henry to be an approaching stranger, the English camp sentinel Pistol halts him with the French challenge, 'Ke ve la?' (Q1 *Henry V*, D3ᵛ; 11.1: F *Henry V*, TLN.1883; 4.1.36). This highlights the fear among the English troops that any stranger might, quite obviously, be French. The dramatic importance of this confrontation is likewise heightened by its close proximity to the previous scene. The augmented Folio text distances these two events with an explanatory Chorus (F *Henry V*, TLN.1790–1842; 4.0.1–53), and a cheerful discussion between Henry and Erpingham about the cloak (F *Henry V*, TLN.1858–81; 4.1.13–35). By contrast, the Q *Henry V* Pistol exchange, which immediately follows the French camp scene, suggests Henry's disguise as a practical and militarily advantageous device for manipulating his troops. It also negates the need for a literary explanation about disguised rulers: the image and the reality are, in Q *Henry V*, plain to imagine or see.

The commonplace nature of Henry's appearance is suggested by Pistol's seeming inability to distinguish the rank of his 'friend': 'art thou Gentleman? / Or art thou common, base, and popeler?' (Q *Henry V*, D3ᵛ; 11.2–4). Henry's reply, that he is 'a Gentleman of a Company' (Q *Henry V*, D3ᵛ; 11.5), is taken by Pistol to mean a gentleman-volunteer serving as pikeman or infantryman and evinces the overall success of the king's disguise.[82] Unlike the decoy 'king' Blunt in *1 Henry IV*, who is mistakenly killed by Douglas while 'marching in [the King's] Coats' (F *1 Henry IV*, TLN.2917; 5.3.25), Henry V appears devoid of military or kingly regalia. In a moment of dramatic irony, which harks back to a long 'comical history' tradition of disguised kings duping their unwitting subjects, Henry introduces himself to Pistol as '*Harry* le Roy' (Q *Henry V*, D3ᵛ; 11.13). At the same time, the king overhears the 'speake lower' exchange between Flewellen and Gower, which in Q begins only twenty-five lines after the scene where the French gain intelligence about the proximity of the English encampment. Flewellen's concern receives Henry's private approbation: 'Tho it appeare a litle out of fashion, / Yet theres much care in this' (Q *Henry V*, D4ʳ; 11.35–6).

What follows is the disguised Henry's discussion with Q's unnamed 'three Souldiers' (Bates, Court and Williams in Folio), the anonymity of whom, so Erne argues, confirms the intrinsic 'orality' of the Q soldiers' functions or 'types', as opposed to their character-specific Folio speech-prefixes.[83] In Q, Henry ironically defends himself from these detractors by describing the 'frolicke' king, whose disregard for the perils of war should act as brave example to his troops: 'he is a man as we are – The Violet smels to him as to vs: Therefore if he see reasons, he feares as we do' (Q *Henry V*, D4ʳ; 11.45–8). Henry's skilful rhetoric counters the Second Soldier's complaints that the King will, 'If his cause be not good', have a 'heauy reckoning to make' on the Last Judgment's 'latter day' (Q *Henry V*, D4ʳ; 11.49–51). The Second Soldier likens the responsibility of a king toward his subjects to that of a master toward his servant or father toward his son, authority figures whom Henry claims cannot personally be held accountable for the misfortunes or misdemeanours of their charges. Henry's pragmatic reaction to this potentially seditious comment is harsh but fair. Even though death might follow an order from master, father or king, because these authority figures 'purpose not their [servant's/ son's/subject's] deaths, whe[n] they craue their seruices' (Q *Henry V*, D4ʳ; 11.60), the same figure should bear no blame for any subsequent unfortunate outcome.

The Soldier's 'latter day' imagery is developed when Henry talks of murderers, thieves and rapists, whose presence among his troops ensures that battle provides a vehicle for executing God's punishment: 'War is Gods Beadel. War is Gods vengeance' (Q *Henry V*, D4ᵛ; 11.63–4). Henry's politic pragmatism endeavours to encourage introspection in his fearful soldiers and deflect blame from his royal personage:

---

[82]   See Roger B. Manning, *Swordsmen: The Martial Ethos in the Three Kingdoms* (Oxford, 2003), p. 23.

[83]   Erne, *Literary*, p. 242.

KING: Euery mans seruice is the kings:
But euery mans soule is his owne.
Therefore I would haue euery souldier examine himselfe,
And wash euery moath out of his conscience:
That in so doing, he may be the readier for death. (Q *Henry V*, D4ᵛ; 11.64–7)

Despite Henry's call for spiritual fortitude and self-accountability, the Second Soldier comments instead that he had 'heard the king, he wold not be ransomde' (Q *Henry V*, D4ᵛ; 11.71). The king would thus rather die among his troops than be captured and ransomed for a safe return home. Bitterly, the Second Soldier explains that Henry had only said this to make them fight: 'But when our throates be cut, he may be ransomde, / And we neuer the wiser' (Q *Henry V*, D4ᵛ; 11.72–3). Henry seems seriously offended by this slur, complaining that the soldier's 'reproofe is somewhat too bitter' and that at any other time he 'could be angry' (Q *Henry V*, E1ʳ; 11.78–9). The ensuing duellistic exchange of gloves sets the scene for Flewellen's later confrontation with the Soldier.

The harshness underlying Q *Henry V*'s kingly disguise is highlighted when Henry invites Flewellen to prove the (falsely accused) treachery of the unwitting Soldier. The duped soldiers' confrontation in Q, although instigated by the dangerously 'playful' whim of the king, bears no relationship to the Folio 'little touch of Harry'. Rather, it represents the politically expedient closure of a cunning though necessary ploy to rally Henry's outnumbered and fractious troops. As with the earlier Q scene, no mention is made of Erpingham or his disguising cloak. There is, however, a subtle change in phrase for the soldier who defends his treatment of the unknown challenger. Henry's initial response to meeting his detractor again, when read in the light of Q's dangerous proximity to the French encampment, is cold and harsh. In the Folio, the King sardonically informs Williams that it was him, 'indeed', he 'promised'st to strike':

KING: And thou hast giuen me most bitter termes.
FLUELLEN: And please your Maiestie, let his Neck answere
for it, if there is any Marshall Law in the World.
KING: How canst thou make me satisfaction?
WILLIAMS: All offences, my Lord, come from the heart: ne-
uer came any from mine, that might offend your Ma-
iestie.
KING: It was our selfe thou didst abuse. (F *Henry V*, TLN.2758–66; 4.8.38–45)

The Q reading of the same scene is sharper and potentially more threatening:

KING: It was I indeed you promised to strike.
And thou thou hast giuen me most bitter words.
How canst thou make vs amends?
FLEWELLEN: Let his necke answere it,
If there be any marshals lawe in the worell.
SOLDIER: My Liege, all offences come from the heart:
Neuer came any from mine to offend your Maiestie. (Q *Henry V*, F2ᵛ–F3ʳ; 17.22–7)

For the King in Q, the 'bitter words' of the Soldier are most offensive and slanderous. Flewellen's suggestion to hang the offender according to 'martial law' is likewise terse and menacing. By contrast, the same exchange in the Folio likens Williams's offence to that of an aristocratic duel. Instead of 'bitter words', Williams has offered 'bitter terms' for which the king requires 'satisfaction'. The chivalric Folio response mockingly highlights the social inequality that precludes a king/commoner duel, and offers Williams the opportunity to defend himself against accusations of treasonous slander.

Both Q's Soldier and Folio's Williams plead pardon for an offence that owes everything to Henry appearing as a common man, rather than to their treasonous intent. The difference between the duped Soldier's response in Q and Williams's plea in F is apparent in their respective descriptions of the king's disguise. In the Folio, to Henry's comment that 'It was our selfe thou didst abuse' (F *Henry V*, TLN.2766; 4.8.45), Williams states the obvious fact that 'Your Maiestie came not like your selfe':

> WILLIAMS: [Y]ou
> appear'd to me but as a common man witnesse the
> Night, your Garments, your Lowlinesse: and what
> your Highnesse suffer'd vnder that shape, I beseech you
> take it for your owne fault, and not mine: for had you
> beene as I tooke you for, I made no offence; therefore I
> beseech your Highnesse pardon me. (F *Henry V*, TLN.2767–73; 4.8.46–51)

Williams's defence is straightforward and honest, his integrity and deference rewarded by a glove filled with crowns. In Q, the Soldier's response is subtly different, following directly as it does from the Soldier's pledge that his heart is innocent of offence:

> SOLDIER: You appeard to me as a common man:
> Witnesse the night, your garments, your lowlinesse,
> And whatsoeuer you receiued vnder that habit,
> I beseech your Maiestie impute it to your owne fault
> And not mine. For your selfe came not like your selfe:
> Had you bene as you seemed, I had made no offence.
> Therefore I beseech your grace to pardon me. (Q *Henry V*, F3ʳ; 17.27–32)

In both versions, Henry is accused of appearing as a 'common man' who, under cover of darkness and with lowly garments and demeanour, gains unwelcome personal insight from his unsuspecting soldiers. The fault for this mistake rests firmly with the king.

A difference is evident between what Henry 'received under that habit' in Q and what he 'suffered under that shape' in Folio. Williams's reference to 'shape' reflects the 'guise' or 'disguising' of the Folio escapade. It was Henry's 'shape', his outward physical appearance muffled in Erpingham's cloak, which led to mistaken identity. In Q, the Soldier refers not to some physical 'shape', but to a simple theatrical garment; Henry 'received' unwanted information because of the 'habit' – the apparel or costume – which made him appear not like himself, but like the 'common man' he 'seemed'.[84] A similar incident, possibly inspired by *Henry V*, is described by Sir William Cornwallis, who claims that the Roman '*Anthony* … neuer sped better, then when his Attire differed not from the common Souldiours'.[85] Like Anthony, Henry is not 'cloaked' but attired like a 'common man'. Likewise, in Shakespeare's *King John* (*c.* 1596, Chamberlain's; published 1623), Philip the Bastard describes his 'habit and deuice, / Exterior forme, [and] outward accoutrement', along with his deceitful 'inward motion', as the masking shield for delivering his 'sweet poyson' (F, TLN.220–23; 1.1.210–13). Henry V's 'habit' or apparel in Q, referenced materially in the Bastard's 'habit' and 'outward accoutrement', suggests therefore a simple stage property immediately recognizable as a costume addition for any theatrical 'King Henry'. So established and conventional is this stage property that it requires no additional Folio explanation or plot adjustment to appreciate the physical change – the disguising of regal identity – that its discarding or donning represents.

A conventionalized 'Henry V' costume is itemized in Philip Henslowe's 1598 Admiral's Men's inventory for the Rose playhouse: 'Item, Harye the v. velvet gowne'.[86] Obviously stock 'Henry V' attire, a similar 'gowne' is mentioned in *1 Edward IV*, when Hobs enters the royal court accompanied by the still-disguised Edward. Having seen travelling actors playing 'kings' at Tamworth, Hobs believes he can recognize his monarch among the courtier throng, since one of them wears a '*long beard, and a red gowne*' (*1 Edward IV*, L1ᵛ–L2ʳ; 23.48–9). Hobs's inability to distinguish true king from courtier because of the lack of a kingly 'gowne' mirrors the Q Soldier's defensive response to Henry, whose royal status was effectively disguised not by the 'habit' he wore, but by what he did *not* wear. Presumably, the Q texts take for granted that readers will likewise recognize Henry's disguise as a feature common to so many 'comical histories' from the preceding decade. Unlike the specific description of a cloak in the Folio text, the absence of the visual signifiers of kingship suggested by Q reaffirms the 'comical history' heritage of Henry's uncomfortably 'playful' Quarto encounter.

Like Prince Edward's green-attired courtier in *Friar Bacon*, or George a Greene's mistaken identification of the disguised kingly duo of Edward and James, or even Hobs's reaction to his monarch disguised as Ned in *1 Edward IV*, without the visual signifiers of kingship, all these disguised rulers appear as 'courtiers', 'yeomen' or 'thieves' in courtiers' clothes. Common to all is Robin Hood's Lincoln green. Although there is no way of knowing if Henry's Gentleman volunteer might likewise be dressed in green, it is certain that Henry V would appear no different to these earlier disguised rulers. Whether in Quarto 'habit' or Folio 'shape', Henry's appearance remains that of a 'common man', with whom

---

[84] Edmund Coote, *The English Schoole-maister* (London, 1596).
[85] Sir William Cornwallis, *Essayes* (London, 1600), fol. N2ᵛ.
[86] *Henslowe's Diary*, p. 323.

the unwitting subject of his secret encounter can freely and unreservedly express his true opinions. Indeed, Henry's disguised meeting with the Soldier/Williams appears directly analogous with the 'king and subject' theme of medieval folktale, its conflict and resolution mirrored precisely in this, the last of Shakespeare's Elizabethan 'Chronicle Histories'. Henry's disguise in Q, like that of his 'comical history' forebears, relies on recognition of an analogue that traces back to the earliest evocations of Robin Hood balladry. The difference between this meeting and previous 'Robin Hood' encounters is that only in the Folio text is it explained in visually explicit literary terms. Both Quarto and Folio *Henry V* evoke a medieval mythical meeting that forges a bridge between the 'comical histories' of the early 1590s, the Shakespearean 'Chronicle Histories', and the disguised ruler plays of the early seventeenth century. Henry might use his disguise for a self-serving political purpose, but this same disguise confirms the charismatic and pragmatic militarism of this heroic figure from Tudor Chronicle history.

That Henry's disguise represents a knowing evocation of the medieval 'king and subject' theme, combined (as in *1 Edward IV*) with a conflation of 'comical history' and far darker anxiety-inducing 'Chronicle History' opportunism, is confirmed by two other 'historical' plays – *1 Sir John Oldcastle* and *When You See Me You Know Me*. These each mirror Shakespeare's conflation of historical subgeneric forms, their disguised ruler episodes being predicated on an awareness of the plot and narrative of *Henry V*. The first, Michael Drayton, Richard Hathway, Antony Munday and Robert Wilson's *1 Sir John Oldcastle* (1599, Admiral's; published 1600), was performed the same year as *Henry V*, at the Globe's nearby rival, the Rose.[87] Written in response to Falstaff's depiction in *1 Henry IV* ('Oldcastle' being the name Shakespeare originally used for his knight), *1 Sir John Oldcastle* represents its authors' attempt to restore the reputation of the famous Lollard martyr and ancestral forebear of the late William Brooke, tenth Baron Cobham.[88] Sir John 'Jockey' Oldcastle, as we recall, had already appeared at 'Gadshill' as a thieving companion to Prince Henry in *The Famous Victories of Henry the Fifth* (*c.* mid-1580s). *1 Sir John Oldcastle* incorporates the narrative of Henry V's rule up until his departure for France, with, presumably, the enactment or consequences of the Agincourt adventure and the king's return with Princess Katherine in the lost sequel, *2 Sir John Oldcastle*. Falstaff makes the link between *1 Sir John Oldcastle* and *1 Henry IV* immediately apparent. More importantly, *1 Sir John Oldcastle* also corrects historical 'errors' up to and including those in *Henry V*.[89] How it does so tells us much about the reception and perception of Shakespeare's disguised ruler by late sixteenth-century admirers and detractors alike.

---

[87]   Michael Drayton, Richard Hathway, Antony Munday and Robert Wilson, *The First Part of the True and Honorable Historie of the Life of Sir John Old-castle* (London, 1600). Through line numbers from W.W. Greg (ed.), *The Life of Sir John Oldcastle* (Oxford, 1908).

[88]   Gary Taylor, 'The Fortunes of Oldcastle', *SS*, 38 (1985): 85–100.

[89]   Jonathan Rittenhouse (ed.), *1 Sir John Oldcastle* (New York, 1984), pp. 29–37; Gurr, *First Quarto 'Henry V'*, pp. 28–9.

Oldcastle, Thievery and Henrician Disguise

In *1 Sir John Oldcastle*, King Henry disguises himself in order secretly to observe a Protestant uprising: 'Well, Ile to Westminster, in this disguise, / To heare what newes is stirring in these brawles' (*Oldcastle*, F2ʳ; TLN.1362–3). In the process, he learns of a pro-Plantagenet plot to usurp and murder him, sponsored by King Charles of France. On his way from Eltham Palace, Henry is accosted by the thieving Parson, Sir John of Wrotham, a self-professed 'woolf ... cloathed in sheepes coate' (*Oldcastle*, B3ʳ; TLN.306). Significantly, as the Parson proudly announces, his parish includes Gadshill (*Oldcastle*, F4ʳ; TLN.1526). At the Parson's challenge, 'Stand true-man saies a thiefe', the disguised Henry replies, 'Stand thiefe, saies a true-man, how if a thiefe?', a response that ironically alludes to Henry's own disreputable Gadshill past (*Oldcastle*, F2ʳ; TLN.1365–6). Thief and victim then embark on an exchange replete with Robin Hood imagery. The king's request to know who is accosting him is answered by the Parson's emphatic, 'A good fellow', to which Henry responds, 'So am I too' (*Oldcastle*, F2ʳ; TLN.1371–2). Reminiscent of the 'good fellow' roysters in *1 Edward IV*, and alluding to the Hood/Goodfellow analogue of thieving opportunism, the Parson commands his victim to 'play the good fellowes part' and 'deliuer [Henry's] purse' (*Oldcastle*, F2ʳ; TLN.1373–4). Henry convinces the Parson that he is a chamber servant to the king, and thus of future use should the robber require a royal pardon. Now assured, the Parson describes how he first 'fell to the trade' of thieving because he too was robbed on the way to London, by none other than King Henry in league with 'that foule villaino[u]s guts ... Falstaffe' (*Oldcastle*, F2ᵛ; TLN.1416–19). For the Parson, this heinous act (an explicit allusion to the Gadshill robbery in *1 Henry IV*) is justification for his own subsequent immorality. In this 'king and subject' confrontation, the disguised Henry learns that his wayward past has directly affected this once honourable subject's life.

The play's reliance on Robin Hood imagery becomes even more apparent in the comic episode that follows. Seeing the benefit of the chamber servant's courtly connections, and echoing the glove exchange with Williams in *Henry V*, the Parson shares a broken gold angel coin with his victim as a means of future recognition. In the subsequent military encampment scene, king and courtiers (still in disguise) lure the Parson to play dice in order to win back Henry's stolen money. Before the Parson loses all, then gambles the exchanged half angel (thus revealing his true identity), Henry ironically describes the highwayman who previously waylaid him. Pretending not to recognize his gambling companion as the Blackheath thief, Henry claims to see a similarity between the Parson and his earlier assailant, even though 'that thiefe was [dressed] all in greene' (*Oldcastle*, F4ᵛ; TLN.1568). Henry's comment, the only evidence describing the Parson's thieving costume, repeats the commonplace colour for any good-fellow robber, especially one associated with the disguised ruler adventurism of Henry V. Later, when Oldcastle's clownish steward Harpoole is accused of Protestant sympathies by the Bishop of Rochester, he defends his ownership of certain 'English bookes', and declares that he will 'not part with' any, especially his 'Robin Hood, and other such godly stories' (*Oldcastle*, H2ʳ; TLN.1956–9). Several elements within *1 Sir John Oldcastle* thus prove that Robin Hood and the disguised adventures of Henry V were inseparable for the play's late sixteenth-century playwrights and audience.

There are, however, more subtle allusions to *Henry V* in *1 Sir John Oldcastle* that highlight the political expediency of royal disguise. The Parson's initial enquiry of Henry – 'What art thou, thou seem'st a gentleman?' (*Oldcastle*, F2ᵛ; TLN.1391) – is reminiscent of Pistol's 'art thou Gentleman?' challenge in *Henry V*. Later, when discussing his journey to observe the rebel factions, Henry confirms the unusualness of such disguised surveillance, especially since spying traditionally is conducted not by a king, but by his 'Sentinells' and 'Lords' (*Oldcastle*, TLN.1457–8). With self-deprecating irony, Henry explains the typical royal response, whereby kings normally remain 'at rest in bed', not choosing 'to watch themselues', but rather to 'sleepe' while 'rebellion and conspiracie, / Reuel and hauocke in the common wealth' (*Oldcastle*, F3ʳ–F3ᵛ; TLN.1461–5). His description of the sleeping monarch, oblivious to rebellion that threatens his rule, supports Henry's belief (held likewise by his *Henry V* counterpart) that secret surveillance is only effective when conducted by a disguised king in royal person. Henry's admission that such secrecy is possible because he has long considered himself a 'perfect night-walker' or nocturnal thief (*Oldcastle*, F3ᵛ; TLN.1477) highlights the symbolism of royal disguise so closely associated with Robin Hood thievery.

'Night-walker' imagery also appears in Samuel Rowley's *When You See Me You Know Me* (*c.* 1603–1604, Admiral's/Prince Henry's[?]; published 1605), a play which, like *1 Sir John Oldcastle*, embeds a disguised ruler 'comical history' adventure within its more serious 'Chronicle History' portrayal of religious dissent and pro-Protestant jingoism. Performed most likely by the same acting personnel who staged *Oldcastle*, now based at the Fortune playhouse, *When You See Me You Know Me* presents King Henry VIII recovering swiftly from the untimely death in childbirth of his queen, Jane Seymour. With a mixture of cold-hearted glee and genuine political desire for knowledge through secret surveillance, Henry elects to travel 'in some disguised shape / To visit *London*' (*When You*, D1ʳ; TLN.930–31).⁹⁰ His purpose is 'to walke the round' of his various policing Watchmen, to 'obserue' how well they apprehend the 'night-walkers' who 'hourely passe the streets, / Committing theft, and hated sacriliege' (*When You*, D1ʳ; TLN.931–5). Unlike *Oldcastle*'s Henry V who, five years before, acknowledges the appropriateness of the 'night-walker' soubriquet for himself, Rowley's Henry VIII embarks on his disguised ruler adventure to expose 'night-walker' criminality in his subjects. In an interesting reworking of the 'hardship of rule' trope, Henry complains how, despite a king's exhaustive efforts 'To toyle himselfe in … high state affaires' (*When You*, D3ʳ; TLN.1055), neglectful law officers, corrupt royal servants and scheming cardinals continue to dupe the innocent into false imprisonment and ignominious death. Only through secret disguise, which prompts the comical irony of his arrest and incarceration in London's Counter prison, can Henry experience

---

⁹⁰ Samuel Rowley, *When You See Me You Know Me* (London, 1605). Through line numbers from F.P. Wilson (ed.), *When You See Me You Know Me* (Oxford, 1952).

first-hand how 'much wrong Kings men may do: / The which their maisters nere consent vnto' (*When You*, E3ʳ; TLN.1354–5).

Henry's arrest follows a bloody encounter with one night-walker, the infamous Black Will. The narrative of this meeting of disguised king and dangerous outlaw mirrors the familiar 'king and subject' theme. Black Will, a self-confessed murderer of two foreign 'Marchants of the *Stilliard*' (*When You*, D3ʳ; TLN.1068–9), is punished less severely than he deserves because he unwittingly proves himself a fervent supporter of 'his Maiestie' (*When You*, D3ᵛ; TLN.1092). Black Will's crimes, while not fully pardoned, are regarded with leniency by the king who recognizes that, if Black Will 'can breake through watches with egres and regres so valiantly', he could do the same fighting 'amongst [his] countries enemies' (*When You*, E3ʳ; TLN.1373–5). Incarcerated in prison until conscripted for war, Black Will still swears allegiance to Henry: 'Ile liue and dye with thee sweet King' (*When You*, E3ʳ; TLN.1382). Henry's treatment of Black Will provides no comic resolution to this 'king and subject' episode. It displays instead the military pragmatism of the nation's ruler who recognizes the benefit of patriotic fervour in one skilled at venturing undetected through 'enemy' lines.

Even before Henry and Black Will first meet, the Robin Hood imagery of their subsequent encounter evinces itself. Echoing the disguised confrontation on the eve of Agincourt, and confirming yet again the Hood/Goodfellow analogue of kingly disguise, Henry VIII is challenged on entry into London by Prichall the Cobbler, lantern-bearer to the Watch. Prichall's 'Stand, who goes there?', is greeted with Henry's ironic response, 'A good fellow' (*When You*, D2ᵛ; TLN.1038). Despite the suspicious circumstances of this strange encounter, and the king's cryptic response about the 'little businesse that [he has] in hand' (*When You*, D2ᵛ; TLN.1044), the sleepy Cobbler (a shoemaking good-fellow by Gentle Craft association) still allows this stranger free passage, to commit 'murder, rapine, theft, or sacriledge' without the least hindrance or examination (*When You*, D2ᵛ; TLN.1051). Almost immediately, Henry confronts the notorious Black Will himself, the king now asking the villain, 'Art thou a good fellow?' (*When You*, D3ᵛ; TLN.1104). Echoing the dramatic irony of Henry V's encounter with his Agincourt troops, Black Will enquires if he 'May … speake freely' with this stranger, with assurance that he 'wilt not tel the king ont?' (*When You*, D3ᵛ; TLN.1105). Henry's ironic response, that 'the King shall know no more … then thou telst him', is balanced by Black Will's equally ironic statement, 'And I tell him any thing let him hang me' (*When You*, D3ᵛ; TLN.1107–9). Black Will is reassured not only by Henry's knowingly evasive answer, but also his disguised appearance. It convinces the outlaw that, 'if a fat purse come ith way, [the stranger] wouldest not refuse it' (*When You*, D3ᵛ; TLN.1110–11). Like many disguised kings before him, Henry VIII looks like a good-fellow purse-taker to this, the 'chiefe commander of all the Stewes' (*When You*, D3ᵛ; TLN.1112).

Black Will invites his new companion on a journey through the streets of London. Immediately, they encounter more Watchmen who, yet again, challenge the strangers as 'good fellows':

FIRST WATCHMAN: Stand, who goes there?
BLACK WILL: A good fellow: come close, regard them not.
SECOND WATCHMAN: How shall we know thee to be a good fellow?
BLACK WILL: My names *Blacke Will*.
FIRST WATCHMAN: Oh, God giue yee good night, good Maister
Blacke William. (*When You*, D3ᵛ; TLN.1104–25)

The extent of Henry's localized political problems is confirmed by the corrupt
Watchmen who, whether through fear or bribery, allow a known criminal to pass
freely around London. They even greet him with overly-familiar civility. Only
after experiencing first-hand the corrupt inequities of prison life can the king
return to court and confront the far greater threat from Cardinal Wolsey, whose
ambitions to gain the Papacy threaten the life of Henry's new queen, Catherine
Parr. This Chronicle evocation of Tudor political and religious strife, written
during an uncertain period of regime change, includes a 'comical history' episode
of disguised 'king and subject' encounter that recalls *Henry V*. It illustrates not
the uniqueness of Henry's disguise on the eve of Agincourt, but the commonplace
nature of its re-enactment of an age-old theme founded on the medieval imagery
of Robin Hood.

Rowley's jingoistic, pro-Lutheran, anti-Catholic play captures the anxiety
of a nation unsure of its situation in the wider theatre of European power. For
Rowley, as for Drayton, Hathway, Munday and Wilson five years before, such
Chronicle portrayal of political uncertainty is inconceivable without the addition
of a 'comical history' disguised ruler for comic effect. The unifying factor of these
plays appears to be Shakespeare's *Henry V*, with Henry's pre-Agincourt disguise
representing a bridge between the medieval 'comical histories', via the factual
narratives of the 'Chronicle Histories', to the principal disguise plot protagonists
of the seventeenth century. Henry might not wear Erpingham's 'cloak' in Q *Henry
V*, but in both Quarto and Folio, Henry metaphorically clothes himself in several
centuries of historicized mythology when confronting his frightened soldiers
poised perilously near the French army.

In cases like these, when historicized mythology combines with the myth of
national and dynastic supremacy, the disguised ruler acquires a more sinister,
anxiety-inducing persona. *Henry V* is a significant example of this conflation of
forms, with Shakespeare creating a play both reassuring in its chivalric militarism
and unnerving for its representation of disguised surveillance by the king.
Henry's disguised ruler escapade on the eve of Agincourt leads, via *1 Sir John
Oldcastle*, to the final flowering of the medieval 'king and subject' theme in Henry
VIII's encounter with Black Will. What was to follow, influenced by European
experiments with form, was fundamentally to change the disguised ruler's role
and appearance on the seventeenth-century stage. This disguised ruler revolution
took place not in the large public playhouses, where audiences eagerly followed
their adult actor heroes, but in the confines of the smaller indoor venues of the
City, manned by the 'children' – the young boys and teenagers – of the children's
companies. Paradoxically, the disguised ruler was to come of age through the
inventive medium of youthful performance.

Chapter 2
The Malcontent:
A Play in Two Forms

In the 1980s, critics classified *The Malcontent* as a Jacobean disguised ruler play. As such, it represents Marston's personal expression of 'theatrical solidarity' with his fellow disguised ruler playwrights, written in direct response to King James's accession to the English throne.[1] With its costumed duke travelling incognito to confront his usurpers and restore himself to power, *The Malcontent* explores the moral decline of a fictive Italian court, while supposedly commenting on England's new regime. *The Malcontent* thus appears self-evidently related to the 'first few months of Jacobean politics'.[2] A host of imitators, including Shakespeare, Middleton and Sharpham, then followed Marston's lead, vying to outdo each other's hegemonic/subversive wit.[3] As we have seen, however, the disguised ruler had already manifested himself in several earlier dramas. These decidedly Elizabethan disguised rulers, which include Hal and Henry V, were closely associated with the medieval and Tudor Chronicle tradition and Robin Hood mythology, things quite unconnected to James's accession. Why, then, is *The Malcontent* considered so unique and paradigmatic? Indeed, is its 'Jacobean' status as concrete as recent scholarship might suggest?

Placing *The Malcontent* in an exclusively Jacobean generic grouping nevertheless makes some sense for a number of reasons, over and above its supposed occasionalism. The title-page dating of 1604 on *The Malcontent*'s three quarto editions, the same year that *Measure for Measure* is recorded in royal performance, appears to confirm the simultaneity of both plays. Likewise, the Globe players named in *The Malcontent*'s Induction most likely are the same King's Men who performed *Measure for Measure* at the Banqueting Hall for their kingly patron. What *The Malcontent* and *Measure for Measure* have in common is obvious – a shared motif, a shared date and a shared company.[4] These common features have led critics to assume the effective identity of these plays. What follows is a questioning of the apparent logic of this assumption, whereby it is not *The Malcontent* in comparison with *Measure for Measure* that we consider, but the '*Malcontents*' in comparison with themselves.

---

[1]   See Tennenhouse, *Power*, p. 154.
[2]   Wharton, 'Sexual', p. 183.
[3]   See Tricomi, *Anticourt*, p. 14.
[4]   Henke, *Pastoral*, pp. 50–51.

The Malcontent or the '*Malcontents*'?

In her study of the Children of the Queen's Revels, Lucy Munro states that *The Malcontent* 'stands in many ways as a paradigmatic tragicomedy', adding that it might 'date from the late Elizabethan rather than the early Jacobean period'.[5] This comment highlights the vague history of *The Malcontent* and its chronology in the early modern canon. What little we know of *The Malcontent*'s history comes from a 1604 *Stationers' Register* entry and its appearance that same year in a trio of quarto versions. The *Stationers' Register* for 5 July 1604 (made on the wrong page and then re-entered) states that the 'Enterlude called the Malecontent' is a 'Tragicomoedia'.[6] As we have seen, this generic description echoes Guarini's *Il pastor fido* title-page, which styles his play a '*tragicomedia pastorale*'.[7] In the months following the *Stationers' Register* entry, three quarto editions of *The Malcontent* are published by William Aspley to be sold at his shop in St Paul's churchyard, all printed by Valentine Sims. In the 1920s, W.W. Greg differentiated between the three quartos, calling them QA, QB and QC, and argued that they display a recognizable chronological progression.[8] First came QA, as performed by a children's company, then QB, with only minor amendments by author and/ or censor (both referred to as QA/B hereafter), and finally the QC edition, whose title-page announces its performance 'by the Kings Maiesties servants' at the Globe.[9] With Greg's differentiation in mind, it is possible to see why Munro's statement that *The Malcontent* might not be Jacobean but Elizabethan, while still representing the 'paradigmatic tragicomedy' of early modern English drama, poses an unanswered and problematic question. Which of these quartos of *The Malcontent* should be considered 'paradigmatic' – the shorter QA/B texts or their longer QC cousin? To answer this, we must consider *The Malcontent*'s external and internal historical evidence, and review the way critics interpret so limited a resource.

Described as 'rather a miserable little quarto' by George K. Hunter (the twentieth-century editor of a conflated version of *The Malcontent*), QA *Malcontent* is slightly more than 1,900 lines long, and thus shorter by approximately one quarter than its QC counterpart at 2,500 lines.[10] Although not an entirely new edition, QB *Malcontent* is the same length as QA (several pages remaining typographically identical), with occasional corrections presumed to be authorial

---

[5]   Munro, *Queen's Revels*, p. 106.

[6]   Arber 3, pp. 266–8.

[7]   Guarini, *Il pastor fido* (Venice, 1590), BL 1073.h.27.

[8]   W.W. Greg, 'Notes on Old Books', *The Library*, 2 (1921–22): 49–57.

[9]   Marston, *Malcontent* (London, 1604), *STC* 17479, 17480 and 17481.

[10]   George K. Hunter (ed.), *The Malcontent* (Manchester, 1975; reprinted 1999), p. xxxi. Note, a revised and foreshortened version appears as George K. Hunter (ed.), *The Malcontent*, Revels Student Editions (Manchester, 2000). Unless otherwise directed, all references are to the full 1975 edition.

rather than printing-house amendments.[11] The far longer QC *Malcontent* is an entirely revised edition that includes twelve new sections of dialogue, as well as an Induction; these combined amount to over 600 additional lines.[12] QC *Malcontent* also announces the collaborative efforts of Webster. One explanation for the QC *Malcontent* additions is that they provide comic material for the King's Men's resident clown, Robert Armin.[13] Alternatively, the additional dialogue might replace lost songs, dances and instrumental interludes (traditionally associated with the children's companies), which lengthen the QC version to that of a 'standard' Globe play.[14] Regardless of which theory is correct, since the average length of plays varied from less than 2,000 to 2,800 lines, the QA/B *Malcontent* at over 1,900 lines hardly seems as unduly short as Hunter's 'miserable little quarto' soubriquet would suggest.[15]

Neither QA nor QB *Malcontent* name a playing company. The QC Induction, by contrast, offers clues about the play's early provenance. The Induction introduces the Globe actors Henry Condell, John Lowin, John Sinklo and William Sly, as well as the company's renowned leading player, Richard Burbage, who is credited with playing the 'Malecontent' (QC *Malcontent*, A4ʳ; Induction 87). It appears, though, that the King's Men were not the first to perform the play. Sinklo indicates that he believes 'the play is not so well acted as it hath beene' (QC, *Malcontent*, A4ʳ; Induction 88–9). This comment instantly suggests that *The Malcontent* originated in a repertory other than the Globe's. By way of explanation, the real William Sly, appearing onstage as a metatheatrical playhouse tire-man, berates the antisocial habits of fashionable London gallants:

> SLY: [T]his play hath beaten all your gallants out
> of the feathers: Blacke friars hath almost spoild blacke friars
> for feathers. (QC *Malcontent*, A3ᵛ; Induction 40–42)

Sly attacks those gallants who purchase extravagant wares from Blackfriars feather merchants, scolding them for wearing such over-sized ostentation in their hats and spoiling the view in the small indoor venue. Blackfriars had, since 1599, presented plays by the Children of the Chapel, renamed the Children of the Queen's Revels with Queen Anne's patronage in 1604. Accordingly, Sly's comments are accepted as proof of the play's origins at Blackfriars.[16]

---

[11]   Hunter, *Malcontent*, p. xxxiv.

[12]   Ibid., p. xlviii. Although Hunter notes only eleven extra passages of dialogue, 'Fride frogs are very good & French like too' (2.2.33) is recognized as a QC addition in the text (p. 59).

[13]   Ibid., pp. xlix–li.

[14]   Chambers, *ES* 3, p. 132; Keith Sturgess, *Jacobean Private Theatre* (London, 1987), p. 47; Charles Cathcart, 'John Marston, *The Malcontent* and the King's Men', *RES*, 57 (2006): 43–63 (p. 55).

[15]   Erne, *Literary*, pp. 146–7.

[16]   Chambers, *ES* 3, p. 432.

As if to defend the unusual circumstance of the play's reappearance on the adult stage, Sly interrogates the actor Condell, asking to 'know how [the King's Men] came by this play?':

> CONDELL: Faith sir the booke was lost, and because twas pittie so
> good a play should be lost, we found it and play it.
> SLY: I wonder you would play it, another company having
> an interest in it.
> CONDELL: Why not Maleuole in folio with vs, as Ieronimo in De-
> cimo sexto with them. They taught vs a name for our play, wee
> call it *One for another*. (QC *Malcontent*, A4ʳ; Induction 73–80)

Condell's explanation, that the original playbook of *The Malcontent* was somehow 'lost' and then 'found' by the King's Men, is often considered with a varying degree of literality.[17] Whatever the truth, the King's Men's staging of a 'lost' play appears in response to some other company's decision to perform 'Ieronimo'. By way of confirmation that this was a children's company, Condell employs imagery derived from the printing-house to describe the difference in size between adult and child players. Based on a book published in full sized, once folded folio paper as opposed to eighth sized, four-times folded decimo sexto paper, the 'Folio' adult players will perform *The Malcontent* instead of the smaller 'Decimo sexto' children. Written in the style of a metatheatrical exercise particularly associated with the children's companies, this Induction might indicate the adults' desire both to advertise and to excuse the play's children's company heritage.[18] Sly's comments seem ironically to voice the concerns of a Globe audience who, quite justifiably, might express disquiet at paying to watch a play they had already seen performed elsewhere, but by children.

Ever since Chambers first suggested that Condell's reference to 'Ieronimo' alludes to an actual theft by the Blackfriars children, this has generally been accepted as historical fact.[19] Initially, Condell's 'Ieronimo' was thought to refer to the anonymous *The First Part of Jeronimo* (*c.* 1600–1604, Chamberlain's[?]/ King's Men[?]; published 1605), otherwise known as *1 Jeronimo, with the Wars of Portugal*, a play whose sole association with the Globe is through this *Malcontent* Induction comment.[20] *1 Jeronimo* was supposedly stolen from the King's Men, who retaliated by stealing *The Malcontent*.[21] Alternative opinion soon favoured Thomas Kyd's *The Spanish Tragedy*, also known as *Hieronimo Is Mad Again*

---

[17]   Hunter, *Malcontent*, p. 13n.

[18]   See Munro, *Queen's Revels*, p. 134.

[19]   Chambers, *ES* 4, p. 23; Michael Shapiro, 'Boy Companies and Private Theaters', in Arthur F. Kinney (ed.), *A Companion to Renaissance Drama* (Oxford, 2002), pp. 314–25 (p. 323).

[20]   Emma Smith (ed.), *The Spanish Tragedie* (Harmondsworth, 1998), pp. 140–41.

[21]   Lukas Erne, *Beyond the Spanish Tragedy* (Manchester, 2001), pp. 21–3.

(1587, Strange's Men; published 1592; revived *c.* 1597, Admiral's Men).[22] If the reference to 'Ieronimo' in QC *Malcontent*'s Induction does refer to Kyd's *Spanish Tragedy*, then Condell's comment reflects not an actual 'theft', but rather justifiable outrage at a dangerous new practice: the controversial performance of adult tragedies by the children's companies.

Such outrage was certainly not new, as implied by Rosencraft and Gilderstone's dialogue when discussing the adult 'Tragedians of the Citty', forced into touring by the 'priuate playes' that exploit the 'humour of children' (Q1 *Hamlet*, E3ʳ; 7.264 & 7.273). At least by 1603, as this Q1 *Hamlet* comment confirms, the children's companies (Folio *Hamlet*'s 'ayrie' of 'little Yases' [TLN.1386–7]) were already considered rivals by their adult counterparts. That Kyd's 1580s *Spanish Tragedy* was still in popular demand is likewise demonstrated by its recent revival (and remodelling by Ben Jonson) for the Admiral's Men in 1602.[23] On the other hand, if the 'Ieronimo' of the Induction refers to the anonymous *First Part of Jeronimo*, then this points to the 'acquisition' of a burlesque of Kyd's tragedy by a children's company. Either way, the Induction appears a simple statement of fact about, as well as a defence for, the seeming anomaly of a famous children's play now prominently featured in the adult repertory. If the 'decimo sextos' can perform an adult tragedy like *The Spanish Tragedy* (or even its burlesque prequel), why should the adult 'folios' not perform a children's play like *The Malcontent*? The Induction can be viewed as an adult company response to a new and potentially dangerous playhouse precedent – the playing of old, successful and oft-revived adult plays by the children's companies – a factor that prompts Condell's retaliatory comment, '*One for another*'.

Based on his analysis of the Induction, Chambers conjectures that *The Malcontent* was first performed in 1604, with all three editions published in quick succession thereafter. Accordingly, so he asserts, 'this is Marston's first play for the Queen's Revels after the formation of the syndicate early in 1604', the QC revision following 'later in the same year'.[24] Chambers conflates the arrival of the various syndicate members of Blackfriars (including Edward Kirkham, Samuel Daniel and John Marston) into the year 1604, a chronology that recent historical analysis brings into question.[25] Kirkham actually became a sharer at Blackfriars as early as 1602, whereas Samuel Daniel was not contracted with the syndicate until 1604.[26] Marston's admission to Blackfriars could have occurred at any time following Kirkham's arrival in 1602 and before Daniel's in 1604; *The Malcontent*

---

[22]   Hunter, *Malcontent*, p. 13n.; W. David Kay (ed.), *Malcontent*, 2nd edn (London, 1998), p. xv.

[23]   *Henslowe's Diary*, p. 203.

[24]   Chambers, *ES* 3, p. 432.

[25]   Munro, *Queen's Revels*, pp. 18–20.

[26]   Michael Shapiro, *Children of the Revels* (New York, 1977), p. 25.

might thus have been written when the Blackfriars company was still known as the Children of the Chapel, prior to their royal patent and new name.[27]

Marston's 'Much Borrowing' from Guarini

Chambers's interpretation of the combined title-page, Induction and syndicate evidence is coloured by his refusal to believe that Shakespeare, in creating his disguised duke for *Measure for Measure*, could ever have borrowed a motif from Marston: 'I do not see how it can be so'.[28] This refusal to accept any influence by supposed 'lesser' dramatists, while always assuming that Shakespeare influenced others, is indicative of prevailing negative attitudes to *The Malcontent*. Contentions that *Measure for Measure* predated *The Malcontent* were seriously undermined in the 1960s by critical recognition of Marston's 'much borrowing' from Guarini's *Il pastor fido*.[29] Such 'borrowing' amounts to twenty-one separate instances of Guarinian dialogue, all supposedly derived from a 1602 translation called *Il Pastor Fido*.[30] This 'Englished' version of Guarini's play was translated by an unknown writer known solely, from its dedicatory sonnet by Samuel Daniel, as a 'kinsman' to '*Syr* Edward Dymock'.[31] A possible allusion to Sir Edward's brother Tailboys Dymock (or Dymoke), who published poetry under the pseudonym Robert Cutwode, Daniel's 'kinsman' provides the only authorial clue, and thus the distinctive title for, the 'Dymock' *Il Pastor Fido*.[32] It was this 'Englished' version that was considered Marston's direct source.

As will become evident, belief that the 'Dymock' translation represents Marston's sole access to Guarini is seriously flawed. Marston's interest in *Il pastor fido*, and his belief that audiences and/or readers would recognize his allusions to it, nevertheless leads to his wholesale appropriation of key dramatic dialogue from this influential tragicomedy. Marston employs this appropriated dialogue in a manner familiar to any early modern commonplace book note-taker: to supply pithy maxims, aphorisms or *sententiae* that punctuate the text.[33] That Guarini's *Il pastor fido* was of sufficient international importance to warrant this appropriation is suggested by its almost immediate 1591 re-publication in England by the Italian

---

[27] Munro, *Queen's Revels*, p. 28.

[28] Chambers, *ES* 3, p. 432.

[29] Hunter, 'English Folly', p. 100.

[30] Guarini, *Il Pastor Fido: or The Faithfull Shepheard*, trans. 'Dymock' (London, 1602).

[31] Ibid., fol. A3[v].

[32] See Elizabeth Story Donno (ed.), *Three Renaissance Pastorals* (Binghampton, 1993), pp. xxi–xxiv; Eleri Larkum, 'Dymoke, Tailboys [Thomas Cutwode] (*bap.* 1561, *d.* 1602/3)', *ODNB* (2004) <http://www.oxforddnb.com/index/101006985/Tailboys-Dymoke> [accessed 6 May 2011].

[33] George K. Hunter, 'The Marking of *Sententiae* in Elizabethan Printed Plays, Poems, and Romances', *The Library*, 6 (1951): 171–88.

émigré, Iacopo Castelvetro.[34] A year after this edition appeared in London for his Italian reading clientele, Castelvetro removed to Edinburgh to become the personal language tutor to King James VI and Queen Anne of Scotland.[35] As later testimony confirms, *Il pastor fido* was particularly favoured by the Italophile Anne who, as Queen of England, conferred patronage on the Children of the Queen's Revels in 1604. At the same time, she employed her favourite, Samuel Daniel (author of the 'Dymock' dedicatory epistle), as private licenser of the company's plays. Daniel had already sojourned in Italy in the early 1590s, in the company of his patron Sir Edward Dymock ('kinsman' of the anonymous translator), and enjoyed a personal audience with the famous Guarini.[36] This encounter confirms Daniel's interest in contemporary Italian literature, while also accounting for his epistle to Sir Edward for the 1602 'Dymock' translation.[37] These factors, though especially his desire to pander to the predilections of his new private licenser, might all account for Marston's decision to refer so overtly to Guarini in this, possibly his earliest Blackfriars play.

Marston's appropriation of Guarinian dialogue, apart from linking *The Malcontent* to a 1602 translated text, did nothing to remove the stigma of a secondary association with *Measure for Measure*. Neither did it suggest that the three quarto editions were worthy of individual consideration. Consequently, twentieth-century editions generally conflate all three quartos.[38] A noticeable absence of critical consideration of QA/B *Malcontent* is coupled with a decidedly biased focus on the Globe's QC version, deemed worthy of study because of its association with Shakespeare, and its status as a supposedly definitive authorial text. This bias has been called into doubt by Jason Lawrence's study of educational techniques employed by late sixteenth-century foreign language tutors. Lawrence recognizes a significant difference between the QA/B and QC texts: the borrowings from Guarini's *Il pastor fido* are evident only in QA/B and are absent from the additions to QC.[39] This observation helps to correct the imbalance between critical consideration of the 'Globe' *Malcontent*, to the near exclusion of the shorter 'miserable little quarto' QA/B version. Not completely, however, because Lawrence fails to suggest why QA/B and QC should be so different. This is surprising, since he argues convincingly that many early modern dramatists followed a similar technique to that employed by language tutors when studying and comparing texts in an original language alongside those in translation. The

---

[34]   Guarini, *Il pastor fido*, ed. Iacopo Castelvetro (London, 1591), BL 1071.a.20.

[35]   Jason Lawrence, *"Who the devil taught thee so much Italian?": Italian Language Learning and Literary Imitation in Early Modern England* (Manchester, 2005), pp. 7–9.

[36]   Ibid., pp. 19–61.

[37]   Ibid., pp. 78 & 94–102.

[38]   Only Keith Sturgess (ed.), *John Marston: 'The Malcontent' and Other Plays* (Oxford, 1997), isolates QA/B from QC, claiming that QA/B reflects Marston's 'authentic, original text' (pp. xviii–xx).

[39]   Lawrence, *"Who the devil"*, p. 144.

opportunity to access obscure foreign sources for inspiration was seized on by playwrights keen to demonstrate their fashionable erudition without the necessity (or undeniable trouble) of tiresomely translating difficult texts: assisted plagiarism held the key to narrative diversity. Noticeably, this same argument is not applied to Marston. Despite a thorough examination of *The Malcontent*'s villainous characters, Mendoza and Maquerelle, Lawrence insists that Marston's only access to *Il pastor fido* is via the 'direct source' of the Englished 'Dymock' text.[40]

A reason why Lawrence fails to countenance Marston's use of comparative texts is suggested by traditional criticism that seeks to explain the playwright's obvious linguistic skill in biographical terms. Marston's proficiency is believed to stem from his 'second-generation Italian immigrant' mother, 'at whose knee he had learned the exotic tongue'.[41] Marston's mother, Mary Marston (nee Guarsi), is repeatedly, though inaccurately, described as the 'daughter' of Balthazar Guarsi, Italian barber-surgeon to Katherine of Aragon and Henry VIII.[42] Balthazar, an Italian by birth, was naturalized an English subject in 1521–22, and resided most of his life in London.[43] Mary Marston was not Balthazar's daughter, however, but the daughter of Elizabeth Gray and Andrew Guarsi, Balthazar's son.[44] Marston's mother was thus the *granddaughter* of Balthazar Guarsi. Marston's genealogical link to an Italian-born forebear was thus to his maternal great-grandfather, who had died nineteen years before his birth. It was Marston's maternal grandfather, not his mother, who was child of an Italian surgeon residing in London, and no reference to Andrew Guarsi as a physician appears in the records of the Royal College of Physicians, although Balthazar is well documented.[45] Indeed, the Anglicized choice of forename given to Marston's grandfather by Balthazar suggests little surviving connection with Italy. As the daughter of Andrew and Elizabeth, Marston's mother might be proud of her Italian heritage, but this hardly confirms any competency in her grandfather's native language. There is every possibility that Marston (who was ordained an Anglican priest in 1609) might be content to have his name linked with a famous barber-surgeon to the founder of Anglican Protestantism, Henry VIII.[46] While not illuminating how Marston

---

[40]   Ibid., p. 162.

[41]   Kiernan Ryan, '*The Malcontent*: Hunting the Letter', in Wharton (ed.), *Marston*, pp. 145–61 (p. 148).

[42]   Charles Cathcart, 'Marston, Montaigne, and Lady Politic Would-be', *ELN*, 36 (1999): 4–8 (p. 5); Martin Wiggins, *Shakespeare and the Drama of his Time* (Oxford, 2000), p. 103.

[43]   Margaret Pelling and Frances White, 'GUERSIE, Balthasar', *Physicians and Irregular Medical Practitioners in London 1550–1640: Database* (2004) <http://www.british-history.ac.uk/report.asp?compid=17492> [accessed 6 May 2011].

[44]   W. Reavley Gair (ed.), *Antonio and Mellida* (Manchester, 1991), p. 11.

[45]   William Munk, *Roll of the Royal College of Physicians of London* (2 vols, London, 1861), vol. 1, p. 52.

[46]   James Knowles, 'Marston, John', *ODNB* (2004) <http://www.oxforddnb.com/index/101018164/John-Marston> [accessed 6 May 2011].

acquired his skill in Italian, with the likelihood that, like many of his Inns of Court contemporaries, he gained his linguistic prowess as part of his humanist grammar school or Oxford University education, it does remove the necessity for Marston to rely solely on a translated text when searching for apposite material for *The Malcontent*.[47] The overly simplistic biographical explanation for Marston's proficiency in Italian affects our appreciation of his intellectual and practical ability to access foreign texts in their original language. The borrowings from Guarini's *Il pastor fido* in QA/B *Malcontent* are indicative of this ability.

The significance of Marston's appropriation of Guarini for his QA/B *Malcontent* can only fully be appreciated once an earliest possible date of performance is established. Dating any early seventeenth-century play must accommodate the apparent closure of the playhouses during the 1603–1604 plague outbreaks in London, as Leeds Barroll famously notes.[48] Plays were most likely performed throughout the first few months of 1603 until the traditional Lent closure on Ash Wednesday, 9 March. On 19 March 1603, the Privy Council instruction ordering the 'restraint of stage-plaies' came into force, followed by Elizabeth's death five days later on 24 March.[49] According to Barroll's reckoning, the playhouses remained closed for a further ten months. Barroll's analysis creates a 'closure' pattern that relies on his reading of a group of dependent statistical variables. His propositions are: that the plague caused deaths, that the Privy Council issued a ban on playing in weeks when thirty or more plague deaths were reported, that the playhouses adhered to the Privy Council directive, and that contemporary mortality rates were reliably recorded.[50] A statistical improbability and unreliability in Barroll's argument, however, is suggested by two entries in Henslowe's *Diary*, which imply that the Fortune at least might have begun 'to playe Agayne by the kynges licence' for a short period in May 1603. Henslowe's comment implies that the playhouse managements might have received conflicting communications from the government, or might not have adhered to public directives as strictly as Privy Council or City authorities – or literary historians – believe or desire.[51] The inherent instability of Barroll's statistical conjecture leads Andrew Gurr to describe his findings as at best 'over-insistent', at worst 'wrong'.[52] Although ultimately impossible to confirm or refute Barroll's findings, his study provides a useful chronology of likely play production for the period 1603–1604. James's coronation, therefore, took place on 15 March 1604, almost precisely a year after Elizabeth's death. Twenty-five days later, the Privy Council lifted its injunction against playing.

---

[47] John Hale, *England and the Italian Renaissance*, 2nd edn (London, 1996), p. 9.

[48] Barroll, *Plague*, pp. 70–116.

[49] John R. Dasent (ed.), *Acts of the Privy Council of England: 1542–1631* (46 vols, London, 1890–1964), vol. 32, p. 492.

[50] Barroll, *Plague*, p. 100.

[51] *Henslowe's Diary*, pp. 209 & 225.

[52] Gurr, *Playing Companies*, pp. 91–2.

Up until April 1604, the playhouses might well have suffered continuous closure for thirteen months. First public performances of *The Malcontent* either predate Elizabeth's death in March 1603, occur during a short period of optimism at James's arrival in London in May 1603, or post-date his coronation on 15 March 1604. If *The Malcontent* post-dates James's coronation, it is unlikely to have been performed prior to the lifting of the playhouse ban. This chronology implies initial performance by the Queen's Revels children, double publication with authorial amendments, and transfer to the King's Men for extensive rewrites by Marston and Webster, followed by performance and publication again, all within eight to eleven months.[53] Certainly, such a timescale is possible given the speed with which plays commonly were revised and returned to the repertory.[54] This triple publication is sufficiently unusual, however, to warrant continued debate and conjecture. The triad might indicate a downturn in fortunes for the children's company, with Marston seeking an alternative outlet for his work, or the commercial furore following a theatrical success, or even the quest for publicity in the aftermath of the long playhouse closures.[55] Whatever motivated the appearance of three 1604 quartos, the differences between the QA/B and QC texts challenge any conclusion that two versions of *The Malcontent* were written concurrently for two companies and then hurried through three printed editions.

Given this inconclusive external evidence, scholars have scoured the play for internal clues about its performance history. The noticeable absence of references to John Florio's translation of Michel de Montaigne's *Essayes* (that permeate the texts of Marston's *c.* 1604 *Dutch Courtesan* and 1604 *Fawn*) counters its traditional dating to 1604.[56] Like many of his contemporaries, Marston included references to the very latest literary fashions. The absence of these allusions cannot, however, confirm that *The Malcontent* was originally written prior to Florio's translation. Marston might not have read the 1603 edition immediately, or he might have chosen to forego topical references. More significantly, John Lowin appears to have joined (or rejoined) the King's Men in the twelve months following 12 March 1603.[57] On this date, Henslowe's *Diary* records Lowin riding 'into the *contrey* wth his company [Worcester's Men] to playe' on tour as an actor.[58] If the absence of references to Florio's translation of Montaigne cannot date the

---

[53]   This timescale acknowledges the relatively recent change (1582) from the Julian to the Gregorian calendar. Under the Julian calendar, New Year's Eve was celebrated 24 March. A 1604 title-page might imply publication any time up to 24 March 1605.

[54]   Kastan, *Book*, pp. 14–49.

[55]   Hunter, *Malcontent*, pp. xliii–xlvi; Knutson, *Commerce*, pp. 67–74.

[56]   Michel de Montaigne, *The Essayes*, trans. John Florio (London, 1603); Hunter, *Malcontent*, p. xlvi.

[57]   Lowin is credited with speech-prefixes throughout QC's Induction, but is unmentioned by name in the dialogue. The metatheatrical in-joke of the real actor's presence must thus have been recognizable only in an original live performance setting.

[58]   *Henslowe's Diary*, p. 212.

QA/B or QC versions, and if Lowin could only have appeared with the King's Men sometime after his Worcester's Men sojourn in the country, then a *terminus ad quem* of spring 1603 to 1604 for QC *Malcontent* seems an obvious conclusion. Similarly, parallels to the 'Dymock' *Il Pastor Fido* suggest a *terminus a quo* for first performance of QA/B of 1602. Consequently, QA/B *Malcontent* appears to be the play performed by a children's company (possibly at Blackfriars) sometime between 1602 and early 1603, with QC being performed at the Globe sometime after March 1603, although most likely following the lifting of the 'restraint of stage-plaies' in April 1604.

Available evidence suggests that *The Malcontent* is indeed a play that appeared on the London stage in two distinct versions, written for two distinct repertories, possibly at two distinct times. The variants between these two versions, and the possibility that they might have been written as much as two years apart, counters suggestions that *The Malcontent* represents Marston's sudden, unexpected engagement with the disguised ruler motif following James's accession in 1604. How could the Globe version be a paradigmatic 'Jacobean disguised ruler play' and a paradigmatic tragicomedy, especially if it had already appeared elsewhere in an alternative form? As for Marston's 'sudden' interest in disguised rulers, this ignores his earliest signed compositions for the nearby Children of Paul's company. The distinctive characteristics of the malcontent Malevole have long been recognized in embryonic form in *Antonio and Mellida* (performed 1599) and *Antonio's Revenge* (performed 1600; published together 1602).[59] Likewise, these plays' formal quality, when viewed or read (as their joint publication encourages) as a narrative whole, suggests that Marston experimented with tragicomedy some years before publication of his ultimate 'Tragicomoedia', *The Malcontent*.[60] The *Antonio* plays are thus significant in marking Marston's early use of disguise as a political and romantic instrument within an overarching tragicomic narrative.

The '*Antonio*' Plays and 'Strange Disguise'

In the first *Antonio* play, *Antonio and Mellida*, Duke Andrugio of Genoa (a dukedom later shared with *The Malcontent*), loses a sea battle against his rival, Piero of Venice, and is shipwrecked on his enemy's coast. Andrugio is separated from his son Antonio, whom he believes to be drowned. When Andrugio defiantly remains in full ducal armour, his shipwrecked companion Lucio advises him to clothe himself in a '*sheepeheard gowne*' (*Mellida*, D4ᵛ; 3.1.0.SD). In this 'strange disguise', Andrugio can safely 'slide … / Vnto some gratious Prince and soiourne there, / Till time, and fortune giue reuenge firme meanes' (*Mellida*, E2ʳ;

---

[59]   John Marston, *The History of Antonio and Mellida* and *Antonios Reuenge* (London, 1602); Geoffrey Bullough (ed.), *Narrative and Dramatic Sources of Shakespeare* (7 vols, London, 1957–78), vol. 2 (1958), p. 411; Caputi, *Satirist*, p. 182; David Farley-Hills, *Shakespeare and the Rival Playwrights 1606–1610* (London, 1990), p. 139.

[60]   Doran, *Endeavors*, p. 213; Henke, *Pastoral*, p. 50.

3.1.93–5).[61] Instead of escaping in the same disguise chosen by Paris, Mucedorus, Tamburlaine and the 'blind' Irus, Andrugio remains a fugitive, advertising his noble status with no thought for his personal safety.[62] Rejecting Lucio's advice, Andrugio announces that it matters not 'wh[i]ther, but from whence we fall' (*Mellida*, E2ᵛ; 3.1.116), a defiant statement adapted from Seneca's *Thyestes* (925–6ff.) and repeated (in Latin) by the villainous Mendoza in *The Malcontent* (QA *Malcontent*, C3ᵛ; 2.1.25). For Andrugio, using disguise to escape his persecutors undermines his honour and dignity.

Unbeknownst to Andrugio, Antonio is not drowned, although his safety is also compromised on enemy soil. In contrast to his father, Antonio 'slide[s]' into a decidedly 'strange disguise' (*Mellida*, B2ᵛ; 1.1.28), that of the Amazonian princess 'Florizel'. Possibly influenced by the cross-dressing Pyrocles in Sir Philip Sidney's *Arcadia*, Antonio's 'Amazonian' disguise ensures the young prince's safe access to his enemy's court, and to his equally secret love, Princess Mellida, daughter to the enemy Duke Piero.[63] Despite their failed attempt to elope, and Antonio's feigned death (intended to trick Piero into offering his daughter's hand in marriage), Antonio and Mellida are finally united and betrothed. Before this happens, however, Andrugio arrives at Piero's court, not disguised, but certainly unrecognizable, his face 'Royally casked in a helme of steele' (*Mellida*, I2ᵛ; 5.2.161). Andrugio's decision to reveal himself to his enemy – his appearance recalling that of Blunt's 'semblably furnish'd' decoy king in *1 Henry IV* (F *1 Henry IV*, TLN.2913; 5.3.21) – forces Piero to recognize Andrugio's nobility and agree to Antonio and Mellida's happy reunion.

The comic dénouement to *Antonio and Mellida* contrasts with the tragic events in *Antonio's Revenge*. A year would pass before the Paul's audience would see this violent sequel, with its opening stage direction describing Piero '*smeer'd in* [Andrugio's] *blood, a poniard in one hand bloodie*' (*Revenge*, A2ᵛ; 1.1.0.SD).[64] With a revenge narrative responding both to Shakespeare's *Hamlet* (or posited *Ur-Hamlet*) and Kyd's *Spanish Tragedy*, liberally peppered with more quotations from Seneca, *Antonio's Revenge* not only demonstrates Marston's interest in the disguised ruler, but also illustrates his linking of the feigned 'starke mad[ness]' of Antonio (*Revenge*, E1ʳ; 2.4.9) with the 'Anticke disposition' of Hamlet (Q1 *Hamlet*, D1ᵛ, 5.140). Indeed, Marston's equation of Hamlet's 'Anticke disposition' with a fool's motley reappears in Antonio's disguise when he returns to the Viennese court to avenge his father's death and restore Mellida's honour.[65] As described in his Act 4 entrance, Antonio adopts '*a fooles habit, with a little toy of a walnut shell, and sope, to make bubbles*' (*Revenge*, G1ᵛ; 4.1.0.SD).

[61]   Line numbers from Gair, *Mellida*, and W. Reavley Gair (ed.), *Antonio's Revenge* (Manchester, 1978).

[62]   Gair, *Mellida*, p. 104n.

[63]   Sir Philip Sidney, *The Countesse of Pembrokes Arcadia*, revised edn (London, 1593), Book 1:14.

[64]   Gair, *Revenge*, p. 15.

[65]   Ann Rosalind Jones and Peter Stallybrass, *Renaissance Clothing and the Materials of Memory* (Cambridge, 2000), p. 266.

Fig. 2.1   A medieval French court jester wearing typical fool's motley, and carrying his grotesque bauble as a mock emblem of office

Antonio's appearance mimics the fool's disguise of Prince Edward in *Friar Bacon*, while referencing Hamlet's 'disposition'. Antonio's reasoning, that those that are without 'power, [must] with dissemblance fight' (*Revenge*, E1ᵛ; 2.4.27), provides both motive and means for the disguised revenge narrative that follows. It also highlights Marston's early engagement with a motif associated with the revenging duplicity of tragic heroes like Hamlet and Hieronimo, as well as with their 'comical history' disguised ruler counterparts.

The *Antonio* plays present royal disguise as a theatrical device designed to avert personal threat, as a means to restore ducal power and, ultimately, as an opportunity for bloody revenge. They also confirm Marston's awareness of the disguised ruler long before he composed *The Malcontent*, and certainly before James's accession could prompt subsequent disguised ruler revenging narratives. *The Malcontent* might rival *Measure for Measure* as the paradigm of later Italianate disguised ruler plays, but it cannot be considered as Marston's first foray into this motif. Indeed, for *The Malcontent* to be considered as paradigmatic at all, its two distinct printed versions with their vague chronology must be acknowledged. The difficulty thus remains of deciding exactly *which* of these versions should be accorded primacy: the shorter tragicomic QA/B version with its topical allusions to Guarini, most likely performed at Blackfriars, or the augmented QC version definitely performed at the Globe? Answering this question requires reconsideration of the literary mode for which Marston had already achieved fame and notoriety – verse satire. Notably, Marston disguises his usurped duke as a railing satirist. The link between the choleric Malevole and Marston's controversial earlier verse satires highlights the difference between QA/B and QC *Malcontent*. This conjunction also explains the medical imagery punctuating Malevole's volatile invective.

QA/B *Malcontent*: The Verse Satirist's Dramatic Return

Early in his career, Marston became famous for scurrilous, sexually explicit verse satires that lampoon London society. Adopting the pseudonym 'W. Kinsayder', Marston railed against contemporary vice in *The Metamorphosis of Pigmalions Image* (1598) and *The Scourge of Villanie* (1598; reprinted with additions 1599).[66] These verse satires betray Marston's idealism and obvious indebtedness to the virtuous self-sufficiency of ancient Stoicism, with its imperative to promote political and civil order despite accepting the fluctuating cycles of life. Marston was not, however, simply a Stoic; his satirical verse also reflects Renaissance Neostoicism, as expounded by the sixteenth-century moral philosopher Justus Lipsius in his 1584 *De Constantia* ('On Constancy'). Renaissance Neostoicism's focus on virtuous living reflected its followers' desire to integrate pagan Stoic

---

[66]   John Marston, *The Metamorphosis of Pigmalions Image* (London, 1598), BL 238.b.24, fol. A3ᵛ; *The Scourge of Villanie*, 2nd edn (London, 1599), BLO (8vo.L.550.B.S.), fol. B3ᵛ.

philosophy with Christian doctrine.[67] Marston's 'Kinsayder' persona thus metaphorically represents an acerbic barber-surgeon who purges society of its moral and social ills. This same medical function is associated, paradoxically, as much with Neostoic morality as with Galenic humour theory.[68] These 'purging' verse satires also coincide with late-Elizabethan interest in the chronotopic Golden Age of literary freedom.[69] On 4 June 1599, however, any perceived Golden Age freedom was violently curtailed. At the direction of the Archbishop of Canterbury, John Whitgift, and the prelate of St Paul's Cathedral and Bishop of London, Richard Bancroft, the 1599 'Order of Conflagration' (or so-called 'Bishops' Ban') decreed that Marston's verse satires should 'bee presentlye broughte to the Bishop of LONDON to be burnte' by the public hangman in an overt display of state censorship.[70] 'Kinsayder's' satiric voice was thus silenced.

Fortunately, Marston had an alternative career path, that of playwright. While writing his scurrilous satires, Marston also studied law at London's Inns of Court. Many Inns of Court men, especially those from Marston's Middle Temple, viewed themselves as literary and dramatic innovators, as well as patrons and benefactors of young talent.[71] Marston might have composed or adapted *Histriomastix* (c. 1585–99; published 1610) for a Christmas Revels performance at the Middle Temple.[72] Apart from stylistic evidence, however, there is no absolute proof of Marston's involvement.[73] Still, *Histriomastix* serves as the opening salvo in the so-called 'War of the Theatres'.[74] This 'War' represents a supposed public feud between playwrights and companies, in which Marston's apparent slights are answered by Jonson's *Poetaster* (1601) and Dekker's *Satiromastix* (1601). Whether such a 'War' occurred remains conjectural.[75] Less contentious is Henslowe's 28 September 1599 diary reference to money lent to 'the new poet mr mastone in earnest of A Boocke'

---

[67] See Adriana McCrea, *Constant Minds: Political Virtue and the Lipsian Paradigm in England, 1584–1650* (Toronto, 1997).

[68] Mary Clare Randolph, 'The Medical Concept in English Renaissance Satiric Theory: Its Possible Relationships and Implications', *SP*, 38 (1941): 125–57; Gail Kern Paster, *Humoring the Body: Emotions and the Shakespearean Stage* (Chicago, 2004), p. 4.

[69] See Frances A. Yates, *Astraea* (London, 1973); Roy Strong, *The Cult of Elizabeth* (London, 1977).

[70] Richard A. McCabe, 'Elizabethan Satire and the Bishops' Ban of 1599', *YES*, 11 (1981): 188–94; Lynda E. Boose, 'The 1599 Bishops' Ban, Elizabethan Pornography, and the Sexualization of the Jacobean Stage', in Richard Burt and John Michael Archer (eds), *Enclosure Acts: Sexuality, Property, and Culture in Early Modern England* (Ithaca, 1994), pp. 185–200.

[71] Philip J. Finkelpearl, *John Marston of the Middle Temple* (Cambridge, MA, 1969), pp. 26–7.

[72] Ibid., p. 10.

[73] John Peachman, 'Previously Unrecorded Verbal Parallels Between *Histriomastix* and the Acknowledged Works of John Marston', *N&Q*, 51 (2004): 304–306

[74] James P. Bednarz, *Shakespeare and the Poet's War* (New York, 2001), pp. 83–104.

[75] Knutson, *Commerce*, pp. 75–102.

(title unknown), which suggests Marston's early employment as a playwright by the Admiral's Men at the Rose.[76] While Marston's authorship of *Histriomastix* and the existence of a 'War of the Theatres' remain indefinite, we do know Marston wrote plays for the Children of Paul's between 1599 and 1601.[77] This company of boy actors performed at the small private playhouse within the confines of St Paul's Cathedral, under the direct control of the cathedral's Dean. For Paul's, Marston created the *Antonio* plays, as well as *Jack Drum's Entertainment* (1600; published 1601) and *What You Will* (1601; published 1607). In the *Antonio* plays and *Jack Drum's*, the Marstonian 'Stoic' characters Felice and Ned Planet may denounce various social ills in order to educate and correct the masses, but their satire remains incidental to the plays' overall narratives.[78] Uncontroversial in subject matter and style, and written with a 'cognoscenti' audience of Inns of Court legal wits in mind, these plays were unlikely to attract direct political and religious censure.[79]

Marston's dramatic output, therefore, until 1604 and the publications of *The Malcontent*, suggests that he skilfully, if somewhat humorously, avoided the label of overt satirist. Nevertheless, in his Paul's comedy *What You Will*, Marston overtly alludes to his dubious poetic fame. The play's Epicurean critic, Quadratus, denounces the flattering French gallant, Lampatho Doria, and describes him quite pointedly as a 'Don Kynsayder' (*What You*, C1ᵛ; 2.1.130).[80] Lampatho is excoriated as a 'ragg'd Satyrist' who jealously mocks those less fortunate than himself (*What You*, C1ᵛ; 2.1.143). The Paul's audience would realise that Quadratus refers to Marston's own relatively recent 'Kinsayder' persona, an identification contradicting those 'War of the Theatres' theorists who propose that Lampatho is actually Marston's satirical portrait of his 'rival', Jonson.[81] Regardless of whether the 'War of the Theatres' was real, Marston appears unwilling to engage fully with his satirical past, preferring instead to recall his alter-ego, while distancing himself from those who might condemn Kinsayder's unwarranted return.

The pseudo-Stoic 'medical' aspect of Marston's previous verse satires does, however, fully and unexpectedly re-emerge in *The Malcontent* with the foul-mouthed invective of Malevole.[82] As Altofronto's disguised persona, Malevole makes viciously incisive comments that, resembling the verse satires, aim to purge abuses from the corrupt court, while aiding the banished duke's return. Accordingly, so Philip J. Finkelpearl argues, Altofronto displays a 'virtuous Machiavellianism'.[83]

---

[76] *Henslowe's Diary*, p. 124.

[77] David G. O'Neill, 'The Commencement of Marston's Career as a Dramatist', *RES*, 22 (1971): 442–45.

[78] Janet Clare, 'Marston: Censure, Censorship, and Free Speech', in Wharton (ed.), *Drama*, pp. 194–211 (p. 199).

[79] Finkelpearl, *Temple*, pp. 139 & 176–7.

[80] John Marston, *What You Will* (London, 1607).

[81] Matthew Steggle, *Wars of the Theatres* (Victoria, 1998), p. 57.

[82] Caputi, *Satirist*, p. 193.

[83] Finkelpearl, *Temple*, p. 193.

This complements the 'Mirror for Magistrates' tradition offered by earlier Inns of Court scholars and writers. Despite Samuel Schoenbaum's literal identification of Marston with Malevole's 'hysterical' personality (resembling T.S. Eliot's equally literal analysis of Marston's 'deep discontent and rebelliousness'), Altofronto/ Malevole's outbursts do mark the dramatic return of Marston's 'Kinsayder' persona reconstituted in the fictive disguised ruler's alter-ego.[84]

That a satiric 'Kinsayder', intent on subverting social and moral norms, has reappeared becomes immediately apparent. Malevole's inherent discord manifests through an aural bombardment of '*vilest out of tune Musicke*' that attacks and shocks the senses (QA/B *Malcontent*, B1^r; 1.1.0.SD). This noisy opening introduces the railing malcontent who soon thrusts his head '*Out of his Chamber*' to lambast the new duke and courtiers below (QA/B *Malcontent*, B1^r; 1.2.5.SD). Malevole's outbursts entertain the assembled nobles who consider them the ravings of a fool. They also illustrate the unusual freedom that this spiteful cynic enjoys within the confines of the Genoan palace. Duke Pietro calls on the 'rugged Cur' to leave his upper chamber, thus giving Malevole 'free liberty' to 'trot about and be-spurtle [urinate on] whom [he] pleasest' (QA *Malcontent*, B1^r; 1.2.10–12). Pietro's 'rugged Cur' imagery draws from the Ancient Greek etymological link between 'cynic' and 'dog'. This verbal conflation echoes a similar demand in *Antonio's Revenge*, where the Ghost of Andrugio calls on Antonio 'Once more [to] assume [his motley] disguise, and dog the Court / In fained habit' (*Revenge*, G1^r; 3.5.25–6). In *The Malcontent*, Pietro's similar invitation introduces a detailed description of the malcontent delivered with almost reverential relish:

> PIETRO: This Maleuole is one of the most prodigious affections that euer conuerst with nature; A man or rather a monster; ... his highest delight is to procure others vexation, and therein hee thinkes he truly serues heauen; ... therefore do's he afflict all in that to which they are most affected; the Elements struggle within him; his owne soule is at varience; his speach is halter-worthy at all howers. (QA *Malcontent*, B1^v; 1.2.17–28)

Pietro describes Malevole in Lipsian pseudo-medical terms as one of the most extraordinary 'affections' that ever 'conversed' (or associated) with nature.[85] The term 'affections' is derived from the Latin *affectio* meaning 'hurt and distemper [of] the mind', thus a madman.[86] Pietro's imagery resembles dialogue in *Antonio's Revenge*, which describes the 'mutining affections' of Antonio's troubled mind (*Revenge*, E4^v; 3.2.24). Malevole's mental dis-ease makes his utterances so 'halter-worthy' that, if unrestrained, they could lead him to the hangman's noose. Malevole is spared this ultimate sanction because of his madness, his chief

---

[84] Samuel Schoenbaum, 'The Precarious Balance of John Marston', *PMLA*, 67 (1952): 1069–78 (p. 1070); T.S. Eliot, *Selected Essays*, 3rd edn (London, 1951), p. 229.

[85] Justus Lipsius, *Two Bookes of Constancie*, trans. John Stradling (London, 1594), fol. C4^r.

[86] Thomas Cooper, *Thesaurus Linguae Romanae & Britannicae* (London, 1584).

'delight' being only to 'procure other's vexation', and thus aggravate rather than openly attack those in court. Malevole achieves the 'vexation' of his victims by 'afflict[ing] all in that to which they are most affected', so revealing the corrupt madness of those he attacks.

Pietro explains why Malevole's own 'soul is at variance' (disquieted) through an ancient Stoic (as opposed to Christianized Neostoic) concept, namely the physical theory of existence. According to this Stoic theory, the world and its inhabitants are composed of the four 'Elements' – earth, water, air and fire – and engaged in an ever-repeating cycle of reconstitution and decay.[87] Because these physical Elements have not achieved harmonious equilibrium, they 'struggle within' Malevole's body.[88] This simple philosophical explanation by Pietro for Malevole's madness is steeped in Classical Stoic metaphysics. Classical Stoicism highlights the inevitability of all creative cycles, thus illustrating the futility of striving for wealth and fame in an ever-changing world.[89] Classical Stoicism also holds the medical key, as far as Pietro is concerned, to understanding the 'prodigious affections' of this malcontent in his court. Even so, Pietro stresses how much he likes this mind-troubled monster, who 'giues good intelligence to [the duke's] spirit' and makes him 'vnderstand those weaknesses which others flattery palliate' (QA/B *Malcontent*, B1ᵛ; 1.2.28–30). The malcontent's vexatious 'intelligence' – those incisive and honest remarks which, by their very bluntness, cause offence or unease – contrasts starkly with the palliative administered by Pietro's sycophantic courtiers, which deceptively eases the spiritual pain of ducal responsibility without curing its problems. This key speech, delivered before the eponymous hero emerges onstage, highlights the underlying Stoic conceit of Malevole's 'affected' outbursts. Pietro notably recognizes Malevole's honest railing as an antidote to flattery and duplicity, outbursts that, by their very nature, cure as they curse, probe as they penetrate to the sickness within.

In addition to Pietro's near praise for the malcontent's manic railing, the duke also describes this 'monster' as one who is 'as free as ayre': 'he blowes ouer euery man' (QA/B *Malcontent*, B1ᵛ; 1.3.2–3). Pietro's comments, and the reactions of the courtiers around him, suggest less an angry defensiveness against Malevole's vexations and more a bemused tolerance of this abusive malcontent who fulfils the dual functions of court fool and intelligencer. Even so, for the play's audience, Pietro's reference to Malevole being as 'free as ayre' might seem unexpectedly apposite, given Marston's long association with the politically and theologically volatile mode of verse satire. 'Freedom' and 'satire' should, according to Marston's

---

[87]   Gail Kern Paster, *The Body Embarrassed* (Ithaca, 1993), pp. 7–10.

[88]   Jesús López-Peláez Casellas, 'The Neo-Stoic Revival in English Literature of the Sixteenth and Seventeenth Centuries: An Approach', *Sederi*, 14 (2004): 93–115 (p. 95). Such equilibrium only occurs at the end of the so-called Platonic year, when the four physical Elements are periodically consumed by the primary Element, the intellectual fire or Ether.

[89]   Caputi, *Satirist*, p. 57.

experience following the 'Bishops' Ban', be two irreconcilable concepts. In *The Malcontent*, however, both are personified in Malevole and act as agents for morally justifiable revenge. That Marston recognized this ironic conflation of contradictory concepts is evident from two separate references in the published text, one directed at the play's live audience, the other to its private reader.

Censorship, Freedom and Politic Religion

Certain later editions of *The Malcontent* include a sonnet, Marston's so-called 'Imperfect Ode', addressed to the audience as a Prologue (QB, I2^r and QC, I4^r).[90] Totally absent from QA, this Prologue appears unconventionally in the QB and QC texts. In both QB and QC, it is printed at the end of the play, with QB after the Epilogue, and QC before. Such belated placement reflects the QC Induction comment that the play has 'never a prologue', at least in its adult playhouse form (QC *Malcontent*, Induction, 125–6). The 'Imperfect Ode' therefore possibly represents a textual ghost from the original children's performance.[91] In this Prologue, Marston pointedly refers to that '*olde freedome of a pen*' traditionally associated with Golden Age satirists (QC *Malcontent*, I4^r; Prologue, 13). With its direct address to the audience, the Prologue encourages the play's spectators to revitalize this '*olde freedome*' by limiting the excesses of '*Immodest censure*', thus countering those whose '*too nice-brained cunning*' threatens the artistic liberty of contemporary satire (QC *Malcontent*, I4^r; Prologue, 3 & 8). Malevole might blow over the Genoan court as 'free as ayre', but the Prologue recognizes that only the strength of Hercules could curb those seeking to '*controule*' the play as a whole (QC *Malcontent*, I4^r; Prologue, 9–11). The Prologue thereby acknowledges state and religious censorship, powers easily suggested to an audience whose appetites are whetted by Marston's return to satire's sexually explicit and scandalous mode.

Satiric freedom is also addressed in the introduction to the published playtexts (extant in all editions) entitled 'To the Reader' (QA/B/C *Malcontent*, A3^v–A4^r).[92] This sardonic defence of Marston's printed play is for those who read *The Malcontent* without attending a performance. Despite a flattering appeal to his reader, Marston offers his defiant statement:

> [F]or the rest of my supposed tartnesse, I feare not, but vnto every worthy mind t'wil be approved so generall and honest, as may modestly passe with the freedome of a Satyre. (QA/B/C *Malcontent*, A4^r)

Marston believes his perceived 'tartness' will be tolerated by all 'worthy' readers who recognize the generality and honesty of his attacks. The ultimate irony resides,

---

[90] See *Malcontent*, *STC* 17481, Folger^1 (Hoe).

[91] Hunter, *Malcontent* (2000), p. 23n.

[92] Folio numbers refer to Folger^2 copy of uncorrected QA *Malcontent* text, *STC* 17479.

however, in his evocative plea to accord the play the 'freedome of a Satyre', a 'freedome' so violently curtailed only five years before. Marston's defence of his play in print (like the 'Imperfect Ode' that introduces the potential for salacious satire), rather than confirming the playwright's innocence, highlights the very controversy for which he was famous. Indeed, the publicity value of the 'Bishops' Ban' is suggested by Henslowe's 'new poet mʳmastone' diary entry in September 1599, made only three months after the 'Order of Conflagration'.[93] As T.F. Wharton argues, Marston was thus 'fortunate' enough to be included in the 'Bishops' Ban'. It did not stifle his artistic endeavours. Instead, it enhanced his salacious 'new poet' reputation.[94] Marston's 'modest' request to view *The Malcontent* with the 'freedome of a Satyre' capitalizes on his sensational past, while defending the severity and painfulness of his 'supposed tartnesse'.

Marston's 'To the Reader' defence concludes with the Senecan Latin tag that defiantly taunts '*Me mea sequentur fata*' ('Let my destiny pursue me').[95] As a resounding declaration of defiance, however, Marston boldly adds his initials 'I.M.' to this statement of intent. No longer hiding behind his 'Kinsayder' pseudonym, Marston acknowledges his personal involvement in earlier controversies, while marking those who staunched his poetic output. Marston could still, however, offend his censorious pursuers. A subtle instance of censorship occurs in certain QA texts. Immediately following Malevole's entrance and Pietro's description of him being as 'free as ayre', Pietro asks Malevole, 'whence you come now sir?' (QA/B *Malcontent*, B1ᵛ; 1.3.3). In the earliest uncorrected versions of QA, Malevole provocatively replies, 'From the publick place of much dissimulation, the Church', having been to 'Talke with a Vsurer [to] take vp at Interest' (uncorrected QA *Malcontent*, B1ᵛ; 1.3.4–7).[96] Subsequent corrected QA versions indicate hurried emendation, with the offensive reference to 'the Church' removed by the unusual method of flattening or cutting away the original type, leaving an unsightly blank on the printed page.[97] In her study of censorship, Janet Clare claims that this alteration denotes pressures brought to bear against the printer, Valentine Sims.[98] Certainly Sims was not unused to censure, having been tortured for his role as printer of seditious tracts in the late 1580s 'Martin Marprelate' controversy. The 'Marprelate' enquiry was under the direct supervision of the cleric Richard Bancroft, whose reward for successfully quelling the seditious presses was the

---

[93]   *Henslowe's Diary*, p. 124.

[94]   Wharton, *Marston*, p. 2.

[95]   QA *Malcontent*, fol. A4ʳ. This tag, derived from Hecuba's speech in *Troades* (994), is changed to '*Sine aliqua dementia nullus Phœbus*' ('There is no poetic power without some madness') in later QB editions. Translations by Hunter, *Malcontent*, p. 6.

[96]   Uncorrected *Malcontent* variant BL Ashley 1100.

[97]   Corrected *Malcontent* variant Folger¹.

[98]   Janet Clare, *'Art Made Tongue-Tied by Authority': Elizabethan and Jacobean Dramatic Censorship*, 2nd edn (Manchester, 1999), p. 136.

bishopric of London.[99] It appears no mere coincidence that Sims, well known for his past political and religious indiscretions, should be employed by Aspley to print *The Malcontent*. Malevole's attacks might be described as 'free as ayre' in a play that Marston defends with the 'freedome of a Satyre', but such freedom still does not extend to satire of the Church.

Although 'the Church' is removed from corrected QA versions, the opening scenes of Act 1 remain satirically volatile, thus setting the tone of the play's 'virtuous Machiavellianism'. Malevole's attack on contemporary religious values continues with Pietro asking the malcontent, 'what religion thou art?', to which Malevole replies, 'Of a Souldier's religion' (QA/B *Malcontent*, B1ᵛ; 1.3.8–9). This statement, which likens the changeable nature of religious allegiance to the mercenary capriciousness of European soldiery, seems a relatively uncontroversial response. It is immediately followed, however, by Pietro's enquiry, 'what doost [Malevole] thinke makes most Infidels now?' (QA/B *Malcontent*, B1ᵛ; 1.3.10). Malevole's reply, 'Sects, sects' (QA/B *Malcontent*, B1ᵛ; 1.3.11), accords with contemporary attitudes about religious sectarianism. Separatist 'sects' were often viewed as heretically delusional and the breeding ground of gluttony, drunkenness and lasciviousness. Members of one such sect, the 'Family of Love', came to symbolize the religious 'Infidels' of the nation.[100] This accounts for the lampooning of its sectarian 'doctrine of perfectionism' in *The Family of Love* (*c.* 1607, King's Revels[?]; published 1608), a play attributed to Lording Barry.[101] Malevole directs his ire not just against the 'Family of Love', but against any Puritan sect whose 'seeming Piety' shifts so often that it loses sight of religious truth (QA/B *Malcontent*, B1ᵛ; 1.3.10). Pietro compounds this sentiment through his response, 'O a religious pollicie' (QA/B *Malcontent*, B2ʳ; 1.3.14). Malevole and Pietro are here attacking those same sectarian dissenters that Whitgift and Bancroft denounced as 'Schismatickes' and 'heretikes'.[102] It is, however, Pietro's close association of 'religious' with the Machiavellian term 'policy' that Malevole seizes upon, exclaiming 'damnation on a politique religion' (QA/B *Malcontent*, B2ʳ; 1.3.15). Malevole may abhor Puritan religious extremism, but his blasphemous outburst, and resigned weariness, might be understood by his contemporaries as a pointed attack on those religious authorities whose 'politique religion' prompted Marston's permanent move from verse satire to drama.

---

[99]   Richard A. McCabe, '"Right Puisante and Terrible Priests": The Role of the Anglican Church in Elizabethan State Censorship', in Andrew Hadfield (ed.), *Literature and Censorship in Renaissance England* (Basingstoke, 2001), pp. 75–94 (pp. 77–8).

[100]   Kristen Poole, *Radical Religion from Shakespeare to Milton* (Cambridge, 2000), pp. 11–12.

[101]   Lording Barry[?], *The Famelie of Love* (London, 1608). See Gary Taylor, Paul Mulholland and MacDonald P. Jackson, 'Thomas Middleton, Lording Barry, and *The Family of Love*', *PBSA*, 93 (1999): 213–41.

[102]   Richard Bancroft, *A Sermon Preached at Paules Crosse the 9. of Februarie ... 1588* (London, 1589), fol. A2ʳ.

With his denunciation of 'politique religion', and his belief in both freedom and in a moral justification for his satirical outbursts, Malevole corresponds with the persona of 'Kinsayder'. Why, then, should there be such a long hiatus between Marston's successive engagements with satiric verse and drama? The answer resides with the 'Order of Conflagration', executed in the grounds of Stationers' Hall, which silenced contemporary satirical poetic voices, including Marston's.[103] At the time of the 'Bishops' Ban', Stationers' Hall was situated in the south-west corner of St Paul's Cathedral churchyard, where it remained until 1606. Originally a cathedral property called Peter College – an adjunct to St Paul's and squarely situated in London's publishing district – the building was acquired for the Stationers' Company in 1554.[104] Here, in the Stationers' Hall grounds and within sight of Paul's playhouse and the many booksellers that sold their wares alongside the Cathedral, Marston's verse satires were symbolically executed. In his new role as playwright for the Paul's company, Marston literally worked in the shadow of his censors. It is not surprising, therefore, that Marston's Paul's dramas avoid the contentious satire that made him infamous.[105]

Only after his move to Blackfriars, coupled with imminent regime change, does Marston's satiric mode return. In what appears to be his first play for the Blackfriars company, Marston creates a principal protagonist whose malcontented disguise refashions the satirical cynicism of his earlier 'Kinsayder' persona. Religious disapproval still plagues the printed text of *The Malcontent*, as the disappearance of contentious dialogue demonstrates. By channelling its satire through the fictive character of Malevole, Marston skilfully avoids the harsh censorship of his earlier 'Bishops' Ban' detractors. Malevole's satirical outbursts do not emerge, however, from a subversive poet whose morality is obscured by sexually explicit innuendo. Instead, the malcontent's railing serves as a medical purge, administered to cure the disease of a corrupt Italian court. This reconfiguration of Marston's moral imperative – from topical verse satire to children's company drama – accords with his call for the return to a Golden Age of literary freedom. Only time, and a new dramatic home removed from his original censors, offer Marston the opportunity to 'be-spurtle' those who prompted both his moral repugnance and self-righteous indignation.

The religious threat posed by Marston's call for satirical 'freedome' resonates in a subtle moment of intertextuality between *The Malcontent* and Shakespeare's *As You Like It*. In Marston's QB version, when Mendoza is invited to discuss the disguised Pietro's presence in court, Malevole offers a mischievous question: 'How didst like the Hermite?' (QB *Malcontent*, F4r; 4.3.122). Mendoza replies, 'A dangerous fellow, very perillous … beware an hypocrite':

---

[103]   Arber 3, pp. 677–8.
[104]   Cyprian Blagden, *The Stationers' Company: A History 1403–1959* (London, 1960), pp. 19 & 206–207.
[105]   Clare, 'Censure', p. 200.

MENDOZA: A Church man once corrupted, oh avoyde
A fellow that makes Religion his stawking horse,   (shootes vnder
He breedes a plague: thou shalt poison him.   his belly)
(QB Malcontent, F4ʳ; 4.3.128–30)

Mendoza's decidedly irreligious response condemns this 'Church man' (Pietro's 'Hermite') to an ignominious death. Visually, it also confirms the materiality of Pietro's hermit disguise; to Mendoza and the audience, he is dressed as a monk or friar. Once such a 'Church man' is 'corrupted', so Mendoza argues, he shields the 'plague' of his immorality from public view behind a 'stawking horse' of feigned religious piety. Mendoza's metaphor describes a 'stalking horse', a real or imitation animal that is trained or constructed to allow a hunter's stealthy approach to wary, skittish game. Mendoza's disparaging observation about 'Religion' and plague-infected churchmen here compounds Malevole's earlier remarks about the affected religiosity of those whose 'seeming Piety' shifts and changes with their 'religious pollicie' (QA/B *Malcontent*, B1ᵛ–B2ʳ; 1.3.10–14).

While not a common Elizabethan literary term, Marston's 'stalking horse' imagery appeared in Holinshed's 1586 description of Sir Nicholas Throckmorton's 1554 trial. Implicated in the Protestant 'Wyatt's Rebellion', Throckmorton was suspected of attempting to depose Mary Tudor in favour of Elizabeth. Discussing Throckmorton's successful defence, Holinshed comments on the court's bias, and how 'euerie man of euerie estate did colour his naughtie affections with a pretense of religion, and made the gospell a stalking horsse to bring their euill desires to effect'.[106] Holinshed's reference to the 'gospell' as a 'stalking horsse' complements Mendoza's similarly irreligious comment. 'Stalking horse' imagery also appears in *As You Like It*, when the malcontented Jaques proudly touts Touchstone's verbal skills to the usurped and banished Duke Senior, who predictably resides like '*Robin Hood* of *England*' with his outlawed courtiers in the Forest of Arden (F *As You Like It*, TLN.117; 1.1.101). When Jaques eulogizes the clown for appearing 'as good at any thing, and yet a foole' (F *As You Like It*, TLN.2677–8; 5.4.93–4), Duke Senior responds with perceptive irony:

DUKE SENIOR: He vses his folly like a stalking-horse, and vn-
der the presentation of that he shoots his wit. (F *As You Like It*, TLN.2679–80; 5.4.95–6)

Like the 'Religion' of the hypocritical 'Church man' in Mendoza's scathing comment, Touchstone's 'folly' is likewise a 'stalking-horse', from which the clown can attack his prey. Duke Senior's remark also introduces a subtle *double entendre*, whereby the licensed fool, shielded behind the 'stalking-horse' of his folly, is free not only to attack his social superiors, but also to gain sexual access to unsuspecting females like Audrey. Foolish license is thus commensurate with

---

[106] Raphael Holinshed, *The Third Volume of Chronicles* (London, 1586), p. 1109.

sexual gratification, as Touchstone's 'stalking-horse' allows him metaphorically to ejaculate as he 'shoots his wit'.[107]

The generally unnoted similarity between Mendoza's comments and Duke Senior's description of Touchstone is explained by the traditional belief that the QB text represents a precise record of some performance-specific comic business. Entirely absent from the QA text (F4[r]), but accentuated by its prominent marginal repositioning in QC (G1[v]), QB's 'shootes under his belly' is enclosed in parentheses. Its appearance as a stage direction demonstrates a physical gesture accompanying Mendoza's dialogue.[108] When the QB text is considered not as a stage direction, however, but as a compositorial error, with an extraneous parenthesis placed at the beginning of some mislaid and now reinstated comic dialogue, Mendoza's speech closely parallels Shakespeare's sexual imagery.[109] Read as continuous dialogue, in line with Holinshed's original, Mendoza's speech transforms Shakespeare's metaphor to suggest that the churchman's 'stalking horse' represents the piety of false 'Religion', not the foolery of a licensed and licentious clown. The sexual outcome is nonetheless the same. Mendoza's corrupt churchman, like Touchstone, can hide behind his pious 'stalking horse' to pursue his female prey. This same churchman 'shoots' not the arrows or bullets of a huntsman, nor the 'wit' of a fool, but ejaculatory material that metaphorically 'breedes' a venereal 'plague' in society.

Mendoza's sexual 'stalking horse' imagery links the theologically sensitive and disparaging satire of *The Malcontent* with the Guarinian pastoralism of Shakespeare's *As You Like It*.[110] The 'stalking horse' also aptly describes Marston's return to his satirical past, as he hides this move behind the metaphorical 'stalking horse' of his Blackfriars drama. By making his railing malcontent a disguised duke – a satirical ex-ruler who scourges the court of his usurping rival – Marston masks his return to that mode deemed so controversial in 1599 that his writing was symbolically executed. Marston now reengages with satire through the conduit of Guarini's *Il pastor fido*. Accordingly, understanding why Marston appropriated key dialogue and themes from Guarini will facilitate our appreciation of the shorter QA/B *Malcontent* text as a unique and individual formal entity.

Il pastor fido and *The Malcontent*

In Act 4 scene 5 of *The Malcontent*, Aurelia bewails the loss of her 'deuoted' husband who has purportedly thrown himself into the sea (QA/B *Malcontent*, G1[v]; 4.5.43). Pietro's supposed death is merely a ruse, however, echoing Antonio's

---

[107] Gordon Williams, *A Glossary of Shakespeare's Language* (Atlantic Highlands, 1997), pp. 340–41.

[108] Hunter, *Malcontent*, pp. xxxiv & 115–16n.; Kay, *Malcontent*, p. 94n.

[109] Holger Schott Syme, 'Unediting the Margin: Jonson, Marston, and the Theatrical Page', *ELR*, 38 (2008): pp. 142–71.

[110] Hunter, *Malcontent*, p. 160n.; Henke, *Pastoral*, pp. 96–7.

bogus demise in Act 4 scene 2 of *Antonio's Revenge*. In fact, Duke Pietro, disguised as a hermit, observes ensuing events as they unfold, including his wife's guilty grief as she admits to having accepted the 'adulterous touch' of Mendoza (QA/B *Malcontent*, G1ᵛ; 4.5.46). Her 'ravenous immodesty' and 'insatiate … appetite' have made Pietro a notorious cuckold (QA/B *Malcontent*, G1ᵛ; 4.5.46–7). Since Aurelia's dialogue betrays her honest regret and contrition, the disguised Pietro (like his Shakespearean counterpart Duke Vincentio) becomes both moral commentator and religious confessor as he seeks the 'blessednesse of repentance' from his wife (QA/B *Malcontent*, G1ʳ; 4.5.2). As Aurelia departs to her '[c]ell of shame' (QA/B *Malcontent*, G1ʳ; 4.5.11), imprisoned by Mendoza (himself now a usurping duke), the hooded ex-duke Pietro, accompanied by the disguised ex-duke Altofronto, is left to grieve. Displaying the harsh pragmatism of a Stoic satirist, Malevole commands the duke 'not [to] weep', but take comfort from his Classical and folklore 'betters' who were also made cuckolds by their faithless partners (QA/B *Malcontent*, G1ᵛ–G2ʳ; 4.5.54 & 61). Pietro's pained response – 'Thou pinchest too deepe, and art too keene ['cruel' or 'harsh'] vpon me' (QA/B *Malcontent*, G2ʳ; 4.5.63) – triggers this pragmatic reply:

MALEVOLE: Tut, a pittifull surgeon makes a dangerous sore.
Ile tent thee to the ground. (QA/B *Malcontent*, G2ʳ; 4.5.64–5)

Malevole refers to a surgical procedure, whereby a wound is 'tented' or probed by a surgical instrument, usually covered with absorbent material. This 'tent' opens, distends and cleans an infected wound. Malevole's 'tenting' imagery therefore describes the painful application of harsh truth to the 'dangerous sore' of Pietro's self pity. For Malevole, this aggressive medical intervention ensures the 'patient' benefits from self-knowledge, moral fortitude and resigned Stoic detachment.

That Malevole's comment revives Marston's longstanding pseudo-Stoic medical interests is evident through similar imagery in *The Metamorphosis of Pigmalion's Image*. In his '*Reactio*', a 170-line verse defence inserted between Satires 3 and 4 of *Pigmalion's Image*, Marston attacks the critical 'Censorians' of his work (*Pigmalion's*, E5ᵛ; 104f.). Written several years before Malevole's dismissive remarks, the '*Reactio*' condemns 'mad Chirurgion[s]' who make 'so dangerous an Incision' as to 'whip away the instrument' of a 'Poets Procreation' (E5ʳ; 93–6ff.). This overtly medicalized reference to censorship corresponds with Malevole's later reference to tenting Pietro's 'dangerous sore'. Marston might associate the witless railing of his verse satire detractors to the malicious intervention of a 'mad Chirurgion', but his cure for this witlessness is equally medically associated.

Since Marston had already employed medical imagery in *Pigmalion's Image*, it is somewhat surprising that he should borrow the 'tenting' of Pietro from a recently translated Italian play. As noted, most critics contend that Malevole's surgical metaphor derives from the 1602 'Dymock' *Il Pastor Fido*, recorded in a *Stationers' Register* entry dated 16 September 1601 as 'A booke called the faythfull

Shepheard'.[111] In this translation, Nicander (Nicando in Guarini's original), chief minister to the priest Montano, must reconcile the nymph Amarillis to her doom. Consoling Amarillis for having broken the sacred commandments that demand her virginity and eventual marriage to a man she does not love, Nicander uses this same medical motif:

> NICANDER: How much I grieue for thee: and if I haue
> Piers't with my wordes thy soule, like a Phisicion I
> Haue done, who searcheth first the wound
> VVhere it suspected is: be quiet then
> Good Nimph, and do not contradict that which
> Is writ in heav'n aboue of thee. ('Dymock', L4ᵛ; 4.5.100–105)

In the Italian source for the 'Dymock' translation, Nicando's sympathetic though ultimately ruthless judgement reads:[112]

> NICANDO: *E se t'hò col mio dir cosi traffita,*
> *Ho fatto come suol medica mano*
> *Pietosamente acerba,*
> *Che uà con ferro, ò stilo*
> *Le latebre tentando*
> *Di profonda ferita,*
> *Ou'ella è più mortale.* (*Il pastor*, Z2ʳ–Z2ᵛ; 4.5.150–56)
> [NICANDO: If with my manner I have stabbed you, I have done so with the pitifully healing hand of a surgeon's knife tenting the folds of a deep and mortal wound.]

Guarini clearly refers to Nicando's harsh but honest words working like a surgeon's healing hand (*medica mano*) wielding the scalpel or knife (*ferro*, literally 'iron') with which to tent (*tentando*) the deep wound (*profonda ferita*) with potentially fatal consequences (*più mortale*).

The 'Dymock' translation and Malevole's medicalized dialogue differ, however, in Marston's choice of the verb 'to tent'. In Guarini's Italian, '*tentando*' denotes the procedure whereby the wound is probed by the physician's iron tool. This verb disappears from the 'Dymock' translation, which refers only to the physician who 'searcheth first the wound'. This is surprising, since the verb 'to tent' was a common medical term employed metaphorically by several writers. In the moral interlude *Like Will to Like* (1568), for instance, Ulpian Fulwell's character Newfangle comments derogatorily, 'This hole in thy fury didst thou disclose: / that now may a tent be put in as big as thy nose'.[113] This imagery is echoed in Marston's *Jack Drum's Entertainment* (*c.* 1599–1600, Paul's; published 1601), when the plain-speaking Ned Planet discusses the enormous red nose of

---

[111]   Arber 3, p. 192.
[112]   Guarini, *Il pastor fido* (Venice, 1590), BL 1073.h.27.
[113]   Ulpian Fulwell, *Like Will to Like* (London, 1568), fol. A3ʳ.

the usurer Mamon.[114] Informing the poor Katherine that her lover is murdered (news that drives the unfortunate woman mad), Ned Planet comments on the villainous Mamon's culpability in Pasquil's (supposed) death: 'I, and I thinke the Vsurer made a Tent / Euen of his nose it was so red and neere' (*Jack Drum's*, D4ʳ).[115] 'Tenting' similarly appears in John Lyly's rhetorical prosework, *Euphues and his England* (1580), with the spurning of Euphues' friend, Philautus, by the heartless Camilla. Writing to the pitiless object of his devotion, Philautus berates Camilla for having opened the 'great wounde' of his love, only then, like 'a good Chyrurgian', to put 'in a small tent'.[116]

The verb 'to tent' is particularly associated with Shakespeare. Tantalizingly suggestive of Guarini's dialogue, Rosalind/Ganymede even alludes to the tenting procedure in *As You Like It* when commenting on the heartfelt despair of the unrequited shepherd, Silvius. The shepherd's plaintive rejoinder that Corin 'hast not lov'd', and his desperate cry, 'O *Phebe, Phebe, Phebe*', prompts Rosalind's medically evocative response: 'Alas poore Shepheard searching of [thy wound], / I haue by hard aduenture found mine owne' (F *As You Like It*, TLN.824–7; 2.4.37–40). Although noticeably absent from Q1 *Hamlet* (published 1603), the verb appears fully in Q2 *Hamlet* (*c.* 1600; published 1604 and in editions thereafter), with the prince soliloquising on the hoped-for effect of 'The Mousetrap' on his uncle: 'Ile tent him to the quick' (Q2 *Hamlet*, G1ʳ; 2.2.532; F, TLN.1637).[117] Figuratively, Hamlet intends to probe his uncle's festering conscience. 'Tenting' is further referenced in the 1608 Quarto *King Lear* (Q, D2ᵛ; 1.4.321; 1.4.263–4), the 1609 Quarto *Troilus and Cressida* (Q, D1ᵛ; 2.2.16; 2.2.15–16) and in Folio *Cymbeline* (F, TLN.1792–4; 3.4.112–14).[118] John Webster's *The White Devil* (1612, Queen Anne's Men, Red Bull; published 1612), furthermore, presents Flamineo, stabbed by the villainous Lodovico's henchmen, making a dying call for them to 'Search [his] wound deeper: tent it with the steele that made it' (*White Devil*, M1ᵛ; 5.6.238–9).[119] It is noticeable, however, that, between Fulwell's *Like*

---

[114] John Marston, *Iacke Drums Entertainment* (London, 1601), fol. D4ʳ. For discussion of the nose imagery, see George L. Geckle, *John Marston's Drama* (Rutherford, 1980), p. 52. Mamon's nose is reminiscent of Cleanthes' false nose as 'Leon the Usurer' in Chapman's *Blind Beggar of Alexandria* (*c.* 1595). Mamon also mirrors the anti-Semitic potential of the usurer Pisaro in William Haughton's *Englishmen for My Money* (1598); see Matthew S. Biberman, *Masculinity, Anti-Semitism, and Early Modern English Literature* (Aldershot, 2004), pp. 58–9.

[115] See H. Harvey Wood (ed.), *The Plays of John Marston* (3 vols, Edinburgh, 1934–39), vol. 3 (1939).

[116] John Lyly, *Euphues and his England* (London, 1580), fol. U2ʳ.

[117] See Thompson and Taylor, *Hamlet*; Thompson and Taylor, *Hamlet: 1603 and 1623*.

[118] Quarto line numbers from W.W. Greg (ed.), *'King Lear', 1608 (Pied Bull Quarto)*, reprint of SQF, 1 (Oxford, 1964); Greg (ed.), *'Troilus and Cressida', First Quarto, 1609*, SQF, 8 (London, 1952).

[119] John Webster, *The White Devil* (London, 1612). Line numbers from John Russell Brown (ed.), *The White Devil* (Manchester, 1996).

Will to Like and Webster's *White Devil*, Marston and Shakespeare are the only known playwrights to employ the medical expression 'to tent'. This suggests, yet again, that Marston and Shakespeare had respective knowledge of Guarini's play, in Shakespeare's case most obviously prior to its 'Dymock' translation.

'Dymock's' failure to translate Guarini's clear allusion to tenting might nevertheless be an oversight. This appears unlikely, however, since Guarini also uses '*tentare*' in Amarillis's description of the physical effect of female self-consciousness:

> AMARILLIS: „*Vergogna ch'n altrui stampò Natura*
> „*Non si puo rinegar, che se tu tenti*
> „*Di cacciarla dal cor, fugge nel uolto*. (*Il pastor*, L2ʳ; 2.5.148–50)
> [AMARILLIS: That shame which Nature has stamped in others, you cannot deny, for if you attempt to tent her out of your heart, she will be expressed on your face.]

The '*Malcontenta*' (malcontented) Amarillis (*Il pastor*, L2ʳ; 2.5.125) claims that nature has permanently embedded shame in a woman's soul. If an immodest thought is metaphorically 'tented' out of a maiden's heart, it manifests itself in her delicate cheeks as a blush. This same 'blushing' imagery occurs in Shakespeare's *Coriolanus* (*c*. 1605–1608), when the Roman general exclaims, 'The smiles of Knaues / Tent in my cheekes' (F *Coriolanus*, TLN.2223–4). In the 'Dymock' translation of Guarini's medical description of a blush, there is little to suggest the redness of raw 'tented' flesh:

> AMARILLIS: This shamefastnesse that nature stamps in vs
> Cannot be mastered for if you seeke
> To hunt it from your hart, it flies into your face. ('Dymock', F3ʳ; 2.5.102–4)

'Dymock's' presentation of tenting as 'hunting' and 'searching' elides the excruciating pain this surgery involves. Such pain would be well known in this age before anaesthetic. Only Malevole's specific invocation of the term accurately correlates with Guarini's explicit medical imagery. 'Dymock's' failure to translate Guarini's verb with painful accuracy might be explained by Florio's Italian dictionary, *The Worlde of Wordes*. Here, the famous language tutor defines '*Tentare*' as 'to tempt, to attempt, to assay, to trie, to sound, to goe about a matter, to offer or profer to do anything, to prooue, to handle or feele often, to tempt one to do euill'.[120] Clearly, none of these definitions sufficiently describe the pain caused by the medical instrument 'the tent'. The absence of this verb in the 'Dymock' translation therefore suggests that Marston might have borrowed this medical expression directly from an Italian edition of *Il pastor fido*.

Marston's use of the verb 'to tent' is not the only textual indication that he was studying *Il pastor fido* in the original Italian, while possibly comparing it to the

---

[120] John Florio, *Worlde of Wordes* (London, 1598), p. 416.

'Dymock' translation. Additional anomalies in these two short lines of dialogue further suggest that 'Dymock' was not the sole source for *The Malcontent*'s medical imagery. Firstly, Marston uses the term 'pittiful' to describe the 'Surgeon' who 'makes a dangerous sore' (QA/B *Malcontent*, 4.5.64), the adjective 'pittiful' being an almost direct translation of Guarini's '*Pietosamente*' ('pitifully') (*Il pastor*, Z2^r; 4.5.152). Marston's description of healing hands expressing pity at the pain they are inflicting could derive from Florio's definition for *Pietoso*, meaning 'pitifull, mercifull, ruthfull, compassionate, naturall and louing'.[121] The 'Dymock' translation simply describes the person who 'searcheth first the wound' as 'a Phisicion', with no adjectival description whatsoever ('Dymock', L4^v; 4.5.101–102). Secondly, Malevole's harsh statement that he will 'tent [Pietro] to the ground' (QA/B *Malcontent*, G2^r; 4.5.65), describes the buckling of the man's knees in helpless agony, an image bearing no resemblance to the sanitary, static and somewhat introspective 'Dymock' translation. In Guarini's original, the healing hand reference appears in the line '*Ho fatto come suol medica mano*' (*Il pastor*, Z2^r; 4.5.150). The Italian '*suol*' is the third person singular of '*solere*', defined by Florio as, 'to be woont, to vse, to accustome, to be accustomed'.[122] In *Il pastor fido*, '*suol*' means 'to be used to' or 'to do something as a matter of habit', with Nicando claiming that he has acted 'as is customary' for a healing hand. Marston possibly misinterpreted or reinterpreted Guarini's '*suol*', understanding it to mean '*suolo*', a word likewise defined by Florio as 'a thing that beareth anything on it, the earth, ground'.[123] Malevole's claim that his medical procedure drove a man in agony to the 'ground' thus accords with Florio's Italian definition.

Although only three anomalous words in one short section of *Malcontent* text, these same words provide significant evidence that Marston appropriated the chief minister's evocative imagery from *Il pastor fido* in its original Italian form, not from an 'Englished' text. They suggest, moreover, that Marston must have read and understood the play in its original language, potentially comparing it with 'Dymock's' translation as he wrote *The Malcontent*. This interpretation does not judge the linguistic skills of Marston or 'Dymock'; it simply corrects the continuing critical assumption that the 'Dymock' translation was the 'direct source' for Malevole's Guarinian dialogue. In fact, Guarini's play in its original Italian appears to be a more 'direct source'. Accordingly, the Guarinian 'tenting' dialogue, which exemplifies the pseudo-Stoic imperative of Marston's earlier verse satires, derives from a morally irreproachable Guarinian character who only appears in this short though significant passage. Based on words spoken by Guarini's chief minister, Malevole's 'advice' confirms Marston's familiarity with the original *Il pastor fido*.

That Marston could interpret Guarini from the original Italian is further suggested by his inventive Italian verse in *Antonio and Mellida*. When Mellida

---

[121] Ibid., p. 277.

[122] Ibid., p. 374.

[123] Ibid., p. 407.

disguises herself as a pageboy, thereby mirroring Antonio's own cross-dressing, she escapes her father's court to meet Antonio in the forest. When the lovers are temporarily united, eighteen lines of Italian dialogue unexpectedly punctuate the mock romantic pastoral scene (*Mellida*, G3ᵛ; 4.1.189–206). This verse exchange owes much to Italian *commedia dell'arte*, and to love poetry made famous by cinquecento writers such as Guarini and Torquato Tasso (Guarini's predecessor at the Ferraran court). Tasso's famous *Aminta* (first performed 1573) was itself published alongside *Il pastor fido* in Castelvetro's 1591 London edition of Italian plays.[124] Not re-exhibited in the play's sequel, or in subsequent plays, Marston's possible skill in Italian is reflected by the madrigalesque exchange in *Antonio and Mellida*. Certainly, his Paul's audience would realise that Marston understood Guarinian dialogue in its original Italian. Why, then, five years later, should audiences to *The Malcontent* consider his skill any less?

Since Marston was most likely consulting Guarini's play in Italian, might other passages traditionally associated with 'Dymock' demonstrate a similar direct indebtedness to Guarini? Dialogue between the licentious urban characters Maquerelle and Mendoza, about the duplicity and sexual corruption of the Genoan court, resembles the Italian rather than 'Englished' text.[125] In Act 2 scene 4, Maquerelle promotes the efficacy of sexual dishonesty to her young court 'pupils', Bianca and Emilia. Based on the words of Guarini's Corisca, who asserts '*Non è che un'arte di parere honesta*' ('honesty is nothing but the art to seem so') (*Il pastor*, P4ᵛ; 3.5.64–5), Maquerelle enquires if her charges have 'the art to seem honest?' (QA *Malcontent*, D1ᵛ; 2.4.26). On behalf of the lusting Mendoza, Maquerelle repeats the question when later trying to corrupt Maria, Altofronto's virtuous, imprisoned wife. After Maria's disdainful rejection of this 'Vnhonest creature' (QA *Malcontent*, G4ʳ; 5.3.11), Maquerelle scathingly replies, 'Pish, honesty is but an art to seeme so' (QA *Malcontent*, G4ʳ; 5.3.12). Again inspired by Guarini, Maquerelle adds, 'pray yee what's honesty? what's constancy? but fables feigned, odde old fooles chat, deuisde by iealous fooles, to wrong our liberty' (QA *Malcontent*, G4ʳ; 5.3.12–14). Maquerelle's cynical response mirrors Corisca's speech. Here, after describing her sexual conquest of city gallants, Corisca bemoans the loss of the faithful shepherd Mirtillo, himself in love with the elsewhere-betrothed Amarillis. In the original Italian, Corisca attacks the moral niceties of '*fede*' (honesty) and '*costanza*' (constancy), claiming they are just '*Fauole*' (fables) put about by jealous men to deceive simple girls (*Il pastor*, E1ʳ; 1.3.74–6). 'Dymock' mistranslates '*fede*' as 'faith' in Corisca's complaint, 'What's faith? what's constancy? but fables fain'd / By jealous men: and names of vanitie, / Simple women to deceiue' ('Dymock', C3ʳ; 1.3.59–61). Marston, by contrast, correctly translates '*fede*' as 'honesty', thus demonstrating first-hand knowledge of Corisca's list of 'fables' in the original Italian. Guarini, not 'Dymock', provides Marston with inspiration for the unsavoury character of the ageing panderess, Maquerelle.

---

[124] Torquato Tasso, *Aminta*, ed. Castelvetro (London, 1591), BL 1071.a.20.(2, 3.).

[125] The distribution of Guarini-inspired dialogue is: Maquerelle (seven), Malevole (five), Mendoza (four), Ferneze (two), Pietro (one) and Maria (one).

The threat posed by Maquerelle's human brokerage had already been the subject of Marston's scathing attack in Satire 3 of *Scourge of Villanie*. Here, he describes those 'broking pandars [who] sucke Nobility' (C8ᵛ, 190f.). Marston's fervour is, however, most markedly expressed in Satire 2, when he exclaims:

> O split my hart, least it doe breake with rage
> To see th'immodest loosenes of our age.
> Immodest loosenes? fie too gentle word,
> When euery signe can brothelry afford.
> When lust doth sparkle from our females eyes
> And modesty is rousted in the skyes. (*Scourge*, C2ʳ; Satire 2, 104–109ff.)

Marston's response to such depravity – whereby 'immodest looseness' is so common that every shop sign advertises a brothel-house, when women's eyes sparkle not with love but lust, and when modesty is unceremoniously jostled like a pure white cloud in a thunderous sky – suggests that the sexual deviousness and bawdish tendencies of Maquerelle are not new objects for his disdain. Maquerelle continues to represent all that Marston abhors about corruption and disease-ridden prostitution in London. In return for her sexual indiscretions, including the procurement of young married women whom she prostitutes for financial gain, Maquerelle receives the ultimate punishment as courtier/bawd. Like Mistress Overdone in *Measure for Measure*, she is banished by Duke Altofronto to 'the suburbs', where prostitutes ply their trade in abject poverty (QA/B *Malcontent*, H4ᵛ, 5.6.161). Marston highlights Maquerelle's sexual deviancy through dialogue derived from Guarini's famous Italian tragicomedy, one particularly popular among the cognoscenti that patronized the children's playhouses.

Marston also appropriates Guarinian dialogue for the villainous Mendoza. Following Mendoza's manipulation of Pietro, whereby he informs the duke of Duchess Aurelia's serial adulteries and confides his plot to murder Ferneze in revenge, Mendoza makes an infamous Machiavellian comment: 'Who cannot faine friendship, can nere produce the effects of hatred' (QA *Malcontent*, C3ʳ; 1.7.82–3). This aside, expressed after Pietro exits, also originates with the duplicitous nymph Corisca, providing a direct translation of Corisca's self-congratulatory comment, '*chi non sa finger l'amico / Non è fiero nemico*' (*Il pastor*, K3ʳ; 2.4.22–3). Unlike 'Dymock', who reverses the word order to 'Who cannot friendship faine' ('Dymock', F1ᵛ; 2.4.15), Marston reflects the Italian original. Mendoza similarly echoes Guarini's original lines in his comically passionate misogynistic rant:

> MENDOZA: O that I could raile against these monsters in nature, models of
> hell, curse of the earth, women that dare attempt any thing, … mistresses in
> dissembling, onely constant in vnconstancie, onely perfect in cou[n]terfetting:
> their wordes are fained, their eyes forg'd, their sights dissembled, their lookes
> counterfeit, their haire false, their giuen hopes deceitfull, their very breath
> artificiall. (QA *Malcontent*, C2ʳ; 1.6.85–95)

Like those loose doyens of 'brothelry' whose 'lust … sparkle[s] from [their] female eyes' (*Scourge*, C2ʳ; Satire 2, 106–108ff.), Mendoza's 'monsters in nature' and 'models of hell' are 'mistresses in dissembling', for whom words, eyes, sights, looks, publicly expressed hopes, breath – even their hair – are feigned, forged, dissembled, counterfeit, false, deceitful and artificial. Mendoza's scathing vilification of 'women' comes from Guarini's angry and priapic Satyr, whose rejected love for the nymph Corisca leads him to a vengeful plan to rape her. He ultimately fails, and the hapless Satyr is left alone onstage clutching his victim's periwig in a comic moment that confirms the artificiality of Corisca's coquettish flirtation, as well as her hair.

Initially, the Satyr's railing expresses his frustration at the duplicitous vanity of all women, whose falsehood makes men uncontrollably susceptible to their feigned love:

> SATYR: *Qual cosa hai tu che non sia tutta finta?*
> *S'apri la bocca menti, se sospiri*
> *Son mentiti i sospir, se moui gli occhi*
> *E' simulato il guardo; in somma ogn'atto,*
> *Ogni sembiante, e cio che'n te si uede,*
> *E cio che non si uede, ò parli, o pensi,*
> *O uadi, ò miri, ò pianga, ò rida, ò canti*
> *Tutto è menzogna, e questo ancora è poco.* (*Il pastor*, F4ʳ–F4ᵛ; 1.5.67–74)
> [SATYR: What things do you have that are not all pretence? When you open your mouth, you lie, if sighing, you lie with that sigh, if you move your eyes, you feign with your looks; in addition every act, every semblance, it is your intention to be seen, and what is not seen, or spoken, or thought, or evaded, or contemplated, or cried, or reciprocated, or sung, everything is a lie, and there is still more to complain about.]

Guarini's patterned imagery becomes the 'words', 'eyes', 'sights' and 'looks' of Mendoza's *Malcontent* railing. Mendoza's 'their wordes are feigned' interprets '*S'apri la bocca menti*' ('when you open your mouth you lie'), combined with the verb '*simulato*' ('you feign'). Similarly, his outburst that 'their eyes forg'd', 'their sights dissembled' and 'their lookes counterfeit', reflects '*se moui gli occhi / E simulato il guardo*', a claim that a woman just has to move her eyes to 'feign [her] looks'. Significantly, Guarini links the verb '*sospirare*' ('to sigh') with lying ('*mentire*'). 'Dymock' transposes this 'sighing' reference, placing it before a foreshortened list of deceitful traits:

> SATYR: What is it that they vse, which is not counterfeit?
> Ope they their mouths? they lie: mooue they their eyes?
> They counterfeit their lookes: If so they sigh,
> Their sighes dissembled are. In summe, each act,
> Each looke, each gesture, is a verie lie. ('Dymock', D2ᵛ–D3ʳ; 1.5.52–6)

Since the early nineteenth century, in response to claims that Mendoza's reference to 'sights' (*Malcontent*, 1.6.93) is a mistake or old-spelling archaism, editors of

The Malcontent have changed 'sights' to 'sighs'.[126] Although 'sights' is printed in all three quarto editions, its alteration to 'sighs' gains credence through the Guarinian references in the text. Mendoza's rant, although similar to the 'Dymock' translation, more closely resembles the Satyr's speech in the original Italian. Marston's access to an Italian edition of *Il pastor fido* would account for this similarity, as well as the quarto editions' consistent spelling of the word 'sights'. In consequence, Mendoza's petulant claim that 'their sights [are] dissembled' might be a cynical description of the falsehood of a woman's false glance, rather than an archaic reference to 'sighing'.

Marston gives Mendoza a dramatic monologue instantly recognizable to those familiar with *Il pastor fido*. By assigning this comic set-piece to a misogynistic, predatory villain, Marston distinguishes between the justifiable cynicism of the malcontent Malevole, who is seeking to restore his authority and rescue his wife from imprisonment, and the misogynistic Satyr-like ire of the usurping Mendoza. Despite the common belief that early modern writers and printers failed to differentiate between the Latin satirical mode and the ancient Greek Satyr, Marston actively separates mode and myth in *The Malcontent*, with Malevole personifying the mode and Mendoza the myth. Still, both owe aspects of their personalities to Guarini's *Il pastor fido*. In conjunction with Maquerelle, these three characters individually anatomize and collectively epitomize Marston's verse satire past, announcing to an astute audience the satirist's return, this time shielded from his religious detractors behind the metaphorical 'stalking horse' of a popular foreign play.

Given that Marston plundered Guarini's *Il pastor fido* for QA/B *Malcontent*, it is surprising that the QC text, written specifically for the Globe, bears no sign of additional Guarinian dialogue. Neither are Guarini's experiments with tragicomedy of generic importance for this revised and augmented play. Instead, QC *Malcontent* displays an entirely new generic impulse that leans towards the recently popularized form, city comedy. Guarinian tragicomedy here appears of only incidental significance. Furthermore, QA/B *Malcontent*'s lack of city comedic tendencies suggests a formal difference between it and QC, one that necessitates the determination of whether QA/B or QC should be considered paradigmatic. This shift in generic focus, from QA/B's tragicomedy to QC's 'city tragicomedy', demands further scrutiny.

QC *Malcontent*: 'City Tragicomedy' and Divine Right Controversy

Towards the end of Act 1, in an additional soliloquy inserted into the Globe's augmented QC *Malcontent*, Malevole/Altofronto comments on the freedom gained through his disguise:

---

[126] Robert Dodsley, *A Select Collection of Old Plays*, ed. J.P. Collier, 3rd edn (12 vols, London, 1825–27), vol. 4.

MALEVOLE: Well, this disguise doth yet afford me that
Which kings do seldome heare, or great men vse,
Free speach: and though my stat's vsurpt,
Yet this affected straine giues me a tongue,
As fetterlesse as is an Emperours. (QC *Malcontent*, B3ᵛ; 1.3.161–5)

This amendment appears only fourteen lines before Malevole's QA/B disclosure
to Celso that he is the 'for euer banisht *Altofront* / This *Genoas* last yeares
Duke' (QA/B *Malcontent*, B3ʳ; 1.4.7–8). It reduces the theatrical shock value of
Malevole's subsequent disguise revelation. Its presence also confirms the play's
already established notoriety, since the Globe version seems unconcerned about
disclosing the principal protagonist's true identity so early in the plot. Whether
or not its audience noticed this narrative adjustment, the additional QC dialogue
specifically highlights the satirical conceit of the original QA/B play. Malevole's
overt reference to '*Free speach*', that truth spoken by the sanctioned malcontent
which is 'seldome' heard by kings, echoes the sentiment behind Marston's plea
to his reading public. Like the 'freedome of a Satyre' evoked in Marston's 'To
the Reader' preamble (extant in all quarto texts), Malevole now demands the
equivalent 'freedom' in the Genoan court of his usurping rival. Marston's familiar
cry for a return to a supposed Golden Age of satirical freedom, now voiced by the
malcontented Malevole, seems particularly apposite for this Globe version of the
play, presented so soon after the arrival of the nation's new king. For audiences
at the adult *Malcontent*, performed by the newly-named King's Men, Malevole's
comment must have resonated with political topicality. Oddly, *Il pastor fido*
no longer claims significance in this evocation of 'Free Speech' by a usurped,
disguised duke. Guarini's voice is strangely silent in the new material written for
the Globe's augmented QC text.

If *Il pastor fido* is no longer relevant for Marston's QC *Malcontent*, might
Guarini's fall from artistic favour be evident in other ways as well? An answer lies
in the generic structure of QC, a play that retains all its QA/B dialogue (including
that derived from Guarini), while adding sections, scenes and a new character.
Nothing in this QC version, however, builds on the Guarinian tragicomedy of
its QA/B forebear. Guarini may provide the generic blueprint for what becomes
Jacobean tragicomedy, but this model is sidelined by those who adapt the QC text
for adult performance. A close comparison of QA/B with QC thus demonstrates
a shift in generic focus between the two '*Malcontents*'. QA/B's Italianate
tragicomedy becomes QC's hybrid Anglo-Italianate 'city tragicomedy'. This
generic adjustment subtly indicates the play's change in company ownership.
As previously noted, criticism of *The Malcontent* tends to overlook this formal
distinctiveness, treating QC as a 'definitive' text, not only because it confirms the
play's Jacobean anti-court bias, but also because of its links to Shakespeare and the
Globe.[127] This teleology ignores the wider generic implication of commissioning
two established playwrights, Marston and Webster, to augment the QC text.

---

[127] Tricomi, *Anticourt*, p. 13.

Webster's involvement is announced on the QC title-page, which declares that he provides the 'additions' to Marston's 'Augmented' play (QC *Malcontent*, A1ʳ). As will become evident, Webster's collaborative 'additions' fundamentally alter the formal cohesion of QA/B *Malcontent*, allowing QC *Malcontent* to be reinvented in its 'city tragicomedic' form.

It is possible to trace this alteration in generic focus because of two separate though complementary analyses of QC *Malcontent* by George K. Hunter and David J. Lake. These isolate, and accredit responsibility for, the augmentations to Marston or Webster respectively. Hunter's stylistic analysis of QC's additional dialogue differentiates between the two authors by comparing extant examples of their work.[128] By contrast, Lake's linguistic analysis isolates specific word choices that suggest Marston's or Webster's separate involvement in specific scenes.[129] Hunter and Lake come to similar conclusions, each apportioning the same additions to QC *Malcontent* between each author, although for differing reasons. Accordingly, it is now accepted that Marston and Webster were independently responsible for their respective QC additions.[130] Not only does such analysis highlight the generic differences between QA/B and QC *Malcontent*, arising from a collaborative adaptation for adult performance, it also confirms that the three quarto texts represent two distinctive versions of the play: the children's QA/B *Malcontent* by Marston and the adult QC *Malcontent* by Marston and Webster.

Of the twelve sections of dialogue added to QC *Malcontent*, two of these offer entirely new scenes (1.8 and 5.1). Ten of the twelve sections provide dialogue for the disguised Duke Altofronto/Malevole. A new character, the clown Passarello, does not exist in QA/B, and only appears in four of the additional QC sections. Similarly, the corrupt Lord Bilioso, an incidental fawning courtier in QA/B, appears in six of the additional sections. Stylistic and linguistic evidence suggests that Marston was involved in seven of the additional QC sections. Webster's participation, therefore, extends to five sections, including the two completely new scenes. Although Marston and Webster worked in isolation, with Webster entirely responsible for Passarello, the collaborators clearly shared the enhancement of Bilioso's role. Marston's additions more than double Bilioso's original QA/B dialogue; those attributed to Webster almost double this same amount again.

Comparison of the QA/B and QC texts confirms that the more despicable features of Bilioso's character and dialogue, which form the basis for Tricomi's anti-court 'warnings for the new king', exist only in the QC sections attributed to Webster.[131] Only there does Bilioso attract Malevole's wrath, the old lord being branded a 'notorious wittally pander to [his] owne wife' (QC *Malcontent*, D2ʳ;

128 Hunter, *Malcontent*, pp. xlvi–liii.

129 David J. Lake, 'Webster's Additions to *The Malcontent*: Linguistic Evidence', *N&Q*, 226 (1981): 153–8.

130 See David Gunby, David Carnegie and MacDonald P. Jackson (eds), *The Works of John Webster* (3 vols, Cambridge, 2007), vol. 3, pp. 309–11; Cathcart, 'Marston', pp. 43–7.

131 Tricomi, *Anticourt*, pp. 13–24.

2.3.35–6). Likewise, only in Webster's additions does Bilioso's arrival prompt the resumption of Altofronto's 'Malevole' persona after the disguised duke speaks privately with Celso. A QC stage direction indicates that Altofronto '*shifteth his speach*' to sound like Malevole (QC *Malcontent*, B4ʳ; 1.4.44.0.SD). The same direction is absent from the QA/B text, possibly suggesting that a child actor's voice here might sound less convincing. Finally, only in Webster's additions does Bilioso transform from a mildly annoying court presence into a complicit 'old Courtier', whom Malevole likens to a 'pigeon house' that is 'smooth, round, and white without, and full of holes and stinke within' (QC *Malcontent*, C1ʳ; 1.4.85–7). Accordingly, Tricomi's anti-court argument that the 'catamite of state', Bilioso, 'sells his integrity for profit and [is] the male counterpart (in spirit) to Maquerelle', describes QC *Malcontent*, but bears little relevance for QA/B.[132] In QA/B, and in the QC additions attributed to Marston, Bilioso does not represent courtly satire. Malevole's derogatory comments, focusing on this elderly courtier's corruption, only occur in the QC sections attributed to Webster. Thus, if critics read Bilioso as the personification of Stuart court corruption, it is important to recognize that this topical anti-court bias is entirely absent from the Marstonian emendations to the same character.

Recent literary criticism, which focuses on topical and localized satire as indicators of subversive anti-court intent, ignores *The Malcontent*'s origin in two forms, written during two distinct creative periods. With this differentiation in mind, however, varied instances of topicality in the QC additions can be interrogated more accurately. As noted, QA/B remains firmly rooted in Italy. QC's augmentation shifts the emphasis from Italy to England, with derogatory remarks aimed primarily at Jacobean London. This topical localization continues through satirical swipes against the Welsh. Notably, a few references to Scots appear less politically sensitive and more humorous. All these, however, appear in QC additions that are Websterian in style and language.

The City of London also attracts localized humour through Bilioso's complaints that he is unwilling to travel as ambassador to Florence dressed, as his wife recommends, all in black. Bilioso sees it as unnecessary to rely on this mourning colour to denote the severity of his mission, and resents being advised to 'weare [his] hat in cipers' in the manner of a grieving 'Aldermans heire' (QC *Malcontent*, E3ʳ; 3.1.101–2).[133] 'Cipers' or 'cypress' is the material used for transparent black veils worn round the hats of male mourners. Bilioso is here describing the fashionable headdress of a City of London dignitary's son, in mourning for his dead father. This London-specific comment is attributed to Webster. Similar Anglocentricity, as spoken by the clown Passarello, is likewise attributed solely to Webster. When describing Maquerelle's decrepit appearance in Act 1, Passarello reminisces how he previously 'was wont to salute her [to greet Maquerelle with an erection] as our English women are [saluted] at their first landing in *Flushing*'

---

[132] Ibid., p. 18.

[133] An alderman is a civic dignitary second only to the City of London's Lord Mayor.

(QC *Malcontent*, C4ᵛ; 1.8.34–5). This analogy transforms Maquerelle into one of the whores who followed their English soldiers to the famous Netherlands garrison town of Flushing (modern-day Vlissingen) during the Dutch war. The Globe audience would immediately recognize this topical reference, however inconsistent it might seem within the Italian locus of the QA/B original. Later, Passarello taunts those 'gentlemen [who] visit brokers', or the 'knights [who] send venison to the citty. / Either to take vp more money, or to procure longer forbearance' (QC *Malcontent*, H1ᵛ; 5.2.19–21). Passarello is condemning English country property holders who mortgage their estates to city usurers, as well as knights who bribe their creditors with homebred venison, in order to borrow more funds or stave off foreclosure. These passages all allude to contemporary social issues of specific English concern, with the City of London now depicted as the site of tension for an ever-expanding urban population.[134] All belong to Webster.

Further Anglocentricity provides a linguistic clue to Webster's personal involvement in the scene, as discernible through several overt references to 'England'. Critics have long noted Webster's fondness for incorporating the word 'England' into his plays.[135] Malevole tells Mendoza, for example, that he will either 'go raile vpon some great man', 'or else go marry some rich *Genoan* lady and instantly go trauaile' (QC *Malcontent*, H4ʳ; 5.4.22–4). To Mendoza's incredulous query, 'Trauaile when thou art married[?]', Malevole replies, 'I tis your yong Lords fashion to do so, though he was so lasy being a batcheller, that he would neuer trauaile so farr as the Vniuersity yet when he married her tales of, and *Catsoe for Ingland*' (QC *Malcontent*, H4ʳ; 5.4.25–30). Malevole's description of these young noblemen, who, when married to rich women, acquire the sudden urge to rush 'tales off' (to turn tail) to England, adds a localized immediacy to this humorous image. The Anglicized irony of Malevole's description is compounded by his suggestion that the English are particularly blessed because 'there [are] no Brothelhouses there' (QC *Malcontent*, H4ʳ; 5.4.31). To Mendoza's incredulous enquiry, 'Nor courtesans?', Malevole answers, 'Neather; your whore went downe with the stewes and your punke came vp with your Puritan' (QC *Malcontent*, H4ʳ; 5.4.32–4). This refers to the 'stewes' or brothels of the Southwark Bankside, close by the Globe. Although originally protected by royal warrant, the 'stewes' were effectively 'put down' in 1546.[136] Ironically for Malevole, the 'whore' may have disappeared but, through Puritan semantics, she is replaced by the prostitute 'punke'. These topical allusions to social problems in London are noticeably absent from the QA/B text, not only because of the play's new status in the Globe repertory, but also because all are derived from Webster's specific additions to the play.

Revised for performance in an adult Jacobean playhouse under the direct patronage of the king, QC *Malcontent*'s shift in satiric focus might justify wary scrutiny by contemporary political authorities. Nevertheless, commentary about

---

[134] Gibbons, *City Comedy*, pp. 76–7.
[135] Lake, 'Additions', p. 157.
[136] Hunter, *Malcontent*, pp. 143–4n.

the morality of court life, as opposed to broader civic considerations, still emerges in the new scene in Act 1 between Malevole and Passarello. In this strangely incongruous exchange, the disguised duke becomes nothing more than a 'straight-man' or comic feed for the new clown.[137] Reinforcing subtle intertextuality between *The Malcontent* and *As You Like It*, the scene echoes similar dialogue between Touchstone and Jaques in Shakespeare's play (F *As You Like It*, TLN.2617–76; 5.4.35–94).[138] Malevole asks Passarello why 'great men begge fooles?' (QC *Malcontent*, C4ʳ; 1.8.22). The clown's reply, that 'As the Welchman stole rushes, when there was nothing else to filch; onely to keepe begging in fashion' (QC *Malcontent*, C4ʳ; 1.8.23–4), alludes to the great at court who 'begge' for the property of fools. Such 'begging' was an acceptable, if demeaning, English court practice. Because a fool was forbidden to own property, his person and possessions belonged to the Crown. Courtiers could thus 'beg' their monarch for his fool's revenue to supplement their incomes.[139] For Passarello, this 'begging' by the privileged few is tantamount to theft. Passarello compares the practice of the courtier 'stealing' from the fool to contemporary perceptions of the Welsh as a nation of thieves, who will even steal the humble rushes strewn on the floor. Employing a popular prejudice against the Welsh, Passarello's comment also attacks immoral practices in the English court. As with other localized allusions in QC, this reference is attributed to Webster alone, and demonstrates, yet again, the topical Anglicization of the revised play. These satirical attacks are not, however, directed against the king, but against corrupt and acquisitive courtiers and citizens, targeting anyone who might threaten the fragile social cohesion of a nation adjusting to regime change.

These instances of QC dialogue, with their Anglocentric topicality and immediacy, contrast starkly with the Italocentric narrative of revenge and usurpation of QA/B. As with the other examples of localized humour, Malevole's ironic social observation and Bilioso's xenophobic jibes stem from the pen of Webster. In consequence, those aspects of QC *Malcontent* that purportedly illustrate the play's anti-court, anti-Scottish topicality – thus justifying its status as the paradigmatic Jacobean disguised ruler play – can no longer be considered proof of Marston's disguised ruler 'solidarity'. Rather, they suggest the adaptation and re-location of the play's original satire (against sexual immodesty and corruption in an Italian court) not by Marston, but by his QC collaborator, Webster. It is Webster's involvement in the adaptation of QC *Malcontent* that alters the play's satiric focus, even though QC is often erroneously considered the 'definitive' Marstonian text. Webster's involvement also provides the most convincing evidence for a generic distinction between QA/B and QC, with his Anglocentric dialogue transforming the play away from an Italianate tragicomedy to its new hybrid 'city tragicomedic' form.

---

[137] Kay, *Malcontent*, p. xxxi.

[138] Hunter, *Malcontent*, p. 160n.

[139] Ibid., p. 52n.

The localized topicality of Webster's additions does not suggest, however, that they were perceived as specific attacks against James. Rather, the changes to Marston's QA/B original appear to be generalized critiques against the corrupt practices of London lawyers, citizens and courtiers. Indeed, QC's city comedy satire, as anti-citizen as it is anti-courtier in focus, suggests an astute business decision to resituate the original play's Italian locus and humour to the familiar environs of London. The King's Men apparently considered the 'literariness' of the QA/B children's version, with its pointed aphorisms drawn from Italian tragicomedy, of less commercial value than the latest fashion for topical city comedy. The play's move to the Globe creates an entirely new version of *The Malcontent*, which reflects its change in company ownership, and its successful adaptation to accommodate the adult performers who now present it.

Nevertheless, one specific QC addition *does* include an overt and contentious reference that *was* considered sufficiently 'anti-Jamesian' to be subtly altered by an apparent act of censorship. In the play's masque dénouement, which echoes the revenge ending of *Antonio's Revenge*, Altofronto/Malevole describes how he has 'seene strange accidents of state':

> MALEVOLE: The flatterer like the Iuy clip the Oke,
> And wast it to the hart: lust so confirm'd
> That the black act of sinne it selfe not shamd
> To be termde Courtship.
> O they that are as great as be their sinnes,
> Let them remember that th'inconstant people,
> Loue many Princes meerely for their faces,
> And outward shewes: and they do couet more
> To haue a sight of these then all their vertues,
> Yet thus much let the great ones still conceale,
> When they obserue not Heauens imposd conditions,
> They are no Kings, but forfeit their commissions. (QC *Malcontent*, I3ᵛ; 5.6.137–49)

Malevole describes how he has observed two vices of court. Firstly, the parasitic flatterer who, like the poisonous ivy that kills the great oak, destroys the court's moral heart, and secondly, sexual corruption which, in the guise of virtuous courtship, masks its true 'sin' of base lust. More important is the explicit warning to those 'Princes' and 'Kings' who dissemble to 'conceal' their moral corruption. The 'inconstant' people yearn to see outward displays of princely pomp, rather than catch 'sight' of those virtues that should be their rulers' true moral arbiters. Those 'Kings' who fail to adhere to 'Heaven's imposed' moral precepts, however, must, with Machiavellian skill, continue to dissemble (as Altofronto has done), or else 'forfeit their commissions'.[140] Malevole's criticism seemingly legitimates

---

[140] Machiavelli, *The Discourses*, ed. Bernard Crick (London, 2003), p. 396.

the right to remove a dishonest or unvirtuous monarch from his/her throne, a right James vehemently refuted in *The True Lawe*.[141]

In several corrected versions of QC, the provocative references to absolutist 'Princes' and 'Kings' are altered to the more innocuous word 'men' (*Malcontent*, 5.6.144 & 149). In view of James's personal interest in the potentially treasonous assertion in Malevole's new speech, and public awareness of the king's 'divine right' polemic, it is not surprising that this contentious comment is diluted in the corrected QC texts. This censorship, almost certainly instigated by the deputy Master of the Revels (later Sir) George Buc, alters a politically volatile passage attributed not to Webster, but to Marston. Unlike the Anglicized satire in the dialogue of Bilioso and Passarello, Malevole's contentious remarks display all the hallmarks of Marstonian stylistic and linguistic authorship.[142] Thus, it is Marston's voice, yet again, being censored. Webster's satire might be anti-courtier and anti-citizen in its topicality, but only Marston's is deemed sensitive enough to threaten the political stability of England's new regime. Perhaps Buc himself censored the remark, rather than anger his king with the inherent republicanism of its message.

Malevole's '*Free speech*' dialogue in Act 1 praises his malcontent's disguise as an apt means of delivering harsh advice 'which kings do seldome heare' (QC *Malcontent*, B3ᵛ; 1.3.162–3). In the later censored dialogue of Act 5, addressed to 'Princes' and 'Kings' who might 'forfeit their commissions' if they violate religious precepts, or fail to demonstrate their true 'vertues', Marston develops this theme. Unlike the generalized Anglocentric satire of Webster, whose topical immediacy goes unchecked, Marston's political satire cannot escape the censor's pen. Like those references to 'the Church' that are hurriedly erased from corrected QA editions (Folger¹ QA *Malcontent*, B1ᵛ; 1.3.5), Marston's allusion to 'Princes' and 'Kings' receives an equally swift excision. The uncomfortable republicanism that could be read into Malevole's speech results in the removal of both 'Princes' and 'Kings'. In their stead appear 'men', whose 'forfeit [of] their commissions' poses no threat to the political hierarchy. Although not as extreme as the 'Order of Conflagration', and seemingly not at the behest of the Church (since the religious argument remains intact), this censorship demonstrates that Marston could still, in his final augmentation to QC, unsettle those nervous about public comment on James's 'divine right' monarchy. Censorship of QC in print need not represent censorship of the play in performance, but it confirms that Marston's reputation as a troublemaker remained intact, a factor likely adding to the commercial value of Marston and Webster's *The Malcontent* for the Globe.

The simultaneous 1604 publication of QA/B and QC *Malcontent* – or the '*Malcontents*' – offers a unique insight into the formal development of the early modern playtext. It also foregrounds Marston's satiric imperative by highlighting the mode's impact on the virtuous Machiavellianism of his malcontented protagonist. Marston's *The Malcontent* is indeed paradigmatic, therefore, not

---

[141]   King James, *True Lawe*, fol. D4ᵛ.

[142]   Clare, '*Art*', pp. 32–7.

because of its 'Jacobean disguised ruler play' status, but because it introduces Italianate tragicomedy to the English stage. Most significantly, however, it is only the shorter QA/B *Malcontent* that deserves the title 'paradigm'. QC *Malcontent*, while retaining its tragicomic roots, is adapted, augmented and altered so fundamentally by Webster as to make the original QA/B tragicomedy almost unrecognizable. Since the paradigmatic status of *The Malcontent* resides solely in its tragicomic QA/B form – a play whose heritage seems more closely associated with the closing years of Elizabeth's reign than the opening years of James's – then perhaps the paradigmatic 'Jacobean disguised ruler play' title should after all pass to that other Globe repertory offering, *Measure for Measure*.

Chapter 3
Measure for Measure:
Conventionality in Disguise

In *Measure for Measure*'s long final act, the Duke, returning to Vienna without his disguise, excuses himself from the proceedings that cast serious doubt on his deputy's integrity. Without properly explaining his withdrawal (although the audience knows he will change into his Friar's robes), the Duke reminds Angelo and Escalus of their judicial duties: 'I for a while / Will leaue you; but stir not you till you haue / Well determin'd vpon these Slanderers' (F *Measure*, TLN.2635–7; 5.1.254–6). Before their combined authority can 'determine' the case against Angelo's 'Slanderers', these magistrates must interrogate the elusive Friar Lodowick. Somewhat pre-empting this interview, Escalus asks the hapless Lucio for his opinion of the friar:

> ESCALUS: Signior *Lucio*, did not you say you knew that Frier *Lodowick* to be
> a dishonest person?
> LUCIO: *Cucullus non facit Monachum*, honest in nothing but in his Clothes. (F
> *Measure*, TLN.2638–41; 5.1.257–60)

As audience/reader, we sense the comical danger in Lucio's arrogant response, given his propensity for slandering the Duke. Not surprisingly, therefore, Lucio employs a medieval proverbial commonplace, which translates as 'the cowl does not make the monk', to suggest Friar Lodowick's underlying dishonesty.[1] Escalus's enquiry about whether Lucio 'knew' Friar Lodowick is particularly ironic given the gallant's earlier surprise, expressed inadvertently to the disguised Duke himself, that Vienna's ruler should 'vsurpe the beggerie hee was neuer borne to' (F *Measure*, TLN.1582–3; 3.1.341). Although this comment might suggest Lucio's recognition of the mendicant friar, he appears not to make this connection. Consequently, Escalus demands that Lucio recount the 'most villainous speeches' made against the Duke by the 'vnreuerend, and vnhallowed Fryer' (F *Measure*, TLN.2684; 5.1.299). Significantly, Lucio invokes the Duke's religious disguise as ultimate proof of this friar's untrustworthiness. In the context of so many similarly disguised rulers in the 'comical histories' of the 1590s, the Duke's appearance as a holy friar/hermit is as commonplace as Lucio's derogatory proverb is dangerously ironic.

As we have seen, critics have long viewed *Measure for Measure* as a paradigmatic 'Jacobean disguised ruler play' that makes an explicit statement about

---

[1]   Shakespeare had already used the proverb in *Twelfth Night* (1.5.48–9) and would, in Anglicized form, in *Henry VIII* (3.1.23).

Fig. 3.1   Sophie Thompson as Isabella and Mark Rylance as the Duke in
                  'Friar Lodowick' disguise, in *Measure for Measure* at Shakespeare's
                  Globe, London (2004)

English society and politics following James I's accession. In league with *The Malcontent*, it supposedly spawned a disguised ruler phenomenon that flourished early in James's reign. A difficulty immediately arises, however, when considering *Measure for Measure* in such an occasionalist context: no version of the play exists prior to its 1623 First Folio publication. *Measure for Measure* is a sole surviving, possibly posthumously adapted, play. Its 'adaptation' could date from any time after 1618, when the scrivener Ralph Crane apparently began transcribing several of Shakespeare's comedies for the King's Men. Even the Duke's character-name, 'Vincentio', might be an invention of Crane's, whose extant work for the company dates up to 1625.[2] Whether the Folio text was transcribed from an authorial manuscript or playbook, or interpolated by later dramatists (hence its inclusion in the Middleton canon as a conjectural 'adaptation'), is a matter for continued debate.[3]

An 'original' version of *Measure for Measure* can be dated with some certainty to a performance by the King's Men at Whitehall on 26 December 1604, as part of the 1604–1605 Christmas royal entertainments. The Revels Accounts records the presentation 'By his Ma[tis] plaiers: On S[t] Stiuens night in the [Banqueting] Hall [at Whitehall] A play caled Mesur for Mesur' by the playwright 'Shaxberd'.[4] The Christmas court plays offered by the King's Men included versions of *Comedy of Errors* (28 December 1604), *Love's Labour's Lost* (*c*. 1–6 January 1605), *Henry V* (7 January 1605), Jonson's *Every Man out of His Humour* (8 January 1605) and *Every Man in His Humour* (2 February 1605), which all originally date from the 1590s.[5] These suggest that the King's Men determined not to present anything but previously performed plays for James's entertainment. It is unlikely, therefore, that *Measure for Measure* received its debut at a private performance before the king.[6] The Revels Accounts evidence suggests, though, that *Measure for Measure* was written sometime between 1603 and 1604. Unlike *The Malcontent*, it is thus irrefutably Jacobean.[7] It might even represent Shakespeare's earliest offering as a Jacobean dramatist.

The tantalizing reference to a performance of *Measure for Measure* so early in James's reign supports an occasionalist reading of the play, since it could gauge public reaction to unfolding political events. The 1623 version's uncertain textual integrity, however, means that apparently topical comments might represent later, post-compositional interpolations. It is therefore unwise to consider Shakespeare's

---

[2]   See T.H. Howard-Hill, *Ralph Crane and Some Shakespeare First Folio Comedies* (Charlottesville, 1972), pp. 99–102 & 127–8.

[3]   Taylor and Lavagnino (eds), *Thomas Middleton and Early Modern Textual Culture: A Companion to the Collected Works* (Oxford, 2007), p. 681. See also Taylor and Jowett, *Reshaped*, pp. 175–6; Taylor 'Mediterranean', pp. 243–69.

[4]   TNA: PRO, Audit Office, Accounts, Various, AO 3/908/13.

[5]   Chambers, *ES* 4, pp. 171–2.

[6]   Goldberg, *James*, p. 231.

[7]   Lever, *Measure*, p. xxxi; Eccles, *Measure*, p. 300; Gibbons, *Measure*, p. 1.

disguised Duke as wholly dependant on the Stuart accession. Similarly, the revival of *Henry V* twelve nights after *Measure for Measure*'s Boxing Day performance might simply indicate a 'disguised ruler' theme for the King's Men's offerings. As our discussion of *Henry V* has shown, the medieval heritage of Henry's Agincourt disguise reflects a motif so conventional that *Measure for Measure* would seem an appropriate dramatic equivalent in the court's revels season. Continuing to read *Measure for Measure* within a restrictively Jacobean context elides the conventionality of its disguised ruler. In fact, *Measure for Measure*'s Duke alludes to the conventionality of his disguise in a scene drawn from the unspoken expectation of 'comical history' wooing romance. This convention's absence, therefore, represents the true subversiveness of the Duke's disguised ruler subterfuge.

The Disguised Duke's 'Comical History' Heritage

Act 1 scene 3 of *Measure for Measure* begins with the Duke's arrival onstage with Friar Thomas. As the scene progresses, the Duke informs Thomas that he intends to appear 'as 'twere a brother of [the friar's] Order', in which guise to 'Visit both Prince, and People':

> DUKE: Therefore I pre'thee
> Supply me with the habit, and instruct me
> How I may formally in person beare
> Like a true Frier. (F *Measure*, TLN.336–40; 1.3.44–8)

After so many disguised ruler adventures staged in the 1590s, the Duke's decision to disguise himself should merit no further comment. Obviously, Friar Thomas will facilitate a practice made commonplace by generations of romance narratives.

Still, *Measure for Measure* actually subverts this conventionality before the Duke specifies his chosen disguise. The scene thus commences mid-conversation, with the Duke admonishing the friar for his understandable, but mistaken presumption:

> DUKE: No: holy Father, throw away that thought,
> Beleeue not that the dribling dart of Loue
> Can pierce a compleat bosome: why, I desire thee
> To giue me secret harbour, hath a purpose
> More graue, and wrinkled, then the aimes, and ends
> Of burning youth. (F *Measure*, TLN.290–95; 1.3.1–6)

The Duke rebukes Friar Thomas for insinuating a romantic motive for this secretive sojourn in the monastery. For Friar Thomas, and the play's first audiences, such a mistake is natural, especially since youthful desire 'burning' in a statesman's heart traditionally gives rise to those convoluted romance narratives that finally resolve themselves in self-enlightenment and a safe return to power. The Duke forcefully

Fig. 3.2   Anna Maxwell Martin as Isabella and Ben Miles as the Duke in a
            contemporary *Measure for Measure* at the Almeida Theatre, London
            (2010)

counters what we presume was Thomas's offstage remark, however, by asserting
that the 'dribling dart of Loue' (Cupid's arrow being 'dribbed' or fired short or
wide of the mark) cannot 'pierce' his 'compleat bosome'. Figuratively alluding to
his 'bosome' as the seat of his secret thoughts and emotions, the Duke suggests
that his metaphorical breastplate ('compleat' being perfect and without defect)
is so well-armoured that romance and wooing intrigue cannot penetrate to his
heart. His real 'purpose', so he explains, is 'More grave and wrinkled' than simple
youthful romance. *Measure for Measure*, so the Duke's defensiveness suggests,
will definitely *not* be a romantic 'comical history'.

    This short scene-setting dialogue reflects the typicality of royal disguises in
romantic contexts. The Duke's opening protest presumes, therefore, that audience
and reader will recognize his disguise as a subversion of contemporary comedic
practice. The subversion extends, moreover, to several conventional plot elements
that were already a mainstay of 'comical history' drama. One play that combines
these plot elements into its disguised ruler narrative is the anonymous *Fair Em*

(*c.* 1589–91, Strange's Men; publication date unknown).[8] *Fair Em* introduces disguised ruler subterfuge, sexual manipulation, substitution and unsatisfactory marital unions into a plot that may fruitfully be compared with *Measure for Measure*.[9] Although not a direct source for *Measure for Measure*, *Fair Em* nevertheless contextualizes the Duke's protestations, while demonstrating the conventionality of his subsequent disguised actions.

The title-page to the 'Pleasant Commodie, of faire *Em*', locates its performance in London by 'Lord Strange his seruaunts', almost certainly prior to the playhouse plague closures of 1593.[10] *Fair Em* also most likely predates 1592, since it does not appear in Henslowe's list of plays for the 1592–93 Rose season.[11] Surviving in two early quarto editions, *Fair Em* is a foreshortened or corrupted text that suffers, so W.W. Greg first commented, from 'rather drastic cutting'.[12] Its brevity, which might be linked to adaptation for a private performance in Lancashire, nonetheless leaves enough intact for its plot conventions, theatrical devices and motifs to be compared with the later *Measure for Measure*.[13] The plot similarities between these two plays account for its brief inclusion in the Shakespeare Apocrypha; it was bound in a volume in King Charles II's library marked on the cover, 'Shakespeare'.[14] Although Edmond Malone was sceptical of this attribution, the 1870s critic Richard Simpson argued forcefully for Shakespeare's authorship, as did Felix E. Schelling in 1908.[15] E.K. Chambers's description of Simpson's conjecture as 'hopelessly uncritical' settled the question of Shakespeare's authorship of *Fair Em*.[16]

Set during the time of William the Conqueror, *Fair Em* presents the story of the eponymous Em, a supposed miller's daughter from Manchester, who is actually the child of Sir Thomas Goddard, a disguised English knight fleeing England's tyrannical new monarch. The tyrant is King William, Duke of Saxony. Em is wooed by three disguised courtiers who remain in England against their king's wishes, rather than participate in their sovereign's mission to marry the Danish princess, Blanch. These courtiers' ensuing adventures bring Sir Thomas and his daughter out of hiding. They lead to the unhappy maiden's betrothal, not to her beloved, but

[8]   Anonymous, *A Pleasant Commodie, of faire Em the Millers daughter of Manchester* (London, n.d.).

[9]   See Marliss C. Desens, *The Bed-Trick in English Renaissance Drama* (Newark, 1994), who mentions *Fair Em*, but makes no connection to *Measure* (pp. 38 & 42).

[10]   *Faire Em*, fol. A1ʳ.

[11]   W.W. Greg (ed.), *Fair Em* (Oxford, 1927), p. vii. Through line numbers from this edition.

[12]   Ibid., pp. ix–x.

[13]   See Standish Henning (ed.), *Fair Em* (New York, 1980), pp. 19–24.

[14]   Ibid., p. 29.

[15]   See Henning, *Fair Em,* pp. 51–3; Richard Simpson, *The School of Shakspere* (2 vols, London, 1878), vol. 2, pp. 339–405; Felix E. Schelling, *Elizabethan Drama 1558–1642* (2 vols, Boston, 1908), vol. 1, pp. 191–2.

[16]   Chambers, *ES* 1, p. 377n.

to the man who woos her most persistently. King William, meanwhile, deputizes Duke Dirot and Earl Demarch as 'substitutes to rule [his] Realme' (*Em*, A3ʳ; TLN.79). For the play's original audience, William's subsequent journey resonates negatively with King James VI of Scotland's October 1589 expedition to meet his fifteen-year-old Danish princess, crowned later as Queen Anne. The disguised ruler plot unfolds as King William decides to present himself in Denmark as the courtier '*Robert* of *VVindsor*' (*Em*, A3ʳ; TLN.81), a choice later echoed in Henry V's Agincourt pseudonym, 'Harry le Roy'.

On his arrival in Denmark, the disguised William immediately impresses Princess Blanch. Unfortunately, he reacts to her far less favourably. Viewing his future bride as 'worse featurde, vncomly, nothing courtly' (*Em*, B1ʳ; TLN.217), he offensively exclaims that he 'neuer sawe a harder fauourd slut' (*Em*, B1ʳ; TLN.219). William is far more interested in the Swedish princess Mariana, a captive who is awaiting ransom and betrothed to the Danish marquis Lubeck (the ambassador sent to England to accompany William to Denmark). More beautiful than Blanch, Mariana attracts William's lustful attention, forcing Lubeck to abandon his own marriage plans in favour of helping win Mariana for William. Lubeck's embassy thus mirrors Lacy's mission in *Friar Bacon*. The Dane reluctantly, albeit obediently, accepts this commission, although Blanch's jealousy and Mariana's love for Lubeck impede William's plan. To escape, Mariana hatches a substitution plot with the unfortunate Blanch. With Machiavellian skill, the favoured lady elects to 'poynt some place for to meete' secretly with William (*Em*, C4ʳ; TLN.751), ostensibly to be spirited away by the disguised king back to England. There, so William believes, they can be married and Mariana crowned queen. William agrees to Mariana's plan and accepts her request that she remain masked for the journey. He also accedes to her wishes that he does 'not seeke by lust vnlawfully / To wrong [her] chast determinations' until after their marriage (*Em*, D1ʳ; TLN.801–2). William then speeds back to England, not accompanied, as he believes, by Mariana, but by the substituted Princess Blanch.

In response, Blanch's father, King Zweno, invades England to rescue his daughter. Confronted by the victorious and irate Zweno, William admits that he has been duped by the trick of substitution. He agrees to accept whatever punishment the Dane might 'set downe' (*Em*, F1ʳ; TLN.1364) in an uncomfortable scene of public humiliation that predates Angelo's 'Triall' and 'Confession' in *Measure for Measure* (F *Measure*, TLN.2753–4; 5.1.364). Blanch then kneels before her father, begging forgiveness for 'errors' which were only 'led by loue' (*Em*, F1ʳ; TLN.1381–2). Blanch's kneeling submission, later echoed in Mariana's similar pleading in *Measure for Measure*, is rewarded by her father's forgiveness and command for William to 'take [his] daughter' as 'wife': 'For well I am assured she loues thee well' (*Em*, F1ʳ; TLN.1389–90). In a traditional romantic comedy setting, this decision would lead to general rejoicing and happy conciliation. Analogous to the fraught marital alliances in *Measure for Measure*, however, William's rejection of Zweno's demands betrays a harsh and bitter distrust of women in general, and of marriage in particular:

WILLIAM: Let Maistres nice goe Saint it where she list,
And coyly quaint it with dissembling face.
I hold in scorne the fooleries that they vse,
I being free will neuer subiect my selfe
to any such as shee is vnderneth the Sunne.
… Conseit hath wrought such generall dislike
Through false dealing of *Mariana*,
That vtterly I doe abhore their sex.
They are all disloyall, vnconstant, all vniust. (*Fair Em*, F1ᵛ; TLN.1394–1405)

William's complaints against the 'false dealing' of 'Mistress Nice' (Mariana), whose coy 'dissembling face' and 'fooleries' have tricked him into eloping with the disguised Blanch, threaten not only his personal security, but also that of the English nation. This king will never 'subject' himself to any 'she', especially since marriage implies a diminution of absolute kingly power. William's wrath is only assuaged when the three courtiers who have wooed the fair Em arrive with the unfortunate girl. Perceiving Em's constancy, and her resolute forgiveness though utter rejection of her original suitor, the fickle Lord Manville, William 'see[s] that women are not generall euils' (*Em*, F2ᵛ; TLN.1489). Forced to reappraise the unfortunate Blanch, he now recognizes her 'modest countenance' and 'heauenly blush' (*Em*, F2ᵛ; TLN.1491). With a magnificent *volte face*, he negotiates the transfer of ownership of Blanch from father to future husband, demanding that Zweno 'receiue a reconciled foe, / Not as [his] friend, but as [his] sonne in law' (*Em*, F2ᵛ; TLN.1493–4). Thus, Blanch marries William and England gains the crown of Denmark at Zweno's death.

Only Em's marital fate remains undecided, even though her true identity is revealed. Enforcing his patriarchal authority over Em's body, William asks her father if, as king, he might bestow the maiden where he deems fit. Sir Thomas agrees. William asks Em her opinion of Lord Valingford. Although not the girl's favourite, Valingford has, as William notes, been persistent and *relatively* honourable in his wooing. Em's enigmatic reply recalls the silence of Isabella that has troubled so many commentators of *Measure for Measure*.[17] Confirming that she 'restes at the pleasure' of her king, Em agrees to be Valingford's wife, not because of his love, but 'for his desert' (*Em*, F3ᵛ; TLN.1540). Like Isabella, whose 'desert' for unknowingly assisting the Duke is the 'benefit' of royal marriage, Em resignedly accepts her sovereign's 'pleasure' and agrees to marry her most 'deserving' suitor. The assembled parties exit to William's haunting demand 'that preparation may be made, / to see these nuptials solemly performed' (*Em*, F3ᵛ; TLN.1545). Little here suggests the merry dénouement of a romantic comedy. *Fair Em*, like *Measure for Measure*, ends with prospective marriages tainted with deceit and disappointment. William is tricked into recognizing the worth of Blanch, just as Angelo is tricked into recognizing Mariana's loving commitment.

---

[17]   See Cohen, 'Mistress', pp. 454–6; Laura Lunger Knoppers, '(En)gendering Shame: *Measure for Measure* and the Spectacles of Power,' *ELR*, 23 (1993): 450–71.

When the protagonists of *Fair Em* or *Measure for Measure* finally depart from the stage, the subsequent marriages will undoubtedly be 'solemly', as opposed to joyously, 'performed'.[18]

Like the solemnly performed nuptials in *Fair Em*, solemn obligation overshadows the Duke's offer to the silent Isabella in *Measure for Measure*: 'What's mine is yours, and what is yours is mine' (F *Measure*, TLN.2936; 5.1.530). This standard husband's pledge could suggest equality in marriage, but to the very end this *deus ex machina* duke manipulates Isabella. Demanding that his newly-wedded deputy and his future bride accompany him into the Viennese 'Pallace', the Duke offers to 'show' not all of 'What's yet behinde', but only that which is 'meete [they] all should know' (F *Measure*, TLN.2937–8; 5.1.531–2). The Duke thus decides what the assembled parties should 'know' of preceding events. Even as he reclaims his authority, the Duke demurs from revealing all about the secret subterfuge that enabled Angelo to act as corrupt law-enforcer in his absence. Isabella, moreover, could easily condemn the unwarranted trauma caused by his disguised ruler antics. Like *Fair Em* a decade before, *Measure for Measure* offers vexed marital alliances without satisfactory resolution. Shakespeare might or might not have known *Fair Em*, but this earlier play presages the very plot conventions that make *Measure for Measure* so distinctive in the Shakespeare canon.

The Duke's dismissal of Friar Thomas's initial romantic explanation for his ruler's absence and secret return highlights the play's subversion of this 'comical history' convention. Shakespeare obviously expected his audience to recognize the romantic heritage preceding the Duke's friar's disguise. James's accession, in this instance, seems of no consequence whatsoever. Even so, critics still regard *Measure for Measure*'s purported occasionality as its most significant feature, not least because of Shakespeare's apparently lifelike caricature of King James in the character of the Duke. Unfortunately, our recognition of this seeming caricature stems not from contemporary reaction to the nation's new monarch, but from later political commentators desiring to assassinate the character of an already discredited Scottish king. Returning to the Duke's conversation with Friar Thomas illuminates these issues further.

King James, Occasionality and *Measure for Measure*

After Friar Thomas is rebuffed for his justifiable misinterpretation of his ruler's intentions, the Duke explains the real reason for his secret return to Vienna:

> DUKE: We haue strict Statutes, and most biting Laws,
> (The needfull bits and curbes to headstrong weedes,)

---

[18]   Marissa Greenberg, 'Crossing from Scaffold to Stage', in Cohen (ed.), *Historical Formalism*, pp. 127–45 (p. 141).

Which for this foureteene yeares, we haue let slip. (F *Measure*, TLN.309–11;
1.3.19–21)

The Duke, referring to himself with the *Pluralis Majestatis* or royal 'we', invokes
images of reined horses and leashed hunting dogs to describe the 'strict Statutes'
and 'biting Laws' of Vienna that remained unenforced. The Duke has 'let slip'
the leash and lost control. As he admits, this laxity has led to Vienna's unstable
state of near sexual anarchy. With surprising candour, Friar Thomas observes
how, rather than delegate responsibility to Angelo, 'It rested in [the Duke's] Grace
/ To vnloose this tyed-vp Iustice', thus making it seem 'more dreadfull' in the
eyes of the populace (F *Measure*, TLN.322–4; 1.3.31–3). This remark provokes a
pragmatic response:

> DUKE: I doe feare: too dreadfull:
> Sith 'twas my fault, to giue the people scope,
> Twould be my tirrany to strike and gall them,
> For what I bid them doe: For, we bid this be done
> When euill deedes haue their permissiue passe,
> And not the punishment. (F *Measure*, TLN.326–31; 1.3.34–9)

Claiming concern that the sudden reimposition of Vienna's 'strict Statutes' could
leave him open to accusations of unanticipated 'tirrany', the Duke admits to
diverting the brunt of his subjects' displeasure to Angelo. Again using the royal
'we', the Duke justifies this duplicity by claiming to test Angelo's integrity:
'hence shall we see / If power change purpose: what our Seemers be' (F *Measure*,
TLN.345–6; 1.3.54). Fundamental to the Duke's response is the need for 'euill
deedes' to receive their true 'punishment'. The current sexual depravity of the
Viennese state, and the necessary punishment of moral offenders, ostensibly
motivates the Duke's disguise.

Traditional criticism of *Measure for Measure* correlates the Duke's eagerness
for strict statutes, and accompanying fear of public resistance, with the real
King James. Some insist that the Duke *is* James. The 1991 Oxford editor N.W.
Bawcutt sensibly warns against such analogous readings, advising that it 'would
best be sceptical about excessive claims for royal presence' in the Duke's role.[19]
Bawcutt's caution contrasts sharply with his 1991 Cambridge counterpart, Brian
Gibbons, who announces 'no doubt' that aspects of the Duke were 'intended to
be recognized as allusions to the new king'.[20] Gibbons's comments echo those
of his Cambridge forebears, Sir Arthur Quiller-Couch and John Dover Wilson,
whose 1922 Cambridge edition (in reprint as late as 1950) maintained that 'James
I's dislike of crowds' was 'historic fact', and that 'any doubt upon the matter

---

[19]   N.W. Bawcutt (ed.), *Measure for Measure* (Oxford, 1991), p. 5.
[20]   Gibbons, *Measure*, p. 22.

Fig. 3.3   Mark Rylance as the Duke in *Measure for Measure* at Shakespeare's
                  Globe, London (2004). Rylance's costume consciously evokes the
                  traditional image of King James in contemporary portraiture (see
                  below)

Fig. 3.4   Portrait of King James showing the costume influence for the 2004
             Globe production of *Measure for Measure*. Painting by John Critz
             the Elder (*c*. 1552–1642), *King James I of England*, 1042 x 838 mm,
             oil on canvas, *c*. 1610, National Maritime Museum, Greenwich,
             London

... should be laid to rest'.[21] For these early twentieth-century editors, parallels between the Duke and King James were based on 'historic fact', with Shakespeare 'flattering the king's weakness, a weakness with which [Shakespeare] himself is likely to have had some sympathy'.[22] Biographical analogy, according to the Cambridge editors, held the key to contextualizing *Measure for Measure*. Their comments epitomize the 'Duke as James' theorizing, with its focus on negative aspects of James's personality and reign, and its search for parallels in Shakespeare's drama. That this correlation remains relatively unchallenged is surprising, particularly since twentieth-century revisionist historical research offers an alternative, more sympathetic view of James and his reception in England in 1603–1604. Unfortunately, since many scholars still view *Measure for Measure* as occasionalist political commentary, Shakespeare is seen to offer negative or apologetic perspectives about his new king.

The belief that the disguised Duke represents a thinly veiled caricature of James stems primarily from two famous passages in the play. The first is the Duke's brief explanation to Escalus about his secretive plans to travel 'priuily away' from Vienna:

> DUKE: I loue the people,
> But doe not like to stage me to their eyes:
> Though it doe well, I do not rellish well
> Their lowd applause, and Aues vehement:
> Nor doe I thinke the man of safe discretion
> That do's affect it. (F *Measure*, TLN.76–80; 1.1.67–72)

The Duke purportedly hopes to avoid both the public 'staging' and the consequent 'lowd applause and Aues vehement' (a hendiadys that combines loud clapping with the excessively loud 'hails and farewells') of his adoring public. Not only does the Duke not 'rellish' these noisy farewells, he also expresses concern over the 'safe discretion' of any man who ostentatiously does 'affect it'.

The second supposed allusion to James occurs in Angelo's description of his physical reaction to meeting with Isabella:

> ANGELO: So play the foolish throngs with one that swounds,
> Come all to help him, and so stop the ayre
> By which hee should reuiue: and euen so
> The generall subiect to a wel-wisht King
> Quit their owne part, and in obsequious fondnesse
> Crowd to his presence, where their vn-taught loue
> Must needs appeare offence. (F *Measure*, TLN.1027–33; 2.4.24–30)

---

[21]   Sir Arthur Quiller-Couch and John Dover Wilson (eds), *Measure for Measure* (Cambridge, 1922; rev. edn 1950), p. 118n.

[22]   Ibid., p. 118n.

Like the subjects who rush to greet their king, Angelo's blood rushes uncontrollably to his swooning, and lusting, heart, stifling the metaphorical 'air' that could aid his moral recovery. Angelo likens this onrush of blood to the 'vn-taught' masses who, from 'obsequious fondnesse', 'quit' their 'owne part' and crowd into the royal presence, thus unwittingly causing offence with their coarse behaviour. Although Angelo pointedly refers here to a 'King', the metaphor enhances Angelo's expression of uncontrollable lust and unexpected passion. Angelo's 'King', therefore, need not correspond to Shakespeare's own ruler. Subjectivity and introspection remain the true focus of Angelo's concern.

The Duke's Act 1 'priuily away' comment offers more specific self-analysis. The true reason for the Duke's travelling 'priuily away' is to embark on an adventure of subterfuge and surveillance, in order to observe Angelo. Indeed, the Duke's original explanation is undermined by his later choice 'To enter publikely' (F *Measure*, TLN.2180; 4.3.88) on his return to Vienna with all the pomp and ceremony appropriate to his rank. The Duke's command to Angelo to 'Giue [him his] hand / And let the Subiect see, to make them know / That outward curtesies would faine proclaime / Fauours that keepe within' (F *Measure*, TLN.2361–4; 5.1.13–16), thus appears both ironic and politically astute. For a Duke who has earlier denounced 'staging' himself to his people's eyes, his later decision belies such self-conscious avoidance of the public gaze, appearing at best spurious, at worst defensive and obfuscatory. As Steven Mullaney suggested in the late 1980s, such spectacle of state corresponds with Queen Elizabeth's 'theatricality of power'.[23] Mullaney here builds on Jonathan Goldberg's argument that James adopted and adapted Elizabeth's theatricality, refashioning it to suit his more distanced, representational attitude to kingship and display.[24]

Explanations for the Duke's manipulation of his deputies abound in topical monarchic readings of *Measure for Measure*. Quiller-Couch and Wilson claim, for example, that the Act 1 and Act 2 passages appear to have been '*additions*, written expressly' for the play's royal auditor at the 'Court performance of 1604'.[25] In the late 1970s, however, Richard Levin derided those who interpret Shakespeare's plays as 'compositions directed at a special audience', in *Measure for Measure*'s case, King James.[26] Levin was particularly scathing about one prominent aspect of the 'Duke as James' theory: the quest for suggestive parallels between the Duke's character and James's political writings, especially his *True Lawe of Free Monarchies* (1598) and *Basilikon Doron* (1599 and 1603).[27] This resulted in what Levin terms an inappropriate 'King James Version' of *Measure for Measure*

---

[23]   Mullaney, *Place*, pp. 10–15.

[24]   Goldberg, *James*, pp. 30–31.

[25]   Quiller-Couch and Wilson, *Measure*, p. 118n.

[26]   Richard Levin, *New Readings vs. Old Plays* (Chicago, 1979), p. 167.

[27]   Jenny Wormald, 'James VI & I, *Basilikon Doron* and *The Trew Law of Free Monarchies*: The Scottish Context and the English Translation', in Linda Levy Peck (ed.), *The Mental World of the Jacobean Court* (Cambridge, 1991), pp. 36–54.

that elides alternative readings.[28] Despite such cautions, Levin's contemporaries continued reading *Measure for Measure* through an occasionalist 'Duke as James' lens, even though its Whitehall performance, as already noted, hardly confirms the play's uniqueness as a court-specific drama.[29]

In reality, however, the 'Duke as James' theory is actually an anachronistic historical construct, whose heritage can be traced to the mid-eighteenth century. The earliest known mention of the 'Duke as James' theory in relation to *Measure for Measure* was not made until 1766, when Thomas Tyrwhitt claimed that Shakespeare meant 'to flatter that unkingly weakness of *James the first*, which made him so impatient of the crowds that flocked to see him, especially on his first coming'.[30] Tyrwhitt justifies this comment through apparently irrefutable historical evidence. Like so much eighteenth-century commentary on James, this 'evidence' relies on partisan hearsay rather than 'historic fact'. Stemming from a post-regicide, pro-Parliament narrative of negativity about the Stuart monarchy, such partisan commentary, full of half-truths, gossip, scandalous fictions and downright lies, became known as Whig historiography.[31] Characterized by Herbert Butterfield in 1931 as a strategy 'introduced for the purpose of facilitating the abridgement of history', Whig historiography presented a grand historical narrative claiming an inevitable progression towards liberal democracy and constitutional monarchy. Whig historiography also became the defining historical principle for describing James's personality and rule, reaching its apotheosis with Thomas Babington Macaulay's *History of England* of 1848.[32] Tyrwhitt, moreover, introduced the 'Duke as James' theory into *Measure for Measure* criticism in direct response to such Whig historiography.

Preceded in 1765 by Samuel Johnson's indignation at '*Angelo's* crimes', Tyrwhitt's 1766 'Duke as James' comments demonstrate how far *Measure for Measure* had captured the imagination of the age.[33] Citing 'some of our Historians', Tyrwhitt discusses how James 'restrained' the crowds who flocked to him, offering 'A Manuscript in the *British Museum*' as primary evidence:

> Sir *Symonds D'Ewes*, in his Memoirs of his own Life, has a remarkable passage with regard to this humour of *James*. After taking notice, that the King going to Parliament, on the 30*th of January*, 1620–1,
> "spake lovingly to the people, and said,

---

[28]   Levin, *Readings*, p. 167.

[29]   See Ivo Kamps and Karen Raber, *Measure for Measure: Texts and Contexts* (Boston, 2004), pp. 124–7.

[30]   Thomas Tyrwhitt, *Observations and Conjectures upon some Passages of Shakespeare* (Oxford, 1766), p. 36.

[31]   Herbert Butterfield, *The Whig Interpretation of History* (London, 1931), pp. 24–6.

[32]   Thomas Babington Macaulay, *History of England from the Accession of James II* (5 vols, London, 1848–55), vol. 1 (1848).

[33]   Samuel Johnson (ed.), *The Plays of William Shakespeare* (8 vols, London, 1765), vol. 1, p. 378.

"*God bless ye, God bless ye;*" he adds these words,
"contrary to his former hasty and passionate custom,
"which often, in his sudden distemper, would bid a
"pox or a plague on such as flocked to see him." (Tyrwhitt, 36–7)

For Tyrwhitt, the most convincing proof of James's 'unkingly weakness' comes not from the early years of his reign when *Measure for Measure* was first performed, but from a manuscript reminiscence about the year 1621 (old-style calendar 1620) written by the parliamentarian and procedural historian, Sir Simonds D'Ewes. D'Ewes relates this experience in his handwritten *Autobiography* (*c.* 1637), an unpublished, self-edited account of his life up to 1635 (based on memory and personal documents) intended only for his family.[34] D'Ewes's *Autobiography* was not published until 1845, over two centuries later.[35] His discursive narrative describes personal, national and international affairs and anecdotes in chronological sequence. D'Ewes recalls, for instance, how once 'not without some danger', he positioned himself in a throng of well-wishers to see 'his Matie passe to Parliament in state' on his 'short progresse from Whitehall to Westminster'.[36] This moment in the young D'Ewes's life, however fleeting, is seized upon by Tyrwhitt to explain two passages in Shakespeare's *Measure for Measure*.

It is important to remember, however, that D'Ewes's testimony recalls an event towards the end of James's life that occurred when D'Ewes was an impressionable nineteen-year-old newcomer to London. As recently as September 1620, four months prior to the state occasion he recalls, D'Ewes had been forced by his overbearing father to leave Cambridge University and embark on a career at the Inner Temple. Only a year old when James acceded to the English throne, and educated variously in Dorset and Suffolk, D'Ewes's only prior experience of the metropolis came from occasional sojourns with his father and grandfather, whose legal duties kept them in London for the seasonal Terms.[37] D'Ewes's 1620s comment about James's customary behaviour should, therefore, be seen most plausibly as a regurgitation of family hearsay and gossip about the king's early reign, rather than an account drawn from personal experience.

At the same time, any response to Tyrwhitt's reliance on this eminent 'witness' demands recognition of D'Ewes's anti-Stuart predisposition and, as his Victorian editor J.O. Halliwell accurately described it, his insufferable pedantry.[38] In 1643, six years after penning his autobiography, D'Ewes famously aligned himself

---

[34]   Sir Simonds D'Ewes, *Autobiography*, BL MS Harley 646, fols 53–4.

[35]   J.O. Halliwell-Phillips (ed.), *The Autobiography and Correspondence of Sir Simonds D'Ewes* (2 vols, London, 1845), vol. 1, pp. 169–70.

[36]   D'Ewes, *Autobiography*, fol. 54.

[37]   Andrew G. Watson, *The Library of Sir Simonds D'Ewes* (London, 1966), pp. 2–3.

[38]   Wallace Notestein (ed.), *The Journal of Sir Simonds D'Ewes* (New Haven, 1923), p. x.

with the parliamentary side.[39] D'Ewes was a parliamentary sympathiser and private commentator on political history, his first published work on Elizabethan parliaments appearing in 1682, thirty-two years after his death. His observations were, however, seized upon by later Whig historians, who recognized the value of his unsympathetic portrait.[40] Nevertheless, they did not enter the public domain until much later, after D'Ewes's private papers were sold in 1705 and acquired for the earl of Oxford's library. Following the earl's death in 1741, they became part of the Harley MSS at the British Museum.[41] Writing some twenty years after a select few gained access to these documents, Tyrwhitt recognized material that could prove valuable in the arsenal of Whig propaganda, even though this commentary originated long before D'Ewes's legal and political skills made him an invaluable though self-important asset to the nation's government.

Tyrwhitt's use of D'Ewes to interpret *Measure for Measure* demonstrates the practice of Whig historiographers who pored over newly available manuscripts for the least sign of anti-Stuart feeling. Reflecting such procedures, Ralph Houlbrooke traces the genesis of Whig historiography to the fall of the Stuart monarchy (Charles I's execution in 1649) and the subsequent publication of memoirs that 'purported to uncover James's personal weaknesses and the more unsavoury aspects of his regime'.[42] The dry, ironic and cynical character assassination of James as 'a Slave' to his 'Favourites' in Sir Anthony Weldon's memoirs of 1650, for instance, set the tone for subsequent moralizing exposés about the king's supposedly unrestrained homosexual proclivity.[43] Like Weldon, Francis Osborne (1658) also attacked James's sexuality, claiming that the king openly and 'amorously conveyed' his affection to his '*Favorites* or *Minions*' as if he had 'mistaken their Sex, and thought them Ladies'.[44] With anti-theatrical homophobic fervour, Osborne describes James's propensity for 'kissing [his favourites] after so lascivious a mode in publick, and upon the Theater as it were of the world, [which] prompted many to Imagine some things done in the Tyring-house, that exceed my expressions no less then they do my experience'.[45] Such prejudiced and rabidly anti-Scottish 1650s polemics had a lasting influence on subsequent histories of James.

---

[39]   J.M. Blatchly, 'D'Ewes, Sir Simonds, first baronet (1602–1650)', *ODNB* (2004) <http://www.oxforddnb.com/index/101007577/Simonds-DEwes> [accessed 6 May 2011].

[40]   Sir Simonds D'Ewes, *The Journals of All the Parliaments* (London, 1682).

[41]   Watson, *Library*, p. 62.

[42]   Ralph Houlbrooke, 'James's Reputation 1625–2005', in Houlbrooke (ed.), *James VI and I: Ideas, Authority, and Government* (Aldershot, 2006), pp. 169–90 (p. 171).

[43]   Sir Anthony Weldon, *The Court and Character of King James* (London, 1650), fol. A3ᵛ.

[44]   Francis Osborne, *Traditionall Memoyres on the Raigne of King Iames* (London, 1658), p. 127.

[45]   Ibid., p. 128. See Thomas Alan King, *The Gendering of Men, 1600–1750* (Madison, 2004), pp. 70–6; Michael B. Young, *King James and the History of Homosexuality* (New York, 2000), pp. 36–63; David M. Bergeron, *King James and Letters of Homoerotic Desire* (Iowa City, 1999), pp. 147–219.

Fig. 3.5   Howard Brenton's 2010 play, *Anne Boleyn*, at Shakespeare's Globe, London, depicting King James and George Villiers in passionate homoerotic embrace, in line with traditional Whig propaganda

Character assassinations they undoubtedly are, but Weldon's and Osborne's testimonies never mention James's avoidance of public exposure. In fact, in another of his anti-Stuart, anti-Scottish polemics, *A Cat May Look Upon a King* (1652), Weldon describes the 'Entrance of King *James* into this Kingdome, with as much pomp and glory as the World could afford', a description that belies assertions of kingly reticence against public display.[46] Similarly, Osborne recalls how, when he saw the king's 'Progress after his Inauguration' in July 1603, James was 'dres'd' in an outfit, 'as *Greene* as the grasse he trod on, with a *Fether* in his Cap, and a *Horne* instead of a Sword by his side'.[47] James's flamboyantly rustic attire, evocative of Robin Hood, appears in the context of an unusual degree of political awareness:

> He that evening parted with his Queene, and to shew himself more uxorious
> before the people at his first coming than in private he was, he did at her Coach
> side take his leave, by Kissing her sufficiently to the middle of the Shoulders, for
> so low she went bare all the dayes I had the fortune to know her. (Osborne, 55)

James's overtly sexual public display of affection for his wife and queen, as well as his ostentatious invocation of an English mythical figure, displays none of what Tyrwhitt was, a century later, to describe as James's 'unkingly weakness'. Unsavoury as Osborne's character assessment of James might be, neither he nor Weldon actually portray James's antisocial, politically incompetent or reclusive behaviour.

Although Weldon and Osborne represent typical post-regicide negative responses to the Stuart monarchy, alternative views about James were also being expressed. Sir William Sanderson's 1656 description of James as a wise and intelligent monarch, who was by nature more reserved than popular, for example, represents a pro-Jamesian polemic.[48] Thus, as Houlbrooke notes, by 1660, 'two sharply opposed views of James had been established', with James either a 'wise, far-sighted, eloquent, open-hearted king', or an extravagant and weak apologist for Roman Catholicism, prone to 'stretching of the crown's prerogative'.[49] Sharply opposed views indeed, but neither the arch-vilifiers Weldon or Osborne, nor the arch-apologist and supporter Sanderson, indicate that James avoided or feared all public display. Quite the reverse; their comments suggest a reserved and intellectual statesman who, through manipulation of his public persona, employed state spectacle as an adjunct to successful rule.

As Sanderson's positive appraisal of James's character confirms, bipartisan attitudes toward the Stuart king remained the norm throughout the closing decades of the seventeenth century. By the early eighteenth century, James was finding further support from royalist or 'Tory' apologists such as the earl of Clarendon

---

[46] Sir Anthony Weldon, *A Cat May Look Upon a King* (London, 1652), p. 85.

[47] Osborne, *Memoyres*, p. 54.

[48] Sir William Sanderson, *A Compleat History* (2 vols, London, 1656), vol. 1, pp. 507–13; Sanderson, *Aulicus Coquinariae* (London, 1650), pp. 200–205.

[49] Houlbrooke, 'Reputation', p. 176.

(1702) and Laurence Echard (1707), who both describe his great perspicacity and sound judgement.[50] Unfortunately for James, however, Whig animosity towards the king and his regime became the predominant eighteenth-century stance. This negativity was epitomized by John Oldmixon, whose *The History of England* (1730) not only accuses James of abusing English law and custom 'notoriously' for his personal political gain, but also proclaims that the Gunpowder 'Plot was of the King's own making', with James 'privy to it from first to last'.[51] Clearly, Tyrwhitt's 1766 'memoir' evidence illustrates the critical tradition of such anti-Stuart Whig historiography. Tyrwhitt's comments also demonstrate how Whiggish influences now permeated contemporary consideration of Shakespeare, at least with regard to *Measure for Measure*.

Towards the end of the eighteenth century, Edmond Malone (1790) developed Tyrwhitt's argument in a similar Whiggish tone. Writing twenty-four years after the publication of Tyrwhitt's *Observations*, Malone comments that the same Act 1 and Act 2 'passages … seem intended as a courtly apology for the stately and ungracious demeanour of King James I … written not long after his accession'.[52] From Malone's perspective, Shakespeare was not flattering James. Rather, he was apologising for his monarch's unattractive 'demeanour', with 'stately' used in the pejorative sense of haughty, domineering and arrogant. Apparently drawing upon Osborne and Tyrwhitt's prior criticism, Malone's uncomplimentary description marks a turning point in critical consideration of *Measure for Measure*. For Malone, *Measure for Measure* could now be read as justification for the inevitable bloody outcome of later years, even if it was not directly involved in the inexorable decline of the Stuart monarchy.

That Malone's 'courtly apology' theory was generally accepted by his contemporaries is suggested by its repetition in George Steevens's 1793 edition of *Shakspere*.[53] Even so, the Malone theory also had its detractors, as evinced by George Chalmers's scathing 1799 rebuttal of those 'commentators' (Malone and Steevens), offering arguments for the apparent '*stately* and *ungracious* demeanor of King James': 'No,' exclaims Chalmers, '[t]he fault of this prince was *too much familiarity*, and not stateliness; he was good natured, and not ungracious; he did not like to *stage* himself to the people's eyes; because he delighted in retirement, in

---

[50]   Edward Hyde, first earl of Clarendon, *The History of the Rebellion and Civil Wars in England* (3 vols, Oxford, 1702–1704), vol. 1, p. 9; Laurence Echard, *The History of England* (3 vols, London, 1707–1718), vol. 1, p. 979.

[51]   John Oldmixon, *The History of England* (London, 1730), pp. 14 & 27. See Pat Rogers, 'Oldmixon, John (1672/3–1742)', *ODNB* (2004) <http://www.oxforddnb.com/index/101020695/John-Oldmixon> [accessed 6 May 2011].

[52]   Edmond Malone (ed.), *The Plays and Poems of William Shakspeare* (10 vols, London, 1790), vol. 1, p. 344.

[53]   George Steevens (ed.), *The Plays of William Shakspeare* (15 vols, London, 1793), vol. 1, p. 568.

the company of a few, in study, and in writing'.[54] Chalmers apparently harbours no doubt that Shakespeare's Duke is correlative to James. Indeed, he remarks 'that the character of *the Duke*, is a very accurate delineation of that of King James, which Shakspeare appears to have caught, with great felicity, and to have sketched, with much truth'.[55] The debate about *Measure for Measure*, according to Chalmers, revolves not around whether Shakespeare caricatured his king, but whether such caricature should be considered offensive or complimentary. Unconsciously pre-empting the twentieth-century 'King James Version' controversy and its fascination with textual negotiation, Chalmers notes that, '[k]nowing that King James's writings ... had been, emulously, republished, in 1603, by the London booksellers, in many editions, Shakspeare could not fitly give a closer parody'.[56] While Chalmers clearly considers *Measure for Measure* a 'parody' of contemporary Jacobean political thought, he never intimates that such parody implies Shakespeare's condemnation of his king: 'Shakspeare did not intend to make an apology, but merely to give *traits of character*'.[57] Whether those '*traits of character*' are derogatory or not, Malone, Steevens and Chalmers demonstrate how entrenched the concept of the 'Duke as James' theory had become by the beginning of the nineteenth century.

By 1849, Charles Knight could reaffirm that Chalmers had made a 'random hit' with his description of the Duke's character traits, claiming them an 'accurate' though good-natured 'parody' of James.[58] Knight's subsequent comparison of the Duke with James betrays his own Whiggish distaste for the Stuart monarch. Despite the fact that 'James was a pedant, and the Duke is a philosopher', Knight observes, 'there is the same desire in each to get behind the curtain and pull the strings which move the puppets'.[59] Knight scorns James's pedantry. For him, the 'desire' of both Duke and king to manipulate situations and subjects to their advantage links the Shakespearean character and the historical monarch. Such less-than-flattering observations are not surprising since Knight's *Studies of Shakspere* was published a year after the first two volumes of Macaulay's *History of England* (1848). Recognized as the archetypal Whig historian, Macaulay writes an unabashedly partisan history that (following Weldon's and Osborne's lead) describes James's implicitly homosexual 'fondness for worthless minions, ... [his] cowardice, his childishness, his pedantry, his ungainly person and manners, [and] his provincial accent, [all making] him an object of derision'.[60] Macaulay's distinctive 1848 reference to James's 'pedantry' is reflected in Knight's own 1849

---

[54]   George Chalmers, *A Supplemental Apology for the Believers in the Shakspeare-Papers* (London, 1799), p. 408.

[55]   Ibid., p. 404.

[56]   Ibid., pp. 404–405.

[57]   Ibid., p. 409.

[58]   Knight, *Studies*, p. 319.

[59]   Ibid., p. 319.

[60]   Macaulay, *History of England*, 11th edn (1856), vol. 1, p. 73.

description of James as a 'pedant'. Furthermore, the resurgence of interest in the 'Duke as James' theory in Shakespeare criticism from the 1850s onwards appears directly linked to the prevailing popularity of Macaulay.

Macaulay's pervasive negativity towards James, and its repeated application by Shakespeare scholars to *Measure for Measure*, also influenced Victorian understandings of the Duke. It was not, therefore, until George Bernard Shaw's 1898 comment about the play's coming of age that *Measure for Measure* criticism developed its socially-oriented literary and historical significance.[61] Shavian social commentary also ensured that, by the first decade of the twentieth century, serious doubts were being expressed about the now entrenched 'Duke as James' theory. Charlotte Porter and Helen A. Clarke, Bostonian editors of a complete works based on the First Folio (1903–1905), for instance, argue that the 'dislike of public adulation' in *Measure for Measure* is more reminiscent of *Coriolanus*, 'rather than James'.[62] As Americans, Porter and Clarke were apparently immune to the partisan excesses of British Whig vitriol (a possible reason why their notes were unceremoniously dropped from the thirteen volume British edition published in 1906, of which only seventy-five copies were printed). Their remarks were contemporaneous with historical reappraisals of James's character, most notably P. Hume Brown's scathing 1902 description of Macaulay's history as 'false and cruel and vindictive'.[63]

Despite these significant doubts, 'Duke as James' theorizing remains evident in the occasionalist source study of the German scholar Louis Albrecht (1914), which describes *Measure for Measure* as '*vorschwebte*' ('envisioned') by Shakespeare to be '*Huldigungsakte für den neuen König bei seiner Thronbesteigung in England zu gestalten*' ('shaped as a homage for the new king on the occasion of his accession in England').[64] Albrecht also champions Chalmers's argument that the play was directly influenced by *Basilikon Doron*.[65] Even so, Albrecht does not criticize James's personality, believing instead in Shakespeare's intent to flatter his monarch through analogy. Albrecht's non-judgemental pre-First World War comment is countered, however, by the post-war remarks of Quiller-Couch and Wilson, whose 1920s 'historic fact' about Shakespeare's complicity in providing topical socio-political commentary is itself suspiciously dependant on the partisan 'facts' disseminated by earlier Whig historians.[66] Their interpretation confirms

[61]   Shaw, *Plays*, vol. 1, p. xxxi.

[62]   Charlotte Porter and Helen A. Clarke (eds), *The Complete Works of William Shakespeare* (12 vols, New York, 1903–1905).

[63]   P. Hume Brown, *History of Scotland* (3 vols, Cambridge, 1900–1909), vol. 2 (1902), p. 186.

[64]   Louis Albrecht, *Neue Untersuchungen zu Shakespeares Mass für Mass* (Berlin, 1914), p. 164. Translation mine.

[65]   Ibid., p. 131.

[66]   Quiller-Couch and Wilson, *Measure*, p. 118n.

that the 'Duke as James' theory was now entrenched in twentieth-century British criticism, where it would set the theorizing tone for the next thirty years.

Not until 1953, in fact, did a critic question the 'Duke as James' theory's validity.[67] Mary Lascelles's reassessment coincides with a notable shift in historical focus, exemplified by D. Harris Willson's 1956 historical treatment of James, which suggests that the Scottish king made an unusually favourable impression on observers in 1603, only losing their faith and adulation after perceived failures in his government and foreign policy after 1612.[68] Willson's modest reappraisal of James's reception was subsequently developed by William McElwee, who, in 1958, embarked on the first of many revisionist historical treatments of James.[69] McElwee notes that, rather than deriding the 'lowd applause and Aues vehement' of the 'mobs of well-wishers' that greeted his journey to London, James actually enjoyed his new-found popularity.[70] As example, McElwee cites James's first 'Speach to Parliament', 19 March 1603, where the new king expresses 'thankefulnes' for the 'ioyfull and generall applause' he received on entering Parliament, and from his English subjects:[71]

> [S]hall it euer bee blotted out of my minde, how at my first entrie into this Kingdome, the people of all sorts rid and ran, nay rather flew to meet mee? their eyes flaming nothing but sparkles of affection, their mouthes and tongues vttering nothing but sounds of ioy, their hands, feete, and all the rest of their members in their gestures discouering a passionate longing, and earnestnesse to meete and embrace their new Soueraigne. ('Speach', 19 March 1603)

According to McElwee, there is little here to suggest that James, at this early stage in his rule, was perceived as reticent or unwilling to receive the adulation of his people. On the contrary, such esteem appeared a welcome change from the relative inattention of James's Scottish subjects and perfectly in accord with a widespread optimism and general English relief that the 'tired, old queen' had finally gone.[72]

Shakespeare critics, however, selectively ignored Willson's alternative historical interpretation of James's political standing, and McElwee's subsequent historical evidence of James's reception. By the late 1950s, David Lloyd Stevenson was still rehearsing a negative debate about the 'Jamesian' character of the Duke in *Measure for Measure*, although a decisive sea-change in historical appreciation of James's skill as a ruling monarch was about to be announced by Mark H.

---

[67]   See Mary Lascelles, *Shakespeare's 'Measure for Measure'* (London, 1953), pp. 108–109.

[68]   D. Harris Willson, *King James VI & I* (London, 1956), pp. 166–8 & 196.

[69]   William McElwee, *The Wisest Fool in Christendom* (London, 1958).

[70]   Ibid., p. 111.

[71]   Neil Rhodes, Jennifer Richards and Joseph Marshall (eds), *King James VI and I: Selected Writings* (Aldershot, 2003), pp. 293–4.

[72]   Keith M. Brown, 'Monarchy and Government in Britain, 1603–1637', in Jenny Wormald (ed.), *The Seventeenth Century* (Oxford, 2008), pp. 13–50 (p. 14).

Curtis's 1961 reappraisal of the 'Hampton Court Conference and its Aftermath'.[73] By contrast, Stevenson offers a familiar full expression of the 'King James Version' of *Measure for Measure* according to Chalmers's late eighteenth-century model and Albrecht's subsequent early twentieth-century source study. Likewise, Ernest Schanzer (1963) comments that, 'taken together', the 'idealized image' in the various character traits of the Duke seem 'too uniquely characteristic of James to be dismissed as mere accidental likenesses'.[74] In his Arden 2 edition, J.W. Lever (1965), although cautious not to suggest the Duke was an 'exact replica' of James, agrees that 'a number of [James's] personal traits went to the making' of the Duke.[75]

Even by the 1970s, Lever's opinion still held sway, despite over a decade's revisionist rethinking of James's personality and political legacy.[76] The 'demolition' of the Whig version of Stuart history was not completed, however, until the work of Conrad Russell (1976) and Kevin Sharpe (1978).[77] It is perhaps no coincidence that, while revisionist historians were restoring James's reputation as a skilful king and politician, Levin (1979) was wryly coining his 'King James Version' label.[78] Still, Levin's argument against the false occasionality of the 'King James Version' of criticism was fiercely contested by Goldberg (1983), who branded Levin a 'skeptic' who 'attacks straw men'.[79] For Goldberg, *Measure for Measure* is undoubtedly a political 're-presentation', whereby the 'power of theater bears a royal stamp'; thus, Shakespeare wrote the Duke not as an occasionalist caricature of his king, but as a 'role that represents [Shakespeare's] powers as playwright as coincident with the powers of the sovereign'.[80] Likewise, the Duke, according to Goldberg, represents Shakespeare's 'coincidence' (his exact agreement) with Stuart divine right rule as expressed in James's political writings. Goldberg's commentary on *Measure for Measure* appears, however, to rely on traditional negative readings of James's politics and regime. As an early new historicist, Goldberg seems unaware of contemporary developments in revisionist historical thinking, especially studies by Maurice Lee Jr and Jenny Wormald. These historians each highlighted the

---

[73]   David Lloyd Stevenson, 'The Role of James I in Shakespeare's *Measure for Measure*', *ELH*, 26 (1959): 188–208, and Stevenson, *The Achievement of Shakespeare's 'Measure for Measure'* (Ithaca, 1966), pp. 134–66 (p. 134); Mark H. Curtis, 'The Hampton Court Conference and its Aftermath', *History*, 46 (1961): 1–16.

[74]   Ernest Schanzer, *The Problem Plays of Shakespeare* (London, 1963), pp. 123–4.

[75]   Lever, *Measure*, pp. xlix–xl.

[76]   Marc L. Schwarz, 'James I and the Historians: Towards a Reconsideration', *JBS*, 13 (1974): 114–34.

[77]   Houlbrooke, 'Reputation', p. 185; Conrad Russell, 'Parliamentary History in Perspective, 1604–1629', *History*, 61 (1976): 1–27, and Russell, *Parliaments and English Politics 1621–1629* (Oxford, 1979), pp. 85–203; Kevin Sharpe (ed.), *Faction and Parliament* (Oxford, 1978).

[78]   Levin, *New Readings*, p. 167.

[79]   Goldberg, *James*, p. 286n.

[80]   Ibid., p. 232.

achievement of James's Scottish government, as well as his energy, informality and accessibility, thus emphasising the contemporary belief of his English subjects that they were adopting a new king whose experience far outweighed negative opinions about his personal demeanour.[81] Goldberg does not address these issues, concentrating instead on his single 'fact': that the 'Duke represents James's Divine Right claims'.[82]

Echoes of Whiggish mistrust also appear in Leah Marcus's 1988 description of the Duke's 'mythos of power' as synonymous with that adopted by James.[83] Although Marcus argues that the 'King James Version' of *Measure for Measure* has often been 'dismissed as impossibly reductive', she still suggests that 'many parallels' exist between the Duke and James, sufficient to introduce a 'remarkably Jacobean *style*' to the Duke's 'activities'.[84] Underlying Marcus's description of this 'Jacobean *style*' is her unquestioning acceptance of the same Whiggish facts that had created the 'King James Version' of *Measure for Measure* that she finds so reductive. For Marcus, the argument against a 'King James Version' of the play rests solely on her assumption that Shakespeare would have been foolhardy to admonish his king so openly. Similarly, Gary Taylor and John D. Jowett (1993) claim that, '[c]learly, James's distaste for crowds became visible, at least to discerning observers, very early'.[85] Taylor and Jowett base their conclusion not on James's public speeches to Parliament, nor on D'Ewes's memoir evidence, but on a private letter from Thomas Wilson of 22 June 1603, which refers obliquely to public dismay at James's inaccessibility, and equally private journal entries by Queen Elizabeth's Master of Requests, Sir Roger Wilbraham (written sometime between April and July 1603), which comment on the 'offence' caused to James by those who 'thronge at Court'.[86] Taylor and Jowett do not note that these same references also share a common complaint. Wilson's letter claims that the 'people ... desyre some more of that generous affabilitye wch ther good old Queen did afford them'.[87] Likewise, Wilbraham's journal complains that the Queen would 'labour to entertayne strangers and sutors & her people', a 'courtlie courtesie' no

[81]   Maurice Lee Jr, *Government by Pen: Scotland under James VI and I* (Urbana, 1980); Jenny Wormald, *Court, Kirk and Community: Scotland 1470–1625* (London, 1981), pp. 143–59; Wormald, 'James VI and I: Two Kings or One?', *History*, 68 (1983): 187–209. Also Tricomi, *Anticourt*, pp. 3–4.

[82]   Goldberg, *James*, p. 236.

[83]   Marcus, *Puzzling*, p. 163.

[84]   Ibid., pp. 164 & 177.

[85]   Taylor and Jowett, *Reshaped*, p. 173.

[86]   Ibid., pp. 172–3. Harold Spencer Scott (ed.), *The Journal of Sir Roger Wilbraham* (London, 1902), p. 56.

[87]   Thomas Wilson's letter appears in John Nichols (ed.), *The Progresses, Processions, and Magnificent Festivities, of King James the First* (4 vols, London, 1828), vol. 1, p. 188.

longer proffered by the king.[88] Both Wilson and Wilbraham find a difference in court practice following the death of Queen Elizabeth that apparently accords with the 'Duke as James' theory of kingly reserve and distance. They also privately bemoan this new circumstance, in Wilson's case understandably since in 1601 he had penned a lengthy justification for James's right to accede to the English throne.[89]

The private grievances of two English courtiers, apparently reacting to their king's refusal to 'entertayne strangers and sutors', can, of course, be read as biographical observations about their new monarch. Expressed in the aftermath of James's arrival with his privileged Scottish entourage, they might also be read as personal complaints about changes in the distribution of privilege and power.[90] Wilbraham, as Master of the Court of Requests since at least 1600 (the post was transferred in 1603 to Wilbraham's rival Sir Julius Caesar), was in the privileged position to observe unscrupulous courtiers abusing the non fee-paying benefit of the nation's tribunal for the poor.[91] Unwilling to pander to the 'thronge' of wealthy petitioners who appeared at 'every back gate & privie dore', the new king, as Wilbraham declares, showed great 'wisdome' in avoiding suitors whose outlandish requests might have caused 'the damage of the crowne & government'.[92] Wilbraham's comments (ignored by Taylor and Jowett) confirm the opinion of revisionist historians who, arguing against traditional Whig interpretations of James, describe the new king as far less amenable towards those wealthy suitors who sought further to line their pockets at the expense of the nation. As Peter R. Roberts notes, two such petitioners, Richard Fiennes (Lord Say and Sele) and the ex-Irish campaigner Francis Clayton, separately pleaded to the king for respective monopolies to tax playgoers and performances at the public playhouses.[93] These audacious ploys were, as Roberts suggests, 'either abandoned in the face of insuperable obstacles or rejected by the king as unacceptable'.[94] If categorically refused by James, the king's response could easily engender disgruntled private correspondence and journal entries from the snubbed pair.

---

[88]   Wilbraham, *Journal*, p. 59. See also Robert Ashton (ed.), *James I by his Contemporaries* (London, 1969), p. 7.

[89]   A.F. Pollard, 'Wilson, Sir Thomas (d. 1629)', rev. Sean Kelsey, *ODNB* (2004) <http://www.oxforddnb.com/index/101029690/Thomas-Wilson> [accessed 6 May 2011]; F.J. Fisher (ed.), *'The State of England, Anno Dom. 1600' by Sir Thomas Wilson* (London, 1936).

[90]   Keith M. Brown, 'The Scottish Aristocracy, Anglicization and the Court, 1603–38', *HJ*, 36 (1993): 543–76 (pp. 548–9).

[91]   Wilbraham, *Journal*, p. xii.

[92]   Ibid., pp. 56–7.

[93]   Peter R. Roberts, 'The Business of Playing and the Patronage of Players at the Jacobean Courts', in Houlbrooke (ed.), *Writings*, pp. 81–105.

[94]   Ibid., p. 102.

Whatever our own response to the theatrical implications of such a brash attempt to tax playgoers and performances, this episode provides further proof that the supposedly recognizable political 'style' of James's rule, as one of unlimited patronage and favouritism, can be countered by revisionist historical study. Likewise, contemporary responses to James's sixteenth-century writings suggest confused and inconsistent opinions about the king's perceived regime 'style'. Available in print prior to James's arrival in London, political texts like *Basilikon Doron* and *The True Lawe* might offer a flavour of his technique of power; their diverse and contradictory messages ensured that they could never be read as blueprints for the Jacobean 'style' of government.[95] Similarly, comments about James's lack of political interest and dedication deserve to be interrogated. On 26 December 1604, the date of *Measure for Measure*'s court performance, no fewer than twenty-one documents were signed by James, a workload matching previous and subsequent working days, and one which counters his reputation as a lax and disinterested ruler.[96] If the 'style' of James's reign could, as early as 1604, not be pinpointed by contemporary complainants, it seems particularly unlikely that a Globe playwright should develop such a close relationship with government and with his royal patron as to parody, satirize or comment on its/his efficacy or direction.[97]

Our continued acceptance of 'Duke as James' parallelism, and belief in the supposed subversion of a recognizable Jacobean 'style' of governance, clearly relies on perspectives about James's government that suited the bias of Whig historians. Literary critics promoting a 'Jacobean style' for *Measure for Measure* unwittingly accept this partisan appraisal of James. As Diana Newton argues, it is 'only by taking a holistic view of James's early years, and considering all the aspects of his first years in England simultaneously, that [we can] get closer to an understanding of his English reign'.[98] A 'holistic view' permits James to emerge as 'energetic, vigorous, intelligent and flexible', managing his new kingdom 'shrewdly, effectively, and even innovatively'.[99] Newton's comments would have been inconceivable to a Whig historian. They likewise appear inconceivable to Shakespeare commentators wishing to detect an anxiety-inducing, 'divine right' principle in the Jacobean 'style' of *Measure for Measure*'s Duke. The Whig interpretation of James's rule needs to be expunged from critical appraisal of

---

[95]   Jenny Wormald, 'James VI and I (1566–1625)', *ODNB* (2004) <http://www. oxforddnb.com/index/101014592/James> [accessed 6 May 2011].

[96]   *Calendar of State Papers Domestic: James I, 1603–1610* (1857): 164–82, ed. Mary Ann Everett Green, *British History Online* <http://www.british-history.ac.uk/report.aspx?compid=14995> [accessed 6 May 2011].

[97]   Daniel Fischlin and Mark Fortier (eds), *Royal Subjects: Essays on the Writings of James VI and I* (Detroit, 2002), pp. 22–3.

[98]   Diana Newton, *The Making of the Jacobean Regime* (Woodbridge, 2005), pp. 141–6 (p. 146).

[99]   Ibid., p. 146.

Measure for Measure in order for the Duke's disguised adventure to be appreciated in its true Jacobean context.

Since Whig historiography appears to hold the key to the 'Duke as James' theory and its application to *Measure for Measure*, then might this approach also offer an alternative, earlier source for Tyrwhitt's 1766 observation, generally regarded as the first to equate Shakespeare's Duke with James? In fact, that early and significant Whig historian, John Oldmixon, writing thirty-six years before Tyrwhitt's discussion of *Measure for Measure*, uses Shakespearean language to analyse the king's personality. The likelihood that Oldmixon, an impassioned champion of Shakespeare, was aware of *Measure for Measure* might account for his conscious or unconscious allusion to this drama in his own Whiggish, anti-James polemic.

Oldmixon and Shakespeare's 'True Sublimity'

As noted, Oldmixon's 1730 *History of England* represents a Whig history that took issue with pro-Stuart 'Tory' historiographers like Clarendon and Echard. Repeating the familiar soubriquet of the new or second 'Solomon' to describe James's learning, knowledge and wisdom, Clarendon and Echard defended the king's memory.[100] For Oldmixon, this 'glorious Title of second *Solomon*' proffered a falsehood that affronted his Whig sensibilities.[101] Oldmixon's intention, what he deems 'My Design', was 'to show' not James's inherent wisdom and learning, but 'how he and his Posterity ... made this once flourishing and glorious Kingdom, a Scene of Misery and Disgrace'.[102] With his 'Design' firmly established, Oldmixon describes James's accession to the English throne with imagery more befitting a fallen angel than a philosopher king:

> Such a Beginning of a Reign promis'd very little Good in the Course of it, but so much Care was taken to gild the Appearance that the Darkness had not its full Effect on the Minds of the people. (*History*, 17)

Oldmixon significantly comments not on negative receptions of the king by his new nation, but on the way his satanic 'Darkness' was carefully 'gilded', shielding his true evil intent from his adoring subjects' 'Minds'.

Oldmixon's crusading 'Design', which shows the devastation James supposedly wreaked on his unfortunate new kingdom, also develops the concept of a suspicious and reclusive monarch, one reflecting those aspects of the Duke's behaviour in *Measure for Measure* that drew Tyrwhitt's attention. Having made

---

[100] Clarendon, *History of the Rebellion*, vol. 1, p. 9; Echard, *History of England*, vol. 1, p. 979. See James Doelman, *King James I and the Religious Culture of England* (Woodbridge, 2000), pp. 76–9.

[101] Oldmixon, *History*, p. 10.

[102] Ibid., p. 11.

a particularly scathing condemnation of James's appearance as 'far from being handsome', Oldmixon describes how 'The King had been almost ten Months in *England*, but had not been seen much abroad':[103]

> He naturally did not love to be look'd at, for, as has been said, he was not very handsome, and had no Relish of the Formalities of State. Some attribute it not to the Disagreeableness of his Person, but to the Shyness of his Temper, and some to his Timorousness, there being more Danger in a Crowd than in a few attendants. (*History*, 21)

Oldmixon's analysis of James's attitude to the 'Formalities of State' echoes the Duke's excuse for travelling 'priuily away', because he does not 'rellish well' the 'lowd applause' of his people. Disagreeable to behold, shy, timorous and threatened with danger by the 'Crowd', James bears a demeanour that, according to Oldmixon, accords with a monarch whose outward 'Appearance' 'gild[s]' the true 'Darkness' beneath. It also demonstrates Oldmixon's conscious or unconscious reliance on imagery derived from passages in *Measure for Measure*.

James's purported timorousness and irascibility further appears a few lines later, when Oldmixon discusses the king's first procession through the City of London after the plague that greeted his arrival a year earlier:

> Having summon'd a Parliament to meet the 19th of *March* [1604], he went on the 15th with his Queen and the Prince to the *Tower*, riding through the City amidst the continu'd Acclamations of the Multitude, which did not affect him as they affected his Predecessor Queen *Elizabeth*. Whether it was that the Noise disturb'd him, or that he did not think them real, 'tis most certain, when the People have been impatient of Access to him, he has often had them dispers'd with Force, and sometimes with Curses. (*History*, 21–2)

This public pageant, complete with ornate triumphal arches designed and erected by Stephen Harrison and with speeches supplied by Thomas Dekker, Ben Jonson and Thomas Middleton, had been delayed until it was deemed safe for the royal family to emerge from plague quarantine in the Tower of London.[104] Again, following the descriptions of James by Weldon and Osborne, and perhaps influenced by recently discovered commentary by D'Ewes (who could not have been an eye-witness since he was a two-year-old toddler in 1604), Oldmixon thus adds to the image of James that is uncannily reminiscent of Shakespeare's Duke.

If Oldmixon was indeed comparing Shakespeare's Duke and the real King James, what in this Whig historian's background might account for this? Significant, here, is Oldmixon's appreciation of Shakespeare in his 1728 literary

---

[103] Ibid., pp. 10 & 21.

[104] Stephen Harrison, *The Arches of Triumph* (London, 1604); Thomas Dekker, *The Magnificent Entertainment* (London, 1604); Ben Jonson, *Part of the Entertainment, through the Cittie of London, Given to James I. 1604* (London, 1604).

study, *An Essay on Criticism*, published two years before his *History of England*.[105] In *An Essay on Criticism*, Oldmixon attacks not only Alexander Pope, but also the 'Royal Historiographers' Clarendon and Echard.[106] His most intense derision, however, is reserved for John Dryden, who (along with Davenant, Colley Cibber and Nahum Tate) wrote Restoration adaptations of Shakespearean dramas, 'in Imitation of *Shakespeare's* Stile'.[107] Oldmixon scorns Dryden's observation 'that *Shakespear* himself did not distinguish *the blown puffy Stile from true Sublimity*', although he accepts Dryden's negative description of France's poetic heritage, agreeing that the 'Latter is incontestable': 'They [the French] have nothing of *Epick* Poetry so good as our King *Arthur*; neither are their *Corneille* and *Racine* a Match for our *Shakespear* and *Otway*'.[108] According to Oldmixon, Shakespeare was unequivocally the nation's supreme dramatist:

> Our *Shakespear* shone on the Stage, with all the Qualities of a Dramatick Poet, and *Diction* in particular, when the ... *French* Stage was Barbarous. His Style has its Beauties now, and is newer than many who have since Writ, and for a while with Reputation. (*Essay*, 29)

For Oldmixon, Shakespeare's dramatic skill was as commendable as James's personality was despicable. Notably, Oldmixon himself was, at the turn of the eighteenth century, an aspiring though less than successful playwright, with several plays spanning a variety of formal genres performed professionally on the London stage.[109] He thus evinced far more than a passing interest in drama. Inevitably, therefore, Oldmixon must have known *Measure for Measure* when composing his *History* in 1730 and describing James's lack of 'Relish of the Formalities of State', particularly since he was writing in the immediate aftermath of renewed interest in the play's unadapted form.[110] Whether from seventeenth-century editions of Shakespeare, or from reprinted examples of individual Shakespeare plays offered by London's booksellers, Oldmixon would undoubtedly have had access to *Measure for Measure*.[111]

Regardless of whether Oldmixon was consciously employing imagery derived from *Measure for Measure*, or was adopting Shakespeare's language in the belief

---

[105] John Oldmixon, *An Essay On Criticism* (London, 1728).

[106] Ibid., p. 55.

[107] John Dryden, *All for Love* (London, 1678), title-page.

[108] Oldmixon, *Essay*, pp. 45 & 54; Dryden, *Essay of Dramatick Poesie* (London, 1668).

[109] See John Oldmixon, *Amintas. A Pastoral* (London, 1698); *The Grove, or Love's Paradice. An Opera* (London, 1700); *The Governour of Cyprus: A Tragedy* (London, 1703).

[110] Robert D. Hume, 'Before the Bard: "Shakespeare" in Early Eighteenth-Century London', *ELH,* 64 (1997): 41–75 (p. 60).

[111] See Thomas Astley, *Books Printed For and Sold By Thomas Astley* (London, 1727), whose catalogue lists *Measure* in a single playtext edition (p. 8).

that his favourite playwright was sending a coded message about his kingly patron, Oldmixon's description of James bears sufficient similarity to the dialogue isolated by Tyrwhitt over thirty years later to suggest a source for the later writer's observation. Tyrwhitt's Whiggish and Jamesian interpretation of *Measure for Measure* might represent not only his own reading of the play, but also his response to an idea first suggested by the equally Whiggish commentary of Oldmixon, whose adulation for Shakespeare has largely gone unnoticed. More famous as a Whig historiographer than as a failed playwright and literary commentator, Oldmixon shields Shakespeare from any Whiggish suspicion that his plays condoned his despised kingly patron. Like Macaulay's later Whig historiography, which fuelled Charles Knight's support for Steevens, Malone and Chalmers, Oldmixon's Whig historiography provides similar fuel for Tyrwhitt's partisan criticism.

Revisionist history's reappraisal of James's early political career in England is only now entering criticism of *Measure for Measure*.[112] This belated acknowledgement of James's political skill probably emanates from the strength of new historicist considerations of *Measure for Measure* from the mid-1980s onwards. These overlooked the Whiggish tendencies of the old-fashioned sources that underpinned new historicism's purportedly radical revisioning. Predicated on Oldmixon, and on other Whig historiographers, anti-James attitudes inherent in new historicist studies of anxiety, hegemony and subversion in *Measure for Measure* unwittingly renew the conventional partisan pursuits of such biased historiography. Only through the release of *Measure for Measure* from its falsely imposed Whiggish heritage can the play's complex engagement with the social and theatrical culture of its time truly emerge.

The Generic Complexity of *Measure for Measure*

Despite the problematic origins of both Whig and new historicist political approaches to the play, *Measure for Measure*'s opening lines do provide a tantalizing statement about the nature of government and legitimate rule:

> DUKE: Of Gouernment, the properties to vn-fold
> Would seeme in me t' affect speech & discourse,
> Since I am put to know, that your owne Science
> Exceedes (in that) the lists of all aduice
> My strength can giue you. (F *Measure*, TLN.6–10; 1.1.3–7)

Although what follows appears initially to be an exposition of the true function 'Of Gouernment', the Duke's self-deprecating speech actually develops into a flattering endorsement of Escalus's skill in better understanding the 'properties' of good rule. The Duke, fearful that any attempt personally to 'vnfold' these

---

[112] Andrew Hadfield, *Shakespeare and Renaissance Politics* (London, 2004), pp. 182–200; Hadfield, *Shakespeare and Republicanism* (Cambridge, 2005), pp. 205–206.

'properties' might be misconstrued as unwarranted affectation rather than eloquent expressiveness, cautiously admits being 'put to know' (implying compulsion rather than self-discovery) the extent of Escalus's 'Science'. Indeed, Escalus's knowledgeable 'Science' far exceeds the 'lists' (a possible pun on state catalogue or roll) of prudent 'aduice' that the Duke's 'strength' can offer. Rife with potential meaning, the Duke's 'strength' evokes not only his intellectual superiority, but also his physical, moral, regal or legal attributes, as well as his military prowess. Escalus's own 'strength', however, outweighs even that of his duke.

These opening lines confirm Escalus's superior intellect and his practical ability to act as ruler in the Duke's absence. They also predispose the audience to a political focus for this apparently serious, potentially tragic play. Indeed, Escalus's name, which sounds like the 'scales of justice' (though actually is derived from the Latin *scala* or 'ladder'), evokes Shakespearean tragedy by recalling the just '*Prince* Eskales' of Verona, whose judgement brings order to the feuding Capulets and Montagues (Q2 *Romeo and Juliet*, 1.1.88.0.SD).[113] Escalus's own superior skill in the 'Science' of good 'Gouernment' suggests a generic potential, whereby *Measure for Measure* might likewise engage with the romantic mode and tragic form. The overwhelming impression given an audience hearing the Duke's effusive praise is that all is safe in Escalus's more than worthy hands. This optimistic tenor vanishes when the 'able' Escalus, still clutching his 'commission', is demoted to 'secondary' to Angelo, the deputized ruler of Vienna (F *Measure*, TLN.52; 1.1.46–7).

This opening dialogue has received much conjectural analysis, especially by scholars focusing on the play's political message. Deeming it presented in a 'manner that characterizes [the play's] proceedings throughout', Goldberg argues that the Duke's 'disquisition on the nature of rule' foreshadows the 'final unsettling refigurations' of the play's dénouement.[114] Goldberg also claims that the Duke's opening remarks 'provide a mirror for the cultural situation of the play', as well as introduce its 'central concerns', most important of which is the Duke's disguise and its analogous representation of the 'combination of absence and presence through which James claimed authority'.[115] For Goldberg, the Duke's 'presence-in-absence' most 'genuinely seems to reflect James's government', with the combining of Angelo and Escalus's power becoming a conscious attempt to rule through division.[116] Angelo's confusion when deputized so unexpectedly is only matched, so Goldberg maintains, by a similar confusion among the audience/ reader, who 'cannot know how far Angelo represents the Duke', nor 'why the Duke has chosen Angelo, or even if he knows why':

---

[113] Q2 *Romeo and Juliet*, STC 22323. Line numbers from W.W. Greg, *Romeo and Juliet, Second Quarto, 1599*, SQF, 6 (London, 1949). 'Escalus' is also named as a non-speaking character who accompanies Bertram and Paroles as they enter by the walls of Florence in *All's Well* (3.5.75).

[114] Goldberg, *James*, pp. 233 & 235.

[115] Ibid., p. 235.

[116] Ibid., p. 235.

What we can know is that the exercise of sovereign power and dramatic power
as the play opens depends upon the enactment of substitutions whose analogical
force remains mysterious. (Goldberg, 233–4)

A similar attitude to the 'mysterious' force of *Measure for Measure*'s 'enactment
of substitutions' appears in Andrew Hadfield's analyses of the 'republican' nature
of Shakespeare's plays.[117] For Hadfield, this opening speech offers a dramatic
admission that the Duke has overlooked his officers' inability to control vice,
either in others or in themselves. As such, it introduces a dominant trope in
Measure for Measure of a nation whose laws are ineffectively administered, and
whose governor absents himself from visible rule. This reading offers Shakespeare
in active engagement with a 'republican tradition' of political discourse.[118] This
'republican tradition' is not presented, however, as a specifically Shakespearean
invention. Rather, as Hadfield argues, it emerges in English literary and dramatic
works throughout the sixteenth and early seventeenth centuries.[119] Particularly
significant for a non-occasionalist reading of *Measure for Measure* is Hadfield's
contention that this play engaged with republicanism, 'after the republican
moment'.[120] Shakespeare's intention was thus to create an analogous Vienna/
London, whose 'problematic autocracy' represents the human fallibility and
weakness of a permanently divided society.[121] For Hadfield, *Measure for Measure*
is an 'interrogative' and 'counselling' play that 'questions the aims and ideals
of the new dynasty', without overtly confronting or alienating Shakespeare's
important new patron.[122]

Measure for Measure sits uncomfortably, however, in the chronology of
Shakespeare's so-called 'republican' repertoire: earlier works such as *Titus
Andronicus* (*c.* 1589, published 1594), *The Rape of Lucrece* (1594), or *Julius
Caesar* (*c.* 1599) more readily engage with the 'republican moment' towards the
end of Elizabeth's reign. The accession of James removed the political immediacy
of active debate, and the 'republican moment' (and thus the opportunity for
significant change) was lost. In consequence, so Hadfield argues, the play represents
an expression of 'fear' that the 'change of ruler and dynasty will, in fact, bring no
change at all': 'Instead of the transformation that had been hoped for – and, of
course, feared – there would simply be more of the same'.[123] Such a reading is not
intended to suggest Shakespeare's prescience of the civil conflict and regicide that
befell the House of Stuart several decades later. Still, it suggests a concern that
Measure for Measure fails to fit neatly into its confining occasionalist designation.

---

[117] Hadfield, *Politics*, pp. 182–200; Hadfield, *Republicanism*, pp. 205–14.

[118] Hadfield, *Republicanism*, pp. 52–3.

[119] Hadfield, *Politics*, p. 191.

[120] Hadfield, *Republicanism*, pp. 205–29.

[121] Ibid., p. 214.

[122] Hadfield, *Politics*, p. 199.

[123] Ibid., p. 200.

This continued reliance on occasionalist readings not only fuels belief in the apparent decadence of James's personality and regime, it also spuriously confirms a long-term decline in English drama.[124] Although Hadfield stresses his own revisionist credentials by acknowledging James's value as an English monarch, his consideration of the opening dialogue of *Measure for Measure* relies on Whiggish (mis)readings of the play. It becomes problematic, for Hadfield, to square the opening remarks of the Duke with a wider interest in republicanism, but in a strictly Jacobean context. By contrast, when read neither as political commentary, nor as republicanism 'after the republican moment', the Duke's discussion with Escalus acquires an alternative tragic generic implication. Indeed, only following the approximate mid-point of the play, when the disguised Duke steps in to 'Vouchsafe a word' with the distressed Isabella (F *Measure*, TLN.1375) and the blank verse is replaced by less formal prose, does the audience's generic expectation shift away from tragedy to the new form of tragicomedy. *Measure for Measure* thus follows upon Marston's formal experiments with Italianate tragicomedy in QA/B *Malcontent*, while acknowledging the city-comedic immediacy of Webster's QC additions.

A possible reason for the apparent generic instability of *Measure for Measure* might be the coincident appearance of Shakespeare's disguised ruler drama alongside QC *Malcontent* in the same 1604–1605 Globe season. Both plays were likely also performed by the same actors. What better way to promote the generic innovativeness of the King's Men than to include two complementary 'disguised rulers' in the same repertory? As *Measure for Measure* opens, the subtle political potential for tragedy provides a fitting setting for the subsequent hubris and moral decline – the self-absorbed sexual deviancy – of Angelo's insatiable lust for a young novitiate. Only after the Duke interposes between the distraught and resolute Isabella and her death-fearing brother does the tragicomic potential of the play present itself. Although *Measure for Measure* largely conforms to Guarini's precept that 'tragicomedy is not made up of two entire plots, one of which is a perfect tragedy and the other a perfect comedy, connected in such a way that they can be disjoined without doing injury to either', its divided structure comes uncomfortably close to a tragic/comic duality.[125] Guarini's warning that tragicomedy is not 'a tragic story vitiated with the lowliness of comedy or a comic fable contaminated with the deaths of tragedy' appears, by Shakespeare, to go unheeded. Jean E. Howard notes this possibility when she suggests that Shakespeare subverts the generic structure of tragicomedy at the very moment that English drama was developing its tentative rules of expression.[126] Still, *Measure*

---

[124]   See James Knowles, '"Tied / To Rules of Flattery?": Court Drama and the Masque', in Michael Hattaway (ed.), *A Companion to English Renaissance Literature and Culture* (Oxford, 2000), pp. 525–44 (pp. 535–36).

[125]   Guarini, 'Compendium', p. 507.

[126]   Ibid., p. 507; Howard, 'Difficulties of Closure', in Braunmuller and Bulman (eds), *Shakespeare to Sheridan*, pp. 113–28.

for Measure appears to be Shakespeare's attempt to conform to Guarini's principle of creating 'from the two [tragedy and comedy] a third thing that will be perfect of its kind and may take from the others the parts that with most verisimilitude can stand together'.[127]

Regardless of whether Shakespeare actually constructs a play that is 'perfect of its kind', or whether he subverts Guarini's precepts as a radical exercise in generic experimentation, *Measure for Measure* employs narrative twists of plot that are recognizably tragicomic. When read as conscious generic subversion, the Duke's opening speech, his effusive support for his elderly advisor, and his subsequent deputizing of a less worthy substitute, all suggest Shakespeare's skilful manipulation of his audience. Whether received by a 'democratic' audience at the Globe or an elite audience at court, *Measure for Measure* provides both entertainment and intellectual flattery to all who appreciate the play's formal subversion.

Measure for Measure was not the only Jacobean play, however, to adopt and adapt the age-old disguised ruler for narrative effect. Two near contemporaries to *Measure for Measure*, traditionally considered less anxiety-producing disguised ruler dramas, are performed by the children's companies in and around the St Paul's Cathedral district of the City. One is written by Thomas Middleton, the other, once again, by Marston. Inevitably, Middleton's *The Phoenix* and Marston's *The Fawn* also remain haunted by 'King James Version' readings of their disguised ruler adventures. With the Whiggish heritage of Jamesian analogy in mind, it is important to interrogate these generically conservative, socially topical evocations of London's court and legal systems, to highlight the inherent medievalism that conventional historicist critical responses often ignore.

---

[127] Guarini, *Compendium*, p. 507; Foster, *Tragicomedy*, p. 55.

Chapter 4
The Phoenix and *The Fawn*:
Law, Morality and the
Medievalism of Disguise

The second act of the censored manuscript, *The Second Maiden's Tragedy* (1611), renamed *The Lady's Tragedy* in the *Oxford Middleton*, presents Helvetius, father of the long-suffering Lady, trying to convince his daughter to marry the nation's Tyrant.[1] Unsuccessful in this, he then recommends she become the Tyrant's mistress instead. Helvetius's shameful suggestion is overheard by the Lady's true love, the usurped king Govianus, who discharges his pistol to fright the conniving old man. Reeling from his near-death encounter, Helvetius acknowledges the unsavouriness of his proposition:

> HELVETIUS: This was well searcht indeed and wthout favouringe
> blessing reward thee, such a wound as myne
> did need a pittiles surgion. (*Lady's Tragedy*, TLN.793–5; 2.1.113–15)

Helvetius's dialogue echoes Altofronto/Malevole's response to the usurping and usurped Duke Pietro, when, like 'a pittifull surgeon', he makes 'a dangerous sore' to search the 'deepe' and 'keene' wound of Pietro's plight (QA/B *Malcontent*, G2ʳ; 4.5.63–5). For the Lady's father, the pitiless precision of Govianus's surgical procedure exposes the metaphorical 'wound' of his own immoral suggestion. Govianus receives Helvetius's 'blessing' for his medical intervention, and for his faithfulness.

In this murder-fuelled tragedy, attributed to Thomas Middleton and written for the King's Men perhaps seven years after they performed QC *Malcontent*, not only does Helvetius's response recall Marston's earlier medical analogy, but the play itself also obliquely mirrors its disguised ruler forebear. Like Altofronto, Govianus is a usurped king, forced into imprisoned exile by the wicked Tyrant, an immoral character reminiscent of Mendoza. Also like Altofronto, Govianus returns in disguise to avenge his loss of power, as well as the imprisonment and attempted seduction of his beloved. Unlike Altofronto, who releases his wife from incarceration, Govianus cannot prevent his Lady's prison-bound suicide. This tragic event triggers the poisoning revenge plot. Disguised as an artist, Govianus is charged with painting the stolen corpse of the Lady to satisfy the necrophiliac desire of the Tyrant. Instead of fulfilling the Tyrant's sick fantasy, the disguised

---

[1]   W.W. Greg (ed.), *The Second Maiden's Tragedy 1611* (Oxford, 1909). Line numbers from Julia Briggs (ed.), *The Lady's Tragedy*, in *Oxford Middleton*, pp. 833–906.

Govianus murders the usurper by poisoning the paint he lovingly applies to the Lady's dead body. The Tyrant kisses the painted corpse and Govianus's revenge is complete. Although generically dissimilar to *The Malcontent*'s tragicomedy, *The Second Maiden's* (*Lady's*) *Tragedy* parallels Marston's disguised ruler narrative, its dark and disturbingly tragic ending ameliorated by Govianus's welcome return to power.

Whether the playwright (most likely Middleton) was consciously alluding to *The Malcontent*, was influenced by Guarini's *Il pastor fido*, or was responding to other literary medical imagery, is unknowable. Regardless, this 1611 tragedy redeploys the disguised ruler, thereby potentially undermining critical claims that Middleton only included the motif in his first solo drama, *The Phoenix* (published 1607), written for the Children of Paul's sometime near the beginning of James's reign.[2] The inherent occasionalism of such an early Jacobean dating often leads, so its editors Lawrence Danson and Ivo Kamps argue, to an unhelpful comparison between *The Phoenix* and *Measure for Measure*.[3] *The Phoenix* is thus reduced to a reflexive response to *The Malcontent* or the experimental model for Marston's and/or Shakespeare's 'Jacobean' disguised rulers. It also perpetuates the notion that Middleton wrote his play in the wake of the Stuart accession. In response to this associative dating, Albert H. Tricomi describes *The Phoenix*'s anti-court (as opposed to anti-Jamesian) satire as an example of the play's 'militancy', whereby it avoids direct condemnation of James, while attacking the excesses of his entourage.[4] Militancy indeed, although for Tricomi such militancy manifests itself as Middleton's failure to engage in a battle fought by other disguised ruler playwrights against the person of the king.

An occasionalist reading of *The Phoenix*'s 'militancy' colours the editorial commentary of Danson and Kamps, who conclude that this play represents Middleton's 'angry denunciation and political optimism' at the arrival of James.[5] Their argument relies on a strictly Jacobean chronology for the play, written with the 'newly installed reform-minded monarch' in mind.[6] Such specificity equates *The Phoenix*'s reforming narrative with Jamesian divine-right rule. Peppered with advice-book aphorisms akin to sixteenth century humanist 'mirrors for princes' discourse, *The Phoenix* offers its reforming didactic within a decidedly medieval and Tudor morality tradition.[7] Unfortunately, these elements add to the apparent hegemonic conservatism of its disguised ruler narrative. Middleton's role as optimistic hegemonist thus continues to trouble modern commentators, especially

---

[2]   Scene and line numbers from Lawrence Danson and Ivo Kamps (eds), *The Phoenix*, in *Oxford Middleton*, pp. 91–127.

[3]   Ibid., p. 91.

[4]   Tricomi, *Anticourt*, p. 16.

[5]   Danson and Kamps, *Oxford Middleton*, p. 94.

[6]   Ibid., p. 93.

[7]   See Quentin Skinner, *The Foundations of Modern Political Thought* (2 vols, Cambridge, 1978), vol. 1, pp. 118–28.

those seeking to identify the Stuart king with *The Phoenix*'s title and/or principal protagonist.[8]

The spectre of King James yet again explains why critics like Danson and Kamps describe the 'angry denunciation and political optimism' of *The Phoenix*, thus guaranteeing the play's anomalous situation in the disguised ruler canon.[9] As this study of 'Duke as James' parallelism in *Measure for Measure* shows, however, such Whig-inspired 'Phoenix as James' analogy hunting should be approached cautiously. Reading *The Phoenix* in an occasionalist timeframe elides its true 'militancy'. If *The Phoenix* is indeed Middleton's 'first solo effort as a dramatist' (as its Oxford editors presume), and if it does predate QA/B *Malcontent*, then its militant optimism is far easier to explain.[10] As the playwright of an Elizabethan rather than Jacobean play, Middleton could be excused for not introducing either anxiety or an experimental new form into his disguised ruler drama, since Marston's tragicomic paradigm had yet be written and James had yet to accede to the throne. Likewise, if *The Phoenix* was written in response to Marston's QA/B *Malcontent*, anxiety would similarly be absent because the Anglicized topicality of Webster had yet to alter Marston's tragicomedy into its subversive QC form. Finally, if the play postdates QC *Malcontent*, this might explain the city-comedic focus of its reforming narrative. Since critics are adamant that *The Phoenix* predates *Measure for Measure*, the loss of an anti-Jamesian Whig agenda for Shakespeare's play effectively negates similar consideration of *The Phoenix* as a non-subversive text.[11] Regardless, therefore, of whether *The Phoenix* predates or postdates QA/B or QC *Malcontent*, Middleton's true innovation remains his decision to combine medieval morality didacticism and city comedy topicality in an overtly Italianate disguised ruler play. This conflation elevates Middleton's 'first solo effort' into a unique and generically individual example of disguised ruler drama, while offering an alternative model for Marston's later disguised ruler sequel, *The Fawn*.

The Phoenix as Proto-City Comedy

The *Stationers' Register* entry for 9 May 1607 describes 'A Booke called The Phenix'.[12] The play itself was published the same year, its title-page announcing that it 'hath beene sundry times Acted by the *Children of Paules*, *And presented before his* Maiestie'.[13] As with *The Second Maiden's* (*Lady's*) *Tragedy*, Middleton's name does not appear in the entry, or on the 1607 or 1630 quarto editions. It was not

---

[8]   See Danson and Kamps, *Oxford Middleton*, p. 93.

[9]   Ibid., p. 94.

[10]   Ibid., p. 91.

[11]   Bullough, *Sources*, vol. 2, p. 411; Pendleton, 'Disguised' p. 83; J. Bradbury Brooks (ed.), *The Phoenix* (New York, 1980), p. 70.

[12]   Arber 3, p. 348.

[13]   Thomas Middleton, *The Phoenix* (London, 1607).

until 1661 that the publisher Francis Kirkman first ascribed *The Phoenix* to 'Tho. Middleton' in his catalogue of English plays.[14] Since Kirkman, few have doubted Middleton's authorship.[15] The 1607 title-page mention of '*his* M*aiestie*' prompted E.K. Chambers to describe the 'only available' date for a court performance (based on a Chamber Accounts entry for an unknown Paul's play) as 20 February 1604, a feasible though unprovable supposition.[16] The play's traditional dating to *c.* 1603–1604 is based, therefore, on Chambers's suggestion, and on the presumption that Middleton was either directly responding to, or responsible for, the supposed 'rash' of disguised ruler plays that accompanied James's accession.[17] As we have seen, however, the uncertain chronology of QA/B *Malcontent* ensures that *The Phoenix* cannot even be considered unequivocally Jacobean; it could first have been acted in the small private Paul's playhouse during the closing years of Elizabeth's reign.

We will probably never know whether *The Phoenix* either represents Middleton's response to Marston's success at Blackfriars, or if it aroused Marston's and/or Shakespeare's professional interests attracting responses from them.[18] It is likewise impossible to judge how much *The Phoenix*, like *The Malcontent*, might have changed between earliest performance and eventual 1607 publication, although anomalous plotlines suggest that the published play had altered over time. For example, the corrupt courtiers Lussurioso and Infesto are accused in its final scene of 'ryotouslye' gambling their wealth and 'adulterously' offering married ladies of court for sexual gain (*Phoenix*, I3ʳ; 15.90–100). These evocative plotlines appear nowhere else in the text. Condemned quite specifically by the Prince/Phoenix, who claims he 'was both hyr'd and led' into colluding with their nefarious activities (*Phoenix*, I3ʳ; 15.104), Lussurioso and Infesto seem part of some missing narrative, whose absence suggests adaptation in the years preceding *The Phoenix*'s quarto appearance. As the censored manuscript of *The Second Maiden's* (*Lady's*) *Tragedy* confirms, such alteration might be in response to external interference, while they might simply stem from Middleton's inexperience as a dramatist.

Even though there are minor inconsistencies in the plotlines of incidental characters, the surviving narrative of *The Phoenix* follows a consistent and predictable 'episodic' flow, from ironic first-hand experience of vice and malice, to a morality dénouement of retribution, forgiveness and ducal abdication in favour of a worthy successor.[19] The play's principal protagonist is the Prince, referred to in his speech-prefixes as 'Phoenix', son to the ageing Duke of Ferrara. Mindful of the problems caused by his lenient rule (an obvious plot similarity with *Measure for Measure*), the Duke sends his son abroad to learn the art of good governance. Publicly, the Prince accepts his father's commission and announces his desire to

[14]   W.W. Greg, *A Bibliography of English Printed Drama to the Restoration* (4 vols, London, 1939–59), vol. 3 (1957), pp. 1338–52.

[15]   Brooks, *Phoenix*, pp. 25–63.

[16]   Chambers, *ES* 3, p. 439; *ES* 4, p. 169.

[17]   Tennenhouse, *Power*, p. 154; Tricomi, *Anticourt*, pp. 13–14.

[18]   Pendleton, 'Disguised', p. 86.

[19]   Danson and Kamps, *Oxford Middleton*, p. 93.

journey in foreign lands in disguise. Privately, he admits to his servant/companion
Fidelio that he will remain in Ferrara to shield his ageing father from unknown
dangers. The Prince rightly distrusts the Machiavellian courtier, lord Proditor,
who is plotting the old Duke's death in the Prince's absence. In his disguise, the
Prince/Phoenix gains first-hand knowledge of Proditor's corruption. Ferrara's
corrupt legal system is also exposed, in particular the dishonesty of Justice Falso,
and his co-conspirator, the lawyer Tangle. When the Prince/Phoenix eventually
returns to his father's court (hired by the unsuspecting Proditor to assassinate the
Duke), he reveals his true identity. Vice is exposed and Proditor is banished. More
importantly, the scene focuses on the theatrical 'cure' of the law-mad Tangle, with
whom most of the play's legalistic humour resides. As a play that mercilessly
satirizes the legal profession – suggesting either a conscious attempt to appeal
to law students and qualified professionals from the Inns of Court, or as comic
revenge for fifteen years' legal wrangling over Middleton's family inheritance –
The Phoenix is as topically disparaging of lawyers and magistrates as it is of those
stock Italian court figures whose libidinous and fawning behaviour threatens the
security of the Ferraran state.[20]

The corrupt Italian court is central to *The Phoenix*'s representation of vice
and intrigue. Like the augmented QC *Malcontent*, however, *The Phoenix* uses
its Italian locus to make thinly-veiled satirical swipes at London citizenry and
court aristocracy. An English legal system that exploits rather than represents
its less educated, more gullible clients is likewise exposed. It is not surprising,
therefore, that Brian Gibbons classed *The Phoenix* as an 'exemplary' early
Jacobean city comedy, adapted from coney-catching pamphlets and a European
commedia dell'arte convention, as well as sixteenth-century Estates Morality and
a Jonsonian 'humours' model.[21] Accordingly, so Gibbons argues, *The Phoenix*
'demands to be placed first' in the Jacobean city comedy canon, since it shows
the 'clearest evidence of imitation of early Jonson and Marston'.[22] Whether, as
Michael Shapiro argues, *The Phoenix* represents a 'cross' between city comedy
and 'archaic semi-allegorical' Elizabethan court plays, or, in Martin Wiggins's
words, a 'curious combination of city comedy and political melodrama',
Middleton's play remains decidedly London-centric in its Italianate pretensions.[23]
It might likewise be an 'exemplary' proto-city comedy as Gibbons suggests, but
it certainly is not tragicomic. This immediately distances *The Phoenix* from its
disguised ruler cousins, *Malcontent* and *Measure for Measure*. It also points to a
far earlier composition date than traditional Jamesian analogy might suggest. Even
so, the 'Phoenix as James' fallacy continues to haunt critical studies of the play,
thereby ignoring the possibility of equally aristocratic, though less regal recipients
for its analogous flattery.

---

[20]   Gary Taylor, 'Thomas Middleton: Live and Afterlives', *Oxford Middleton*, pp. 25–
58 (p. 31).

[21]   Gibbons, *City Comedy*, p. 84.

[22]   Ibid., p. 78.

[23]   Shapiro, *Revels*, p. 54; Wiggins, *Shakespeare*, p. 107.

The 'Phoenix as James' Fallacy

The 'exemplary' generic status of *The Phoenix* and uncertainty over its dating make it impossible to confirm any specific recipient/s for Middleton's advice-laden narrative. Nonetheless, a commonplace critical assumption (that mirrors similar 'Duke as James' analysis of *Measure for Measure*) is that Middleton intended to flatter or advise his new monarch. To this end, Middleton employed his 'Phoenix as James' analogy to educate his king in good government.[24] With the advent of new historicist criticism, *The Phoenix*'s apparent lack of political agenda ensured its effective sidelining as a lesser example of what Tennenhouse terms Jacobean disguised ruler 'solidarity'.[25] Tennenhouse thus gives *The Phoenix* only passing mention.[26] *The Phoenix*'s Prince might be considered, in Thomas A. Pendleton's words, 'a textbook figure of sagacious majesty' and thus complimentary to James, but Middleton's representation of virtuous rule guaranteed its relative neglect by those seeking the play's anxiety-inducing subversiveness.[27] As noted, however, the negatively nuanced 'King James Version' of disguised ruler analysis, upon which such 'Phoenix as James' commentary is based, is seriously undermined by our awareness of the post-regicide, anti-Stuart bias of Whig historiography. Revisionist history's reappraisal of James has demonstrated the king's relative popularity early in his reign. This popularity might account for the apparent lack of anxiety-inducing subversion in Middleton's didactic play. The idea that Middleton was educating or flattering his 'newly installed reform-minded monarch' could be no more than anachronistic wishful thinking by critics eager to discover an anti-Stuart message in *The Phoenix*.

That 'Phoenix as James' theorizing has a long critical tradition is unsurprising, since this analogy was first suggested in mid- to late nineteenth-century editions written when Whiggish animosity towards James was reaching its height.[28] Indeed, such is the strength of the analogizing model that even the play's title is considered Middleton's direct (and surprisingly unsubtle) attempt to evoke his king: 'Prince Phoenix' and James are oft considered one and the same. This identification presents Middleton as flattering his monarch by linking him with the legendary bird from classical mythology.[29] Its fiery regeneration ensured the phoenix's status as a symbol for solitary wisdom, self-sacrifice and rebirth, imagery which Middleton purportedly used to compliment James. Despite the very plausible assumption

---

[24]   See Marilyn L. Williamson, '*The Phoenix*: Middleton's Comedy *de Regimine Principum*', *RN*, 10 (1957): 183–87; Stevenson, 'James I', pp. 188–208.

[25]   Tennenhouse, *Power*, p. 154.

[26]   Ibid., p. 157.

[27]   See Pendleton, 'Disguised' p. 82; Farley-Hills, *Rival*, pp. 139–40; Redmond, 'Italianate', p. 202.

[28]   Alexander Dyce (ed.), *The Works of Thomas Middleton* (5 vols, London, 1840), vol. 1; A.H. Bullen (ed.), *The Works of Thomas Middleton* (8 vols, London, 1885), vol. 1.

[29]   Danson and Kamps, *Oxford Middleton*, p. 91.

that *The Phoenix* is Middleton's allusion to this mythical bird, another heritage for wisdom and didactic forthrightness can be traced elsewhere to the Phoenix of Homer's *Iliad* (Book 9). Homer's Phoenix is trusted with convincing Achilles of his duty to the Greek cause. The diplomatic skill of this 'old knight' ensures that he is later hailed as the '*perfect Courtier*' (and, in a marginalia comment, the '*Instructor of a Prince*') in the fourth book of Sir Thomas Hoby's 1561 translation of Castiglione's *The Courtyer*.[30] Persuasive didacticism and the Phoenix of Homer provide fitting alternatives to mythical-creatured 'Phoenix as James' analogy, which figures the legendary bird as synonymous with the miraculous arrival of the Stuart king, metaphorically born out of the 'ashes' of Tudor rule.[31]

There is, of course, no denying that James was heralded in numerous publications as a 'phoenix' arising out of Elizabeth's ashes. Likewise, prior to the accession, that James was specifically associated with the famous bird following publication of his allegorical poem, 'The Phoenix', in his collection of verses entitled *Essayes of a Prentise* (1584).[32] James even concluded his *Essayes* with the 'verie wordis' used to describe the creature in Pliny the Elder's first-century *Naturalis Historia*.[33] Dedicated to his disgraced kinsman Esmé Stewart, James's poem represents his 'high-handed' rejection of the 'mirrors for princes' advice offered him in the wake of this scandal (although it did not prevent James's own advice-book foray fifteen years later with *Basilikon Doron*).[34] James's 'The Phoenix' promotes Esmé Stewart's rebirth from the ashes of disgrace, offering convenient imagery for expressing hope for his kinsman, and displeasure at those seeking to advise their king. James's reliance on 'phoenix' imagery to express his own analogous agenda highlights the ubiquity of this mythical image in early modern panegyrical responses not only to James, but also to his English counterpart and predecessor, Elizabeth. During this time, the phoenix also described the noble qualities of the late lamented Sir Philip Sidney, as well as that ultimate 'phoenix', Jesus Christ.[35]

Shakespeare's own phoenix inspired verse, 'Let the bird of lowdest lay' (traditionally known as 'The Phoenix and the Turtle'), a thirteen stanza poem included in Robert Chester's 1601 *Love's Martyr*, further demonstrates the popularity of such imagery, even though its aristocratic recipient remains a mystery.[36] Not so *The Phoenix Nest* (1593), '*Written on the death of the Right Honourable the Earle of Leicester*', a collection of work 'Set foorth' by the

---

[30]   Baldesar Castiglione, *The Courtyer*, trans. Sir Thomas Hoby (London, 1561), fol. 2S3^r.

[31]   Tricomi, *Anticourt*, p. 16.

[32]   King James VI & I, *The Essayes of a Prentise* (Edinburgh, 1584), fols G2^r–I2^v.

[33]   Ibid., fols P4^r–P4^v.

[34]   Rhodes, Richards and Marshall, *Selected Writings*, pp. 7–8.

[35]   Ivo Kamps, 'Ruling Fantasies and the Fantasies of Rule: *The Phoenix* and *Measure for Measure*', *SP*, 92 (1995): 248–73 (p. 254).

[36]   Robert Chester, *Love's Martyr* (London, 1601), fols Z3^v–Z4^r. See Colin Burrow (ed.), *Complete Sonnets and Poems* (Oxford, 2002), pp. 82–90.

unknown 'R.S., of the Inner Temple', whose 'An Elegie' explicitly likens the ill-fated Sidney to the mythical bird.[37] Accordingly, Middleton could be figuring any number of aristocratic or royal recipients in his play's title. Indeed, Fidelio's panegyric for that 'wonder of all Princes, President, and Glorie, / True Phoenix, made of an vnusuall straine' (*Phoenix*, A4[r]; 1.136–7), praises the unique 'straine' or admixture of good qualities that differentiate this prince from his peers. The description 'True Phoenix' offers a fitting analogy for the solitary wisdom of this 'wonder'. Even so, it does not directly invoke the name of the play's princely protagonist, nor by implication England's Stuart monarch.

Whether or not Middleton's *Phoenix* represents a didactic response to Tudor uncertainty in the light of an unknown succession, or an encomium to a Scottish king, traditional 'Phoenix as James' (or even 'Phoenix as Elizabeth') readings fail to consider the less obvious fact that, as J. Bradbury Brooks argues, 'Phoenix' appears to be the name adopted by the Prince, though only when in disguise.[38] As first noted by Alexander Dyce in the 1840s, scenes 12 and 15 (Acts 4 and 5 in Dyce's edition) commence with Proditor greeting his hired assassin with 'Come hither Phoenix' (*Phoenix*, G3[v]; 12.1) and 'Now Phoenix' (*Phoenix*, I1[r]; 15.1). Dyce claims that these names, 'forming part of a line, cannot be thrown out as a printer's interpolation'.[39] His conclusion, that this was Middleton's 'oversight in the haste of composition', appears correct, although (as Brooks argues) for completely the wrong reason.[40] It is not the scene 12 and scene 15 references to 'Phoenix' that are Middletonian mistakes, but Proditor's scene 2 parting aside: 'I loue to auoide strife, / Not many monthes *Phoenix* shall keepe his life' (*Phoenix*, B2[r]; 2.137–8). This uncomfortably metered line, which might itself be a compositor's or 'printer's interpolation' mistakenly replacing 'the Prince' with its speech-prefix alternative, is the only reference to 'Phoenix' when the Prince lacks his disguise. Throughout the rest of the play, he refers to himself, or is referred to by others, as 'the Prince'. If indeed Middleton's oversight or a compositorial alteration, then *The Phoenix*'s title and speech-prefixes invoke the disguised persona, as opposed to the actual character name, of the play's protagonist. This possibility accords with similar speech-prefixes in *The Malcontent*, *The Fawn* and *The Fleer*. Danson and Kamps ignore this, however, insisting instead that Proditor's scene 12 and scene 15 references to 'Phoenix' are an 'error in the text: Proditor does not know the true identity of the disguised Phoenix'.[41] Representative of attempts to conflate the Prince/Phoenix personas into an identifiable Jamesian unit, such editorial responses add to the perception of royal equivalence between play title and disguised hero, thus fuelling the supposed 'militancy' of Middleton's hegemonic agenda.

---

[37] R.S., *The Phoenix Nest* (London, 1593), fols A1[r]–A3[r] & B1[r]–B4[v].

[38] Brooks, *Phoenix*, pp. 149–52.

[39] Dyce, *Middleton*, vol. 1.

[40] Brooks, *Phoenix*, p. 330n.

[41] Danson and Kamps, *Oxford Middleton*, p. 116n.

Despite the difficulties associated with proving (or disproving) any 'Phoenix as James' analogy, *The Phoenix*'s didacticism is understandably associated with that most famous of 'mirrors for princes' advice-books, James's *Basilikon Doron*. Was Middleton's intention, when commenting on contemporary corrupt practices among London's urban elite, to hold an advice-book mirror to the incumbent regime? Or might *The Phoenix* be his response to recent disguised ruler success in a rival children's company? Topical commentary, moralizing conservatism, commercial contingency and flattering occasionalist analogy could all influence a young playwright seeking, as the play's *'Epilogus'* indicates, 'Fame and Opinion' (*Phoenix*, K3ᵛ). Overt didacticism there undoubtedly is, but it should not overshadow Middleton's true innovation: the conflation of traditional humanist responses to good government with a popular dramatic motif.

Travel/Travail and the Didactics of Disguise

In the opening scene of *The Phoenix*, the Prince describes his desire secretly to 'look into the heart & bowels of [his father's] Dukedome, and in disguise, marke all abuses readie for Reformation or Punishment' (*Phoenix*, A3ᵛ; 1.102–104). This familiarly medicalized description of the Prince's surveillance technique imagines him surgically probing Ferrara's metaphorical skin to expose the cankerous 'heart & bowels' beneath. The same surgical metaphor is later literally enacted with the incisive blood-letting in the final scene. Here, the steady hand of the ex-lawyer Quieto 'sluce[s] the Veyne' of the 'Law-mad' Tangle, from whom the diseased 'issue … burst[s] out' like a 'filthy streame of trouble, spite and doubt' into an awaiting bowl (*Phoenix*, K2ʳ; 15.306–309). Only through medical intervention can peace be restored to a troubled mind, a procedure according with the Prince/ Phoenix's own medicalized observation, 'in disguise', of his father's corrupt and corrupting subjects.

The success with which the Prince's disguised intervention exposes wrongdoers, while foiling the murderous plans of Proditor, is acknowledged on his eventual return to court. Describing the miraculous skill with which his youthful son has achieved the 'Reformation and Punishment' of sins, the Duke comments on the fundamental difference between father and child:

> DUKE: State is but blindness[e, t]hou hadst piercing Art,
> We onely saw the knee, but thou the heart.
> To thee then power and Dukedome we resigne,
> „Hee's fit to raign, whose knowledge can refine. (*Phoenix*, I4ʳ; 15.179–82)

With self deprecating humility, the Duke (personifying the 'State') recognizes his own 'blindness' and abdicates in favour of a son whose 'piercing Art' disregards the bending 'knee' of courtly flattery. The Prince/Phoenix sees instead the true, often dangerous 'heart' of his subjects. The Duke's reference to the 'piercing' nature of his son's 'Art' unwittingly reinforces the medical imagery of the Prince/

Phoenix's original disguised intent. Ultimate proof that the Prince is 'fit to reign', however, resides in his ability to 'refine' his knowledge. The Duke's reference to 'refine' suggests either the clarification of intellect, or, more sanctiloquently, the moral purification and attainment of a higher spiritual state. Whether the Duke is alluding to intellectual and/or spiritual refinement, his comment confirms his son's unique ability – his 'piercing Art' – as a practical skill, learnt from personal experience. We, as audience/reader, however, know that his 'piercing Art' is no more than a Machiavellian use of disguise, made more effective by the gullibility of his victims. This didactics of disguise, the gaining of first-hand experience and intelligence, is the true 'piercing Art' of the youthful Prince.

That Ferrara is in need of a more powerful, potentially Machiavellian ruler has already been noted in the Duke's opening speech:

> DUKE: We know wee're old, my daies proclayme me so:
> Fortie-fiue yeres, I'ue gently ruld this Dukedome,
> Pray heauen it be no fault,
> For there's as much disease, though not to th' eye,
> In too much pittie, as in Tyrannie. (*Phoenix*, A2ʳ; 1.6–10)

The Duke's description of having 'gently ruld' his nation, so reminiscent of the claim by *Measure for Measure*'s Duke that he has 'let slip' Vienna's laws (F *Measure*, TLN.311; 1.3.21), illustrates the fading authority of Ferrara's ducal regime. The Duke's account of a personal rule marred by excessive 'pittie' is often cited as Middleton's overt allusion to the forty-five year reign of Queen Elizabeth (a somewhat heavy-handed example of historical specificity if indeed the case).[42] Regardless of whether Middleton was actually making an ironic historical reference, the old Duke's 'gentle' behaviour engenders a barely discernible 'disease' in Ferrara's body-politic, his 'pittie' proving as malignant as any tyrannical regime. With his own age and ill health in mind, the Duke invokes the truism that 'Kinges haue mortall bodies' (*Phoenix*, A2ʳ; 1.13), while naming his son as rightful heir to the dukedom.

The Duke's comments demonstrate that, despite his best intention, his failing health and ineffectual government have resulted in social corruption and decay. To right these obvious wrongs, he intends to abdicate in favour of his far worthier son, thereby ensuring a government that is strict though non-tyrannical. The scene is set for regime change, although nothing so far foreshadows a disguised adventure for the play's principal protagonist. Indeed, the disguise plot unravels not because a princely heir travels for romance or self-enlightenment, but because of the villainous Proditor's machinations. It is Proditor who alone suggests that, 'Had [the Prince] but trauaile to his time and Vertue' (*Phoenix*, A2ᵛ; 1.23), he might better succeed to royal office. Motivated by a desire to remove the young Prince from the safety of court before his premature enthronement, Proditor opportunistically positions himself to have the Duke assassinated, while implicating the Prince in

---

42   Ibid., p. 91.

his father's murder. 'Trauaile' is the key to Proditor's murderous plan, as well as the Prince/Phoenix's subsequent disguise.

Immediately seized on by the Duke, who agrees that 'Experience quickens, trauaile confirmes the man' (*Phoenix*, A2ᵛ; 1.26), Proditor's advice is soon relayed to the Prince posing as his father's counsel. He may have supported the Prince's 'Serious studyes' in the past (*Phoenix*, A2ᵛ; 1.34), but now the Duke sees his son's need to escape books, 'To see affections actually præsented' (*Phoenix*, A2ᵛ; 1.42). Personal experience, so the Duke advises, 'yeeld[s] more profit' than a lifetime of bookish reading (*Phoenix*, A2ᵛ; 1.43). The Duke proposes 'to moue [the Prince] toward Trauaile', thus giving his son's 'apter [more suitable] power' a firmer 'foundation' (*Phoenix*, A2ᵛ; 1.39–41). The Duke expands on Proditor's initial proposal by explaining the benefit of such 'Trauaile' for Ferrara's future ruler:

> DUKE: The good and free example which you finde,
> In other Countries, match it with your owne,
> The ill to shame the ill, which will in time,
> Fully instruct you how to set in frame,
> A kingdome all in peeces. (*Phoenix*, A2ᵛ–A3ʳ; 1.46–50)

Only through empirical observation abroad can the Duke's heir draw together the fragmentary jigsaw 'peeces' of his own 'kingdome' within a secure unified 'frame'. The didactic sentiment behind the Duke's instruction accords with traditional 'mirrors for princes' counsel. Such advice might be derived from the biblical precedent of that arch-disguiser Jacob. As Robert Albott muses in his book of classical maxims, Jacob, 'hauing gotten vvisedome in trauaile, is sayd i[n] Genesis to haue had the sight of God'.[43] Whatever its basis, the Duke's request confirms the importance of travel as a prerequisite for enlightened wise rule.

This conventional wisdom reappears in George Whetstone's panegyric poem dedicated to the late Sir Philip Sidney, in which the earl's youthful exploits are praised:[44]

> To decke his minde, with Language, and with Lore,
> In greenest youth, to trauaile he was sett:
> By forrayne toyes, he sette but little store,
> Sound knowledge was the Marchandize he fette.
> And he abroade, such worthy praise did gett,
> As Princes when his fame they vnderstoode:
> They honor'd him, by all the meanes they could. (Whetstone, *Sidney*, B2ʳ)

Whetstone's effusive tribute applauds Sidney's quest for 'sound knowledge' from his 'trauaile' abroad. It also echoes encomiastic responses to the earl's death that rely on 'Sidney as phoenix' imagery. In this vein, John Phillips describes 'This *Phenix* sweet *Sidney*' as the 'flower of curtesie', who might 'leade men to

---

43   Robert Albott, *Wits Theater of the Little World* (London, 1599), fols T2ʳ–T2ᵛ.
44   George Whetstone, *Sir Phillip Sidney* (London, 1587).

virtue', while ensuring they 'become carefull louers of their natiue countrie'.[45] Likewise, *The Phoenix Nest*'s introductory defence, 'The dead mans Right', seeks to dispel the slander of 'vngratefull Malecontents' eager to denigrate 'the trauels of so memorable a Noble' as Sidney.[46] Whether or not Middleton consciously intended so specific an allusion, the regularity with which Sidney is invoked both as mythical phoenix and figure of sagacity ensures the wisdom of such foreign 'trauaile' in 'other Countries'. The Prince therefore publicly accepts his father's commission. Unaware, moreover, that his absence was proposed by Proditor, the Prince adds his aphoristic agreement that 'Experience is a Kingdomes better sight' (*Phoenix*, A3ʳ; 1.54). Like a Sidnean aristocrat, he willingly embraces foreign travel, to experience and observe each nation's 'good and free example' and thus consolidate the 'foundation' of his future rule.

Although a self-serving ploy, Proditor's advice represents more than the promotion of his rival's absence abroad. A subtle duality of meaning in Proditor's call for the Prince to 'trauaile', evident in the play's original text, presages a harsher, more dangerous task ahead. The fact that modern editions invariably modernize the spelling to 'travel' constrains the word to its innocuous touristic meaning.[47] For the Prince to embark on his 'travels' implies a pleasant relief preceding his heavy ducal responsibilities. The original spelling of 'trauaile' has, however, far broader connotations. Travail is defined, for example, in Thomas Thomas's 1587 dictionary as, 'To endeauour or labour, to enforce ones selfe to doe a thing, to ascend vp with great paines'.[48] Thomas's definition also refers to a woman's labour in childbirth as 'to travaile with child, or to bring forth'. The obnoxious Captain, stepfather to Fidelio, even conflates these concepts, when he considers 'travel' in foreign lands and 'travail' as laborious task as the same thing. In a scene of uncomfortable dramatic irony that mirrors numerous prior disguised ruler episodes, the Captain discusses the sale of his wife, Castiza. Also the widowed mother of Fidelio, Castiza has attracted the attention of the lusting Proditor. Unaware that he addresses both the Prince and his wife's son, the Captain explains why he now seeks to sell Castiza to the wicked lord. To the Prince/Phoenix's query, 'what if the Duke [or Fidelio] should heare of this?', the Captain replies, 'What and they did, I sell none but mine own: as for the Duke, hee's abroad by this time, and for Fidelio hee's in labour' (*Phoenix*, E2ᵛ; 8.283–8). Prematurely investing the son with his father's ducal authority, the Captain confirms his knowledge of the Prince's journeys. This cryptic response prompts the Prince/Phoenix's further enquiry as to what the Captain means by being 'in labour?' (*Phoenix*, E2ᵛ; 8.289). The Captain wryly answers, 'What call you Trauelling?' (*Phoenix*, E2ᵛ; 8.290). Clearly, for the seafaring husband of Castiza,

---

45   John Phillips, *The Life and Death of Sir Phillip Sidney* (London, 1587), fol. A2ʳ.

46   R.S., *Phoenix*, fols A3ʳ–A4ᵛ.

47   Pendleton, 'Disguised', pp. 86–7.

48   Thomas Thomas, *Dictionarium Linguae Latinae et Anglicanae* (Cambridge, 1587).

and for the play's seventeenth-century auditor/reader, the Prince's mission abroad suggests both travel and travail according to Thomas's laboursome definition.

Although the Prince publicly accedes to his father's wishes, he privately decides to 'stay at home, and trauaile' (*Phoenix*, A3ᵛ; 1.89), intending to 'reforme those fashions that are alreadye in his Countrey' rather than 'bring newe ones in' (*Phoenix*, A3ᵛ; 1.96–7). It is 'reforme', leading to 'Reformation and Punishment', that informs the Prince's actions, his moralistic fervour overriding any apparent disquiet over the manipulation of his father by the 'wilde Nobilitie' of court (*Phoenix*, A3ᵛ; 1.80). Not surprisingly, given the advice-book heritage of the Prince's personal quest for 'Reformation', similar advice appears in James's *Basilikon Doron*. When commenting on the faults among 'all the estates of [his] kingdome', James advises Prince Henry to travel because of a 'fatherly loue' for his people, 'onely hating' as he does 'their vices':

> And because (for the better reformation of all these abuses among your estates) It will be a greate helpe vnto you, to be wel acquent with the nature and humoures of all your subjects, and to know particularlie the estate of euery part of your dominions; I woulde therefore counsel you, once in the yeare to visite the principall parts of the cuntry ye were in. (*Basilikon* [1599], I4ᵛ–K1ʳ)

For James, as for the Prince in *The Phoenix*, travel/travail is meant to acquaint the ruler with 'abuses' that are specifically in need of 'reformation'.

Whether Middleton consciously alludes to *Basilikon Doron* in *The Phoenix* is unclear; similarity in didactic sentiment need not suggest 'King James Version' correspondence.[49] Indeed, that a young, supposedly inexperienced playwright would choose to educate his new king, if at some stage his play was deemed suitable for court performance, seems unlikely. Flattery perhaps, but advice-book didacticism almost definitely not. What seems more plausible is that the Prince adopts his disguise before travelling/travailing in foreign lands as a prerequisite for intellectual development, thereby fulfilling the moral expectations of those who recognize his path towards virtuous non-tyrannical government in a volatile Italian state. *The Phoenix* could, of course, present its didacticism as cryptic commentary on legal and aristocratic corruption in England. If so, it employs a travel/travail tradition already associated via Sidney with the mythical phoenix, whose own longed-for resurrection represented the hope and despair of a nation unsure of its political future. The Prince/Phoenix's 'Reformation' of Ferrara's court and legal system thus transforms the play's advice-book optimism into a politicized message of Machiavellian intrigue and opportunism.

To facilitate this journey of 'Reformation', Middleton introduces a disguised ruler costume that allows his royal protagonist to observe 'abuses' first hand. As in the children's version of *The Malcontent*, *The Phoenix*'s youthful actor adopts a physical disguise that alters his appearance so much that neither father, friend nor enemy recognize him. He appears as 'a priuate Gentleman', who 'notes all, /

---

49   Brooks, *Phoenix*, p. 21.

Himselfe vnnoted' (*Phoenix*, A3ʳ; 1.62–4). If he ostentatiously sported the 'fashion of a prince', rather than this plainer costume, the Prince's venture would be far less successful. As he wryly observes, grand display tends to 'win more flatterie, then profit' (*Phoenix*, A3ʳ; 1.65–6). This same 'priuate Gentleman' disguise also betrays a far darker purpose. When clothed in princely 'fashion', such royal display offers miscreants 'time & warning' by which 'To hide their Actions' (*Phoenix*, A3ʳ; 1.67–8). If the Prince should 'appeare a Sunne', then forewarned criminals would 'run into the shade with their ill deedes' like scurrying malignant insects (*Phoenix*, A3ʳ; 1.68–9). The Prince's choice of disguise receives the enthusiastic approbation of the Duke himself, who commends his son's 'wisdome' in understanding that 'Things priuate are best known through priuacy' (*Phoenix*, A3ʳ; 1.73). This comment is as Machiavellian in tone as his son's subsequent subterfuge. Expanding on his father's observation, the Prince remarks how 'oft betwene Kings Eyes, and subiects Crimes / Stands there a barre of brybes' (*Phoenix*, A4ʳ; 1.120–21). The Prince hopes, however, to expose these exploitations of privilege: 'for how can abuses that keepe lowe, come to the right view of a Prince, vnlesse his lookes lie leuell with them' (*Phoenix*, A4ʳ; 1.116–18). This conscious effort to 'lie leuell' with those he observes defines the mode of the Prince's later disguised appearance.

To guarantee success, the Prince must 'fit [his] bodie to the humblest forme and bearing' of an everyday Ferraran citizen (*Phoenix*, A4ʳ; 1.114–16). Only in this 'forme' can he be sure that his 'labor' will be 'fruitfull' (*Phoenix*, A4ʳ; 1.115–16), a fitting image recalling 'travail' as the pains of birth. His 'humble' disguise's success is confirmed when the Captain is duped into purchasing a divorce from Castiza. Assisted by Fidelio, who also disguises himself like a legal 'Scriuener', the Prince describes how his 'forme and bearing' ensure that the Captain sees him only as 'that common folly of Gentry, the easie-affecting venturer' (*Phoenix*, D2ʳ; 7.2–4). The Prince's costume implies his status as a country-born innocent, newly arrived in the city, who can easily be gulled into parting with his inheritance to fund trading ventures abroad. That his venturer's disguise succeeds becomes evident when the unwary Captain describes the Prince/Phoenix to Proditor. The seafarer calls the Prince an easily-duped 'filthy Farmers sonne', who, despite his pretensions of being a 'Gentleman', cannot escape his rural upbringing (*Phoenix*, D3ᵛ; 8.79–80). The 'filthy Farmers' hard work and thrift might fund his pretentious son's folly, but the Captain still scathingly comments that this supportive 'father's a Iew' (*Phoenix*, D3ᵛ; 8.80). Gentlemanly costume and demeanour, coupled with apparent gullibility and country-born innocence, become the disguising tools with which the Prince can 'lie leuell' with his less honourable subjects.

Surprisingly, having tricked the Captain into releasing his wife from her marital contract in exchange for money, the Prince allows his royal status to be recognized at this dangerous mid-point of the play. With Proditor now absent, Castiza kneels and requests 'pardon' from her 'Lord' (*Phoenix*, E2ᵛ; 8.303) for having defended her husband against his apparent enemies (an image strangely evocative of Mariana and Isabella's plea in *Measure for Measure*). This suggests her recognition of the disguised prince before her. In return, the Prince offers a suitably aristocratic response, requesting her simply to 'Rise' in his royal presence (*Phoenix*, E2ᵛ; 8.304). Although this moment of mid-play recognition invites comparison with the 'king and subject' theme of medieval balladry, it also remains part of the Prince's laboursome 'travail' as a 'priuate Gentleman'. The reforming imperative of his disguised subterfuge directly contrasts with the accidental self-knowledge gleaned from unwitting subjects in traditional 'king and subject' confrontations.

That the Prince dissembles for political, not romantic, ends remains an unwavering theme within the play. His father's aged 'stoop' might be described as 'Without dissemblance' (*Phoenix*, A3ʳ; 1.77–8) – an ironic allusion to the child actor who dissembles the physicality of age on the Paul's playhouse stage – but the Prince's own 'dissemblance' is for the good of the state alone. It is with added irony, therefore, that the Duke receives a letter in the final scene that purports to announce his son's return to court. In it, the Prince proclaims that he has got a 'large portion of knowledge … by the benefit' of his 'Trauaile' (*Phoenix*, I2ᵛ; 15.68–9). There is little doubt for audience/readers that the Prince's 'portion of knowledge' stems not from 'trauaile' in foreign lands, but from his disguise at home. Such 'knowledge' accords, moreover, with an English tradition of medieval and Tudor morality drama, in which a disguised 'everyman' embarks on a redemptive journey.[50] Along the way, he encounters numerous nefarious characters whose wrongdoings are punished, while he gains personal enlightenment. Middleton's reliance on an outdated morality tradition is seemingly at odds with the avant garde experimentation of Marston and Shakespeare, whose tragicomic disguised rulers are regularly associated with *The Phoenix*. It is not tragicomedy, however, but an 'everyman' morality disguise that holds the key to the Prince's 'portion of knowledge' and his subsequent punishment of offenders. This morality tradition points to an inherent medievalism at the heart of Middleton's play. Representative of his distinctive engagement with the disguised ruler, this medievalism also accounts for the underlying hegemonic conservatism of *The Phoenix*'s uncontentious political message.

Medievalism and a Morality Tradition

The violent blood-letting of the lawyer Tangle, the serio-comic cure enacted in *The Phoenix*'s closing moments, provides the final abiding image of the play. No longer law-mad, the lawyer expresses his relief that the surgical procedure has resulted in him feeling 'Compassion in [his] hart, & aboue al, … peaces musick' coursing through his veins: '"Now I'ue least law, I hope I haue most grace' (*Phoenix*, K2ᵛ; 15.343–7). Tangle's religio-musical imagery is developed by the Prince who, having completed his quest to expose corruption and administered his retributive justice, adds his parting aphorism: 'Thus when all hearts are tunde

---

[50]   See Jean MacIntyre, *Costumes and Scripts in the Elizabethan Theatre* (Edmonton, 1992), pp. 13–47.

to Honors strings, / There is no musicke to the Quire of Kings' (*Phoenix*, K2ᵛ; 15.349–50). The meaning of this cryptic maxim is far from clear. It might refer to a choir of royals appreciating the harmonious unity of their subjects' hearts, or imply that kings create the most harmonious governance, whereby they metaphorically play their subjects like well-tuned stringed instruments. Whatever Middleton's intention, these references to 'grace' and a 'Quire of Kings' display a religiosity noticeably lacking in the rest of the play. Given that the Paul's playhouse is so close to, and under the direct control of, St Paul's Cathedral, this absence of overt religious imagery is perhaps unsurprising.

Nonetheless, the Prince/Phoenix's 'Quire of Kings' evokes Roman Catholic angelology, which traditionally depicts not kings, but a 'Quire of Angels'. As a religious concept, the 'Quire of Angels' represents an angelic host of heavenly singers, divided into nine distinctive ranks in descending order, the highest being the Seraphim and Cherubim, and the lowest, the common Angel. Such medieval Catholic imagery appears regularly in Shakespeare's plays, most memorably when Horatio calls for 'flights of Angels' to sing Hamlet to his rest (F *Hamlet*, TLN.3850; 5.2.303), and when Lorenzo, in *Merchant of Venice*, invokes planetary 'harmony' when romancing Jessica:

> LORENZO: There's not the smallest orbe which thou beholdst
> But in his motion like an Angell sings,
> Still quiring to the young eyed Cherubins. (F *Merchant of Venice*, TLN.2472–4;
> 5.1.59–61)

Middleton transforms the medieval nine-tiered angelic choir into a decidedly secular 'Quire of Kings', suggesting that earthly rulers hold equal, if not superior, spiritual power to their holy counterparts. Catholic angelology offers a blueprint for the Prince/Phoenix's earthly divine-right rule, while highlighting the explicit medievalism of the play's ending.

That *The Phoenix* displays a certain medievalism has long been recognized.[51] 'Poised', as Brooks argues, at a 'crucial point' between long-established and new forms of comedy, *The Phoenix* reflects both a liminality and diversity that differentiates it from its disguised ruler cousins, *Malcontent* and *Measure for Measure*.[52] Liminal perhaps, but *The Phoenix*'s exposure of villainy through the contingency of disguise also bears a marked similarity to two anonymous plays from the 1590s, *A Knack to Know a Knave* (*c*. 1592, Strange's; published 1594) and *A Knack to Know an Honest Man* (1594, Admiral's; published 1596).[53] In *Knack to Know a Knave*, a play discussed with the 'comical histories' of the 1590s, the character Honesty (whose personifying name indicates his morality heritage) is deputized by King Edgar and sent in disguise to seek out abuses.

---

[51] See Muriel Bradbrook, *The Growth and Structure of Elizabethan Comedy* (London, 1955), pp. 160–61.

[52] Brooks, *Phoenix*, pp. 70 & 104.

[53] Anonymous, *A Knacke to Know an Honest Man* (London, 1596).

Honesty is punningly described by Brooks as a 'kind of one-man vice squad', who single-mindedly and secretively journeys through his ruler's land, exposing and punishing the Vice figures in the play.[54]

Despite its Italianate narrative, the sequel to *Knack to Know a Knave*, *Knack to Know an Honest Man*, also evokes an English morality past. Thus, when the Venetian Sempronio is wounded by his jealous friend Lelio and left for dead, he is revived by the hermit Phillip. His invalid patient is magically disguised in the same habit as his hermit saviour. Phillip then forces Sempronio to renounce his former life and embrace that of a 'cynike pure' (*Honest Man*, B4r; TLN.315).[55] While disguised, Sempronio adopts the personifying morality character-name, 'Penitent experience' (*Honest Man*, C1v; TLN.392), and swears to conceal his true identity. Sempronio/'Penitent Experience' then becomes servant to the Duke of Venice's son, Fortunio. After plot twists, followed by Sempronio's offer to exchange places on the scaffold with his condemned friend Lelio, Phillip finally permits his disguised patient to reveal himself as Sempronio. It is the morality figure 'Penitent Experience', then, who has learned the knack to know an honest man, a knack evolving from the friar-like hermit's disguise that offers him easy access to all sections of Venetian society.

The morality character-names evident in both *Knack* plays, combined with their overarching concern with reforming vice, offer an obvious context for appreciating the medievalism of Middleton's *Phoenix*.[56] *The Phoenix* likewise includes character-name personifications, although Middleton's are distinctly Italian, as befits the play's Ferraran location. 'Proditor' derives from the Italian *proditóre*, which Florio defines as 'a traitor, a villain, a deceiuer, a betrayer, an accuser, a discloser'.[57] Similarly, ten of the fourteen principal characters in *The Phoenix* are traceable to definitions in Florio's dictionary. Middleton's use of personifying character-names appears to contradict Raphael Falco's argument about the medieval and Reformation roots of early modern drama.[58] Falco distinguishes between 'symbolic names' used in late sixteenth- and early seventeenth-century plays, and the 'full personifications' of their morality forebears.[59] Indeed, he describes it as 'naive evolutionism' to associate morality character-names that personify a virtue

[54] Ibid., p. 136.

[55] Through line numbers from Henry De Vocht (ed.), *A Knack to Know an Honest Man* (Oxford, 1910).

[56] For discussion of morality character-name personifications, see Helen Cooper, *Shakespeare and the Medieval World* (London, 2010), pp. 108–11. For personifications in *King Lear*, especially in relation to the Fool and the disguised Kent, see Michael O'Connell, '*King Lear* and the Summons of Death', in Curtis Perry and John Watkins (eds), *Shakespeare and the Middle Ages* (Oxford, 2009), pp. 199–216 (pp. 203–6).

[57] Florio, *Wordes*, p. 108.

[58] Raphael Falco, 'Medieval and Reformation Roots', in Kinney (ed.), *Renaissance Drama*, pp. 239–56.

[59] Ibid., p. 249.

or vice, such as Honesty or Penitent Experience, with names that symbolically allude to a character's 'humour' (as opposed to their allegorical function), such as Lady Politic Would-Be in Jonson's *Volpone*.[60] Because the later 'symbolic' character-names do not constrain their owners' personalities, they should not be considered direct descendants of the medieval morality personifications.

Falco's caution seems misplaced, however, with regard to *The Phoenix*. When compared with Florio's definitions, the personalities (rather than the humours) of Middleton's characters are confined within an Italian convention that the playwright repeats elsewhere. Thus, the 'luxurious' and 'lustful' Lussurioso and the 'chaste' Castiza of *The Phoenix* reappear in Middleton's *The Revenger's Tragedy* (1606, King's Men; published 1607). Likewise, the 'trustie' and 'faithfull' Fidelio, the 'littel thief' Latronello, the 'stealingly' stealthy Furtivo and the 'false' and 'counterfeit' Falso, all conform to Florio's Italian etymologies. As with *The Malcontent*, where an awareness of Italian allows a full appreciation of Marston's QA/B allusions to Guarini, so with *The Phoenix*, an understanding of Italian reveals the ways that the protagonists personify their character-traits according to morality play tradition.

The inherent medievalism of Middleton's Italianized disguised ruler adventure is further evinced in several miracle play allusions that denote a subtle intertextuality between *The Phoenix* and *The Malcontent*. In *The Phoenix*'s dénouement, when the Prince banishes Proditor for plotting against his father, the initial reaction of the lord is to prostrate himself at his prince's feet, while pleading with him to 'Tread' to 'dust' this 'Serpent [who] on his bellie creepes' (*Phoenix*, I4ʳ; 15.166–7). Proditor's supplication here mirrors the Serpent's banishment from the Garden of Eden (Genesis, 3:14–15). It thus evokes the personification of that ultimate disguised villain, Satan.[61] The miracle play heritage of this moment appears in the fifteenth-century *Fall of Man*, as performed in the York Pageant of the Coopers, in which Eve exclaims, 'A worm, Lord, enticed me theretill' (147f.).[62] God replies, 'Ah, wicked worm, woe worth thee ay!': 'My malison [curse] have thou here / With all the might I may. / And on thy womb [belly] then shalt thou glide' (150–55ff.). The play's audience would see Proditor's belly-creeping as re-enacting the biblical pageantry of the gliding 'worm' or Serpent.

This miracle play provenance for Proditor's grovelling is highlighted by the Prince's demand that the prostrated lord 'Ranckle not [his] foote' (*Phoenix*, I4ʳ; 15.168). With his contemptuous command, 'away', the Prince emphasizes the villain's lowly posture: 'Treason, we laugh at thy vain-labouring strings [*sic*], / Aboue the foote thou hast no power ore Kings' (*Phoenix*, I4ʳ; 15.168–70). In line with nineteenth-century editorial practice, modern editions of *The Phoenix* amend

---

[60]   Ibid., p. 249.

[61]   See Bradbrook, *Growth*, p. 161.

[62]   *The Fall of Man*, The York Pageant of the Coopers, Fifth Cycle, BL MS Add. 35290, in A.C. Cawley (ed.), *Everyman and Medieval Miracle Plays* (London, 1956), pp. 15–22.

'strings' to 'stings' to agree with the preceding 'Serpent' imagery.[63] The 1607 quarto is nevertheless specific in describing 'vain-labouring strings'. By contrast, the 1630 second quarto reads 'vaine-labouring string' in the singular.[64] 'String' is, however, an appropriate spelling if used according to its alternative definition, as a snaring or trapping cord. Proditor would thus be grovelling around the Prince's ankles in an ineffectual attempt to ensnare his royal person.

Regardless of whether 'sting' or 'string' is indeed correct, the Prince tempers his anger towards a character both literally and metaphorically too low to wield 'power' over him. By referring to him as 'Treason', the Prince also directly translates Proditor's Italian character name. This overt reference symbolically unites two complementary images: the villain's act of treachery and his similarity to the miracle play Serpent, doomed to 'glide' on his belly for enticing Adam and Eve's Fall. Proclaiming that 'So vgly are [Proditor's] crimes / Thine eye cannot endure 'em', the Prince passes judgement on his foe:

> PRINCE/PHOENIX: And that thy face may stand perpetually
> Turn'd so from ours, and thy abhorred selfe,
> Neither to threaten wracke of state or credite,
> An euerlasting banishment ceaze on thee. (*Phoenix*, I4ᵛ; 15.194–9)

Proditor threatens the security of the state, as well as the honourable 'credite' of Ferraran society. To counter this danger, the Prince imposes 'euerlasting banishment' on the 'abhorred' villain. Both lenient and derisory, this punishment reflects the play's comic pretensions. Despite his undeserved good fortune, Proditor evinces no gratitude. Instead, with petulant maliciousness, he curses the young prince for his leniency: 'May thy Rule, life, and all that's in thee glad, / Haue as short time – as thy begetting had' (*Phoenix*, I4ᵛ; 15.202–3). The Prince's response, 'Away, thy curse is idle' (*Phoenix*, I4ᵛ; 15.204), is equally dismissive, both of lord and of abuse.

The Prince's moderate penalty for Proditor's crimes distinguishes Middleton's play from that late Elizabethan morality, *A Knack to Know a Knave*. In *Knave*, Honesty dupes the four villains, Cuthbert the Coneycatcher, the Priest, Walter-Would-Have-More the Farmer and Perin the Courtier. These characters receive death sentences involving mutilation and torture (*Knave*, G2ʳ–G4ʳ; TLN.1755–1874). Their punishments are as medieval in their retributive intensity as they are horrific in their execution. By contrast, Proditor's punishment delivers personal humiliation, not bodily pain. Proditor's banishment also parallels Mendoza's sentence in *The Malcontent*. In this play's dénouement, Mendoza pleads for a stay of execution so he can enjoy life until 'fit to die' (QA *Malcontent*, H4ᵛ; 5.6.121). While begging Altofronto for leniency, Mendoza, like Proditor, grovels at his duke's feet before being banished from the dukedom. This usurper's removal is, however, more ignominious than Proditor's: according to the stage direction,

---

[63] Dyce, *Middleton*, vol. 1, p. 402; Bullen, *Middleton*, vol. 1, p. 203.

[64] Middleton, *Phoenix* [Q2] (London, 1630), fol. H4ᵛ.

Altofronto simply '*Kicks out Mendoza*' (*Malcontent*, II^r; 5.6.159.0.SD). Like the stock miracle play Serpents they emulate, Proditor and Mendoza leave the scene as debased individuals. Their exits offer a fascinating instance of medieval intertextuality. Middleton's and Marston's respective audiences would recognize the theatrical convention being invoked, whose medieval heritage is more overtly expressed in Middleton's work. *The Phoenix*'s overarching medievalism, where miracle play imagery and morality reform define the Prince/Phoenix's entire disguised subterfuge, ultimately differentiates this play from *The Malcontent* and *Measure for Measure*.

Middleton's *The Phoenix* thus predicates its entire narrative on medieval morality and advice-book reformation. It relies on the disguised ruler convention to attack widespread corruption, particularly when faced with a tired and ineffectual ruling elite. The Ferraran dukedom of *The Phoenix* figures the barely-disguised City of London. With its proto-city comedy subgeneric status, *The Phoenix* exemplifies Middleton's own generic radicalism. Although *The Second Maiden's* (*Lady's*) *Tragedy*'s necrophiliac ending alludes to the motif, the disguised ruler is only fully evoked in Middleton's earliest extant drama. Shakespeare likewise explores the motif's full potential in *Measure for Measure*, before metaphorically hanging his protagonist's disguising habit up for good. It is left to Marston, somewhat intriguingly, to buck this compositional trend. Marston capitalizes on his dual '*Malcontent*' success by writing one more disguised ruler play, *Parasitaster, or The Fawn*. Written after James becomes king, and following the publication of an influential translation of Montaigne, *The Fawn* offers the most convincing example of external political influences brought to bear on a Jacobean playwright. Eager to display his erudition and commercial dexterity, Marston revisits the motif that brought him such recent theatrical success.

The Fawn: Sixteenth-Century Folly and Disguised Ruler Reprise

In his 1983 review of London's National Theatre production of *The Fawn*, the critic Michael Billington notes the relative obscurity of the play and of its motif:[65]

> I once heard that Jonathan Miller, in his tenure at the National, proposed a season of Disguised Duke plays, which prompted Kenneth Tynan to remark that he couldn't imagine anyone actually saying 'Let's go out tonight darling, and see a Disguised Duke play'. (*Guardian* [15 July 1983], 11)

This conversation, between the National Theatre's 1970s associate director, Jonathan Miller, and the famous post-war theatre commentator, Kenneth Tynan, highlights Tynan's commercial pragmatism when recognizing that lucrative middle-class 'darling' playgoers to Britain's National Theatre might not flock to disguised ruler plays. David J. Houser's 1970s source study probably accounts

---

[65]   Michael Billington, 'Review of *The Fawn*', *Guardian*, 15 July 1983.

for Miller's original interest in such plays, but Tennenhouse's 1982 *Genre* article appears instrumental in triggering a mainstream performance of this rarely-staged Marstonian comedy.[66] Even so, despite Billington's assessment of *The Fawn* as an 'estimable and enjoyable revival' and a 'sprightly Italianate *Measure for Measure*', Tynan dismissed it as obscure Jacobean social commentary. Tynan's focus on the dubious commerciality of disguised ruler drama is unwittingly ironic, since such plays *were* popular on the Jacobean stage. Indeed, so popular do they appear that Marston reprised the motif through the now less familiar children's company comedy, *Parasitaster, or The Fawn* (*c.* 1604–1605, Queen's Revels/ Paul's; published 1606).[67]

Written, like QA/B *Malcontent*, for the Blackfriars children sometime after Marston's Globe collaboration with Webster, *The Fawn* presents Hercules, the fully-functioning (as opposed to usurped) Duke of Ferrara, as disguised ruler protagonist. Hercules is, as Lucy Munro observes, a 'superannuated prodigal' based on the trickster hero of Greek and Roman New Comedy.[68] His disguise allows him secretly to sojourn in the neighbouring dukedom of 'Urbin' (Urbino), ruled by Duke Gonzago. Here he observes corruption in his rival's court, although primarily he hopes to facilitate his son's marriage to Gonzago's daughter. Traditionally classed as a lesser example of Jacobean disguised ruler play because of its relative dearth of obvious political bite, *The Fawn* displays a greater dependence on advice-book morality and 'comical history' disguise than its malcontented forebear. By condemning folly and flattering deceit, it manifests a trope that spans sixteenth-century humanist discourse, from Erasmus's *Praise of Folly* (1511), through Machiavelli's *Il principe* (*The Prince*) of 1532, to Montaigne's *Essais*, first published in 1580 and translated by Florio in 1603.[69] Located in Urbino, the play is situated in the birthplace of Castiglione's 1528 *Il libro del cortegiano*, translated as *The Courtyer* in Hoby's 1561 London edition. *The Fawn* resonates with nostalgia, reflected not only in its advice-book morality, but also in its 'comical history' heritage, its disguised ruler ensuring the patrilineal continuance of his dynasty. This nostalgic generic conventionality possibly reflects Marston's abandonment of tragicomic experimentation in favour of a more traditional comedic form.

Variously named 'Fawne', 'Fawnus' or (more rarely) 'Faunus', the disguised Hercules is the fawning 'parasitaster' of the play. *Parasitaster*, which appears nowhere but the title-page, might represent a mocking association with Jonson's *Poetaster* (1601, Chapel Children, Blackfriars; pub. 1602).[70] Jonson's *Poetaster* satirizes Marston as the failed poet 'Crispinus', forced by the purging 'Pill' of Jonson's alter-ego 'Horace', and 'a little with [Marston's own] Finger', to vomit up

---

[66]   Houser, 'Purging', pp. 993–1006; Tennenhouse, 'Representing', pp. 139–56.

[67]   John Marston, *Parasitaster, or The Fawne* (London, 1606).

[68]   Munro, *Queen's Revels*, p. 46.

[69]   Desiderius Erasmus, *Encomium Moriae* (Basel, 1515).

[70]   Ben Jonson, *The Poetaster* (London, 1602).

his overblown verbiage (*Poetaster*, 5.3.499–501).[71] Although similar to Jonson's play-title, *Parasitaster* nevertheless actually derives from Terence's *Adelphoe* (160 BCE), in which the word contemptuously describes a young boy who is believed to be hovering about the elderly Micio's house (779f.). Marston's title thus evokes the 'court parasite', one of those obsequiously 'knowing creatures' (Q1 *Fawn*, F2^v; 3.1.535), who, according to Hercules, 'lurke in Courts' (Q1 *Fawn*, F2^v; 3.1.532).[72] These self-serving parasites keep 'broade eyes, soft feet, long ears, & most short tonge', while employing 'quicke hammes, wide armes and most close heart' in over-expansive displays of courtly bowing (Q1 *Fawn*, F2^v; 3.1.534–6). The court parasite also recalls medieval Vice figures and classical parasitic tricksters, whose malicious, sycophantic advice causes suffering to their victims. Traditionally, these Vice figures receive harsh punishment when discovered.[73] For Hercules/Fawn, the suffix '-aster' suggests that the duke's disguised character personifies not the mock poet (as in *Poetaster*), but the mock parasite.[74] *Parasitaster* thus fittingly describes this seeming parasite, who flatters in order to advance in a foreign court. Once there, he uses flattery publicly to humiliate the immoral, pompous and devious. Unlike the Vice figures of old, this mock parasite will, because of his 'incomplete resemblance', escape the harsh reckoning of his morality forebears.

As prelude to his mock parasite adventure, Hercules leaves his dukedom in his brother's safe hands, having 'vowd to visit the Court of *Urbin* in some disguise' (Q1 *Fawn*, A4^r; 1.1.19–20). He then removes his ducal robes, those grand physical emblems of 'Ceremonious soverainty', 'statefull Complements' and 'secret artes of *Rule*' (Q1 *Fawn*, A4^r; 1.1.37–9). Hercules needs far less ostentatious clothing in order to appear as a credible 'officer to the Prince' and a 'yeoman of the bottles' (Q1 *Fawn*, B3^v; 1.2.222–6).

Thus newly arrived, the fawning parasite ingratiates himself with Urbino's self-absorbed duke, who quickly elevates Hercules/Fawn to court favourite and ducal confidant. This successful insinuation is not prompted, however, by malice or reforming zeal, but by the 'cooler bloud' of Hercules' son Tiberio, which manifests itself in the young prince's apparent lack of interest in women (Q1 *Fawn*, A4^r; 1.1.24–5). Duke Hercules hopes to awaken Tiberio's manly feelings, thus encouraging a fruitful, politically expedient marriage. Hercules has already sent Tiberio as ambassador to Urbino, charged with wooing Gonzago's daughter, Princess Dulcimel, ostensibly on Hercules' behalf. The unwitting Tiberio's dormant libido is successfully ignited, and the couple are clandestinely married, despite Gonzago's efforts to keep daughter and ambassador apart.

The play concludes with a mock trial or '*Cupids* parliament' (Q1 *Fawn*, I1^r; 5.1.156), arranged by Hercules/Fawn as a court entertainment. This parliament

---

[71]   Ibid., fol. M3^v. See Charles Cathcart, *Marston, Rivalry, Rapprochement, and Jonson* (Aldershot, 2008), p. 68. Line numbers from Tom Cain (ed.), *Poetaster* (Manchester, 1995).

[72]   E.P. Vandiver, Jr, 'The Elizabethan Dramatic Parasite', *SP*, 32 (1935): 411–27.

[73]   Ibid., pp. 426–7.

[74]   David A. Blostein (ed.), *Parasitaster or The Fawn* (Manchester, 1978), p. 74n.

Fig. 4.1   Bernard Lloyd as Duke Hercules, disguised as the obsequious
              Fawn, humouring the adulterous Donna Garbetza (Jane Evers) in
              the National Theatre's 1983 London production

arraigns, charges and condemns the most ruthless, deceiving and feckless members
of Urbino's court, and banishes them to a 'ship of fools'. The final revelation,
that the fawning parasite is actually Duke Hercules, occurs when the formerly
disguised ruler enters (as the marginalia stage direction stresses), '*in his owne
shape*' (Q1 *Fawn*, I4^{v}; 5.1.469.1.SD). Like 'that shape' the disguised Henry bears
in Folio *Henry V* (F *Henry V*, TLN.2770; 4.8.48–9), so Hercules' '*owne shape*'
suggests him reassuming his original ducal costume. The boy actor need only
'change [his] face' (possibly by removing a false beard) to deliver the play's
Epilogue (Q1 *Fawn*, I4^{v}; 5.1.480).[75]

Predictably, the dating of Marston's second disguised ruler play remains
tenuous. The *Stationers' Register* records 'A playe called the *ffaune*' on 12 March
1606, entered with this caveat: 'PROVIDED that he shall not put the same in
prynte before he gette alowed lawfull aucthoritie'.[76] This conditional entry suggests
the play's prior performance in an unlicensed, possibly uncensored state.[77] More

---

[75]   See Will Fisher, 'Staging the Beard: Masculinity in Early Modern English Culture',
in Jonathan Gil Harris and Natasha Korda (eds), *Staged Properties in Early Modern English
Drama* (Cambridge, 2002), pp. 230–57 (p. 255n.). Charles Wentworth Dilke (ed.), *Old
English Plays* (6 vols, London, 1814–16), vol. 2, p. 405, replaces '*shape*' with '*Dress*'.

[76]   Arber 3, p. 316.

[77]   See Clare, *'Art'*, p. 42.

atypically, *The Fawn*, like *The Malcontent*, is presented by two separate acting companies, indicated by its dual 1606 quarto editions (designated Q1 and Q2).[78] Q1's title-page states that it was 'DIVERS times presented at the blacke Fri*ars, by the Children of the Queenes Maiesties Reuels*'. In 1606, such a company ascription could be anomalous if, as the title-pages of Blackfriars plays like *The Isle of Gulls* (1606), *The Fleer* (1607) and *Law Tricks* (1608) suggest, the children had lost the favour (and the right to use the royal title) of their patron, Queen Anne.[79] Certainly for Chambers, the retention of '*Queenes Maiesties Reuels*' on *The Fawn*'s title-page suffices for a playing date between 1604 and 1605, despite there being no definitive evidence that such a company ascription represents an accurate chronological record. *The Fawn*'s motific association with *Malcontent* and *Measure for Measure* adds weight to Chambers's conjecture, but vagaries of publication and inconsistencies in title-page publicity weaken historical certainty about repertorial attribution.[80] Despite such uncertainty, the second (Q2 *Fawn*) edition's title-page note, '*and since at Powles*', associates the play with both of London's children's companies. *The Fawn* thus appears to have been staged at Blackfriars and at Paul's.

For the most part, Q2 *Fawn* retains much of Q1's standing type. This coincidence led Fredson Bowers to suggest 'an unlawful attempt' by Marston and/ or his publishers to flout the Stationers' Company rules, which limited print-runs to between twelve and fifteen hundred copies before a workman could be paid again for the same job.[81] Even if the two quartos do represent an attempt to defraud printing house employees, the Q2 title-page still suggests that *The Fawn* transferred from Blackfriars while the Paul's boys were most likely performing their own disguised ruler drama, Middleton's *Phoenix*. The apparent dual ownership of *The Fawn* has long been explained by the transfer to Paul's in 1605–1606 of the Blackfriars manager, Edward Kirkham, his move a successful attempt to undermine the ill-fated Paul's company, which closed abruptly in 1606.[82] Acknowledging that *The Fawn* accompanied this move, Chambers even tentatively attributes differences between Q1 and Q2 to this transfer: 'I do not like explaining discrepancies by the hypothesis of a revision, but if Kirkham revived the *Fawn* at Paul's in 1606, he is not unlikely to have had it written up a bit'.[83] Chambers's 'hypothesis' fails to explain the relatively minor changes that this 'bit' of 'writing up' represents.

---

[78]   *Fawn*, STC 17483 and 17484.

[79]   Munro, *Queen's Revels*, p. 21.

[80]   Chambers, *ES* 3, p. 432. For the possible link between title-pages and playbill publicity, see Stern, *Documents*, pp. 36–62.

[81]   Fredson Bowers, *Principles of Bibliographical Description* (Oxford, 1949), p. 110.

[82]   Chambers, *ES* 2, pp. 22 & 51; *ES* 3, pp. 432–3.

[83]   Chambers, *ES* 3, p. 433.

Links between the transfer of *The Fawn* from Blackfriars to Paul's and Kirkham's allegedly 'Trojan Horse' move remain uncertain.[84]

The two company names on Q2 *Fawn*'s title-page indicate a relative fluidity between the children's repertories, one that was neither isolated nor unidirectional.[85] Indeed, the reissued title-page to Middleton's *A Trick to Catch the Old One* (*c*. 1609) describes the play as 'often in Action, both at Paules, and the Black-Fryers', suggesting a reverse transfer back to Blackfriars from Paul's.[86] This kind of movement could account for the inter-company associations of *The Fawn*'s title-page. With the acquisition and performance of *The Malcontent* by the King's Men, the Blackfriars children might have felt the loss of a popular and presumably lucrative play, which was replaced by Marston's *Fawn*. Alternatively, they might have continued performing QA/B *Malcontent* while the adult QC version was simultaneously staged at the Globe (thus negating common notions about 'rivalry traditions').[87] This scenario makes *The Fawn* a welcome addition that is enhanced by association with Marston's earlier disguised ruler drama. Similarly, *The Fawn* might have entered the Paul's repertory when boys disguised as voyeuristic rulers, in plays like *The Phoenix*, were obviously popular. *The Fawn*'s transfer from Blackfriars would prompt only minor revision to its printed text. Still, whatever the rationale behind *The Fawn*'s two quarto editions, Q1 and Q2 remain substantively similar, other than their 'finicky alteration[s] of no great importance'.[88]

Critical responses to *The Fawn* have frequently been uncomplimentary and dismissive.[89] In the nineteenth century, commentators displayed familiar Whiggish tendencies when identifying the pompous and self-congratulatory rhetorician, Duke Gonzago, as Marston's caricature of King James.[90] Such Jamesian analogy is based on Gonzago's boastful description of himself as a 'philosopher [who has] spoke / With much applause' (Q1 *Fawn*, B3ʳ; 1.2.174–5), who has 'reade *Cicero de Oratore*' (Q1 *Fawn*, H1ᵛ; 4.1.614), and whose daughter calls him a 'royally wise, and wisely royall Father' blessed with 'eloquence' (Q1 *Fawn*, E4ᵛ; 3.1.345–6). Nineteenth-century responses to Marstonian caricaturing led to Albert Upton's 1929 claim, for instance, that it is 'scarcely credible' that Marston 'could have

---

[84]   See Brian Jay Corrigan, *Playhouse Law in Shakespeare's World* (Cranbury, 2004), pp. 82–3

[85]   Ibid., p. 82–3.

[86]   Middleton, *A Tricke to Catch the Old-one* (London, 1608), *STC* 17896a, fol. A1ʳ; Valerie Wayne (ed.), *A Trick to Catch the Old One*, in *Oxford Middleton*, pp. 373–4.

[87]   See Lucy Munro, 'The Humour of Children: Performance, Gender, and the Early Modern Children's Companies', *Literature Compass*, 2 (2005): 1–26.

[88]   Blostein, *Fawn*, p. 51.

[89]   See Freeburg, *Disguise*, p. 166; Hunter, 'English Folly', p. 106; Houser, 'Purging', p. 1004; Tennenhouse, *Power*, p. 157; Pendleton, 'Disguised', p. 83. For a defence of *Fawn*, see Joel Kaplan, 'John Marston's *Fawn*: A Saturnalian Satire', *SEL*, 9 (1969): 335–50 (pp. 336–7).

[90]   See Robert Cartwright, *Shakspere and Jonson* (London, 1864), p. 118n.; Bullen, *Marston*, vol. 1, p. xliii.

drawn in ignorance a satirical portrait so like his sovereign'.[91] According to Upton, *The Fawn* offers Marston's conscious, albeit foolhardy, response to his king, even though Marston's *c.* 1605 marriage to the daughter of William Wilkes, one of King James's favourite chaplains, makes this reading particularly unlikely.[92]

As the above discussion about *Measure for Measure* demonstrates, Whig-inspired critical responses to James, such as Upton's, rely on a false and anachronistic understanding of the king, tainted by selective historical discourse of long standing. Despite this, Philip J. Finkelpearl considers Upton's 'modest and sensible' identification of 'Gonzago as James' as incontrovertible, even though this would represent the 'only full-length portrait of a ruling sovereign in early modern drama'.[93] Similarly, Albert H. Tricomi sees Gonzago's 'inveterate' use of the royal 'we' – the *Pluralis Majestatis* invoked by Shakespeare's Duke in *Measure for Measure* (F, TLN.309; 1.3.19) – as an 'unexceptionable context' for arguing the intentional satire of James.[94] Tricomi further reveals his Whiggish tendencies when discussing the two quarto versions, claiming that the 'revised *Fawn* [Q2] treats more explicit Jacobean issues, in places even satirizing James's complacent self-regard'.[95] Tricomi places undue emphasis on the description of Gonzago as 'a weake Lord of a selfe admiring wisedome', which is appended to the character's name, although only in Q2's list of *Interlocutores* (Q2 *Fawn*, A3ᵛ). Within the body of the play, there is no evidence for Marston's 'finicky alteration' affecting Gonzago's character, or anything resembling King James. Indeed, the play's broad anti-folly focus has prompted alternative Gonzago identification as analogous with Shakespeare's Polonius.[96] Nevertheless, critics such as Frank Whigham describe *The Fawn* as a specific attack against James and his court, with Marston creating a 'typifying or capturing photograph, a Foucauldian monument', complete with its own geographic and temporal presence.[97]

In the same book that Whigham evokes this 'Foucauldian monument', Linda Levy Peck takes issue with traditional 'Gonzago as James' analysis, asserting that such negative conjecture is based on 'a fiction that came to be current in [James's] lifetime and which bloomed in the hothouse of Commonwealth propaganda'.[98] Despite Peck's caution, she offers an alternative target for Marston's 'deliberately multivalent' satire, namely supporters of Prince Henry (the recipient of *Basilikon Doron*) and Queen Anne. In this reading, the positive character of the disguised Hercules reflects Marston's monarch, while that 'renow[n]ed Ladie' Philocalia,

---

[91]   Upton, 'Allusions', p. 1053.

[92]   See Knowles, 'Marston', *ODNB*.

[93]   Finkelpearl, *Middle Temple*, p. 223.

[94]   Tricomi, *Anticourt*, p. 22.

[95]   Ibid., p. 14.

[96]   Cathcart, *Rivalry*, p. 65.

[97]   Whigham, 'Flattering', p. 137.

[98]   Linda Levy Peck, 'Ambivalence and Jacobean Courts', in Smith, Strier and Bevington (eds), *Theatrical City*, pp. 117–36 (pp. 117 & 136).

companion to Princess Dulcimel, represents a complimentary reference to James's queen.[99] The 'noble industries' and 'pitie' of Philocalia make her a suitable 'lady for *Ferraraes* Duke' (Q1 *Fawn*, E2ʳ; 3.1.153–66). Ultimately, therefore, 'Gonzago as James' theorizing is replaced by 'Philocalia as Anne' identification in another attempt to isolate specific royal recipients for Marston's hegemonic/subversive wit.

Once again, negativity about James, his wife and his son, colours our perception of this play that supposedly panders to Queen Anne's factional court. The 'factional' argument lacks credence, however, since there is no evidence that the queen or prince ever attended a performance at Blackfriars or Paul's.[100] Their only likely exposure to Marston's plays was through children's performances at court, where explicit and/or offensive satire might easily be expunged or amplified according to prevailing taste. Likewise, the importance of royal patronage should not be over-estimated. Court performance, and thus court patronage, was a cost-effective means of producing royal entertainment at a fraction of the outlay for self-funded Stuart masques.[101] Economic pragmatism rather than factional didacticism seems more important for the aristocratic patrons of London's playhouse companies.

Royal or noble patronage sustained commercial viability, but a playhouse needed wider audiences in order to guarantee economic survival. *The Fawn*, for instance, seems particularly suited to the legal wits of the City's Middle and Inner Temple, a group who probably remained decidedly Anglocentric in their artistic tastes due to the incompatibility of the Scottish and English legal systems.[102] Since only two of nearly eleven thousand entrants to the Inns of Court between 1590 and 1639 were Scottish, the City's legal fraternity offered a stable, identifiably English, source of income for the children's companies.[103] This demographic possibly accounts for the surprisingly gentle mockery offered in the children's company plays. These same playgoers, joined by City merchants and intelligentsia, created what Jenny Wormald describes as the 'visible hostility' of certain Londoners towards the 'appalling spectacle of "Scotsmen on the make"'.[104] For such a legally-trained, inherently anti-Scottish audience, the disguised ruler motif would be less significant than the late-medieval and sixteenth-century heritage of *The Fawn*'s exposure and punishment of folly. This advice-book morality presumably arose from Marston's and his father's training in London's Middle Temple. Marston's disguised ruler, moreover, appears to relish the sixteenth-century heritage of his advice and legal disputation.

---

[99]   Ibid., p. 118n.

[100]   Munro, *Queen's Revels*, pp. 33–4.

[101]   Kathleen E. McLuskie and Felicity Dunsworth, 'Patronage and the Economics of Theater', in John D. Cox and David Scott Kastan (eds), *A New History of Early English Drama* (New York, 1997), pp. 423–40 (pp. 428–9).

[102]   Finkelpearl, *Middle Temple*, pp. 227–9.

[103]   Brown, 'Scottish Aristocracy', p. 555.

[104]   Jenny Wormald, 'Gunpowder, Treason, and Scots', *JBS*, 24 (1985): 141–68 (p. 160).

Morality, Madness and the 'Ship of Fools'

The innocent and sexually neglected wife of Don Zuccone, Donna Zoya, feigns a pregnancy to punish her foolish husband. Zuccone's folly manifests itself in insane, unwarranted jealousy. Zoya's 'pregnancy' prompts him to divorce her in a fit of impotent rage. Defined in Florio's 1598 *Worlde of Wordes* as 'a shauen pate', 'a gull' and 'a ninnie', 'Zuccone' thus fittingly describes the physical and/ or 'humorous' traits of its owner. Marston's verbal ploy contrasts with the Florio-inspired personifications employed in Middleton's *Phoenix*, whereby a name like Proditor personifies 'treason' in the play. In *The Fawn*, Zuccone is merely the defining feature of the 'ninnie', whose jealousy earns him the 'contempt of women, and the shame of men' (Q1 *Fawn*, G4ᵛ; 4.1.536). Now the butt of Hercules/Fawn's scoffing disdain, this 'ninnie' confesses his faults and pleads for advice from his harsh critic. In response, Hercules/Fawn offers the following coldly pragmatic counsel:

> HERCULES: Hang your selfe you shal not, marrie you cannot, ile tell yee what you shal do, there is a ship of fooles setting foorth, if you make good meanes & intreat hard, you may obtaine a passage man, be maisters mate I warrant yow. (Q1 *Fawn*, G4ᵛ–H1ʳ; 4.1.511–14)

Hercules/Fawn's Act 4 condemnation precedes his masque-like 'Cupid's parliament', where those accused of sexual and moral misconduct are arraigned by 'Drunkennes, Sloth, Pride, & Plenty', '*followed by* Folly, Warre, Beggary *and* Laughter' (Q2 *Fawn*, H4ᵛ; 5.1.139.0–3.SD).[105] Resembling the *Prince d'Amour* Christmas revels of 1597–98, which were performed by law students of the Middle Temple, this 'Cupid's parliament' would appeal to Blackfriars patrons for whom heightened legalistic word-play and mock trial pronouncements provided nostalgic reminders of their own saturnalian student days.[106] In this instance, Hercules/Fawn uses the opportunity merely to humiliate the jealous husband by advising him to seek passage on that stock trope for folly and madness, the 'ship of fooles'. Zuccone is denied any hope of escape through suicide or even a degrading remarriage, since not even a 'waiting woma[n] of three bastards, a strumpet nine times carted or a hag whose eies shoot poison' (Q1 *Fawn*, G4ᵛ; 4.1.532–3) would agree to such a partnership. Embarkation, rather than incarceration in death's shroud or a loveless marriage, awaits this shaven-pated jealous 'ninnie'.

Marston's 'ship of fooles' can be traced to late-medieval European poetry. The 'ship of fools' was a fictive vessel in which the foolish and insane were sent to a far-off island, in hopes of recovering their lost reason.[107] 'Ship of fools'

---

[105]   Q1 *Fawn*, fol. H4ᵛ (5.1.139.3.SD) reads 'Slaughter', not 'Laughter'.

[106]   Kaplan, 'Saturnalian', pp. 335–50.

[107]   Peck, 'Ambivalence', p. 124.

imagery regained popularity in the 1590s.[108] Thomas Nashe, for instance, in his dedicatory epistle to Sir Philip Sidney's *Astrophil and Stella* (1591), describes keeping 'pace with [the] Grauesend barge' (that ferried Londoners the twenty-two miles back and forth along the Thames on every tide) in his own 'ship of fooles'.[109] Nashe's ship bears unscrupulous lawyers and gullible provincial victims to London for the lucrative legal Terms. Repeated by authors such as Michael Drayton and Gabriel Harvey, the same imagery appears in Thomas Dekker's 1604 plague pamphlet, *Newes from Graues-end* (augmented by Middleton), whose satiric 'Epistle Dedicatory' again invokes the Gravesend ferry, while condemning all 'Rymesters, Play-patchers, Iig-makers, Ballad-mongers, & Pamphlet-stitchers' into being 'prest to serue at sea in the ship of Fooles'.[110] 'Ship of fools' imagery thus pervaded late-sixteenth and early seventeenth-century satire.

This metaphorical 'ship of fools' was originally derived from Sebastian Brant's *Das Narrenschiff* (1494), a long, moralizing and non-ironic German poem, translated into Latin by Jacob Locher and republished in 1497 as *Stultifera Navis*.[111] Brant's poem heralded the sixteenth-century *narrenliteratur* or 'fool's literature', of which Erasmus's *Praise of Folly* is an early, albeit ironic example.[112] Described in Michel Foucault's 1961 discourse, *Folie et déraison* (*Madness and Civilization*), as a 'strange "drunken boat"' – whose 'crew of imaginary heroes, ethical models, or social tropes embarked on a great symbolic voyage which would bring them, if not fortune, then at least the figure of their destiny or their truth' – Brant's 'ship of fools' offered passengers a chance to rediscover reason through prolonged isolation from their communities.[113] Brant's ship was based, so Foucault somewhat anecdotally argues, on the ritual 'expulsion of madmen' on supposedly 'real' ships that sailed along the Rhineland waterways and Flemish canals.[114] Foucault offers no firm evidence for these ships, though he argues that Brant reinterpreted these material vessels to create his 'highly symbolic' evocation of 'madmen in search of their reason'.[115]

Whether actual ships served as floating asylums, or as depositories for social misfits, remains unclear. Nevertheless, Brant's exposure of assorted follies

---

[108] See C.W. Brooks, *Pettyfoggers and Vipers of the Commonwealth* (Cambridge, 2004), pp. 30–31.

[109] Sir Philip Sidney, *His Astrophel and Stella* (London, 1591), fol. A4ᵛ.

[110] Thomas Dekker, *Newes from Graues-end* (London, 1604), fol. B1ᵛ; Gary Taylor (ed.), *News From Gravesend*, in *Oxford Middleton*, pp. 134–5.

[111] Sebastian Brant, *Das Narrenschiff* (Basel, 1494); *Stultifera Navis,* trans. Jacob Locher (Basel, 1497).

[112] Erasmus, *Praise of Folly*, trans. Betty Radice (Harmondsworth: 1993), pp. xliii–xliv.

[113] Michel Foucault, *Madness and Civilization*, trans. Richard Howard (London, 2001), pp. 5–7.

[114] Ibid., pp. 6–8.

[115] Ibid., p. 7.

Fig. 4.2   'Madmen' in fool's motley jostle for position aboard Sebastian Brant's 'Ship of Fools' (1494)

and vices gained notoriety and popularity following the London publication of
Alexander Barclay's 1509 translation of Locher's Latinized edition, under its
Englished title, *The Ship of Fooles* (1509).[116] Republished again as late as 1570,
Barclay's expanded and highly personalized interpretation of Brant's metaphorical
ship appears in *The Fawn* as a natural depository for Urbino's miscreant citizens and
courtiers. Like Foucault's floating asylums, the 'ship of fools' in Marston's *Fawn*
transcends commonplace metaphor. This symbolic ship figuratively manifests
on an offstage sea, complete with captain, cabins and freight-holds.[117] The ship's
material presence becomes so credible that the clownish Dondolo, whom Gonzago
promotes to 'Captain' of the vessel (Q2 *Fawn*, E2ʳ; 2.1.142), informs Hercules/
Fawn that the 'fooles that were appointed to waight on *Don Cupid*' (those morality
personifications who later lead the legalistic revelry) 'haue launcht out their ship
to purge their stomackes on the water' (Q2 *Fawn*, H3ᵛ; 5.1.46–8). The *mal de mer*
of these drunken revellers enhances Marston's 'ship of fooles' imagery, elevating
it, as Peck argues, to the most 'striking image' in this most 'anti-Castiglione, anti-
Urbino' of plays.[118]

The Fawn invokes Brant's *Narrenschiff*, not only with its overt 'ship of fooles'
imagery, but also with its Zuccone/Zoya subplot of insane marital jealousy. This
Brantian dimension to the play emerges from Section 32 of the 1570s Englished
edition of *Ship of Fools*, entitled: 'Of him that is gelous ouer his wife, and watcheth
her wayes without cause or euident token of her misliuing'.[119] Brant's original
verse, printed first in Locher's Latin, then in the English translation by Barclay,
appears sympathetic to '*chast*' wives like Donna Zoya who are cursed by their
husbands' jealousy: '*Thus is it foly, and causeth great debate / Betwene man and
wife, when he by gelousy, / His wife suspecteth*'.[120] In Barclay's poetic farewell or
'*Lenuoy*', the tone is less salutary and more misogynistic.[121] Barclay admonishes
all '*women* [to] *liue wisely, and eschewe / ... wilde company*', and especially to
'*Haunt no olde queanes that nourish ribaudry*' or '*wanton wooers* [that] *are full of
flattery*'.[122] Barclay advises wives, on fear of being '*rauished by handes violent*',
ever to '*Be meke, demure, bocsome, and obedient*'.[123] Zuccone's obvious guilt
and Donna Zoya's equally obvious innocence thus accord more closely with a
Brantian moral ethos than with Barclay's scare-mongering rhetoric.

---

[116] Brant, *The Ship of Fooles*, trans. Alexander Barclay (London, 1509).

[117] Blostein, *Fawn*, p. 29, accords the 'Ship of Fools' an onstage status as an actual
scene-property moved on wheels.

[118] Peck, 'Ambivalence', p. 124.

[119] *Ship of Fooles*, STC 3546, fol. L3ʳ.

[120] Ibid., fol. L3ᵛ.

[121] Brant's verse echoes Gonzago's self-congratulatory praise when explaining 'the
morality or lenuoy' of his sentential observations (Q1 *Fawn*, I3ᵛ; 5.1.388).

[122] *Ship of Fooles*, STC 3546, fol. L4ʳ.

[123] Ibid., fol. L4ʳ.

This Brantian context ensures that Zuccone's jealousy remains the focus of Hercules/Fawn's scorn. Zuccone's punishment reflects his foolishness. Threatened with embarkation on the metaphorical 'ship of fools', Zuccone escapes this humiliation through a timid acceptance of his wife's every demand. Foremost among these is an absolute sexual freedom that guarantees Zuccone's future as a notorious cuckold. Other Urbino courtiers face harsher fates. Those guilty of transgressions such as 'plurality of Mistresses' (Q2 *Fawn*, I1ʳ; 5.1.212), 'abusing … subjectes with false money' (Q2 *Fawn*, I2ʳ; 5.1.262), incestuous adultery or braggartly seduction, are all escorted to the ship by the morality personification of 'Folly' himself, 'without eyther baile or main-prize' (Q2 *Fawn*, I2ʳ; 5.1.280–81).

For Marston, overcoming folly and deceit provides the principal motive for Hercules' disguised ruler adventure. Hercules attacks his victims not with harsh satire, but by encouraging their foolish and deceitful behaviour. His retributive justice relies on the theory of self-correcting folly.[124] Such self-reform ensures that it is Duke Gonzago, and not Hercules/Fawn, who has 'labord to haue all the fools shipt out of his dominions' (Q2 *Fawn*, G1ᵛ; 4.1.233). As Dondolo ironically comments, Gonzago's insistence on ejecting the foolish from his land guarantees that he can 'play the foole himselfe alone without any riuall' (Q2 *Fawn*, G1ᵛ; 4.1.236). Hercules need not satirize his victims; they incriminate themselves in a feast of fawning sycophancy. This strategy leads Charles Larmore to label *The Fawn* as Marston's ultimate rejection of satire and rationality, which he replaces with a scepticism towards Stoic self-control and constancy.[125]

Marston's scepticism represents a movement away from life's sensual pleasures, which found its fullest expression in the late sixteenth-century writing of Michel de Montaigne. Indeed, much of *The Fawn* is influenced by Montaigne; over thirty-five separate passages originate directly from Florio's recent translation of Montaigne's *Essayes*. Most of these references stem from the fifth chapter of Book 3, '*Vpon some uerses of* Virgill', which highlights Montaigne's free-thinking libertinism through its provenance in an erotic passage about Venus and Vulcan in the *Aeneid* (8:387–92 & 404–6ff.).[126] Exploring the tribulations of marriage, love, sex, jealousy and infidelity, Montaigne sympathizes with women who, like Marston's Donna Zoya, are 'much more easie to accuse': '*I say, that both male and female, are cast in one same moulde; instruction and custome excepted, there is no great difference betweene them*'.[127] Montaigne's perspectives on female sexuality align more closely with Brant's views than with Barclay's. Echoes of Montaigne also resonate through Marston's treatment of Zuccone, when this foolish lord is

---

[124] See Blostein, *Fawn*, p. 2; R.W. Ingram, *John Marston* (Boston, 1978), p. 127.

[125] Charles Larmore, 'Scepticism', in Daniel Garber and Michael Ayers (eds), *Cambridge History of Seventeenth Century Philosophy* (2 vols, Cambridge, 1998), vol. 2, pp. 1145–92 (p. 1147).

[126] Montaigne, *Essayes*, trans. Florio, fols 2V3ʳ–2Z1ʳ.

[127] Ibid., fol. 2Z1ʳ.

threatened with the 'ship of fooles', a punishment not remitted until he agrees to his wife's demand for sexual freedom.

Throughout, late-medieval metaphor combines with late sixteenth-century scepticism to create the sexual comedy of *The Fawn*. Marston's reliance on literary material from the sixteenth century is not restricted, however, to Brantian imagery, Erasmian irony or Montaignean ideal selfhood. *The Fawn* also betrays Marston's invocation of the familiar 'comical history' heritage of his disguised ruler/wooing ambassador plot. Not content with subtle allusion, Marston explicitly quotes from *Friar Bacon and Friar Bungay*, a popular exemplar of that tradition, incorporating its themes into *The Fawn*'s disguised ruler narrative.

Tiberio's Wooing Embassy and the 'Far-Fam'd Friar'

On his first meeting with Dulcimel, *The Fawn*'s Tiberio presents the young princess with Hercules' 'perfect counterfeit' as a painted love-token from the old duke (Q2 *Fawn*, B2^r; 1.2.108). Dulcimel questions the 'true proportion' of Hercules' portrait, the best that any 'Painters Art' could yield, and wonders at the aged suitor's effrontery in 'send[ing] a counterfeit to mooue [her] loue' (Q2 *Fawn*, B2^r; 1.2.108–12). Tiberio offers a somewhat undiplomatic response: if her 'eie dislike the deader peece', she should 'behold' the ambassador before her as a 'true forme and liuelier image', for 'such [Tiberio's] Father hath beene' (Q2 *Fawn*, B2^r; 1.2.116–18). Dulcimel's rejoinder is both barbed and witty:

> DULCIMEL: My Lord, please you to scent this flower.
> TIBERIO: Tis withered Ladie, the flowers scent is gone.
> DULCIMEL: This hath been such as you are, hath been sir[. T]hey say in
> *England*, that a farre fam'd Frier had guirt the Island round with a
> brasse wall, if that they could haue catched, *Time is*, but *Time is*
> *past*, left it still clipt with aged *Neptunes* arme. (Q2 *Fawn*, B2^r; 1.2.119–25)

Not only does Dulcimel suggest that Hercules' likeness is as true to life as a withered flower whose scent has died with age, she also alludes to the 'farre fam'd' Friar Bacon, who has 'guirt the Island round' with his 'brasse wall'. If the painter of Hercules' portrait could have captured a more truthful though less flattering representation of her suitor, then Dulcimel's suspicions about this 'counterfeit' might not have been roused.

The original uncorrected Q1 spelling of 'far found Frier' (Q1 *Fawn*, B2^r; 1.2.123) suggests that Marston, or his printer, deliberately emphasized Friar Bacon's presence when amending the Q2 text to 'far fam'd Frier'. In Q2, the allusion to *Friar Bacon* is substantially heightened and confirmed. Indeed, the whole episode mirrors Princess Eleanor's receipt of Edward's 'louely counterfeit' in *Friar Bacon*, where Eleanor undertakes the 'perrils' of travel to see her future husband for herself, once being shown his 'comly pourtrait' (*Bacon*, C1^v; 4.22–30). Unfortunately, like Friar Bacon's failed attempt to ring the English Isle with a wall of brass to fend off all intruders (a topical, jingoistic image following the 1588 Armada threat), so Hercules' portrait also fails, since Dulcimel deems it an over-romanticized image of an ageing duke whose '*Time is past*'. The success of Dulcimel's dismissive imagery relies on audience recognition of the *Friar Bacon* narrative, where the friar fails in his magical quest by sleeping through the fateful utterances of the brazen head: 'Time is', 'Time was' and 'Time is past' (*Bacon*, G2ᵛ; 11.53, 65 & 75).

The princess's derogatory comments are not the only allusions to *Friar Bacon* within *The Fawn*. In the 'Cupid's parliament', Lord Granuffo speaks for the first time. Granuffo's status as a learned man in Urbino's court depends upon him never opening his mouth to prove the contrary. His silence flatters Gonzago, whose pomposity thereby remains unchallenged. When forced to comment on the justice of 'An Act against mummers, false seemers, that ... [seem] wise onely by silence' (Q2 *Fawn*, I3ʳ–I3ᵛ; 5.1.371–3), Granuffo utters this inane response: 'Iust sure, for in good truth, or in good sooth, when wise men speake, they still must open their mouth' (Q2 *Fawn*, I3ᵛ; 5.1.381). With unbridled astonishment, Hercules/Fawn declares that 'The brazen head haz spoken' (Q2 *Fawn*, I3ᵛ; 5.1.382), an allusion to the magical 'head' in *Friar Bacon*. Granuffo's sudden utterance resembles *Friar Bacon*'s stage illusion, where an actor's metalized head 'magically' comes to life. *The Fawn* invokes that moment when, after many patient years, the brazen head speaks its seven fateful words about 'Time', before falling silent forever (*Bacon* G2ᵛ; 11.53–75). This explicit reference to such a famous 'comical history' illustrates Marston's decision to foreground this popular adult play in his latest disguised ruler offering.

The Fawn's overt references to *Friar Bacon* are not surprising, given the overall plot of Marston's nostalgic comic construction. As David J. Houser remarks, *The Fawn*'s retributive disguised ruler is likewise reminiscent of that earlier 'morality' drama, the anonymous *A Knack to Know a Knave* (*c.* 1592).[128] As noted above, the disguise narrative and character personifications of *Knack to Know a Knave* reappear in Middleton's *Phoenix*. Nevertheless, *Knack to Know a Knave* also presents the wooing intrigue of King Edgar, who sends his courtier Ethenwald as ambassador to the lady Alfrida. Ethenwald predictably falls for Alfrida, who changes places with her kitchen maid in an attempt to fool the king. Although Alfrida's ruse is discovered, King Edgar cannot consummate his adulterous union. The king's employment of Ethenwald as a wooing ambassador closely mirrors Prince Edward's lustful endeavours in *Friar Bacon*. Like Edgar, Edward is also thwarted by Lacy's loving defence of Margaret. Whether *Friar Bacon* directly influenced the unknown playwright of *Knack to Know a Knave* is unclear, but Marston clearly uses the same plot premise in his play. He deliberately alludes to *Friar Bacon*, a play still popular enough to be immediately recognizable to the *Fawn*'s children's company audience. In fact, *Friar Bacon* was revived in December 1602 for an adult performance by the Admiral's Men at Elizabeth's

---

[128]   Houser, 'Purging', p. 993.

Fig. 4.3   The brazen head speaks while Miles and Friar Bacon sleep, from
              Friar Bacon's 1630 title-page

court. This version, so Henslowe's *Diary* suggests, included an additional
Prologue and Epilogue by Middleton, written either before or contemporaneously
with his own disguised ruler drama, *The Phoenix*.[129] The well-known *Friar Bacon*,
rather than the obscure *Knack to Know a Knave*, informs the wooing narrative of
Dulcimel and Tiberio. Tiberio's ambassadorship thus parallels Lacy's wooing of
Margaret. Although this young prince is not surveilled through a distant 'glass
prospective', he is nonetheless observed by an all-seeing father who, like the
angry Prince Edward, is likewise a disguised ruler.

    Friar Bacon's influence similarly appears through Hercules' manipulation of
his son. When Hercules, still disguised as Fawn, tries to convince Tiberio to woo
for himself, rather than for his ageing father, the duke evokes a commonplace
about the loneliness of kingly rule. 'Fawn' informs Tiberio that 'fathers or friends,
a crowne, / And loue hath none, but all are allied to themselues alone' (Q2 *Fawn*,
F2ʳ; 3.1.502–3). Hercules' remark echoes Lacy's observation in *Friar Bacon* that
'love makes no exception of a friend, / Nor deems it of a prince but as a man'
(*Bacon*, D1ʳ; 6.58–9). By successfully convincing his son to act for himself,
Hercules guarantees the continuation of Ferrara's ancestral line. This dynastic
pragmatism enables a marriage that will unite the dukedoms of Ferrara and Urbino
when Gonzago dies. Such union becomes necessary because Urbino suffers the
same threat to its dynasty encountered by the sixteenth-century Tudors: the lack
of a patrilineal successor. As the father of a daughter, Gonzago's line must end.

---

[129] *Henslowe's Diary*, p. 207.

Hercules' proactive pragmatism, coupled with Gonzago's lack of a successor, provides the focus for Marston's exploration of disguised ruler power. Hercules' quest to sustain his ducal line relies on an explicit intertextuality between *The Fawn* and *Friar Bacon*, evinced by overt quotations from this significant and popular 'comical history' in the disguised ruler tradition. Audiences could enjoy *The Fawn* on various levels – as eroticized drama, as comic entertainment, as xenophobic or localized satire – but, as with so many of the children's company plays, law and disputation drive the momentum of its moralizing Italianate comedy. A similar engagement with disguised ruler intrigue and legal chicanery appears in *Law Tricks*, a play Tennenhouse includes in his 'solidarity' list of disguised ruler dramas.[130] This city comedy conflates several familiar Anglocentric themes into its Italianate prodigal child narrative.

Law Tricks, Disguise and the Prodigal Child

John Day's *Law Tricks* (*c*. 1604–1607, Queen's Revels, Blackfriars[?]/King's Revels, Whitefriars[?]; published 1608) was not entered in the *Stationers' Register* until 28 March 1608.[131] Published in quarto that same year, its title-page identifies it as 'diuers times Acted by the Children of the Reuels'.[132] Chambers believed that this company ascription correlated with ownership by the children at Blackfriars.[133] *Law Tricks* could thus have been staged as early as 1604, although it more likely appeared 1605–1606, because of its apparent association with other disguised ruler dramas. Chambers also equates the absence of any reference to 'Queen' on the title-page's promotional statement (as opposed to the 'Queen's' title-page presence on *Fawn*) as historical evidence for the supposed loss of Anne's patronage at Blackfriars in early 1606.[134] Accordingly, since Chambers, *Law Tricks* has remained firmly dated to the middle years of the decade. Critical enthusiasm is mixed for the alternative suggestion, that the title-page refers to ownership, adoption or adaptation by the King's Revels children at Whitefriars between 1607 and 1608.[135] Although company ownership and dating remain uncertain, the play's incidental and strangely isolated depiction of a disguised ruler has much in common with the satirical treatment of the legal profession in *The Phoenix*, as well as with the abuse of married women in both *Phoenix* and *Fawn*.

---

[130] Tennenhouse, *Power*, p. 154.

[131] Arber 3, p. 372.

[132] John Day, *Law-Trickes* (London, 1608). Through line numbers from John Crow (ed.), *Law Tricks* (Oxford, 1950).

[133] Chambers, *ES* 3, pp. 285–6.

[134] See also Munro, *Children*, p. 21.

[135] Giorgio Melchiori (ed.), *Insatiate Countess* (Manchester, 1984), pp. 12–13 & 45n.; Charles Cathcart, 'Authorship, Indebtedness, and the Children of the King's Revels', *SEL*, 45 (2005): 357–74; Munro, *Queen's Revels*, p. 174.

That Day intends to introduce a disguised ruler into the narrative of *Law Tricks* is, at the play's beginning, far from obvious. In the opening scene of Act 1, Ferneze, Duke of Genoa (a dukedom shared with Marston's Andrugio and Altofronto), learns that his daughter, Emilia, has been kidnapped by marauding Turks. Immediately travelling to nearby '*Pisa*' to trace his 'lou'd *Emilia*', Ferneze deputizes his bookish son Polymetes to rule the 'widowed Duke-dome' in his absence (*Law*, B2[r]; TLN.220–22). Ferneze insists that his son should temporarily 'possesse' the 'chaire' of state (an obtuse hint at Angelo's deputyship in Vienna if such is intended), while invoking the commonplace that this office will 'fill [Polymetes] with care' (*Law*, B2[r]; TLN.223–4). Even so, there is little to suggest this austere young prince, whose 'robe of learning' and 'strict contemplation' make him shun 'Publique assemblies, [and] knightly exercise', will either fail in his commission, or warrant his father's disguised observation (*Law*, B1[r]; TLN.147–50).

Unbeknownst to all, Emilia has already escaped the Turks and disguised herself secretly in Genoa as the servant 'Tristella'. Tristella attracts amorous attention from her unsuspecting brother (Polymetes) and her lascivious uncle-by-marriage, Count Lurdo. With comic skill, she avoids the incestuous advances of both. Emilia/Tristella will, in the play's final act, disclose her true identity and be reunited with her father. Her joyous return ensures all wrongdoers are forgiven. The dominant plot of the play thus is not the disguised ruler, but the 'law tricks' of the unscrupulous Lurdo, uncle to Emilia and Polymetes and brother-in-law to the duke. The play's full title, *Law-Trickes or, Who Would Have Thought It*, marks this overriding concern with the intrigue of Lurdo, who uses 'law-trickes' to accuse his wife, the Countess, of adultery in order to gain a divorce. In a plot that echoes Castiza's plight in *The Phoenix*, the Countess proves her innocence, though only after she has feigned her own death by poison. Her miraculous resurrection, invoking the mythical 'Phoenix' regularly mentioned in the play, exposes her husband's legal chicanery. In this legalistic principal plot, the voyeuristic intervention of a disguised ruler is of no consequence, not even when Lurdo's wicked scheme is revealed in the play's dénouement.

Despite the play's overriding concern with the 'law tricks' of Lurdo, a belated Act 4 stage direction does declare, '*Enter Duke Ferneze disguisd*' (*Law*, F1[v]; TLN.1321.SD). Hinting at the uncomfortable dramatic irony to come, this notation announces the arrival of Ferneze who, like Emilia, has also returned to Genoa, but without knowing his daughter's whereabouts. Intent on testing his son's virtue, the duke disguises himself as a humble messenger, the 'sad reporter of … newes' that Polymetes' 'father' has died (*Law*, F2[r]; TLN.1329). Polymetes is now no longer a diligent scholar, having been transformed, like one from Ovid's 'Metamorphosis' (*Law*, F2[r]; TLN.1332), into a corrupt and profligate prince. He receives his disguised father's report with unbridled glee and triumphantly declares himself Duke Polymetes. At the same time, he decides how best to squander the 'countlesse masse of wealth' his 'father [has] bequeath'd [him] at his death' (*Law*, F2[r]; TLN.1350–51). Although privy to his son's heartlessness, Ferneze leaves when perfunctorily dismissed, only to return in full ducal splendour 131 lines later. Ferneze watches with fatherly tolerance as his son feigns madness at the supposed pressures of state responsibility, and pretends to be duped by Polymetes' sudden change into a dutiful, hard-working son. To prove his supposed conscientiousness, Polymetes delegates his equally corrupt friend, Julio, with the task of sweeping the court of 'idle brayn'd and antique parasites', even though Julio is the most significant example (_Law_, G2ᵛ; TLN.1636).

This incidental subplot episode, which includes a disguised ruler's appearance and disappearance, involves a mere 39 lines of dialogue. Polymetes only enjoys a short period of profligate planning for his life as 'an indifferent careles Duke' (_Law_, F2ᵛ; TLN.1365–6), intent on squandering his 'Royall expence' on fashionable clothes, drinking and whoring (_Law_, F3ʳ; TLN.1402). His plans are quickly curtailed when he is informed of the untimely return of 'the Duke [his] father with a greate traine' (_Law_, F3ᵛ; TLN.1463–4). Obviously no longer in disguise, Ferneze re-enters almost immediately, ready to 'startle' his prodigal son by putting 'his wit vnto … present tryall' (_Law_, F4ʳ; TLN.1500–1501). Ferneze privately comments on Polymetes' obvious falsehood, claiming that as a father, he 'can but smile to see how' the prince and his colleagues think 'to leade [him] in an idle maze' (_Law_, G2ᵛ; TLN.1638–40). His fatherly tolerance is tinged with caution, however, as he 'temporize[s], and note[s] the issue' of his unexpected return (_Law_, G2ᵛ; TLN.1641–2). Nevertheless, within a markedly short section of the play (334 lines out of 2318 through lines in total), a prodigal narrative is enacted, which incidentally includes a disguised ruler's 39-line appearance and dismissal. The disguised ruler's dramatic presence is simply a means for exposing the comic decline of a wayward, prodigal prince. Ferneze may keep a wary eye on a son who, unaware of any disguised visitation, now believes he has duped his father, but the disguised ruler is never mentioned again.

Although the disguised ruler makes only a fleeting appearance in _Law Tricks_, the prodigal son motive for the duke's incidental subterfuge accords with several other London comedies of the period. In these, disguised patriarchs, husbands and fathers plot to resolve the financial and/or sexual misdemeanours of their wayward charges, wives and children. The anonymous _London Prodigal_ (_c_. 1604, King's Men; published 1605), Marston's _Dutch Courtesan_ (_c_. 1604, Queen's Revels; published 1605), Dekker and Middleton's _The Patient Man and the Honest Whore_ (1604, Prince Henry's; published 1604) and Dekker's _The Second Part of the Honest Whore_ (_c_. 1604–1605, Prince Henry's; published 1630), as well as Dekker and Webster's _Westward Ho!_ (1604, Paul's; published 1607), each include disguised characters secretly observing profligate behaviour, before leading toward a desired resolution.[136] The incidental disguise episode in _Law Tricks_ may invite comparison with its more famous Italianate disguised ruler associates, but its prodigal son subplot more noticeably resides within a group of plays that

---

[136] Dekker's _Second Part of the Honest Whore_ proved a major influence on Marston's _Dutch Courtesan_.

reflect the broad popularity of this biblical 'organising narrative', rather than the disguised characters who resolve their prodigal issues.[137]

Polymetes in *Law Tricks* represents yet another prodigal character, corrupted by power and forced to feign 'cares-of-state' madness to escape his father's wrath. His actions, like those of so many prodigals before him, arise less from political misrule, and more from the dangers of unhealthy sexual appetites. In Polymetes' case, his unchecked libido results in illicit lust for his own sister. Like Tiberio in *The Fawn*, Polymetes cannot engage with 'Tristella' (Emilia in disguise) except through witty wordplay. His reclusive, scholarly behaviour has left him incapable of 'loue' for any of her 'sex' (*Law*, B4ᵛ; TLN.371). The unwitting siblings' wordplay even reengages with the late-medieval trope so dominant in *The Fawn*. On first meeting Emilia/Tristella, Polymetes begins a sexually nuanced exchange that layers incestuous lasciviousness over the plot. This erotic dialogue follows Emilia's encounter with the clumsy Julio who, as a 'young wooer', proves 'much to[o] rude' to gain the young girl's affections (*Law*, B4ʳ; TLN.366). In response, the disguised princess humiliates the blushing gallant into silent submission. Answering Polymetes' mocking enquiry about whether the crestfallen Julio is, like a stranded ship, 'graueld' in low-lying water, Emilia compounds her brother's nautical imagery by answering on Julio's behalf, 'No, but run a Land' (*Law*, B4ᵛ; TLN.373–4). Emilia's equally disdainful query about whether Polymetes' own 'shipping [is] any better mand?' (*Law*, B4ᵛ; TLN.375) invites a sexually charged exchange between the sparring siblings:

> POLYMETES: Yes, will you board it?
> EMILIA: No, I dare not venter:
> POLYMETES: Make but a shot in iest and you may enter.
> EMILIA: You are a Scholler.
> POLYMETES: I haue seene some Schooles.
> EMILIA: You came not ore i'the last fleet of Fooles.
> POLYMETES: You tooke my roome vp.
> EMILIA: I pray tak't agen.
> Weele haue no women fooles saile amongst men. (*Law Tricks*, B4ᵛ; TLN.376–85)

While they display their skilful wordplay, Polymetes and his disguised sister equate youthful sexual excess with imagery reliant not on a single 'ship', but on an entire 'fleet of Fooles'. Although this short exchange represents only a brief moment in Day's complex Italianate city comedy, it reaffirms the conventionality of the late-medieval 'ship of fools' trope for exploring the folly of sexual desire. In this instance, such folly is made more urgent by the incestuous implication of this erotic chance meeting.

As *The Phoenix* and *The Fawn* had already demonstrated, disguised ruler plays, however formulaic, excited the playgoing public. The motif's influence extended to the prodigal child narrative of *Law Tricks* and beyond. Medieval

---

[137] Munro, *Queen's Revels*, p. 58.

morality and sixteenth-century advice-book imagery remained constant features within these explorations of royal disguise. It is unsurprising, therefore, that disguised rulers should continue to be evoked in plays, inviting parodic comparison with Marston, Shakespeare and Middleton. In 1605, however, an event occurred that overshadowed theatrical expression in the age, an incident so potentially devastating that it united the majority of the nation's subjects behind their monarch. The resulting climate of insecurity and fear – of public uncertainty and private suspicion directed at those seeking to destabilize the Stuart regime in the most murderous way – colours subsequent representations of disguised rulers. Heralding the decline of a longstanding motif, the spectre of terrorism fundamentally altered the way disguised rulers served as agents for social or moral change in the immoral world of London's bustling mercantile city.

Chapter 5
Disguised Ruler Afterlives:
The Spectre of Terrorism

Francis Beaumont and John Fletcher's collaborative venture, *The Woman Hater* (*c.* 1606, Paul's; published 1607), is an Italianate proto-tragicomedy. It predates by up to two years Fletcher's 1608 Blackfriars failure, *The Faithful Shepherdess*, a play that belatedly emulates Guarini's *Il pastor fido*.[1] In *The Woman Hater*'s opening scene, the Duke of Milan discusses the earliness of the hour and his unusual pre-dawn perambulation with his courtiers, Arrigo and Lucio. The Duke enquires if they know why he is 'vp so soone' (*Woman*, A3ʳ; 1.1.9).[2] This so-called 'patterne for all Princes' is rewarded with a progression of proposed political scenarios, his motive being either to execute 'some waightie State plot', 'cure some strange corruptions in the common wealth', 'walke the publique streetes disguised, to see the streetes disorders', or 'secretly [to] crosse some other states, that … conspire against' him (*Woman*, A3ʳ–A3ᵛ; 1.1.10–27). Evoking any number of voyeuristic subterfuges, Lucio's specific reference to his Duke walking the 'publique streets' whets our collective appetite for disguised ruler intrigue within a potentially moralizing, reforming narrative.

Unexpectedly, and despite a belief in the 'waightie' seriousness of their master's venturing, the courtiers suffer the Duke's perfunctory denial, 'It is not so' (*Woman*, A3ᵛ; 1.1.25). With ironic relish, he proclaims instead the true purpose of his night-time meander as being 'Waightier farre':

> DUKE: You are my friendes, and you shall haue the cause;
> I breake my sleepes thus soone to see a wench. (*Woman Hater*, A3ᵛ; 1.1.27–9)

Within the opening moments of this Children of Paul's play, most likely performed alongside *The Phoenix* and the recently-acquired *Fawn* (and possibly, as its 1648 and 1649 Q2 versions imply, later staged by the King's Men), the disguised ruler as serious political overseer is simultaneously evoked and rejected.[3] The Duke's 'Waightier' purpose, an assignation with Oriana, sister of his friend Count Valore, constitutes no more than wooing adventurism by a sexually predatory royal. Oriana's virtue is later called into question by both brother and future husband, her flirtatious manipulation of Gondarino (the 'woman hater' of the play) leading to

---

[1] See Munro, *Queen's Revels*, p. 123.

[2] Line numbers from George Walton Williams (ed.), *The Woman Hater*, in Fredson Bowers (gen. ed.), *The Dramatic Works in the Beaumont and Fletcher Canon* (10 vols, Cambridge, 1966–96), vol. 1 (1966).

[3] Ibid., vol. 1, p. 154.

the denouncement that prompts her to seek sanctuary in one of the nearby 'bawdy houses' (*Woman*, H2ᵛ; 4.2.281). She faces potential execution, her trauma secretly observed by the 'sufficiently disguiz'd' Duke (*Woman*, H2ᵛ; 4.2.288). She also is offered her life in exchange for sexual favours by the sword-wielding Arrigo, who swears (in accord with his Duke's secret command) to 'injoy' her whether she agrees or no (*Woman*, K2ʳ; 5.4.69). Oriana's chaste refusal and acceptance of death, the Duke's subsequent proposal of marriage, and the wronged woman's tersely resigned response – 'My Lord, I am no more mine owne' (*Woman*, K2ᵛ; 5.4.94) – echo the plot of *Measure for Measure*.[4] These traumatic events happen, however, only after *The Woman Hater*'s Duke has dismissed the suggestion that his disguised appearance performs any 'Waightier' purpose, other than 'to see a wench'.

Beaumont and Fletcher take for granted that their Paul's audience would recognize the irony of presenting a disguised ruler *in potentia*, only to have these expectations immediately quashed. By so doing, *The Woman Hater* invites a parodic reminder of the disguised ruler's romantic heritage, the Duke's subsequent revelation evoking 1590s 'comical history' kings whose wooing adventures provide the morally suspect motive for his night-time wandering.[5] Parody indeed, but the 'core of truth' in this opening scene – its ironic evocation of disguised ruler 'State plot' intrigue – also spotlights the ubiquity of the motif, with Beaumont and Fletcher comically rejecting its narrative potential.[6] This Italian duke might walk Milan's 'publique streets', inviting an audience/reader's initial knowing response to his travels/travails. Unlike the Prince/Phoenix or Hercules/Fawn, whose reforming impulses inform their disguised subterfuge, the Duke of *The Woman Hater* resolutely returns to the romantic roots of his becloaked adventure.

What possible motive might there be for Beaumont and Fletcher's comical rejection of the moralizing disguised ruler, and their revisiting of far older romantic intrigue, other than as simple parody? Might there be a more pressing reason why the disguised ruler should fade in political significance, his presence in plays now evoking light-heartedness rather than serious social commentary? Traditional critical responses to *The Woman Hater* see the play as Beaumont and Fletcher's attempt at 'protested political neutrality', motivated by their desire to distance themselves and the Paul's company from the controversies plaguing the neighbouring Blackfriars over the staging of potentially subversive, satirical plays.[7] By 1606, the Blackfriars children had, so Chambers 'inferred' from various title-pages, lost Queen Anne's patronage, and their official private censor, Samuel Daniel.[8] Daniel's removal from his unusually favoured position

---

[4]   Gordon McMullan, *The Politics of Unease in the Plays of John Fletcher* (Amherst, 1994), p. 89.

[5]   Redmond, *Shakespeare, Politics,* p. 11.

[6]   Tiffany Stern, *Making Shakespeare* (London, 2004), p. 79.

[7]   Munro, *Queen's Revels*, p. 9.

[8]   Chambers, *ES* 2, p. 51.

as Blackfriars censor, in direct competition with the Master of the Revels, probably stemmed from nuanced readings of his play, *The Tragedie of Philotas* (*c*. 1604, Queen's Revels; published 1605, with revisions 1607). The conspirator Philotas was, it is suggested, associated with Robert Devereux, second earl of Essex, himself convicted of treason in 1601; Daniel's *Tragedie of Philotas* might thus be perceived as tacitly approving Essex's rebellion.[9] Blackfriars also stood accused of anti-Scottish sentiment in Chapman, Jonson and Marston's *Eastward Ho!* (1605), which resulted (if we are fully to believe his 1618–19 reminiscences in conversation with William Drummond) in Jonson being 'voluntarly imprissonned' with Chapman.[10] Likewise, anti-Union sentiment in Day's *Isle of Gulls* (1606) led to a short incarceration in Bridewell for some of the play's young actors.[11] These scandals, when combined with similar incidents involving Chapman's *The Conspiracy and Tragedy of Charles, Duke of Byron* (1608), and the lost play commonly known as *The Silver Mine*, which reportedly satirized King James's silver mining ventures in Scotland, eventually lead to the children losing their Blackfriars home and providing the King's Men with their new indoor venue.[12] Losing a private playhouse could represent an absolute fall from favour, but this penalty did not prevent the same children's company from later performing at court and on tour, so suggesting a less complete distancing from royal patronage.[13]

Whether or not Beaumont and Fletcher were seeking to distance themselves (and/or the Paul's children for whom they initially wrote) from these Blackfriars scandals cannot definitively be determined. Whatever prompted their disguised ruler parody, its depoliticizing effect seems fortuitous considering the fear that no doubt accompanied performances of *The Woman Hater*. Presented in the aftermath of a significant historical event that oddly receives less literary consideration than the personality traits of the king whose life it threatened, *The Woman Hater* is associated with the Gunpowder Plot of 1605. This sent shockwaves through the nation. From this perspective, disguised ruler parody plausibly becomes a dramatic reaction to the localized political fear of a government made painfully aware of its tenuous hold on power.

---

[9]   See Hugh Gazzard, '"Those Graue Presentments of Antiquitie" Samuel Daniel's *Philotas* and the Earl of Essex', *RES*, 51 (2000): 423–50.

[10]   R.F. Patterson (ed.), *Ben Jonson's Conversations with William Drummond of Hawthornden* (London, 1923), pp. 26–7.

[11]   Chambers, *ES* 2, pp. 51–2.

[12]   Ibid., pp. 53–4; Clare, *'Art'*, pp. 139–48; Munro, *Queen's Revels*, pp. 20–21.

[13]   Munro, *Queen's Revels*, pp. 21–3.

Parody and Gunpowder Plot

In his 1610 polemic, *Popish Pietie* (translated from its 1606 Latin original, *Pietas Pontificia*), Francis Herring voices the concerns of a Protestant establishment coming under attack from foreign Catholic powers: [14]

> He takes his iourney onward, and with speed
> ... to the Brittons comes with equall heed,
> ... by his weed
> A Catholicke: 't hath bene the custome still
> Of Satan, that being clad in truths attire,
> Closer he might deceiue, and play the lier.
>
> Here he was called *Fawkes* or *False,* ...
> A second *Proteus,* that could easly wind
> And turne himselfe to all the shapes i'th towne:
> Fitting the place, he to himselfe assign'd
> New names, ...
> But still the selfe same wicked mind he keepes. (*Popish Pietie,* B3[r]; Stanzas 13–14)

Herring's description of the protean Guy Fawkes, co-perpetrator of 'that horrible and barbarous conspiracie, commonly called the powder-treason' (*Popish,* A2[r]), emanates from the overriding anxiety of the time. The Anglo-Scottish 'Brittons' might appear united according to King James's proclamation calling for the 'blessed Union' of 'England and Scotland, under one Imperiall Crowne', but this fragile, incomplete construct seems shattered by an act of Catholic terrorism.[15] Implicit in Herring's poem is a fear that Satan himself, removing his Jesuit priestly 'weed', might appear in simple Protestant 'attire'. Thus 'clad', Satan can surreptitiously adopt 'shapes i'th towne' (the 1606 version reading '*Tectius*', which can mean 'cloaked' or 'disguised'), as well as 'New names', with which to perpetrate his 'wicked' plans.[16] For Herring, a London physician and avowed Protestant, Guy Fawkes simultaneously personifies Satan, Catholic priest and disguised infiltrator, all of whom are capable of stirring susceptible 'male-contents' into bloody 'powder-treason' (*Popish,* B3[v]; Stanza 15).

The ominous 'powder-treason' or Gunpowder Plot threatened to kill king, queen, at least one royal child, the lords temporal and spiritual, judges, leading members of the Commons, visiting ambassadors and countless innocent bystanders. Its

---

[14]   Francis Herring, *Popish Pietie* (London, 1610).

[15]   King James VI & I, 'Proclamation concerning the Kings Majesties Stile, of King of Great Britaine, &c. Westminster, 20 Oct 1604', in James F. Larkin and Paul L. Hughes (eds), *Stuart Royal Proclamations* (2 vols, Oxford, 1973–83), vol. 1, p. 96; J.G.A. Pocock, *The Discovery of Islands* (Cambridge, 2005), pp. 67–70.

[16]   Francis Herring, *Pietas Pontificia* (London, 1606), fol. A3[r].

averted success remained an issue of 'absolute centrality' in early Stuart politics.[17] Surprisingly, however, as Jenny Wormald argues, the same Plot became 'entirely domesticated' within the nation's calendar.[18] This 'domestication' followed a 'sustained attempt' by the Anglo-Scottish elite to downplay the Plot's significance, thus making 'men celebrate ... rather than shiver at' its potential devastation.[19] To institute this historical and social reconstruction, these same elites promoted an annual festivity capitalizing on the popular esteem James enjoyed in the immediate aftermath of the conspiracy. Henceforth, 'Firework Night', 'Bonfire Night' or 'Guy Fawkes Day' effigy burnings were held every 5 November throughout England, Scotland and Wales (though not Ireland).[20] These 'Bonfire' celebrations, legally mandated until 1859 by an Act of Parliament that appointed 5 November a 'joyful day of deliverance' (3 *Jac.* I, *cap.* 1), remain significant annual events in Britain today, on a par with Halloween in the United States.[21] With political skill and social manipulation, the Gunpowder Plot's origin in religious extremism was thus 'domesticated' into an evening of pyrotechnic glee.

This successful 'domestication' remains evident not only in today's effigy burning, but also, as Wormald notes, in traditional historical scholarship, where the Plot is described as 'dominated by fireworks, Catholic defensiveness, and hostility to the first Scottish king of England'.[22] This typical scholarly focus conflates the absolute success of the Plot's political and social 'domestication' with the pervasive negativity towards James of subsequent Whig historiography. In a similar vein, literary historians have paid scant heed to this political event with regard to 'localized' readings of early modern plays, often discounting the Plot as a 'domesticated' instance of lunatic extremism.[23] For Chambers, the burning of 'folk-custom' effigies merely marks a failed coup with little or no impact on contemporary drama.[24] Ironically, the denial of an occasionalist dimension to post-Plot plays appears as unwarranted as earlier anti-Jamesian dramatic interpretations. If the Plot's 'domestication' limits its significance in early modern dramatic criticism, might it logically also affect our understanding of the disguised ruler motif in its post-Plot form? Parody could thus represent a reconfiguration of the disguised ruler, whose subversive potential is only perceived as threatening after a failed attempt to destroy the monarchy.

---

[17] Richard Dutton, *Ben Jonson, 'Volpone' and the Gunpowder Plot* (Cambridge, 2008), p. 11.

[18] Wormald, 'Gunpowder', p. 142.

[19] Ibid., p. 142.

[20] Roger Lockyer, *The Early Stuarts*, 2nd edn (London, 1999), p. 41.

[21] Chris R. Kyle, 'Early Modern Terrorism: The Gunpowder Plot of 1605 and its Aftermath', in Brett Bowden and Michael T Davis (eds), *Terror: From Tyrannicide to Terrorism* (St Lucia, 2008), pp. 42–55 (p. 55).

[22] Wormald, 'Gunpowder', p. 144.

[23] Dutton, *'Volpone'*, p. 9.

[24] Chambers, *ES* 1, p. 21.

Fig. 5.1   Bonfires and firework pyrotechnics celebrate the 'Wonderfull
               deliverance' from the Gunpowder Plot (1641)

For playgoers attending *The Woman Hater*, this Paul's playhouse parody of a
disguised ruler appears of particular relevance given that some of the conspirators
were executed at nearby St Paul's Cathedral. Of the eight summarily tried and
convicted on Friday 27 January 1606, Guy Fawkes, along with Thomas Winter,
Robert Keyes and Ambrose Rookwood, died at the Old Palace Yard, Westminster,
on Tuesday 31 January.[25] One day earlier, on Monday 30 January, the four lesser
conspirators – Sir Everard Digby, Robert Winter (Thomas's brother), John Grant
and Thomas Bates – were drawn on hurdles through the City of London, its streets
lined with guards recruited from the capital's householders, to be executed in St
Paul's churchyard, the bookselling district of the City only moments from the

---

[25]   Francis S.J. Edwards (ed.), *The Gunpowder Plot* (London, 1973), pp. 225–6; Mark
Nicholls, *Investigating Gunpowder Plot* (Manchester, 1991), p. 55.

Fig. 5.2   The Gunpowder Plot conspirators, dragged in pairs through the
              streets of London, approaching the scaffold prior to their hanging,
              drawing and quartering (1606)

Paul's playhouse.[26] For audience, players and dramatists alike, St Paul's Cathedral
became the site for horrific public displays of state retribution.

The proximity of these acts of sanctioned violence to the Paul's playhouse
suggests that Beaumont and Fletcher could not possibly ignore them. The event is
perhaps reflected in the submissive words of the woman-hater, Gondarino. Rather
than suffer overpowering female attention as punishment for his misogynistic
humour, Gondarino begs the Duke to 'Let [him] be quarter'd ... quickly', a
punishment he can more readily 'endure' than being tied to a chair as Oriana and
her (boy company) ladies force kisses on their unwilling victim (*Woman*, K3ʳ;
5.4.134). The real-life hanging, drawing and quartering of the Gunpowder Plot
conspirators, occurring nearby the playhouse that stages this comical act of torture,
adds a topical immediacy to *The Woman Hater*'s dark humour.

Beaumont and Fletcher's depoliticized parody of the disguised ruler, moreover,
gains a sinister immediacy when viewed as a specific response to these actual
executions staged nearby. If *The Woman Hater*'s innocuous parody responds to
this topical event, it should not be surprising that the disguised ruler is likewise

---

[26]   Nicholls, *Investigating*, p. 55.

parodied in *The Fleer* at the nearby Blackfriars, only a few streets from Paul's. Deemed by Tennenhouse to be the final, least significant example of theatrical solidarity, *The Fleer* nevertheless embraces political controversy in a surprising way.[27] Remarkably, the Blackfriars children perform a play that openly disparages the influx of Scottish citizens arriving with James. In the suspicious 'Gunpowder Plot' climate, such anti-Scottish sentiment was foolhardy, if not treasonous. Whether *The Fleer*'s satire was seen as subversive is unclear, in part because *Eastward Ho!* and *The Isle of Gulls* attracted far greater attention from censors eager to curb criticism of the court's Scottish faction. In *The Fleer*, however, social commentary, sexual innuendo and anti-Scottish satire are expressed openly, its 'parody or self-parody' highlighting disquiet among London's urban population.[28]

The Fleer and Fawkesian Disguise

The usurped duke Antifront, principal protagonist of Edward Sharpham's Blackfriars city comedy, *The Fleer* (1606, Queen's Revels; published 1607), escapes Florence to seek sanctuary in London.[29] Here, he adopts the disguise of 'Fleer', his name representing a facial expression defined by John Palsgrave as the 'vncoueryng of the tethe', as when a 'knaue fleareth lyke a dogge vnder a doore'.[30] This sycophantic leer of the 'fleer' corresponds with Florio's definition as 'foolishly to smile and simper'.[31] On London's streets, the simpering Antifront/ Fleer encounters the ostentatious English courtier, Ruffle. The disguised duke asks why Ruffle is dressed so extravagantly. Ruffle remarks that he has recently been 'at Court', a place where, as Antifront/Fleer ironically suggests, he too has visited, 'but yesterday':

> ANTIFRONT: [W]here I saw a Farmers Son sit newly made a courtier, that sat in the [King's] presence at cardes, as familiar as if the chayre of state had bin made of a peece of his fathers Barne-doore. (*Fleer*, D3ʳ; 2.1.222–6)

Antifront's description of the lowly 'Farmers Son' made royal intimate accords with contemporary images of unworthy subjects ennobled by parvenu 'Scotsmen on the make'.[32] The butt of this derogatory remark recalls Sir Petronel Flash in the notorious Blackfriars city comedy *Eastward Ho!*, who, as one of many 'thirty

---

[27] Tennenhouse, *Power*, p. 154.
[28] Shapiro, *Children*, p. 206.
[29] Edward Sharpham, *The Fleire* (London, 1607). Line numbers from Christopher Gordon Petter (ed.), *The Fleire*, in *The Works of Edward Sharpham* (New York, 1986).
[30] John Palsgrave, *Lesclarcissement de la Langue Francoyse* (London, 1530).
[31] Florio, *Queen Anna's New World of Words* (London, 1611), p. 497.
[32] Wormald, 'Gunpowder', p. 160.

pound Knights' (*Eastward*, F4ʳ; 4.1.168), bought his title from unscrupulous Scottish hangers-on at court.[33]

Antifront's scornful comment reflects an age-old English hatred for Scotland, now manifested as 'open and bitter resentment' of the Scots in London.[34] It also illustrates a general displeasure at King James's Scottish friends and servants, for their immodest behaviour in court, success in gaining favour and perceived contempt for England's aristocracy.[35] By 1605, so Wormald argues, such resentment ran through 'every stratum of English society', especially among the City's 'merchants, lawyers, academics' – that 'stratum' most likely to attend a Blackfriars play.[36] Antifront's explicit anti-courtier (though not necessarily anti-Jamesian) satire, describing his supposed intimate access to the English court, is spoken, however, by a disguised foreigner. Given the contemporary national obsession with foreigners in disguise, it seems politically volatile for Sharpham to offer the Blackfriars children yet another protean infiltrator, able to 'turne himselfe to all shapes i'th towne' according to Herring's fearful Fawkesian model, especially one who resides unrecognized and unknown among the 'Brittons' he so obviously derides.

This localized topicality in Sharpham's play is suggested by the 13 May 1606 *Stationers' Register* record of 'A Comedie called The fleare', entered less than fifteen weeks after the execution of the Gunpowder conspirators. *The Fleer*'s political insensitivity, staged when anti-Fawkesian feeling was still at its height, might be reflected in the additional *Stationers' Register* comment, 'PROVIDED that [the publishers] are not to printe yt tell they bringe good aucthoritie and licence for Doinge therof'.[37] The required 'aucthoritie' was not granted until 21 November 1606, and *The Fleer* remained unpublished until 1607 when its title-page announces: 'The Fleire. As it hath beene often played in the *Blacke-Fryers* by the Children of the Reuells'.[38] The unusual spelling of 'Fleire' is retained in many critical studies because of the relative archaism of the term. The title-page also lacks any mention of 'Queen's' in its children's company name. This absence, so Chambers argued, indicates Queen Anne's disapproval, and the removal of royal patronage from the Blackfriars company following the *Eastward Ho!* and *Isle of Gulls* controversies.[39] Chambers's hypothesis, as noted elsewhere, is inherently problematic, not least because company names and name changes were often inconsistent.[40] Whatever the reason for the company's slightly altered name, *The Fleer* was obviously staged during a period of unusual unrest and fear.

---

[33] Line numbers from Petter (ed.), *Eastward Ho!* (London, 1973).

[34] Wormald. 'Gunpowder', p. 160.

[35] Ibid., p. 157.

[36] Ibid., p. 160.

[37] Arber 3, p. 321.

[38] Ibid., p. 333.

[39] Chambers, *ES* 2, pp. 51–2.

[40] See Munro, *Queen's Revels*, p. 21.

Despite this volatile timing, standard commentary still considers *The Fleer* merely as Sharpham's 'rank imitation' of *The Malcontent*.[41] In consequence, it is often assumed that Antifront (meaning 'oppositional' or 'confrontational forehead') was simply 'named after' Marston's Altofronto (with *la fronte alta* the Italian for 'tall forehead' or 'lofty-brow').[42] These readings overlook Sharpham's possible allusion to the honest whore Bellafront ('beautiful forehead/face'). Sharpham could thus be mirroring Dekker's *Second Part of the Honest Whore*, in which Bellafront's father, Orlando Friscobaldo, is disguised as the servingman 'Pacheco' in order to spy on his daughter as she is unsuccessfully enticed back to prostitution. Any such 'imitations' are unrecognizable in *The Fleer*'s performance setting, however, since the belated revelation that 'Signior *Antifront* yet liues' (*Fleer*, H4ᵛ; 5.5.106) occurs in the final moments of the play. The duke's real name is uttered just twice in the last eleven lines. Rather than confirming Sharpham's allusion to a Marstonian (or Dekkerian) character, the name's absence in the preceding dialogue offers it as an ironic parting glimpse at several famous theatrical forebears. Without the benefit of playtext speech-prefixes, the Blackfriars audience could only speculate about similarities in protagonist names once the play is concluded.

Uncertainty over Sharpham's naming decisions highlights the complexity of this '*pot-pourri* parody' of several plays.[43] *Hamlet*, *Merchant of Venice*, *1 Henry IV* and *Measure for Measure*, *Malcontent*, *Fawn* and *Dutch Courtesan*, *London Prodigal*, the '*Honest Whore*' plays, and *Westward*, *Northward* and *Eastward Ho!*, all add to the intertextual fabric of *The Fleer*. Thus, *The Fleer* presents multiple plots and subplots, each adding parodic intensity. They enliven what G.K. Hunter sees as the 'hideously disorganized' adventures of the banished and disguised duke Antifront, a character described by Michael J. Redmond as 'unashamedly amoral'.[44] Like Duke Senior in *As You Like It* and Prospero in *The Tempest*, Antifront loses his dukedom to his rival, the 'mightie *Piso*', through 'feeblenes' and 'weakenes' (*Fleer*, B1ʳ; 1.1.14–17). Admitting in the play's opening scene both a 'longing' and a 'resolution' to return (*Fleer*, B1ʳ; 1.1.7), Antifront adopts 'some strange disguise' to 'stelth away' from Florence (*Fleer*, B1ʳ; 1.1.25–6). Although the 'strange disguise' of flattering 'Fleer' predominates, Antifront also assumes two further disguises: an Italian apothecary and a prosecuting Doctor of Law. For those in the play's original audience who, like Herring, feared infiltration by a 'second *Proteus*', Antifront's multiple 'disguisement' (*Fleer*, B1ʳ; 1.1.29) and ability to 'deceiue, and play the liar', would simultaneously amuse and disconcert.

Antifront escapes Florence in order to 'redeeme [his] honours lost, and regaine [his] right' (*Fleer*, E2ʳ; 2.1.429–30). He also acts on behalf of the 'true inheritors' of Florence's throne (*Fleer*, B1ʳ; 1.1.13): his daughters, the princesses Florida and Felecia. Like their father, these princesses have been forced into impecunious

41   Tricomi, *Anticourt*, p. 23.
42   Petter, *Fleire*, p. 185.
43   Ibid., p. 214.
44   Hunter, 'English Folly', p. 107; Redmond, *Shakespeare, Politics*, p. 126.

exile. They now reside in 'Englands' capital (*Fleer*, B1ᵛ; 1.2.28). Antifront follows his daughters to London, sardonically describing it as this 'pretty Towne' (*Fleer*, C2ᵛ; 1.3.226). Here, he finds them surviving through prostitution in the guise of notorious Italian courtesans. Unrecognizable to his daughters and unknown to the swaggering gallants, the disguised Antifront/Fleer offers to work as the courtesans' servant and bawd. Ironically admitting to having 'been a Courtier' once himself (*Fleer*, C3ᵛ; 1.3.291), Antifront/Fleer subsequently satirizes this life through mock-courtier titles like 'Ye[o]man ath' Iurdan [pisspot], Gentleman ath' smock and Squire of entertaynment' (*Fleer*, C4ᵛ; 2.1.56–7). In his new 'sute', Antifront/Fleer receives money from his mistresses' many clients. He also learns of his daughters' passions for two English courtiers, Ruffle and Spark, themselves loved by two young Englishwomen, Susan and Nan (who embark on their own 'disguised page' subplot).

Spark and Ruffle's refusal to accept Florida and Felecia's romantic overtures leads inevitably to the princesses' plan to murder the unfortunate young men. They seduce two clients into undertaking the task. The first, the impecunious northern knight Sir John Have-Little, is traditionally labelled as Scottish because he eats 'Oten cake' (*Fleer*, F1ʳ; 3.1.110). As the play's 1986 editor, Christopher Gordon Petter, observes, 'Oten cake' was as regularly associated with Yorkshire and Lancashire.[45] Sharpham's supposedly Scottish satirized knight might actually hail from northern English shires. The second client to be embroiled into the princesses' murderous plan, Have-Little's companion Lord Piso, is also the son of the Florentine Duke Piso, Antifront's usurping rival. Unable to resist their courtesan temptresses, Have-Little and Piso agree to poison Spark and Ruffle. Antifront foils the plot by disguising himself as an Italian apothecary who supplies a sleeping potion instead of poison. The young Englishmen are presumed murdered and Have-Little and Piso are arrested. In a self-consciously complex conclusion, which possibly reflects a wider trend for 'generic stress-points' in plays that subvert audience expectation, Antifront disguises himself a third time as a Doctor of Law.[46] In this semblance, he assists in Have-Little and Piso's trial and betrays his daughters' complicity. Sentenced to death, the contrite Felecia and Florida beg forgiveness and vow to marry Piso and Have-Little before their combined executions. Piso receives news that his father has died in Florence. Believing that his own death is imminent, he restores the banished Antifront to ducal authority. At this late moment in the play, Antifront reveals his true identity before confirming that Spark and Ruffle still live. The death sentences are revoked and the prodigal daughters are free to marry Have-Little and Piso as they promised. It remains only for Antifront publicly to reclaim his dukedom.

This disguised ruler intrigue restores Antifront to ducal authority. Florida's marriage to Piso then ensures a powerful succession to his rule. To achieve this end, Antifront has employed numerous stereotypical disguises, including the

---

[45]   See Petter, *Fleire*, pp. 207–208.
[46]   Munro, *Queen's Revels*, p. 60.

stock Machiavel figure of a poisoning Italian apothecary. Antifront, obviously a 'Catholicke' infiltrator and foreigner in disguise, is thus able to 'turne himselfe to all the shapes i'th towne'. His goal, however, focuses more on exposing immorality among newly-knighted court hangers-on than undermining a regime that parallels contemporary London. It is surprising, therefore, that Sharpham so openly highlights the dangers of admitting Catholic interlopers, obviously prone to equivocation and sophistry, to an audience still reeling from the recent 'horrible and barbarous conspiracie'. The Catholic implication of Fleer's presence in a barely disguised London only adds to the potential danger of Sharpham's disguised ruler plot.

Equivocation and Anti-Catholic Resentment

When the disguised Antifront first arrives in London, he is accosted by the court gallants and their ladies. In response to Have-Little's interrogation, Antifront/Fleer admits to being 'An Italian' (*Fleer*, C3ʳ; 1.3.245), while acknowledging in an aside his recognition of Piso, the son of his usurping rival, among the swaggering group. Although Antifront dismisses facetious comments about his 'melancholie' humour, and ripostes that only a 'mad fellowe [would] loue anie' of them (*Fleer*, C3ʳ; 1.3.253–7), he appears genuinely affronted by Piso's forthright question, 'Why camst thou out of *Italy* into *England*?' (*Fleer*, C3ʳ; 1.3.258). His response is both cryptic and evasive: 'Because *England* would not come into *Italy* to me' (*Fleer*, C3ʳ; 1.3.259). Continuing in this equivocating vein, Antifront parries other questions about his mood, his money and his preferment, only answering Spark's innocent sounding query, 'Who doost serue?', with an unequivocal, 'God' (*Fleer*, C3ᵛ; 1.3.265). Alone on the streets of London, Antifront appears to be defensive and confrontational in equal measure. His response to Spark's offer of employment by 'a couple of Gentlewomen of [his] owne Countrie' (*Fleer*, C3ᵛ; 1.3.276) is to enquire if the young courtier is himself 'an English-man' (*Fleer*, C3ᵛ; 1.3.280–81). Somewhat taken aback, Spark confirms his nationality, whereupon Antifront makes the following observation:

> ANTIFRONT: So I thought indeede, you cannot poyson as well as we Italians, but youle find a meanes to bring a man out of his life as soone. (*Fleer*, C3ᵛ; 1.3.283–4)

This comment anticipates the mock poison plot, while illustrating Antifront's perception of the English as a dangerous, life-threatening race. How far this reflects the mood of the nation (if indeed *The Fleer* was written after the failed Plot) is uncertain. Gunpowder Plot equivocation and Catholic intrigue could nevertheless offer surprising subtexts to this seemingly innocent scene as Antifront appears to epitomize a 'second *Proteus*' in England's midst.

In his critical introduction to *The Fleer*, Petter expresses little doubt the Gunpowder Plot provides a 'pivotal part' of Sharpham's complicated plot structure. *The Fleer*, so Petter argues, represents a 'discerning comment on a King who from

1603 showed utter disdain for the English Common Law': 'What more suitable topic for the witty young men of the Middle Temple!'.[47] This remark betrays Petter's reliance on Whig appraisals of King James. Nevertheless, a 'pivotal' moment does occur in Act 3, when the princesses Felecia and Florida, observed and encouraged by their disguised father, devise their poisoning plot. The courtesans exchange letters from their more pliable admirers (reproduced with *mise en page* precision in the quarto texts), and compare their suitors' suitability. With genuine surprise, Felecia realizes that her sister's letter comes from the 'sonne and heire to Duke *Piso* that now is', a revelation that prompts Florida's impassioned plea, 'O would hee were!' (*Fleer*, E4ʳ; 3.1.35–7). Florida greets this opportunity to seduce the son of her father's usurper with disquieting relish.

Florida's enthusiastic outburst is far more sinister than at first it might appear. By seducing Piso, she could return to Florence and escape her life as a foreign prostitute. In reality, though, her excitement stems from vengeance. Coldly concluding that, 'whosoere he bee', Piso must assist their murderous plans, Florida emphasises the need for his absolute complicity:

> FLORIDA: [He] must bee made a match to giue fire to the hell blacke pouder of our reuenge. …
> FLORIDA: Then shall be thus: these two being earnest suters for our loues, weele graunt vpon condition, that suddenly they murther *Sparke* and *Ruffell,* but first to take the Sacrament if euer it be knowne, as knowne 'twill be, to keep our names vnspotted in the action; this being done –
> FELECIA: Let them challenge vs, wee and our loues are won.
> [B]ut say they should reueale vs.
> FLORIDA: O none will breake a Sacrament to heape vp periury on other sinnes, when death & hel stands gaping for their soules. (*Fleer*, E4ʳ; 3.1.37–50)

For a Blackfriars audience of 1606, the mention of 'hell blacke pouder' and a secret, perjuring 'Sacrament' conjures specific topicality. Florida's repeated reference to 'Sacrament' invokes the Catholic Sacrament of the Eucharist or Holy Communion, one of only two sacraments retained by Protestants, but condemned as superstitious by fundamentalist Puritans.[48] The topical implication of a 'Sacrament', when taken as part of a secret oath, resonates from the confessions of the Gunpowder Plot conspirators. The ringleader, Robert Catesby, admitted that he relied on his co-conspirators' inviolable faith when forcing them to swear an oath of secrecy, made spiritually binding by taking the Sacrament.[49] Administered by a Catholic priest, this Sacrament ensured his compatriots' absolute commitment to their treacherous Plot.[50]

---

[47] Petter, *Fleire*, pp. 183 & 220.

[48] David Lyle Jeffery (ed.), *A Dictionary of Biblical Tradition in English Literature* (Grand Rapids, 1992), pp. 673–5.

[49] Nicholls, *Investigating*, p. 51.

[50] Mark Nicholls, 'Fawkes, Guy (*bap.* 1570, *d.* 1606)', *ODNB* (2009) <http://www.oxforddnb.com/index/101009230/Guy-Fawkes> [accessed 6 May 2011].

The public's awareness of the Sacrament's use in the Plot emerges in the writings of the Jesuit, Robert Persons [or Parsons]. His pro-Catholic polemic, *Answere to the Fifth Part of Reportes* (1606), springs from the pamphlet war between Persons and the cleric Thomas Morton (eventual Bishop of Durham).[51] This text discusses the legal tactics used in the trial of the Jesuit priest, Henry Garnett, who was apprehended the day of Fawkes's trial. According to Persons's ironic 'Epistle dedicatory' to the Attorney General, 'Syr Edward Cooke', Garnett was not part of the so-called '*Iesuites treason*', but a priest who had been told of the Plot 'in *Confession*, … but a very fevv daies before' the 5 November 'discouerie'.[52] Garnett's defence, that he 'neuer gaue anie consent, helpe, hearkening, approbation, or cooperation to the [conspirators]; but contrari-vvise sought to dissuade, dehorte, and hinder' their treasonous act, is underscored by the priest's belief that, because 'bound by the inuiolable seale of that *Sacrament* [priestly confession] not to vtter the same', he was unable to inform the relevant authorities.[53] Regardless of Garnett's innocence or guilt, his Jesuit mission, general equivocation and undeniable association with the Gunpowder traitors guaranteed his hanging, drawing and quartering at St Paul's churchyard on 3 May 1606, only ten days before *The Fleer* was entered in the *Stationers' Register*. Notably, it is generally assumed that Shakespeare references Garnett's execution in *Macbeth*, with the Porter's description of 'an Equiuocator, that could sweare in both the Scales against eyther Scale, who committed Treason enough for Gods sake, yet could not equiuocate to Heauen' (F *Macbeth*, TLN.750–54; 2.3.8–10). The very public association of this treasonous 'equivocator' with the term 'Sacrament', and Florida's exclamation that 'none will breake a Sacrament to heape vp periury on other sinnes', adds to the Catholic imagery of Sharpham's dialogue.

Florida's 'Sacrament' remark, and its easy association with conspiracy and terrorism, emphasises the dark tone underlying Antifront's disguised activities in London. Rather than parodically evoking the disguised ruler motif, *The Fleer* presents a foreign interloper infiltrating and manipulating London's wealthy society. His sojourn among the parvenu knights and other hangers-on ironically highlights contemporary animosity towards those who advanced socially and financially at James's accession. It seems inconceivable, therefore, that Sharpham, when writing his disguised ruler parody, was not aware of the contemporary volatility of his play. *The Fleer*'s allusions to Gunpowder Plot explosives, murderous intrigues, Sacraments and public executions, and the presence of equivocating, multiple disguise-wearing foreigners, all add to the shocking topicality of this entertainment. Seemingly untouched by the censor's hand, a play that has traditionally been viewed as an indictment of James and his court instead criticizes those flattering, fleering new courtiers as they ingratiate their way into the corridors of power. Whether Catholic disguised ruler, Jesuit priest,

---

[51] Robert Persons, *Answere to the Fifth Part of Reportes* (Saint-Omer, 1606).

[52] Ibid., fols ẽ3ʳ–ẽ3ᵛ.

[53] Ibid., fol. ẽ3ᵛ.

Guy Fawkes traitor or impecunious courtier, all threaten the security of a nation made painfully aware of the mortality of their ruling elite. The Gunpowder Plot, possibly the first instance of near-successful terrorist activity on a mass-destructive scale, provides the unsettling new subplot to this Blackfriars drama, written and staged when popularity for the children's companies was on the wane. *The Fleer* also marks the decline of the motif it parodies, as the disguised ruler's presence now highlights a new anxiety. It is not the ruler travelling unknown among his own people that threatens the fragile security of England's island state, but the prospect of anyone, like the feared Guy Fawkes himself, travelling undetected and undetectable through its land.

Post-Plot Disguise: The Embedded Motif

The insidious threat of disguised ruler secrecy is reflected in subsequent seventeenth-century dramas that only fleetingly allude to the motif. Its tragicomic potential appears, for example, in Shakespeare and George Wilkins's *Pericles* (*c.* 1607–1608; published 1609), which mentions regular brothel visits by 'the Lord *Lysimachus* disguised' (Q1 *Pericles*, G3ᵛ; 4.6.17).[54] The Bawd, Pander and Boult's quick acknowledgment of Lysimichus's presence suggests, however, that this 'disguise' merely forestalls embarrassment as the governor negotiates Mytilene's less salubrious streets. Similarly, in Gervase Markham and Lewis Machin's *The Dumb Knight* (*c.* 1607–1608, King's Revels, Whitefriars; published 1608), the King of Cyprus, having conquered Sicily and married its Queen, acquires a disguise after becoming jealous of his wife's flirtatious behaviour.[55] The Iago-like influence of his adviser, Duke Epire, forces the suspicious King to '*enter disguised like one of the guard*', to observe the Queen secretly as she dances a measure at a court entertainment (*Dumb*, G3ᵛ; 4.1.25.1.SD). The King remains onstage for only 52 lines of dialogue before exiting and returning, his disguise thereafter completely forgotten. For this same Whitefriars children's company, John Day's *Humour Out of Breath* (1608, King's Revels; published 1608) presents the usurped Anthonio, Duke of Mantua, who is forced into rural exile with his son and two daughters.[56] His rival, the usurping Octavio, Duke of Venice, in order to spy on his sons, wears the 'strange habit' (*Breath*, C3ᵛ; 2.1.20) of a 'sweete foole' (*Breath*, C4ʳ; 2.1.41). In his fool's disguise, Octavio meets Anthonio's aggrieved and vengeful son, Aspero, and learns that his own sons love Anthonio's daughters.

---

[54] *Pericles, Prince of Tyre* [Q1] (London, 1609); *STC* 22334. Line numbers from W.W. Greg (ed.), *Pericles 1609*, SQF, 5 (London, 1940).

[55] Gervase Markham and Lewis Machin, *The Dumbe Knight* (London, 1608).

[56] John Day, *Humour Out of Breath* (London, 1608). For an occasionalist discussion of this play's 'radical inversion' of disguised ruler conventions, see Michael J. Redmond, '"Low Comedy" and Political Cynicism: Parodies of the Jacobean Disguised-Duke Play', *Renaissance Forum*, 7 (2004) <http://www.hull.ac.uk/renforum/v7/redmond.htm> [accessed 26 April 2011]: paras 1–13 (para. 1).

Although initially intent on preventing the double union, Octavio soon reveals his true identity and, after some persuasion, blesses the marriages.

A tragic evocation of disguised ruler intrigue then occurs in John Mason's tragedy *The Turk* (*c.* 1609, King's Revels; published 1610), which presents the Duke of Ferrara seeking the love of Julia, the Duchess of Florence.[57] Julia's wicked guardian and uncle, the Florentine governor Borgia, manipulates her fortune-seeking suitors in order to secure Julia's inheritance for himself. Rightly suspecting the governor's 'Falsehood and treason', the Duke murders Borgia's Eunuch slave in a moment of reckless fear (*Turk*, F4ᵛ; TLN.1429). As a later stage direction indicates, the Duke then adopts the Eunuch's costume and, thus '*disguisd*', spies on his rival (*Turk*, H3ᵛ; TLN.1913.SD). The unfortunate Duke is subsequently slain by Borgia. In his dying speech, he admits that he 'murthered' Borgia's slave 'and assumd his shape' (*Turk*, H4ʳ; TLN.1948–9). By adopting the 'shape' of the Eunuch slave, which again recalls Guy Fawkes's 'shapes' in *Popish Pietie*, the Duke suffers his untimely and violent demise. While these incidental episodes rely on established disguised ruler imagery, they also reveal an underlying anxiety about the intrinsically deceptive nature of disguise.

The tragic disguised ruler likewise informs Roberto's appearance as a friar in Marston, William Barksted and Lewis Machin's *The Insatiate Countess* (*c.* 1607, King's Revels[?]/Queen's Revels[?]; published 1613).[58] As the Count of Cyprus (the king's domain in *Dumb Knight*), Roberto woos, then loses the sexually voracious countess Isabella. Her infidelity leads Roberto publicly to renounce women, joining instead 'some religious Monasterie' (*Insatiate*, D4ʳ; 2.4.51). When he later appears at the executioner's scaffold '*in Friers weeds*' (*Insatiate*, I1ʳ; 5.1.150.0.SD), offering the condemned Isabella 'Pardon' for her wrongs (*Insatiate*, I1ᵛ; 5.1.191), there is no suggestion that the count is 'disguised'. Rather, this 'Holy Sir', whose religious vocation (and friar's habit) ensures that he is 'so farre … gone from [Isabella's] memorie' (*Insatiate*, I1ᵛ; 5.1.158), is easily recognizable as her 'offended Lord' by condemned woman and audience alike (*Insatiate*, I1ᵛ; 5.1.183). As Giorgio Melchiori suggests, Roberto's hooded appearance here might be a wry allusion to *Measure for Measure*, a play also evoked by *The Insatiate Countess*'s double bed-trick.[59] Such similarities are not surprising, since one of the original sources for Isabella's repentance at execution appears to be the opening poetic complaint in *The Rocke of Regard* (1576), written by George Whetstone, whose *Promos and Cassandra* (1578) is likewise recognized as a source for *Measure for Measure*.[60]

---

[57]   John Mason, *The Turke* (London, 1610). Through line numbers from Joseph Quincy Adams, Jr (ed.), *The Turke* (London, 1913).

[58]   John Marston, *The Insatiate Countesse* [Q] (London, 1613). Line numbers from Melchiori (ed.), *Insatiate*.

[59]   Melchiori (ed.), *Insatiate*, pp. 25 & 171n.

[60]   Bullough, *Sources*, vol. 2, pp. 442–513.

As these instances suggest, the disguised ruler evolved from principal protagonist to incidental motif in only a few years. The disguised ruler's decline from favour apparently coincides with the failed Gunpowder Plot. Real disguised infiltrators threatening the state thus make fictive portrayals of voyeuristic disguisers particularly unsettling. Concurrently, playwrights parody the motif, with its commonplace fool's and friar's costumes offering fleeting moments of comic or tragic intrigue. George Chapman's *May Day* (*c.* 1609, Queen's Revels[?]; published 1611) particularly illustrates this pattern.[61] *May Day*'s title-page reference to being 'diuers times acted at the Blacke Fryers' has led many critics to identify this as a Queen's Revels play, possibly dating from far earlier in the century.[62] The opening stage direction, '*Chorus Iuuenum cantantes & saltantes*' ('youthful Chorus singing and skipping'), is often presumed to denote *May Day*'s children's company heritage (A2ʳ).[63] Unfortunately, this presumption ignores the redundancy of stressing the youthfulness of the play's Chorus should all the performers already be boys or youths. The play's revelatory dénouement moreover supports a later dating for *May Day* of *c.* 1609. Throughout the play, a page called Lionell appears as a boy. In the penultimate act, Lionell even agrees to be 'disguis'd like a woman' to gull the young Francischina, wife to the braggartly *miles gloriosus*, Captain Quintilliano (*May*, I1ʳ; 4.5.29). Only in Act 5 do onstage characters and audience learn the truth: Lionell is actually a woman, called Theagine, who has pretended to be a 'boy' all along. Theagine is now free to marry the young exile Lucretio, who has likewise spent the play disguised, although in his case as the girl Lucretia. Like Lionell/Theagine, Lucretia/Lucretio only reveals her/his true gender and identity in the final scene. As Peter Hyland notes, such cross-gender revelations, concealed from the audience until the final moments of the play, 'deprive disguise of any possible metatheatrical meaning'.[64] Similar delayed exposures of hidden gender occur in Jonson's *Epicoene* (1609, Queen's Revels, Whitefriars; published 1616) and Beaumont and Fletcher's *Philaster* (*c.* 1608–1609, King's Men; published 1620), plays that further suggest a *c.* 1609 dating for *May Day*. For these playwrights, the conventional disguised ruler is no longer useful, since London's novelty-seeking audiences now require alternative, more shocking instances of disguised revelation.

Whatever its original dating, *May Day* provides disguised ruler interest because of its Act 2 exchange between the play's *senex amans*, Lorenzo, and a duplicitous servant called Angelo. Lorenzo is, quite ridiculously, lusting after the married Francischina. Angelo convinces the old suitor to disguise himself to gain access to Francischina's house. Before being persuaded to blacken his face and pretend to be Snail, a local chimney sweep, Lorenzo discusses which 'disguise would serue

---

[61] George Chapman, *May-Day* (London, 1611).
[62] Chambers, *ES* 3, p. 256.
[63] Munro, *Queen's Revels*, p. 175. Translation mine.
[64] Hyland, *Disguise*, p. 105.

the turne' of his romantic adventure (*May*, D3ʳ; 2.4.133–4).[65] Angelo's initial list of disguises – 'Tinkers, pedlers, porters, chimney-sweepers, fooles and Physitians' – is contemptuously dismissed by Lorenzo, as are more elevated disguises such as 'one of the Senate, a graue Iusticer, a man of wealth, a magnifico' (*May*, D3ʳ– D3ᵛ; 2.4.137–43). Lorenzo's own preference appears far more straightforward: 'And yet by my troth, for the safegard of her honour, … me thinks a Friers weede were nothing' (*May*, D3ᵛ; 2.4.144–5). Angelo, however, derides the old lord's suggestion:

> ANGELO: Out vppon't, that disguise is worne thread bare vp-
> on euery stage, and so much villany committed vnder that
> habit; that 'tis growne as su[s]picious as the vilest. (*May*, D3ᵛ; 2.4.146–8)

For Angelo, the friar's disguise is so predictable that it would attract far greater suspicion than its clandestine wearer might expect. Indeed, Angelo likens the 'Friers weede' to that other mainstay of disguised ruler intrigue by adding that, even if Lorenzo 'were stuffed into a motley coate', his face would disclose his true identity (*May*, D3ᵛ; 2.4.153–4). Accordingly, they decide to blacken the old man's face with chimneysweep soot. This short exchange, in a comedy that relies on multiple disguises for comic effect, marks the contemporary rejection of traditional disguise costumes. *May Day* thus presents the barely recognizable afterlife of this once flourishing dramatic motif.

Chapman's *May Day* is also significant when compared with the enigmatic anonymous manuscript, *The Telltale*.[66] *The Telltale*, whose authorship and provenance are completely unknown, has been dated to anytime between *c*. 1605 (because of its apparent association with the 'Jacobean disguised ruler plays'), and the decade 1630–40, because of Nathaniel Brook's 1658 announcement of his intention to print it.[67] In *The Telltale*, the Duke of Florence, suspecting his wife's infidelity, 'purpose[s] Couertly to goe' from his dukedom (*Telltale*, 4ʳ; TLN.255), leaving his general, Aspero, 'a firme warrant' to rule as deputy in his absence (*Telltale*, 4ʳ; TLN.271). Aspero, like Angelo in *Measure for Measure*, proves himself a lascivious tyrant. He imprisons the Duke's wife, Duchess Victoria, and banishes the courtier Picentio, whose only crime is to love the Duke's niece, Princess Isabella. Since Aspero intends to marry the unfortunate princess, he needs to banish Picentio. To avenge this wrong and save Isabella from a forced marriage, Picentio returns to Florence disguised as a French doctor. At the same time, the Duke's sister, Princess Elinor, fearing for her own safety, seeks assistance

---

[65]   Line numbers from Robert F. Welsh (ed.) *May Day*, in Allan Holaday (gen. ed.), *The Plays of George Chapman: The Comedies* (Urbana, 1970), pp. 311–96.

[66]   *The Telltale*, Dulwich College MSS 20. See R.A. Foakes and J.C. Gibson (eds), *The Telltale* (Oxford, 1959), pp. v–viii. Through line numbers from this edition.

[67]   See R.A. Foakes, Peter Beal and Grace Ioppolo, 'The Manuscript of *The Telltale*', Henslowe-Alleyn Digitisation Project (2005) <http://www.henslowe-alleyn.org.uk/essays/telltale.html> [accessed 6 May 2011].

from the faithful Count Garullo. Subsequently disguised 'in his fooles Iackett' or motley (*Telltale*, 8ʳ; TLN.677–8), complete with 'Cap and bauble' (*Telltale*, 24ʳ; TLN.2288), Count Garullo guards the princess in her brother's absence.[68] Unknown to both, the Duke has already returned to spy on the 'mock duke' Aspero (*Telltale*, 18ʳ; TLN.1789), specifically disguised (according to a stage direction) 'like a hermit' (*Telltale*, 10ʳ; TLN.889–90). In his 'hermit' disguise, the Duke appears to all as a 'reuerend man' and 'Confessor' (*Telltale*, 10ʳ; TLN.919), thus reasserting the traditional religious significance of the 'hermit' costume and its visual association with the Duke's habit in *Measure for Measure*.

The fool's and hermit's disguises, so violently rejected by Angelo in Chapman's *May Day*, provide the perfect costumes in *Telltale* to spy on a tyrannical deputy. Indeed, Garullo's original suggestion, prior to being convinced by Elinor's 'real' fool to adopt motley, is to 'Camelionise or Change [him]selfe into the shape of a Chimnysweeper' (*Telltale*, 7ᵛ; TLN.645–6), the very costume Lorenzo chooses for his senile seduction attempts in *May Day*. Whether pre- or postdating *May Day*, *Telltale* relies on the same disguises that generations of actors had worn for portraying wooing or voyeuristic adventurers. In his hermit's disguise, the Duke even subtly mirrors Henry V's Agincourt escapade when he advises his servant Fidelio that his 'next busines', once he has 'sett the Court in some good order', 'ys thus disguisd to ouerlooke the Camp' of his 'rude army' (*Telltale*, 11ʳ; TLN.1003–1006). Evoking the 'hardship of rule' trope, this 'ouerseer' Duke likens himself to 'the sun' keeping a 'watchfull eye ouer the world' (*Telltale*, 11ʳ; TLN.1019–23). Like the sun, all 'kings' who wish to rule with safety and authority must 'moue in a restles sphere', since 'the publique safty ys theyr priuat Care' (*Telltale*, 11ʳ; 1023–6). *The Telltale* thus combines multiple layers of disguised ruler imagery, relating back to the 'comical histories' of the late sixteenth century, as well as to the tragicomic disguises from the early seventeenth century.

Although it is impossible definitively to date *The Telltale*, this play contains an intriguing textual anomaly that offers a chronological clue: the unusual stage direction '*Exiturus*' (*Telltale*, 7ᵃ; TLN.567). '*Exiturus*' appears in five plays by Chapman, including *May Day*, which suggests Chapman as *Telltale*'s putative author.[69] If *Telltale* is the work of Chapman, then Angelo's *May Day* animosity towards the 'Friers weede' or 'motley coate' would suggest that *Telltale* predates Chapman's children's comedy. *May Day* rejects the exact costumes that clothe *The Telltale*'s disguised ruler. Chapman's authorship could also account for the manuscript's inclusion in the Henslowe/Alleyn papers at Dulwich College. Rather

---

[68]   Dulwich College MSS 20, fol. 8ʳ. In Foakes and Gibson, *Telltale*, the reference to 'Iackett' is misspelt 'Iackett' (TLN.678).

[69]   See Alan C. Dessen and Leslie Thomson, *A Dictionary of Stage Directions in English Drama, 1580–1642* (Cambridge, 1999), p. 86. Intriguingly, '*Exiturus*' also appears in the obscure manuscript play, *The Emperor's Favourite* (TLN.2292.SD), bound with the as yet unpublished (though tantalizingly titled) *The Twice Chang'd Friar*. See Siobhan Keenan (ed.), *The Emperor's Favourite* (Oxford, 2010).

than being an obscure drama, as R.A. Foakes, Peter Beal and Grace Ioppolo describe it, which 'has no known connection to Edward Alleyn', *Telltale* would then represent an early Chapman play that capitalizes on Alleyn's well-known disguise as the hermit Irus in *The Blind Beggar of Alexandria*.[70] Regardless of chronology, however, the similarity between the staged disguises of *Telltale* and the dismissed disguises in *May Day* link the texts of both plays.

Despite its obvious fall from favour by the second decade of the seventeenth century, the disguised ruler makes a brief appearance in Shakespeare and Fletcher's collaborative venture, *King Henry VIII* (1613, King's Men; published 1621). In an incidental episode at Cardinal Wolsey's masque, Henry arrives masked and dressed like a shepherd to meet Anne Bullen for the first time (F *Henry VIII*, TLN.753–4.SD; 1.4.65.0.SD). This scene probably derives from the description of Henry's famous Twelfth Night '*maske*' in Hall's *Chronicle*.[71] At this masque, an entertainment newly arrived from '*Italie*' and a '*thynge not seen afore in Englande*', the king and his gentlemen entered '*disguised*' in '*visers*'.[72] Revisualized by Shakespeare and Fletcher, Henry's masked escapade also parallels similar wooing episodes in Elizabethan 'comical histories', while echoing varied bucolic disguises in plays like *Friar Bacon* and *Mucedorus*. The shepherd's costume fails to hide Henry's regal status, and Wolsey easily identifies his 'royall choyce' from among the masked courtiers (F *Henry VIII*, TLN.788; 1.4.89). This episode still indicates, however, that the successful depoliticization and 'domestication' of the Gunpowder Plot allowed a disguised ruler to return, albeit briefly, in a play written eight years after the inheritors of Henry's Tudor crown suffered the terrorist threat of annihilation.

No longer cause for social or political concern, nor of sufficient dramatic interest to warrant overt parody, the disguised ruler in Wolsey's masque provides a fleeting reminder of a Tudor motif. Although the disguised ruler had waned in popular appeal by this time, his presence would still memorably be reinvented once again by a playwright not typically associated with the motif. This playwright was, however, explicitly associated with the Gunpowder Plot, and was subsequently forced to defend his religious affiliation and reputation. The play that revives the disguised ruler as an integral plot protagonist is *Bartholomew Fair*. Its playwright, of course, Ben Jonson.

Bartholomew Fair and the Gunpowder (Sub)Plot

In preparation for his afternoon's fair-booth performance at the annual cloth and horse-trading fair, the puppeteer Lantern (the alternative persona of the hobbyhorse-seller Leatherhead) discusses his past theatrical glories in the final

---

[70]   Foakes, Beal and Ioppolo, 'MSS 20: The Manuscript of *The Telltale*', Henslowe-Alleyn Digitisation Project (2005) <http://www.henslowe-alleyn.org.uk/catalogue/MSS-20.html> [accessed 6 May 2011].

[71]   *Hall's Chronicle*, 'Henry VIII', Year 3 [1511–12], fol. xviʳ (fol. 3C4ʳ).

[72]   Ibid., fol. xviʳ (fol. 3C4ʳ).

act of *Bartholomew Fair* (1614, Lady Elizabeth's Men; published 1631).[73] Leatherhead/Lantern proclaims the array of '*Motions*' (puppet shows) he has 'giuen light to', and catalogues his personal favourites:

> LEATHERHEAD: *Ierusalem* was a stately thing; and so was *Niniue*, and the citty of *Norwich*, and *Sodom* and *Gomorrah*; with the rising o'the prentises; and pulling downe the bawdy houses there, vpon *Shroue-Tuesday*; but the *Gunpowder-plot*, there was a get-penny! I haue presented that to an eighteene, or twenty pence audience, nine times in an afternoone. Your home-borne proiects proue euer the best, they are so easie, and familiar. (*Bartholomew*, K3ʳ; 5.1.7–16)

The '*Gunpowder-plot*' that completes Leatherhead's list of minuscule entertainments presumably celebrates the salvation of the Stuart dynasty with violent theatrics. This occasionalist 'home-borne' project, 'so easie' to enjoy because so 'familiar' to his thrill-seeking audience, proves the most profitable of Leatherhead's 'get-penny' hits. Its dominant position among several sensational '*Motions*' nevertheless evinces the successful 'domestication' of this nine-year-old event in the political and cultural psyche of the English nation.

Although a 'get-penny' hit, the Plot's destructive potential is fully acknowledged through association with Leatherhead's other 'stately' fair-booth offerings. These each present historical or historio-biblical instances of ruin and desolation. Thus, the Roman sack of Jerusalem, the destruction of Nineveh, the fall of Norwich and the razing of Sodom and Gomorrah (with its localized reference to Shrove Tuesday apprentice troubles and attacks on bawdy houses), all pale in comparison with that ultimate money-spinning horror tale, the '*Gunpowder-plot*'.[74] The original Plot might, by 1614, be sufficiently 'domesticated' to allow the corrupt Leatherhead to compare it with other destructive episodes from a real or mythical past, but Jonson's openly satirical reference possesses a far darker political dimension, made more immediate by the playwright's very personal, active involvement in the 1605 events.

Jonson's role in the Gunpowder Plot is well documented.[75] On or about 9 October 1605, he dined with the leading conspirators, including Catesby and Thomas Winter. Unless Jonson was acting as government sponsored *agent provocateur*, his presence at this social gathering must of necessity appear highly

---

[73] Ben Jonson, *Bartholmew Fayre* (London, 1631), *STC* 14753.5. Line numbers from Suzanne Gossett (ed.), *Bartholomew Fair* (Manchester, 2000).

[74] The 'fall of Norwich' probably alludes to Kett's Rebellion of 1549, the last large scale anti-enclosure uprising in southern England. See Anthony Fletcher and Diarmaid MacCulloch, *Tudor Rebellions*, 5th edn (Harlow, 2004), pp. 65–74; Keith Lindley, 'Riot Prevention and Control in Early Stuart London', *TRHS* (5th series), 33 (1983): 109–26 (pp. 109–10).

[75] Martin Butler's illuminating paper, 'Ben Jonson: Catholic dramatist', offered while this book was under revision, was presented at the London Renaissance Seminar, Birkbeck College, University of London, 12 February 2011.

suspicious, especially since he was a well-known Catholic convert.[76] Indeed, Jonson's recusancy resulted in court proceedings being brought against him as late as April 1606. At these, Jonson was forced to deny all wrongdoing, especially the 'seduceing of youthe ... to the popishe religion'.[77] Jonson's association with the Gunpowder Plotters, and his very open Catholic sympathies, makes his apparent immunity in the aftermath of the Gunpowder Plot even more surprising. That Jonson was not accused of complicity might stem from some exemption, or his willingness to assist the newly-created earl of Salisbury, Robert Cecil, in his hurried post-Plot investigations. Two days after the Plot was discovered, Jonson received a warrant from the Privy Council permitting him to inform 'a certaine priest' that, if he agreed to give evidence against the plotters, the priest's freedom to travel to and from Westminster would be guaranteed.[78] As Jonson explained in his detailed letter to Cecil, dated 8 November 1605, the Privy Council's commission was, unfortunately, impossible to fulfil. Supposedly unable to locate the priest, Jonson defends his failure while assuring Cecil that, in the same position, he 'would have put on wings' to do 'his *Maiesty*', his 'Country [and] all Christianity ... [a similar] good service'.[79] Jonson's eagerness to assist and overt patriotic fervour appear to have been successful. He was not implicated in the Plot, although theories about his involvement still surface in critical studies of his plays.[80]

Whatever Jonson's actual role in the Plot and its aftermath, there seems little doubt that when Leatherhead discusses his 'get-penny' motion, some in the audience would recognize the irony of the criminal profiteering from this particular historical event. It is probably no coincidence that Jonson's principal government contact, Cecil, had died 24 May 1612, over two years before the first performance of *Bartholomew Fair*. The elderly statesmen's absence, Jonson's apparent sense of security, and/or the 'domestication' of the '*Motions*' subject matter, all enable Leatherhead's description of his '*Gunpowder-plot*' puppet-show to provide a non-threatening moment of ironic humour. Referenced nearly a decade after the actual event, Leatherhead's 'get-penny' hit also confirms the continued association of this historical occasion with disguised ruler intrigue. From the chronological distance of 1614, Jonson seems perfectly comfortable reminding his audience of the Gunpowder Plot. At the same time, he parodies a motif particularly associated with post-Plot conspiracy and infiltration. Why he does so remains a mystery, although the ghostly presence of one disguised ruler in particular still haunts the 1614 production, a figure only fleetingly alluded to within the play's complex and convoluted narrative.

---

[76]   See Peter Lake, *The Anti-Christ's Lewd Hat* (New Haven, 2002); Ian Donaldson, 'Talking with Ghosts: Ben Jonson and the English Civil War', *BJJ*, 17 (2010): 1–18 (pp. 10–11).

[77]   C.H. Herford, Percy and Evelyn Simpson (eds), *Ben Jonson* (11 vols, Oxford, 1925–52), vol. 1, p. 220–23.

[78]   B.N. De Luna, *Jonson's Romish Plot* (Oxford, 1967), pp. 130–31.

[79]   Herford, Simpson and Simpson, *Jonson*, vol. 1, p. 202.

[80]   Frances Teague, 'Jonson and the Gunpowder Plot', *BJJ*, 5 (1998): 249–52.

Burbage, Field and the Blackfriars Connection

G.R. Hibbard's 1977 edition describes *Bartholomew Fair* as a parodic 'skit' on earlier disguised ruler plays, even though, by 1614, Marston's, Shakespeare's and Middleton's offerings were at least a decade old.[81] Whatever the justification for the play's 'skit' status, the disguised ruler does resurface in *Bartholomew Fair* in the person of Adam Overdo, a Justice of the Peace who travels in disguise, seeking to expose corruption and vice among the fair's stallholders and punters.[82] Michael J. Redmond considers Overdo's escapade as proof of the nation's active discontent with James, particularly regarding his failure to reform England's court.[83] Accordingly, a well-hidden subversive agenda for *Bartholomew Fair* places it in alignment with the disguised ruler plays of the previous decade. In the context of conventional Whig negativity, Redmond's conjectural response to Jonson's supposedly sly allusions to James must be treated with suspicion. It seems highly unlikely some unified political intent would prompt Jonson's adoption of a timeworn motif, especially one he previously and pointedly ignored. There is, however, another reason why Jonson might parody the disguised ruler in *Bartholomew Fair*, one based not on solidarity with earlier subversive drama, but on accommodating the specific skill sets provided by the disparate actors brought together for the play's Hope performance. How and why Jonson achieves this owes much to the unusual circumstances that accompanied the play's performance and appearance in print, and to the status of mature and maturing actors united through serendipity to perform Jonson's complex late comedy.

Critical opinion remains divided between those who consider *Bartholomew Fair* an 'episodic' play, with a 'sparse and disparate narrative' that results in a 'rich mess', and those who view it as a 'complex comic masterpiece' boasting an 'elaborate intertextuality'.[84] Whether mess or masterpiece, the play's absence from the 1616 *Workes* suggests that it was not a particular favourite of Jonson's. In fact, *Bartholomew Fair* was not prepared for publication until 1631, seventeen years after its first performance. This separate quarto edition was supposed to be bound into subsequent *Workes* folios with two other plays, *The Devil Is An Ass* (1616)

---

[81]   G.R. Hibbard (ed.), *Bartholmew Fair* (London, 1977), p. xvi.

[82]   My thanks to John Creaser, editor of *Bartholomew Fair* in David Bevington, Martin Butler and Ian Donaldson (gen. eds), *The Cambridge Edition of the Works of Ben Jonson* (6 vols, Cambridge, 2011), an edition that appeared after this book went to press. Creaser kindly confirms that his own editorial commentary does not consider the disguised ruler in *Bartholomew Fair*.

[83]   See Redmond, *Shakespeare, Politics*, p. 127.

[84]   For the 'episodic', see Gordon Campbell (ed.), *Bartholomew Fair* (Oxford, 1995), p. xx; 'sparse and disparate' and 'rich mess', Stephen Orgel, 'Jonson and the Arts', in Richard Harp and Stanley Stewart (eds), *Cambridge Companion to Ben Jonson* (Cambridge, 2000), pp. 140–51 (p. 146); 'complex comic masterpiece', Gossett, *Bartholomew*, p. 1; 'elaborate intertextuality', William W.E. Slights, *Ben Jonson and the Art of Secrecy* (Toronto, 1994), pp. 152.

and *The Staple of News* (1625–26).[85] Possibly indicating a dispute between printer and an ailing Jonson, this 1631 venture failed, ensuring that 'Bartholmew Fayre: A Comedie, Acted in the Yeare, 1614', was not included in the *Workes* until the 1640 two-volume second folio, published three years after the playwright's death.[86]

The 1640 'first edition' includes a metatheatrical Induction (*Bartholomew*, A4ʳ–A6ᵛ), and a separate Prologue and Epilogue (*Bartholomew*, A3ʳ and M4ᵛ) written specifically for a court performance on 1 November 1614. A mock indenture in the Induction also refers to the 'one and thirtieth day of *Octob*. 1614' (*Bartholomew*, A5ʳ; Induction 69), confirming that *Bartholomew Fair* premiered publicly at the Hope playhouse, one day before its appearance at court. *Bartholomew Fair* was also staged almost precisely two years after the premature death on 6 November 1612 of that beloved eighteen-year-old symbol of Protestantism, Prince Henry Stuart. A year after Henry's death, on 24 February 1613, James's daughter, Princess Elizabeth, married the Protestant Elector of Palatine, Frederick V. This marriage reassured subjects who feared a return to royal Catholicism. *Bartholomew Fair* thus appeared during a period of relative political and religious calm.[87]

The site of the first public performance of *Bartholomew Fair* was Henslowe's Hope playhouse, newly-built on the site of the old Bear Garden close by the Globe. The Hope was a dual-purpose playhouse-*cum*-bearbaiting arena, complete with odiferous 'stockyard atmosphere'.[88] In 1614, it housed the Lady Elizabeth's Players, a company that combined acting talent from the Lady Elizabeth's Men, the (First) Prince Charles's Men, and the remnants of the Blackfriars children. Jonson's association with the Blackfriars children, for whom he occasionally wrote, traces back to 1600.[89] Performed by over thirty characters, *Bartholomew Fair* was written for actors, some of whom had most likely appeared in earlier children's company disguised ruler plays. In fact, one ex-Blackfriars actor is specifically named during a conversation between the puppeteer Leatherhead/Lantern and the unfortunate country esquire, Bartholomew Cokes. Having been relieved of his money and clothing in a series of comical robberies, the gullible Cokes now asks the puppeteer to rate the acting skill of his wooden performers:

> COKES: [W]hich is your *Burbage* now?
> LEATHERHEAD: What meane you by that, Sir?
> COKES: Your best *Actor*. Your *Field*? (*Bartholomew*, L1ᵛ; 5.3.85–7)

Cokes's reference to '*Field*' denotes the actor and playwright Nathan Field, Jonson's personal 'schollar' or protégé, who, as a teenaged performer, appeared

---

[85]   Gossett, *Bartholomew*, pp. 20–21.

[86]   Jonson, *Workes* (2 vols, London, 1640), vol. 2, fol. A2ʳ (*STC* 14754); Herford, Simpson and Simpson, *Jonson*, vol. 1, p. 211.

[87]   Lockyer, *Early Stuarts*, pp. 156–7.

[88]   See W. David Kay, 'Ben Jonson', in Kinney (ed.), *Renaissance Drama*, pp. 464–81 (p. 465).

[89]   Chambers, *ES* 2, pp. 465–9; Gurr, *Playing Companies*, pp. 394–415.

in his Blackfriars productions of *Cynthia's Revels* (1600) and *Poetaster* (1601).[90] When the same children's company relocated to Whitefriars, Field later appeared in Jonson's cross-gendered comedy, *Epicoene* (c. 1609). By 1614, while working for Henslowe, the twenty-seven-year-old Field was entrusted with collecting the company payment for King James's 1 November court performance. The Chamber Accounts entry names 'Nathan ffeilde' as the recipient of ten pounds, 'in behalfe of himselfe and the rest of his fellowes', for their staging of 'Bartholomewe Fayre'.[91] Obviously a member of the Hope company, Field's presence in the Act 5 dialogue implies that he either played Cokes, Leatherhead or the citizen Littlewit, thus adding to the metatheatrical irony of Cokes's enquiry.

It remains unclear whether Jonson was 'renewing a link' with the playhouse company of his early stage successes, comically satirizing his personal 'schollar' (perhaps implying a certain woodenness of performance), or even alluding to Field's father, a fanatical Puritan preacher and supposed inspiration for the hypocritical zealot, Zeal-of-the-Land Busy.[92] Whatever Jonson's true intention, the fictive Cokes clearly believes Field to be the natural inheritor of Richard Burbage's theatrical crown. Field is being compared to the actor who, a decade previously, starred as the disguised 'Malecontent' Malevole in the adult manifestation of QC *Malcontent* (Induction, 86). Around the same time, the same 'malcontent' role at Blackfriars (as well as the disguised protagonists in *The Fawn* and *The Fleer*), might, so William Peery first argued, have been played by the teenaged Nathan Field.[93] No matter whether Jonson is being complimentary to, or satirical about, his young protégé, the metatheatricality of this *Bartholomew Fair* moment, matching the metatheatre of QC *Malcontent*'s Induction, signifies far more than an accidental comparison of two leading early seventeenth-century players. Instead, this moment describes the same players who possibly appeared in the same role at the same time, but on either side of the Thames.

Although *Bartholomew Fair* offers a potential parodic hit at *The Malcontent*, it remains within a pure, comedic form, adhering closely to the classical unities. Jonson's pretensions to be the 'English Horace' no doubt dictated this decorum of character, time and place.[94] No tragicomic dangers or near deaths threaten this fair's clientele. In fact, Jonson was fundamentally opposed to Guarinian theory, as he later expressed to Drummond. His comment, that 'Guarini, in his Pastor Fido, kept no decorum, in making Shepherds speak as well as himself could', provides an aesthetic reason for parodying plays like *The Malcontent*, which wore

---

[90]   Patterson, *Conversations*, p. 15.

[91]   Chambers, *ES* 4, p. 183.

[92]   See Gurr, *Playing Companies*, p. 400; Nora Johnson, *The Actor as Playwright in Early Modern Drama* (Cambridge, 2003), pp. 54–83; David Riggs, *Ben Jonson: A Life* (Cambridge, MA, 1989), pp. 207–208.

[93]   See William Peery (ed.), *Plays of Nathan Field* (Austin, 1950), p. 280.

[94]   Leah Marcus, 'Jonson and the Court', in Harp and Stewart (eds), *Companion*, pp. 30–42 (p. 33).

their Guarinian credentials so openly.[95] As the figure of tragicomedy on his *Workes* title-page demonstrates, however, Jonson must have recognized the importance of the 'mongrell' form, even if he chose not to advance specifically Guarinian pastoralism in his own plays.

Whatever Jonson's view of tragicomedy, he explicitly revives the motif so closely associated with Guarini in its *Malcontent* manifestation. Jonson's own disguised ruler, however, is no duke or prince or king, but a Justice of the Peace, the traditional butt of countless comic situations and characterizations. In *Bartholomew Fair*, Adam Overdo is the Justice in charge of the peripatetic Court of Pie-powders, a summary court at fairs and markets that administers justice to itinerant stall-holders and fairgoers. Its name derives from the French *pieds poudroux* or 'dusty feet'.[96] Overdo is not corrupt or duplicitous. Instead, his pompous self-importance and blindness indicate ineptitude and complacency. In this, Overdo resembles Justice Shallow in *1* and *2 Henry IV* and *Merry Wives*, far more than the despicable Justice Falso in Middleton's *Phoenix*. Jonson's generalized and gentle satire against the magistracy is nevertheless predicated on recognition of a folktale and ballad character whose costume returns Justice Overdo's disguised ruler antics to their 'comical history' roots.

Overdo, Robin Hood and Mad Arthur O'Bradley

When, in the final act of *Bartholomew Fair*, Justice Overdo describes his 'later [meaning 'latest'] disguise', he explains how he has 'borrow'd' the clothes of a lowly 'Porter' (*Bartholomew*, K3ᵛ; 5.2.1), in order to bring transgressors and criminals to justice. Overdo admits that his 'great and good ends' have been interrupted by a series of unexpected mishaps, not least his humiliating confinement in Bartholomew Fair's stocks (*Bartholomew*, K3ᵛ; 5.2.1). Even so, the Justice's resolve has, as he explains, 'neuer [been] destroyed':

> [N]either is the houre of my seuerity yet come, to reueale my selfe, wherein cloud-like, I will breake out in raine, and haile, lightning, and thunder, vpon the head of enormity. (*Bartholomew*, K3ᵛ; 5.2.3–6)

Overdo's exclamation evokes the standard trope of the disguised ruler. His 'seuerity' lies hidden, ready to 'breake out' like a torrential downpour over the metaphorical 'head' of any 'enormity' (any breach of law or morality, transgression or crime). Reminiscent of the 'base contagious clouds' that 'smother vp [Hal's] beautie from the world' in *1 Henry IV* (Q1, 1.2.221–2), Overdo's disguise shields the metaphorical reality of his avenging rain. Hidden beneath his Porter's clothes, Overdo relishes the opportunity to 'reueale' the 'haile, lightning, and thunder' of his true authority. He might be inept when dealing with the thieves, pickpockets,

---

95   Patterson, *Conversations*, p. 7.
96   Gossett, *Bartholomew*, p. 72n.

violent braggarts and whores of the fair, but Overdo's 'houre' of 'seuerity' eventually comes, along with an enlightened recognition of his own fallibility. The Porter does indeed 'reueale' himself, but the outcome is more jovial than severe since the Justice invites all for supper at his home.

As the Porter in Act 5, Overdo achieves a level of self-awareness that eludes most 'Pie-powders' Justices. In all previous acts, however, he has appeared not as a Porter, but in a costume resonating with 'comical history' significance. Overdo makes his first entrance in Act 2 wearing the 'couert' or concealing disguise he adopts for most of the play, his intention being to 'see, and not be seene' (*Bartholomew*, D1ʳ; 2.1.47–8). Ironically, in view of his subsequent misadventures, this legal term 'couert' also invokes security from arrest or debt. Overdo's chosen 'couert' might seem strange, until compared with similar disguised ruler costumes from the 1590s. Overdo appears to his Hope/court audience dressed as 'mad *Arthur of Bradley*' (*Bartholomew*, D4ᵛ; 2.2.126). Arthur of Bradley (or O'Bradley) is a folk character associated with medieval marriage ritual. He is mentioned in the *c.* 1681–84 broadside ballad, *Robin Hood's Birth, Breeding, Valour and Marriage*, whose narrative traces back at least to the fourteenth century.[97] This text describes Robin Hood's wedding to Clorinda, Queen of the Shepherds.[98] At their nuptial celebrations, enthusiastic wedding guests congregate in a 'strange shouting' mass, from which 'all that were in it lookt madly':

> For some ware a Bull-back, some dancing a Morris,
> and some singing Arthur-a-Bradley. (*Robin Hood's Birth*, Stanza 46)

The medieval 'Arthur-a-Bradley' song that some of the 'strange shouting' guests were 'singing' concerns the simple and impoverished Arthur, whose mismatched points and garters are violently removed on his wedding night. This folkloric image was later adopted as a part of common English wedding festivities. Thus, a guest dressed as 'mad *Arthur*' would arrive at the celebrations festooned with ribbons, which were then cut into tiny strips and distributed to fellow revellers as good luck or fertility tokens. This custom appears several times in Samuel Pepys's *Diary*, including his 24 January 1659/1660 description of the scramble to pull 'off Mrs. bride's and Mr. bridegroom's ribbons' as the wedding-night couple were undressed.[99] Likewise, a year later, 26 January 1660/1661, Pepys describes the unfortunate 'Lieutenant Lambert', a gentleman 'with whom' Pepys and his friends made 'very merry by taking away his ribbans and garters, having made him to confess that he [was] lately married'.[100] A barely-disguised analogy for loss both of wedding night clothing and virginity, the 'mad *Arthur*' custom was, less than fifty

---

[97] Child, *Ballads* 3, pp. 214–17.

[98] *Robin Hood's Birth*, Magdalene College, Cambridge, Pepys 2.116–117.

[99] Henry B. Wheatley (ed.), *The Diary of Samuel Pepys* (10 vols, London and Cambridge, 1893–99), vol. 1, pp. 30–31.

[100] Ibid., vol. 1, p. 334.

years after Overdo chooses his particular 'couert', still an opportunity for drunken ribaldry and innuendo.

The traditional costume for any 'mad *Arthur*' is described in the eighteenth-century ballad, 'Arthur O'Bradley O':[101]

> His coat was of scarlet so fine,
> Full trimmed with buttons behind,
> Two sleeves he had, it is true,
> One yellow, the other was blue,
> And the cuffs and capes were of green,
> And the longest that ever were seen. ('Arthur O'Bradley O', Verse 3)

That Overdo's 'mad *Arthur*' costume echoes the ballad is confirmed by the pig-woman Ursla, who notes the Justice's 'garded' or outlandishly ornamented coat (*Bartholomew*, E1ʳ; 2.5.48).[102]

Ursla's description of Overdo's 'garded' clothing also recalls numerous disguised rulers in multi-coloured motley. Memorable from the appearances of Prince Edward in *Friar Bacon*, Antonio in *Antonio's Revenge* and the Duke of Venice in *Humour Out of Breath*, as well as from 'real' fools such as Touchstone in *As You Like It* and Passarello in QC *Malcontent*, the 'garded' motley had, as already noted, a long heritage in disguised ruler subterfuge. A commonplace image for those who rail against human folly, Overdo's disguise would be both familiar and ludicrously anachronistic for the play's 1614 audience.[103] Now lost as a wedding night custom, the Arthur of Bradley tradition offers Overdo the opportunity to observe wrongdoing beneath the motley 'couert' of simple and naive foolishness.

Overdo might figure himself in an outmoded ballad and 'comical history' costume, but Jonson's character-assassination appears far more precise a portrait of a contemporary civic politician than traditional 'Overdo as anti-James' commentary would suggest. As David McPherson argues, Jonson is not just evoking a folkloric tradition, but lampooning a specific London dignitary, who only recently and very openly prefigured Overdo's disguised subterfuge as a precursor to social reform. This dignitary, London's outgoing Lord Mayor, is the true target for Jonson's topical satire.

Topical Satire in Overdo's Disguise

Overdo self-consciously comments on his Arthur O'Bradley motley, whereby people 'may haue seene many a foole in the habite of a Iustice; but neuer till now, a Iustice in the habit of a foole' (*Bartholomew*, C6ᵛ; 2.1.7–9). His justification for dressing in so unusual a disguise is as politically astute as the costume is

---

[101] Alfred Williams (ed.), *Folk-Songs of the Upper Thames* (London, 1923), pp. 271–4.

[102] Gossett, *Bartholomew*, p. 85n.

[103] Hans Holbein's drawing of Folly is reproduced in Betty Radice (ed.), *Praise of Folly* (London, 1974), facing p. 16.

Fig. 5.3   John Quayle as the false-bearded Justice Overdo (left), suffering punishment in the stocks, wearing his motley disguise as 'Mad Arthur' in the RSC's *Bartholomew Fair* (1997)

outlandishly ridiculous. Overdo complains how those who 'liue in high place' are in receipt of 'idle' spying intelligence, not least because 'most … intelligencers [are] knaues' (*Bartholomew*, D1ʳ; 2.1.37–8). In consequence, Justices like himself are 'little better' than 'errant fooles' for 'beleeuing' all they are told (*Bartholomew*, D1ʳ; 2.1.39). Over and above the traditional 'king and subject' theme of bettering the mediated and unreliable intelligence received at court, there is a decidedly pecuniary motive for Overdo's disguise. Overdo proclaims himself 'resolu'd … to spare spy-money hereafter' (*Bartholomew*, D1ʳ; 2.1.40–41). This ruler, in other words, can save money by adopting a disguise and making his 'owne discoueries' (*Bartholomew*, D1ʳ; 2.1.41). Dressed as a character from Robin Hood lore, Overdo uses the lunacy of 'mad *Arthur*' to gain easy, cost-effective access to the less salubrious parts of Bartholomew Fair.

As 'mad *Arthur*', Overdo explains why he chooses the 'habit of a foole'. Claiming his actions are not self-serving, but 'for the publike good', he cites historical precedent: 'thus hath the wise Magistrate done in all ages' (*Bartholomew*, C6ᵛ; 2.1.10–11). Even so, Overdo's 'wise' actions bear a topical, localized precedent as well:

> OVERDO: Neuer shall I enough commend a worthy worshipfull man, sometime a capitall member of this City, for his high wisdome, … who would take … now the habit of a Porter; now of a Carman; now of the Dog-killer, … [or]

a Seller of tinder-boxes; and what would hee doe in all these shapes? mary goe … into euery Alehouse, and down into euery Celler; measure the length of puddings, take the gage of blacke pots, and cannes, … and custards with a sticke; … weigh the loaues of bread on his middle-finger; then would he send for 'hem, home; giue the puddings to the poore, the bread to the hungry, the custards to his children; breake the pots, and burne the cannes, … hee Would not trust his corrupt officers; he would do't himselfe. would all men in authority would follow this worthy president! (*Bartholomew*, C6ᵛ; 2.1.13–28)

As Overdo meticulously explains, his disguise emulates another 'worthy worshipfull man' who has, 'sometime' in the recent past, appeared in the humble 'shape' of several London tradespeople, including that of a 'Porter' as depicted in Act 5. His mission is secretly to observe fraudulent practices among the City's vendors. Thus disguised, the 'worshipfull man' has measured 'puddings', 'pots', 'cannes', 'custards' and 'bread', deciding not to 'trust his corrupt officers', but to 'do't himselfe' instead. Wishing 'all men in authority' would do likewise, Overdo enthuses over the wisdom of such actions and commends his 'mad *Arthur*' disguise as a way to 'follow this worthy president!' [*sic*].

Overdo's historical specificity leads to David McPherson's conjecture that Jonson's Justice is based on a real-life 'worthy worshipfull man': the puritanical reforming Lord Mayor of London for 1613–14, Sir Thomas Myddelton (no relation to the similarly named playwright).[104] McPherson's argument stems from a letter written by Myddelton to the Lord Chamberlain Thomas Howard, first earl of Suffolk, dated 8 July 1614 (shortly before Howard's 11 July promotion to Lord Treasurer). In it, Myddelton mentions his 'reforming' zeal and the 'steps [he has] taken' to investigate corrupt practices in the City.[105] He also explains how he has explored the City's taverns and breweries, taking an exact survey of all 'victualling houses and ale-houses', while noting the excessive alcoholic production and consumption of 'that sweet poison'.[106] Myddelton then determines to limit the 'quantity of beer' produced, as well as the number of establishments entitled to sell it.[107] His prohibitionary fervour extends likewise to enforcing observance of Sabbath trading restrictions, as well as eliminating short weights and measures being offered by unscrupulous bakers and brewers. With ambitious plans for dealing 'with thieving brokers and broggers' who act as 'receivers of all stolen goods', Myddelton's reformative zeal is thus figured in *Bartholomew Fair*.[108] Admitting his use of spies to discover the whereabouts of bawdy houses, Myddelton states that he himself has travelled 'disguised' to visit these 'nurseries

---

[104]   David McPherson, 'The Origins of Overdo: A Study in Jonsonian Invention', *MLQ*, 37 (1976): 221–33 (pp. 225–6).

[105]   Quoted in H.C. Overall and W.H. Overall (eds), *Remembrancia: Archives of the City of London, AD 1579–1664* (London, 1878), pp. 358–9.

[106]   Ibid., p. 359.

[107]   Ibid., p. 359.

[108]   Ibid., p. 359.

of villainy'.[109] For McPherson, Myddelton's 'disguised' undertaking equates with Overdo's disguised mission of reform.

Such a definitive correlation between fictive character and actual Lord Mayor is, of course, impossible to prove. Our knowledge of this mayor's disguising stems only from his private correspondence to Thomas Howard, a member of King James's most trusted inner circle of confidants.[110] Myddelton's letter does, however, illuminate Overdo's unusually precise monologue. As the mayor's letter indicates, a recent real-life City official has disguised himself for the same reason as Overdo. Hence, Overdo's wish that 'all men in authority would follow this worthy president!'. Significantly, all modern editions of *Bartholomew Fair* adjust the spelling of Overdo's exclamation to 'worthy precedent', an understandable alteration when compared with Florio's 1598 secondary definition of '*Presidente*', with its legal/moral sense as '*an example, a patterne, or a president* [e.g. 'precedent'] *to follow or shew to others*'.[111] However, Overdo might actually be referring to the 'worthy president' according to its original *Workes* spelling, with 'president' being the actual 'worthy worshipfull' Mayor Myddelton himself. Thus, Florio's primary definition of '*Presidente*', as '*a president, a lieutenant, a captaine, a gouernour, a prouost, a viceroy, a chiefe, a defender, a ruler or president, he that hath authoritie in a prouince next vnder a King*', and Florio's earlier definition of '*Edeti*' as '*chiefe magistrate or president*', both confirm that 'president' as presiding magistrate, and 'president' as prior example, had identical early modern spellings.[112]

If Overdo's 'worthy president' does refer to an authority figure rather than the precedent set by his deeds, this reference strengthens the argument that Jonson is here alluding to an identifiable character in contemporary politics. Indeed, unrelated research on *Measure for Measure* notes Mayor Myddelton's well-known title as 'President' and founder, in 1613, of the Bridewell Prison's 'Black Room'.[113] Open to select fee-paying voyeuristic visitors, Myddelton's 'Black Room' was the site where accused (invariably female) felons were publicly whipped until released from their ordeal by the 'knocking' of the president's hammer. Furthermore, Myddelton's letter to Howard confirms that nefarious persons discovered in 'lewd houses' were punished 'according to their deserts, some by carting and whipping,

---

[109] Ibid., p. 358.

[110] It was Howard who first spotted the large pile of brushwood beneath the palace at Westminster, thus foiling the 1605 plot. See Pauline Croft, 'Howard, Thomas, first earl of Suffolk (1561–1626)', *ODNB* (2004) <http://www.oxforddnb.com/index/101013942/Thomas-Howard> [accessed 6 May 2011].

[111] Florio, *Wordes*, p. 292.

[112] Ibid., pp. 292 & 115.

[113] Richard Wilson, 'Prince of Darkness: Foucault's Shakespeare', in Nigel Wood (ed.), *Measure for Measure* (Buckingham, 1996), pp. 133–78 (pp. 146–7). Overall and Overall, *Remembrancia*, p. 3n. Also Charles Welch, 'Myddelton , Sir Thomas (1549x56–1631)', rev. Trevor Dickie, *ODNB* (2004) <http://www.oxforddnb.com/index/101019685/Thomas-Myddelton> [accessed 6 May 2011].

and many by banishment', but specifically by sending the 'swarm of loose and idle vagrants' to enforced 'work in Bridewell'.[114] Ursla invokes this specific punishment while haranguing the prostitute Alice for attacking the Justice's wife, Mistress Overdo. Alice assumes Mistress Overdo to be a 'privy rich' harlot, who is trying to 'call away [male] customers' from the 'poore common whores' that ply their trade at the fair (*Bartholomew*, I4ᵛ; 4.5.69–71). Having shouted abuse at each other, Ursla defiantly describes how Alice was herself lately 'both lash'd, and slash'd … in *Bridewell*', to which Alice replies with vitriolic incisiveness about Ursla's ample girth: 'I, by the same token, you rid that weeke, and broake out the bottome o'the Cart' (*Bartholomew*, I4ᵛ; 4.5.78–81). Although a commonplace accusation for any woman engaged in the sex trade (Bridewell is sometimes considered analogous with the prison in *Measure for Measure*), the specifics with which Ursla and Alice attack each other accord with contemporary perceptions of the 'President's' prison and its corrective function.[115]

The Bridewell of which Myddelton was 'President', and where Alice received her lashes and slashes, was the infamous 'house of correction' constituted by the 1598 'Vagrancy Act' for the 'Payne and Punyshment of Rogues Vagabondes and Sturdy Beggars'.[116] Here, the travelling homeless, petty thieves, pickpockets, children, and women accused of prostitution and bastardy were likewise 'lash'd' and 'slash'd' by the official sanction of regularly-enforced Acts of Parliament.[117] Bridewell's principal charge was the punishment of sexual sin, its 'correction' administered through hard labour as well as regular floggings at the Bridewell whipping post.[118] Nevertheless, despite the goals of puritan moralists like Myddelton, Bridewell's proportion of 'sexual' criminals fell from 84 percent in the early 1560s to 38 percent in 1600–1601.[119] The prison was crowded from then on with 'swarms of loose and idle vagrants', as the Mayor describes them, who flocked to London to escape rural poverty and hunger.[120] This shift in focus, away from the punishment of sexual offences towards the incarceration of vagrants, hardly reflected, however, a softening of moral purpose. Rather, it represents a

---

[114] Overall and Overall, *Remembrancia*, p. 358.

[115] William C. Carroll, *Fat King, Lean Beggar* (Ithaca, 1996), pp. 97–124 (p. 114); Duncan Salkeld, 'Literary Traces in Bridewell and Bethlem, 1602–1624', *RES*, 56 (2005), 379–85 (p. 381); Salkeld, 'Making Sense of Differences: Postmodern History, Philosophy and Shakespeare's Prostitutes', *Chronicon*, 3 (2007) <http://www.ucc.ie/chronicon/3/salkeld.pdf> [accessed 5 May 2011]: 7–35 (pp. 29–35).

[116] Paul Slack, *Poverty and Policy in Tudor and Stuart England* (London, 1988), pp. 126–7; Slack, *The English Poor Law, 1531–1782* (Cambridge, 1995), pp. 10–13.

[117] John Pound, *Poverty and Vagrancy in Tudor England*, 2nd edn (London, 1986), pp. 53–7.

[118] Slack, *Poverty*, p. 93.

[119] Ibid., p. 93.

[120] Overall and Overall, *Remembrancia*, p. 358.

pragmatic response to those 'swarms' that left little time for anything else.[121] The harsh treatment of prisoners in Bridewell's 'Black Room' is actually somewhat surprising, given Myddelton's personal prison experience; Myddelton had himself been committed to Newgate in 1603 for refusing to accept his office as City Alderman, a post he swiftly assumed thereafter.[122] Eleven years later, the same Alderman, now the 'third Welsh Lord Mayor' of London, treats 'idle vagrants' with little regard, despite his own earlier imprisonment.[123]

Overdo's disguised meanderings reflect the actions of a contemporary political figure, while expressing a general dislike of all puritanical and/or hypocritical attempts to curb drinking and whoring in the City of London. This does not explain, however, the reason for Jonson's overt references to a reforming individual. A possible explanation may nevertheless be inferred from an entertainment that corresponded with Myddelton's mayoral investiture. *The Triumphs of Truth* (1613) was written by Thomas Middleton for this inauguration, when the new Lord Mayor progressed through the City and along the Thames to Westminster, there to swear allegiance to the Crown.[124] Presented a year before *Bartholomew Fair*, *Triumphs of Truth* makes no reference to disguise in its narrative, although, as Richard Wilson argues, it celebrates Mayor Myddelton's personal 'zeal' for the flogging of prostitutes in Bridewell.[125] The Bridewell 'President' thus analogously appears as 'Zeal, the champion of Truth', whose 'right hand [holds] a flaming scourge ... [as] chastiser of Ignorance and Error'.[126]

The dating of *Triumphs of Truth* does, however, contextualize Jonson's Myddeltonian commentary. As the *Stationers' Register* for 3 November 1613 indicates, *Triumphs of Truth* was presented on Myddelton's 'Lord Maiours Day octobris 29, 1613'.[127] Prior to the late seventeenth century, the pageant at Westminster celebrating the incumbent Lord Mayor of London's oath-taking occurred on the same date each year (Sundays excepted). It was staged the day after the religious festival of St Simon and St Jude (28 October), when the 'Silent Ceremony' of mayoral swearing-in was conducted at the City's Guildhall. These pageants were the most important events in the civic calendar, with the whole City '*en fête*' for their celebration.[128] The actual day of Myddelton's 1613 pageant can be deduced from earlier correspondence between the City dignitary and letter-writer, John Chamberlain, and the diplomat Sir Dudley Carleton (himself wrongly

---

[121] Slack, *Poverty*, p. 94.

[122] Alfred B. Beaven (ed.), *The Aldermen of the City of London* (2 vols, London, 1908–13), vol. 2 (1913), p. 176.

[123] Ibid., p. 176.

[124] David M. Bergeron (ed.), *The Manner of his Lordship's Entertainment* and *The Triumphs of Truth*, in *Oxford Middleton*, pp. 959–76.

[125] Wilson, 'Darkness', pp. 147–8.

[126] Bergeron, *Oxford Middleton*, p. 970 (209–214ff).

[127] Arber 3, p. 536.

[128] Caroline M. Barron, *London in the Later Middle Ages* (Oxford, 2004), pp. 151–2.

implicated in the Gunpowder Plot). Dated 3 November 1612, Chamberlain's letter refers to the 'Lord Mayors Feast' to celebrate the oath-taking of Myddelton's predecessor, Sir John Swinnerton.[129] This 'Feast', to which Prince Henry and the Count Palatine had been invited, was held 'on Thursday last'.[130] It was preceded by a pageant written by Thomas Dekker entitled *Troia-Noua Triumphans* or *London Triumphing*, whose title-page announces its staging 'on the Morrow next after *Simon* and *Iudes* day, being the 29. of *October*, 1612'.[131] The event suffered the inauspicious absence of Henry, who fell ill with typhoid two days before the 'Feast', only to die a week later on 6 November. Counting back from the letter's date of 3 November, the 'Thursday last' that Chamberlain refers to is thus, according to the 'New' or Gregorian calendar, Thursday 29 October 1612.

A year later, Myddelton's own Lord Mayor's pageant (with its staging of Middleton's *Triumphs of Truth*) thus fell on the following calendrical weekday, Friday 29 October 1613. The year after that, in 1614, the incumbent Sir Thomas Hayes, successor to Mayor Myddelton, celebrated his Lord Mayor's pageant on Saturday 29 October. The title-page date of Jonson's Prologue and Induction (which appears to correspond with the Gregorian calendar) claims that *Bartholomew Fair* was first performed at the Hope on 31 October (a Monday), with the court performance held the next day, 1 November (a Tuesday), All Hallows' Eve and All Hallows' Day respectively in the Christian liturgical calendar. These same Hope/court entertainments thus occurred on the earliest possible performance dates after Hayes's Saturday staging of his Lord Mayor's pageant, and the Friday St Simon and St Jude Day retirement of Mayor Thomas Myddelton. This chronology suggests a topical immediacy for Overdo's actions, with Jonson alluding to a London Mayor who had just resigned his post following his allotted year in office. Despite the play lampooning a contemporary authority figure only days after his removal from office, the timing of *Bartholomew Fair* ensures that Jonson sidesteps accusations of satirical slander against the current Lord Mayor of London. The most powerful person in the City of London is now Lord Mayor Sir Thomas Hayes. Sir Thomas Myddelton, no longer in office, is thus available for, and prone to, ridicule.

That Jonson sought, perhaps ironically and disingenuously, to circumvent any specific associations between Overdo and the City's ex-mayor is suggested by the Scrivener's mock indenture in the play's Hope Induction. Here, the Scrivener asks the audience not to speculate on 'what *Mirror of Magistrates* is meant by the *Iustice*' (*Bartholomew*, A6ʳ; Induction 146). Later, when Overdo delivers his mock classical oration calling upon all '*London*' to 'Harken vnto [his] *labours*, and but obserue [his] *discoueries*', he describes himself as an '*example of Iustice*, and *Mirror of Magistrates*' (*Bartholomew*, M5ᵛ; 5.6.34–5). With self-righteous pomposity, Overdo adds that he is 'the true top of formality, and scourge of

---

[129]   Quoted in R.T.D. Sayle, *Lord Mayors' Pageants* (London, 1931), pp. 97–8.

[130]   Ibid., pp. 97–8.

[131]   Thomas Dekker, *Troia-Noua Triumphans. London Triumphing* (London, 1612), fol. A1ʳ.

enormity' (*Bartholomew*, M5ᵛ; 5.6.35–6). Overdo's oratory subtly echoes Zeal, that 'scourge' and 'chastiser of Ignorance and Error' from Middleton's *Triumphs of Truth*.[132] The Justice's invocations of '*Mirror of Magistrates*' are generally interpreted either as allusions to William Baldwin and George Ferrers's *A Mirror for Magistrates* (1559), or to George Whetstone's *Mirour for Magestrates of Cities* (1584), which is often cited as a source for *Measure for Measure*.[133] If the reference alludes to Whetstone, Overdo would thus be likening himself to a real London Mayor whose propensity for reforming subterfuge mirrors Whetstone's advice to 'haue visible Lightes, in obscure Corners'.[134] *Bartholomew Fair*'s '*example of Iustice*', who makes his '*discoueries*' with Whetstonian fervour, thus emulates the 'olde fantastical Duke of darke corners' in *Measure for Measure* (F, TLN.2249–50; 4.3.147).

Whomsoever Jonson was actually satirizing, it appears that the Hope/court audience would recognize the topical humour of Justice Overdo's foolish disguise. Overdo is thus a fitting, as well as ironic, parody of similar theatricalized disguised ruler adventurers. This last full expression of Jacobean disguised ruler subterfuge is enacted, however, not by a king, prince or duke, but by a self-confessed scrivener-turned-Justice, whose motive is both commercial and moral in its secretive intent. With Overdo, the disguised ruler as voyeuristic overseer becomes the butt of comic abuse. His powers no longer strike 'king and subject' awe or fear in a suspicious populace. Instead, this disguised ruler becomes the unwitting victim of dramatic irony, as audience and reader laugh at his incredulity, and at his subsequent humiliation by the very villains he seeks to reform.

---

[132] Bergeron, *Oxford Middleton*, p. 970.

[133] Herford, Simpson and Simpson, *Jonson*, vol. 10, p. 177; Campbell, *Bartholomew*, p. 505n.; Gossett, *Bartholomew*, p. 42n.; McPherson, 'Origins', p. 226. See Paul Budra, '*A Mirror for Magistrates' and the De Casibus Tradition* (Toronto, 2000).

[134] George Whetstone, *A Mirour for Magestrates of Cyties* (London, 1584), fol. A3ᵛ.

Afterword
The Sting in *The Wasp*'s Tail

Historical certainties about the early modern playhouses are few and far between. Definitive evidence about the society in which the playhouses thrived is likewise sparse. It is little wonder, then, that early modern playtexts are deemed of such central importance for our understanding and analysis of the period in which they were written. This positioning is, however, inherently problematic. The plays that have survived, upon which so much historical conjecture is based, represent only a fraction of those written for and performed on London's stages. Of Henslowe's extensive list alone, barely one third remain extant in print or manuscript form.[1] Furthermore, recent historicist critical trends have imbued the extant early modern canon with historical and political nuances that reflect our own predilections and prejudices far more than those of its original creators. In Shakespeare studies, this historicizing of the canon prompts another investigation, not aimed at discovering the definitive authorial text, but searching for the text as 'originally performed'.[2] Such a quest, of significance for appreciating a play's reception when first conceived, written and staged, effectively denies a theatrical afterlife for the play, and for the collaborative and creative processes involved in its evolution.[3] The 'originally performed' playtext is, moreover, itself a hypothetical construct, anachronistically imposed by commentators largely raised in an age of opening nights and 'first night' press reviews. Early modern plays, by contrast, were purchased outright for the repertory. They were regularly restaged, revised and possibly drastically rewritten to ensure their ongoing topicality. They were constructed to be resources as portable and mutable as the actors whose skills and personalities breathed new life into old characters.

The disguised ruler plays neatly fit this paradigm. A small group of playwrights from the early seventeenth century might have recognized the potential of this age-old motif, only to discard it as social, political and artistic pressures dictated. This does not mean that the disguised ruler suddenly disappeared from the playhouse stages. Far from it. The likelihood is that, in any playing month of any year until the closures of 1642, some tiring-house or backstage changing area would shield a wooing king as he adopted his illicit disguise, or a usurped duke as he prepared for secret revenge. A popular play was too valuable a commodity to remain unperformed, and it seems likely that the disguised ruler plays continued to enjoy lively existences on the Jacobean and Caroline stages. Indeed, the continued

---

[1]   Andrew Gurr, 'Shakespeare's Playhouses', in Kastan (ed.), *Companion*, pp. 362–76 (p. 373).

[2]   Wells and Taylor (eds), *Oxford Shakespeare*, p. xv.

[3]   Greenblatt (gen. ed.), *Norton Shakespeare*, p. 78.

success of QC *Malcontent* is evident from the Caroline diary of John Greene, who mentions seeing this specific play at Blackfriars in February 1635, ten years after Charles I succeeded his father's throne.[4] Greene's diary offers tangible evidence that disguised rulers, though no longer appearing in print, were still masquerading for their playgoing public.

The likelihood that the disguised ruler play remained, to use Leatherhead/ Lantern's phrase, a 'get-penny' hit, is confirmed by the motif's appearance in several plays from the first half of the seventeenth century. As Overdo's presence in *Bartholomew Fair* demonstrates, the imagery and intertextuality of such disguises are only discernible to an audience familiar with earlier disguised ruler drama. Whether introduced for comic, tragic, romantic, parodic or subversive effect, disguised rulers appear long after Elizabeth's death and James's accession faded in England's collective memory.

On the late-Jacobean and Caroline stage, the disguised ruler remains of incidental narrative appeal, largely because of its heritage in the King's Men's repertory. Hence, John Fletcher parodies the disguised duke in his Italianate comedy, *The Chances* (1617, King's Men; published 1647), a play performed only a year after Shakespeare's death.[5] Based on one of Cervantes' Spanish *Novelas ejemplares* ('Moral or Instructive Tales') entitled *La Señora Cornelia* (1613), *The Chances* presents a farcical romp of mistaken identity. In one scene, the Spanish gallant Don John, having come to the aid of a stranger who is outnumbered in a street brawl, loses his 'hat i'th scuffle' (*Chances*, 3A3^v; 2.1.45).[6] The stranger (who is actually the Duke of Ferrara) offers his own hat in recompense, which Don John accepts before continuing on his night-walking adventures. Elsewhere, the young aristocrat Constantia is offered sanctuary by Don John's friend, Don Fredrick. On seeing Don John for the first time in his new hat, Constantia mistakes him for her 'Lord the Duke', her lover and the father of her child (*Chances*, 3A4^v; 2.3.29). In this subtle reversal of the disguised ruler motif, it is Don John who is mistaken for a duke, the stranger of 'noble breeding' he assisted in the earlier brawl (*Chances*, 3A4^r; 2.1.102). The Duke's assailants were Constantia's brother, Petruchio, and his violent associates, all seeking revenge for the young woman's dishonour. When Petruchio finally meets his sister's lover, the Duke assures his future brother-in-law that he might have 'enjoy'd' Constantia, but that she is actually his 'wife, contracted before Heaven' (*Chances*, 3B3^r; 3.4.47–53). Duke and mistress now wait for Petruchio's fury to pass in order to receive 'the Churches approbation', so legitimizing their marital contract and their child (*Chances*, 3B3^r; 3.4.56). This

---

[4]   E.M. Symonds, 'The Diary of John Greene (1635–59)', *EHR*, 43 (1928): 385–94 (p. 386).

[5]   Francis Beaumont and John Fletcher, *Comedies and Tragedies* (London, 1647).

[6]   Line numbers from George Walton Williams (ed.), *The Chances*, in Bowers, *Beaumont and Fletcher*, vol. 4 (1979).

similarity to the plight of Claudio and Juliet in *Measure for Measure* complements the disguise motif evoked elsewhere in the comedy.[7]

Other plays belonging to the King's Men make passing reference to the disguised ruler. For romantic effect, the friar's costume returns in Lodowick Carlell's tragicomedy, *The Deserving Favourite* (c. 1622, King's Men; published 1629).[8] This complex drama presents a Duke who is insanely jealous of his ward, Lysander. Both Duke and Lysander love Clarinda. Shown that Lysander is Clarinda's true love, the Duke duels with the young man, who supposedly kills him. Although Lysander is charged with murder, the Duke actually survives and is secretly nursed to health by the forest-dwelling Hermit. Disguised as 'A Gentleman' (*Deserving*, M1[r]; TLN.2792), the Duke returns to court, reconciles himself to Lysander's love for Clarinda and, revealing his true identity, saves Lysander's life. At this, the Hermit likewise '*puls off his beard*' to reveal himself the banished Count Orsinio (*Deserving*, M3[v]; TLN.2977.SD). Orsinio confirms that Lysander, swapped at birth, is Clarinda's brother, thus leaving her free to accept the Duke's original marriage proposal.

The 'hermit' costume appears also in the anonymous *The Fatal Marriage or A Second Lucretia* (c. 1630–1640, King's Men; MS).[9] In this text, Prince Lodowick, son of the Duke of Piacenza, loves the woodsman's daughter, Isabella. Because of her lowly birth, the Duke attempts to prevent their union, but the young lovers hide in the forest. The Duke follows the pair, '*disguis'd*' (*Fatal*, 153[a]; TLN.1617.SD) in the holy habit of a 'father' (*Fatal*, 153[a]; TLN.1643). Strongly opposed to the match, the Duke begrudgingly relents, prompting the woodsman to reveal himself as Ferdinand of Parma. Isabella is thus of noble birth and the Duke gladly accepts her as daughter-in-law. Likewise, in Davenant's *The Wits* (1633–34, King's Men; published 1636), the miserly Sir Tyrant Thrift, guardian of the 'Inheratrix' Lady Ample, reportedly departs his home, 'With his warp'd face close button'd in his Hood, / That Men may take him for a Monke disguis'd' (*Wits*, C2[v]; 2.1.6–7).[10] Although only a brief allusion, this reference to a 'Monke disguis'd' reconfirms the ubiquity of this disguising habit as the perfect costume for furtive rulers, patriarchs and tyrannical guardians.

In contrast to such romantic disguises, Davenant's earlier salacious tragedy, *The Cruel Brother* (1626–27, King's Men; published 1630), presents a sinister

---

[7]   Taylor, 'Mediterranean', p. 253.

[8]   Lodowick Carlell, *The Deseruing Fauorite* (London, 1629). Through line numbers from Charles H. Gray (ed.), *Lodowick Carliell: 'The Deserving Favourite'* (Chicago, 1905).

[9]   *The ffatall Maryage or A Second Lucreatya*, BL MS Egerton 1994. Through line numbers from S. Brigid Younghughes and Harold Jenkins (eds), *The Fatal Marriage* (Oxford, 1959).

[10]   William Davenant, *The Wits* (London, 1636). Line numbers from Robert Blattès (ed.), *The Wits* (Grenoble, 1983).

Duke of Sienna.[11] Under cover of night, the Duke 'creepe[s] within [his] Cloke' to rape the wife of his court favourite, only to be mistakenly murdered by his own minions (*Cruel*, G2ʳ). Likewise, James Shirley's *The Duke's Mistress* (1635–36, Henrietta's Men; published 1638) presents a lustful Duke whose fondness for his mistress threatens his authority, and results in a plot to murder him.[12] A stage direction, '*Enter the Duke, disguis'd*' (*Duke's*, K1ᵛ; 5.4.1.0.SD), suggests how he escapes his fate, returns to his virtuous wife and shows remorse for his licentious behaviour, but not before the stage is strewn with bloodied corpses. These episodes depend on audience recognition of the disguised ruler's timeworn motif. Though no longer of sufficient theatrical importance to merit an entire play, the disguised ruler can still provide a swift and identifiable plot mechanism to further the romantic or tragic narrative.

One final instance confirms the motif's continued dramatic importance, for at least one unknown late-Caroline dramatist. The disguised ruler is a significant subplot character in *The Wasp or Subject's Precedent* (*c.* 1636–40, King's Revels[?]; MS).[13] This incomplete and enigmatic drama survives only in manuscript form, and is missing its final two pages. It was possibly performed by Charles I's King's Revels Company who, between 1636 and 1639, shared occupancy of the Salisbury Court with Queen Henrietta's Men.[14] *The Wasp* might thus have been staged as little as a year after John Greene saw the King's Men perform *The Malcontent* at Blackfriars.[15] This coincidence would account for the similarity between *The Wasp*'s disguised protagonist and his railing counterpart, Malevole. More intriguingly, this self-acclaimed 'Comical History' (*Wasp*, 1ª) is bound together with *John of Bordeaux* (*c.* 1590–94), the incomplete sequel to *Friar Bacon*. As noted in the previous discussion about Elizabethan disguised rulers, *John of Bordeaux* is attributed to Greene because of its 'Friar Bacon' subject matter. The disguise episodes in *John of Bordeaux* and *The Wasp* have thus offered an understandable, albeit simplistic explanation for their being bound together. The presence of Percy/Perce characters in both plays, however, seems more important. In *The Wasp*, 'Percy' is the woodsman's disguise of the noble baron Tom Archibald, the 'subiects president' of the play (*Wasp*, I9ª; TLN.1886). In *John of Bordeaux*, Perce is the servant to Friar Bacon who momentarily disguises himself to escape Turkish captors in the 'beest appariell' of the emperor's son, Selimus (*Bordeaux*, 3[25]ª; TLN.217). Since it is possible that 'Percy' and 'Perce' were both pronounced the same (their names sounding like 'Per-cee' when spoken aloud), these characters would attract the interest of the Percy family of

[11]   William Davenant, *The Cruell Brother* (London, 1630), BL 644.b.17.

[12]   James Shirley, *The Dukes Mistris* (London, 1638). Line numbers from Kim Walker (ed.), *The Duke's Mistress* (London, 1988).

[13]   *The Waspe or Subjects President*, Alnwick Castle MS.507, fol. 2ª. Through line numbers from J.W. Lever (ed.), *The Wasp* (Oxford, 1976).

[14]   Ibid., p. xv.

[15]   Symonds, 'Diary', p. 386; Bentley, *JCS* 1, p. 123.

Alnwick Castle, for whose library the two manuscripts were bound together. It is not disguise, therefore, that probably unites these manuscripts, but the vanity of an aristocratic family finding their name perpetuated among the pages of two otherwise disparate plays.

For whatever reason *The Wasp* was combined with *John of Bordeaux*, it remains a significant drama that 'consciously or unconsciously' recalls 'the most celebrated plays of the age, especially their stage situations'.[16] *The Wasp* is thus a remarkable example of Caroline intertextuality that reintroduces the disguised ruler to its 'comical history' past. The play's historical setting is Roman Britain as ruled by its foreign overseer, the Prorex Marianus. Its title, *The Wasp*, reflects the eponymous character-disguise of Gilbert, the Baron of Claridon. Having lost his lands to the Prorex's court favourite and 'fawneing parasite', the Machiavellian intriguer Varletti (*Wasp*, 8[b]; TLN.662), Baron Gilbert feigns his own death. Although a political move, Gilbert's motive, as his trusted servant Howlet perceives, is also 'to put his wives constancy & sonnes Honesty to the tryall' (*Wasp*, 4[b]; TLN.233–4). Gilbert's caution is justified because his son, Geraldine, is indeed intent on duping his mother out if her inheritance. Meanwhile, the grieving Countess Claridon adopts a new identity, going to reside in the rural hamlet of Walthamstow, there to live 'maryed … to Vesta's monastery' (*Wasp*, 8[b]; TLN.688). She shuns all male company and, with Geraldine's self-interested support, renounces her right to property ownership, instead seeking to become a 'Vestal Virgin' nun. Geraldine uses his 'trick' of 'comon Lawe' to 'foole or fright' his mother out of her widow's (half) legacy (*Wasp*, 7[a]; TLN.486–91), but his ploy is not without danger. Although unconcerned about the moral implications of his actions, Geraldine worries about equally corrupt 'Court wits' who might maliciously accuse him of being without the 'wit to manage' his newly-acquired wealth. If successful, they might 'beg' the 'fooles paradice' (his preferment) 'over [Geraldine's] eres' (*Wasp*, 8[b]; TLN.698–700). Geraldine's position and wealth, in other words, could be lost if fellow courtiers prove him a witless fool. This allusion to the denial of property rights for court 'fooles' echoes Malevole/Passarello's discussion about 'great men [who] begge fooles' at court (QC *Malcontent*, C4[r]; 1.8.22). Whether a conscious or unconscious allusion, Geraldine's concern subtly mirrors a far earlier disguised ruler exchange only recently performed (as John Greene's diary confirms) on the Blackfriars stage.

Regardless of whether the author of *The Wasp* intended so precise an intertextual allusion to *The Malcontent*, Gilbert's costume as 'Wasp' is surprisingly specific in its evocation of a far earlier disguised ruler image. This becomes evident upon Gilbert's return onstage after feigning illness and death. A stage direction instructs the actor playing Wasp how to present his new persona to the audience: 'Enter Clarydon, throw of[f] his cloke Apeare disguisd as the waspe' (*Wasp*, 12[a]; TLN.1072–3.SD). Accordingly, as he discards his masking cloak, Gilbert bids

---

[16] Lever, *Wasp*, p. xvii.

farewell to 'old' Claridon, '& welcome mʳ waspe', while explaining his 'disguisd' appearance:

> GILBERT: In this fantastick
> & ridiculous habit Tyme gives me Leave to play the foole, &
> make a foole both of the Tyme & my self too, & fooleing in
> this Censorious age, is a fashion that some
> of yʳ witts will vouchsafe to walk in – yoʳ Timonist or as
> we call e'm Tyme-ist is yʳ onely man – for he is allowd or
> at least takes allowance, to raile at Authority, gird at
> governement & vnder pretence of strikeing at pety Abuses
> in others, begets & generates greater in himself – & in
> this swarme do I but buz and make a noise. (*Wasp*, 12ᵃ; TLN.1074–83)

Gilbert thus imitates those 'witts' who personify the misanthropic stoic, Timon of Athens. To do this, he adopts the 'fantastick & ridiculous habit' of a court fool, whose motley costume covered many disguised rulers from the late-1580s and 1590s. Claiming to suit his actions to the 'Tyme' and its 'Censorious age', Gilbert likens his Wasp disguise to the countless 'swarme' of 'allowd' or tolerated 'Timonists' who, with malcontented malice, 'raile at Authority, gird at governement'. These hypocrites strike at 'pety Abuses' in others, while begetting and generating the same 'Abuses' in themselves. Compared to this ranting 'swarme' of buzzing Timons, Gilbert/Wasp's anthropomorphic 'buz' seems but an ineffectual 'noise'.

Disguised in this 'fantastick & ridiculous habit', Gilbert/Wasp clandestinely woos his newly-widowed wife to make trial of her faithfulness. To accomplish this, he enters the grieving Countess's employ as a servant and attempts to seduce her. The Countess soon falls 'most Horibly in Love' with the railing 'foole', and asks if the Wasp's attentions demonstrate his 'stomach to mary' (*Wasp*, 13ᵇ; TLN.1302). This ironic moment, when a grieving widow succumbs to the advances of her own disguised husband, is accompanied by Wasp's equally ironic admission that he recognizes the Countess's true identity (*Wasp*, 14ᵃ; TLN.1326). Reminiscent of 'king and subject' dialogue in the 'comical' and 'Chronicle' histories from the 1590s, Gilbert/Wasp assures the Countess that the 'Love' he owes her 'husband, for whose sake [he] carefully' observes her, guarantees that her 'life & Honors [are as] safe in [his] kepeing' as in Gilbert's 'owne being alive' (*Wasp*, 14ᵃ; TLN.1325–7). The Wasp's 'gentile fayre & becomeing' service convinces the unsuspecting Countess that, though she has 'vowd a single life', she should marry her fool (*Wasp*, 14ᵃ; TLN.1330–38). With utmost speed, Wasp offers a solution to the Countess's dilemma. As 'a good Ieast', and 'to gull the world & make [them]selvs merry', Wasp suggests entering into a 'private Maryage', whereby they appear to all as 'man & wife' (*Wasp*, 14ᵃ; TLN.1342–5). Claiming in all innocence to love Wasp 'as derely as the Count thats dead', the Countess agrees to this 'private Maryage' (*Wasp*, 14ᵇ; TLN.138). Still, although she 'can deny [Wasp] nothing', their 'private Maryage' offers the fool no access to the Countess's 'bed', since her Vestal vows forbid sexual communion (*Wasp*, 14ᵇ; TLN.1385–6).

This 'private Maryage' contract, echoing Claudio and Juliet's prenuptial arrangements in *Measure for Measure*, allows Gilbert/Wasp to gain full control of the widow's 'tenants & howshold servants', giving him 'governement of all' (*Wasp*, 14ᵃ; TLN.1353–4).[17] Geraldine cannot steal from his mother, and the Countess's freedom from 'vnruly suiters' is guaranteed (*Wasp*, 14ᵃ; TLN.1348).[18] As Gilbert/Wasp wryly concedes in an aside, this 'Ieast' is indeed a 'good' one, especially since the audience see him as 'a cuckold' for having brokered his own illicit marital arrangement (*Wasp*, 14ᵇ; TLN.1390). Later, upon realising her mistake, the unfortunate Countess pleads with the Prorex to release her from her 'private Maryage'. She accuses the 'poore Beggerly fellow', whom she kept 'of Allmes' to be her 'foole & make [her] freinds merrye' (*Wasp*, 20ᵇ; TLN.2060), of deforesting her property, destroying her houses and overtaxing her poor tenants. Producing a written paper to confirm her 'private' marital status (*Wasp*, 20ᵇ; TLN.2077), the Countess forces Gilbert to reveal his true identity. Gilbert then presumably removes his motley costume, thus saving his wife's reputation and (his own) money. This revelation provokes the Countess's undeservedly contrite apology, 'pardon my Ignorance' (*Wasp*, 20ᵇ; TLN.2102). No longer disguised, Gilbert watches as his son and Varletti prove their unsuitability as rulers of the British Roman colony. The closing dialogue, however, has been lost with the last page of the manuscript.

In this late example of a play relying so heavily on the disguised ruler convention, an English baron adopts the character of a railing misanthrope to foil his prodigal son's wicked plans. All this happens in an ancient Britain governed by an unwelcome, though ultimately worthy foreign power. *The Wasp* could offer veiled criticism of Charles I's court favourite, George Villiers, first duke of Buckingham, who was assassinated in 1628.[19] Alternatively, it might represent criticism of King Charles himself, who, following the dismissal of his third Parliament in 1629, embarked with his Privy Council on over a decade of unchecked and isolated 'Personal Rule'.[20] Whether subtle condemnation or tacit support for England's isolated king, the political message in *The Wasp* remains an enigmatic mystery. *The Wasp* is, however, not a disguised ruler parody or ludicrous burlesque, but a joyous pastiche presented nearly thirty-five years after James's accession. Written only a few years prior to the ordinance of 2 September 1642, which demanded that 'publike Stage-Plays shall cease', *The Wasp* appears at a liminal moment in theatre history.[21] It is *The Wasp* that demonstrates the continued

---

[17] B.J. Sokol and Mary Sokol, *Shakespeare's Legal Language* (London, 2000), pp. 289–307.

[18] B.J. Sokol and Mary Sokol, *Shakespeare, Law, and Marriage* (Cambridge, 2003), pp. 93–100.

[19] Lever, *Wasp*, p. xvii.

[20] Barry Coward, *The Stuart Age*, 2nd edn (London and New York, 1994), pp. 165–82; Lockyer, *Early Stuarts*, pp. 282–95.

[21] Bentley, *JCS* 2, p. 690; Gurr, *Playing Companies*, pp. 385–6.

dramatic relevance of a motif that did not suddenly disappear in the first decade of the seventeenth century, but which continued to influence drama for decades to come. While plays that immediately followed the golden years of disguised ruler drama might parody an overused motif, *The Wasp* reintroduces the disguised ruler with refreshing originality. It is *The Wasp*, therefore, that truly stands as the last early modern disguised ruler play.

As *The Wasp* demonstrates, the repertory system, with its constant search for novelty and commercial success, helped perpetuate the disguised ruler in various guises. His antics are rewritten and revised to suit the prevailing political and social climate. Of the comparatively few plays that have survived to the twenty-first century, a significant number introduce a disguised ruler, so pointing to the motif's continual refashioning. This offers considerable insight into the commercial expectations of a repertory system based, as so many of Shakespeare's plays confirm, on the revamping of age-old narratives and conventions. Frequently repackaged for the early modern stage, the disguised ruler continued to excite, entertain, enthral, amuse and shock for many decades. The true revelation, however, is that, throughout this period, the disguised ruler in a friar's habit, a fool's motley, a Lincoln-green outlaw's costume or a gentleman's borrowed garments, was never far from the public's imagination, or from the playhouse stages.

Bibliography

Manuscript Sources

Alnwick, Northumberland, Alnwick Castle MS 507
London, British Library MS Add. 35290
London, British Library MS Egerton 1994
London, British Library MS Harley 646
London, Dulwich College MSS 20
London, The National Archives of the UK: Public Record Office, Audit Office, Accounts, Various, AO 3/908/13

Printed Primary Sources

Albott, Robert, *Wits Theater of the Little World* (London, 1588)
Anon., *The Emperor's Favourite,* ed. Siobhan Keenan (Oxford: Malone Society Reprints, 2010)
———, *Faire Em* (London, n.d.)
———, *Fair Em,* ed. W.W. Greg (Oxford: Malone Society Reprints, 1927)
———, *Fair Em: A Critical Edition,* ed. Standish Henning (New York: Garland Publishing, 1980)
———, *The Famous Historie of Fryer Bacon* (London, 1627)
———, *The Famous Victories of Henry the fifth* (London, 1598)
———, *The Fatal Marriage,* ed. S. Brigid Younghughes and Harold Jenkins (Oxford: Malone Society Reprints, 1959)
———, *The True Chronicle History of King Leir* (London, 1605)
———, *The History of King Leir,* ed. W.W. Greg (Oxford: Malone Society Reprints, 1907)
———, *John of Bordeaux, or The Second Part of Friar Bacon,* ed. W.L. Renwick and W.W. Greg (Oxford: Malone Society Reprints, 1936)
———, *A Knacke to Knowe a Knave* (London, 1594)
———, *A Knack to Know a Knave*, ed. Richard Proudfoot (Oxford: Malone Society Reprints, 1963)
———, *A Knacke to Know an Honest Man* (London, 1596)
———, *A Knack to Know an Honest Man*, ed. Henry De Vocht (Oxford: Malone Society Reprints, 1910)
———, *Look About You*, ed. W.W. Greg (Oxford: Malone Society Reprints, 1913)
———, *The Merry Deuill of Edmonton* (London, 1608)
———, *The Merry Devil of Edmonton*, ed. Nicola Bennett (London: Nick Hern, 2000)
———, *A Mery Geste of Robyn Hoode* [Copland] (London, 1560)
———, *Mucedorus* (London, 1598)

————, *The Telltale*, ed. R.A. Foakes and J.C. Gibson (Oxford: Malone Society Reprints, 1959)

————, *The Wasp or Subject's Precedent*, ed. J.W. Lever (Oxford: Malone Society Reprints, 1976)

————, *The Weakest Goeth to the Wall* (London, 1600)

Astley, Thomas, *Books Printed For and Sold By Thomas Astley* (London, 1727)

Baldwin, William and George Ferrers (eds), *A Myrroure for Magistrates* (London, 1559)

Bancroft, Richard, *A Sermon Preached at Paules Crosse the 9. of Februarie* […] 1588 (London, 1589)

Barry, Lording, *The Famelie of Love* (London, 1608)

Beaumont, Francis and John Fletcher, *Comedies and Tragedies Written by Francis Beaumont and John Fletcher* (London, 1647)

————, *The Dramatic Works in the Beaumont and Fletcher Canon,* ed. Fredson Bowers (10 vols, Cambridge: Cambridge University Press, 1966–96)

Billington, Michael, 'Review of The National Theatre Company Production of The Fawn', *Guardian,* Friday 15 July 1983, p. 11

Brant, Sebastian, *Das Narrenschiff* (Basel, 1494)

————, *Stultifera Navis,* trans. Jacob Locher (Basel, 1497)

————, *The Ship of Fooles,* trans. Alexander Barclay (London, 1509)

————, *The Ship of Fooles,* trans. Alexander Barclay (London, 1570)

Carlell, Lodowick, *The Deserving Favorite* (London, 1629)

————, *Lodowick Carliell: His Life, A Discussion of His Plays and 'The Deserving Favourite',* ed. Charles H. Gray (Chicago: University of Chicago Press, 1905)

Castiglione, Baldassare, *The Courtyer of Count Baldessar Castilio*, trans. Sir Thomas Hoby (London, 1561)

Cawley, A.C. (ed.), *Everyman and Medieval Miracle Plays*, The Everyman Library (London: J.M. Dent, 1956)

Chalmers, George, *A Supplemental Apology for the Believers in the Shakspeare-Papers* (London: Thomas Egerton, 1799)

Chapman, George, *The Blinde Begger of Alexandria* (London, 1598)

————, *The Blind Beggar of Alexandria,* ed. W.W. Greg (Oxford: Malone Society Reprints, 1929)

————, *May-Day* (London, 1611)

————, *The Plays of George Chapman: The Comedies,* ed. Allan Holaday (Urbana: University of Illinois Press, 1970)

Chester, Robert, *Loves Martyr* (London, 1601)

Child, Francis James (ed.), *The English and Scottish Popular Ballads* (5 vols, Mineola: Dover Publications, 2003)

Cooper, Thomas, *Thesaurus linguae Romanae & Britannicae* (London, 1584)

Coote, Edmund, *The English Schoole-maister* (London, 1596)

Cornwallis, William, *Essayes* (London, 1600)

D'Ewes, Sir Simonds, *The Autobiography and Correspondence of Sir Simonds D'Ewes, Bart., During the Reigns of James I and Charles I,* ed. J.O. Halliwell-Phillips (2 vols, London: Richard Bentley, 1845)

————, *The Journal of Sir Simonds D'Ewes*, ed. Wallace Notestein (New Haven: Yale University Press, 1923)

————, *The Journals of All the Parliaments During the Reign of Queen Elizabeth Both of the House of Lords and House of Commons* (London, 1682)

Dasent, John R., *Acts of the Privy Council of England: 1542–1631* (46 vols, London: HMSO, 1890–1964)

Davenant, Sir William, *The Cruell Brother* (London, 1630)

————, *The Wits* (London, 1636)

————, *The Wits, comédie en cinq actes*, ed. Robert Blattès (Grenoble: *Université des langues et lettres*, 1983)

Day, John, *Humour Out of Breath* (London, 1608)

————, *Law-Trickes or Who Would Have Thought It* (London, 1608)

————, *Law Tricks*, ed. John Crow (London: Malone Society Reprints, 1950)

Dekker, Thomas, *The Magnificent Entertainment* (London, 1604)

————, *Newes from Graues-end Sent to Nobody* (London, 1604)

————, *The Second Part of the Honest Whore* (London, 1630)

————, *The Shomakers Holiday. Or The Gentle Craft* (London, 1600)

————, *The Shoemaker's Holiday*, ed. R. L. Smallwood and Stanley Wells (Manchester: Manchester University Press, 1979)

————, *Troia-Noua Triumphans. London Triumphing* (London, 1612)

Dilke, Charles Wentworth (ed.), *Old English Plays* (6 vols, London, 1814–16)

Dodsley, Robert (ed.), *A Select Collection of Old Plays*, ed. J.P. Collier, 3rd edn (12 vols, London, 1825–27)

Drayton, Michael, Richard Hathway, Antony Munday and Robert Wilson, *The First Part of the True and Honorable Historie of the Life of Sir John Oldcastle, The Good Lord Cobham* (London, 1600)

————, *The Life of Sir John Oldcastle, 1600*, ed. W.W. Greg (Oxford: Malone Society Reprints, 1908)

————, *1 Sir John Oldcastle: A Critical Edition*, ed. Jonathan Rittenhouse (New York: Garland, 1984)

Dryden, John, *All for Love; or, The World Well Lost* (London, 1678)

————, *Essay of Dramatick Poesie* (London, 1668)

Echard, Laurence, *The History of England* (3 vols, London, 1707–18)

Edwards, Richard, *Damon and Pithias* (London, 1571)

————, *Damon and Pythias*, ed. Arthur Brown (Oxford: Malone Society Reprints, 1957)

Erasmus, Desiderius, *Encomium Moriae (Stultitiae Laus)* (Basle, 1515)

————, *Praise of Folly*, trans. Betty Radice (London: Folio, 1974)

————, *Praise of Folly*, trans. Betty Radice (Harmondsworth: Penguin, 1993)

Field, Nathan, *The Plays of Nathan Field*, ed. William Peery (Austin: University of Texas Press, 1950)

Florio, John, *Queen Anna's New World of Words, or Dictionarie of the Italian and English Tongues* (London, 1611)

————, *The Worlde of Wordes* (London, 1598)

Fulwell, Ulpian, *Like Will to Like* (London, 1568)

Gilbert, Allan H. (ed.), *Literary Criticism: Plato to Dryden* (New York: American Book Company, 1940; repr. Detroit: Wayne State University Press, 1962)

Grafton, Richard, *An Abridgement of the Chronicles of England* (London, 1563)

Greene, Robert, *The Honorable Historie of frier Bacon, and frier Bungay* (London, 1594)

———, *Friar Bacon and Friar Bungay,* ed. Daniel Seltzer (London: Edward Arnold, 1964)

———, *Friar Bacon and Friar Bungay,* ed. J.A. Lavin (London: Ernest Benn, 1969)

———, *A Pleasant Conceyted Comedie of George a Greene, the Pinner of Wakefield* (London, 1599)

———, *The Comedy of George a Green,* ed. W.W. Greg (Oxford: Malone Society Reprints, 1911)

Guarini, Giovanni Battista, *Compendio della poesia tragicomica* (Venice, 1601)

———, *Il pastor fido tragicomedia pastorale* (Venice, 1590)

———, *Il pastor fido tragicomedia pastorale,* ed. Iacopo Castelvetro (London, 1591)

———, *Il Pastor Fido: or The Faithfull Shepheard,* trans. Dymock (London, 1602)

Hall, Edward, *The Union of the Noble and Illustre Famelies of Lancastre & York* (London, 1542)

Harrison, Stephen, *The Arches of Triumph* (London, 1604)

Haughton, William, *Englishmen for My Money* (London, 1598)

Henslowe, Philip, *Henslowe's Diary,* ed. R.A. Foakes and R.T. Rickert, 2nd edn (Cambridge: Cambridge University Press, 2002)

Herring, Francis, *Pietas Pontificia* (London, 1606)

———, *Popish Pietie, or The first part of the historie of that horrible and barbarous conspiracie, commonly called the powder-treason* (London, 1610)

Heywood, Thomas, *The First and Second Partes of King Edward the Fourth* (London, 1599)

———, *The First and Second Parts of King Edward IV*, ed. Richard Rowland (Manchester: Manchester University Press, 2005)

Holinshed, Raphael, *The Firste Volume of the Chronicles of England, Scotlande, and Irelande* (London, 1577)

———, *The Third Volume of Chronicles* (London, 1586)

Hyde, Edward, 1st Earl of Clarendon, *The History of the Rebellion and Civil Wars in England* (3 vols, Oxford, 1702–1704)

Jonson, Ben, *'The Alchemist' and Other Plays*, ed. Gordon Campbell (Oxford: Oxford University Press, 1995)

———, *Bartholmew Fayre: A Comedie, Acted in the Year 1614* (London, 1631)

———, *Bartholomew Fair*, ed. G.R. Hibbard (London: Ernest Benn Limited, 1977)

———, *Bartholomew Fair*, ed. Suzanne Gossett (Manchester: Manchester University Press, 2000)

———, *Ben Jonson: The Man and His Work*, ed. C.H. Herford and Percy and Evelyn Simpson (11 vols, Oxford: Clarendon Press, 1925–52)

———, *The Cambridge Edition of the Works of Ben Jonson*, ed. David Bevington, Martin Butler and Ian Donaldson (6 vols, Cambridge: Cambridge University Press, 2011)

———, *Part of the Entertainment, through the Cittie of London, Given to James I. 1604* (London, 1604)

———, *The Poetaster* (London, 1602)

———, *Poetaster*, ed. Tom Cain (Manchester: Manchester University Press, 1995)

———, *The Workes of Benjamin Jonson* (London, 1616)

———, *The Workes of Benjamin Jonson* (2 vols, London, 1640)

Jonson, Ben, George Chapman and John Marston, *Eastward Ho!*, ed. C.G. Petter, New Mermaids (London: Ernest Benn, 1973)

King James, VI & I, *Basilicon Doron* (London, 1603)

———, *Basilikon Doron* (Edinburgh, 1599)

———, *The Essayes of a Prentise, in the Diuine Art of Poesie* (Edinburgh, 1584)

———, *King James VI and I: Selected Writings*, ed. Neil Rhodes, Jennifer Richards and Joseph Marshall (Aldershot: Ashgate, 2003)

———, *The True Lawe of Free Monarchies* (Edinburgh, 1598)

Knight, Stephen and Thomas H. Ohlgren (eds), *Robin Hood and Other Outlaw Tales* (Kalamazoo: Medieval Institute Publications, 1997)

Kyd, Thomas, *The Spanish Tragedie* (London, 1592)

———, *The Spanish Tragedie*, ed. Emma Smith (Harmondsworth: Penguin, 1998)

Larkin, James F. and Paul L. Hughes (eds), *Stuart Royal Proclamations, 1603– 1625* (2 vols, Oxford: Oxford University Press, 1973–83)

Lipsius, Justus, *Two Bookes of Constancie*, trans. John Stradling (London, 1594)

Lyly, John, *Euphues and his England* (London, 1580)

Macaulay, Thomas Babington, *History of England from the Accession of James II* (5 vols, London: Longman, 1848–55)

———, *History of England from the Accession of James II*, 11th edn (5 vols, London: Longman, 1856)

Machiavelli, Niccolò, *The Discourses*, ed. Bernard Crick, trans. Leslie J. Walker, revised Brian Richardson (London: Penguin, 2003)

Markham, Gervase and Lewis Machin, *The Dumbe Knight* (London, 1608)

Marston, John, *The History of Antonio and Mellida* and *Antonios Revenge* (London, 1602)

———, *Antonio and Mellida*, ed. W. Reavley Gair (Manchester: Manchester University Press, 1991)

———, *Antonio's Revenge*, ed. W. Reavley Gair (Manchester: Manchester University Press, 1978)

———, *The Dutch Courtezan* (London, 1605)

———, *The Insatiate Countesse* (London, 1613)

———, *The Insatiate Countess*, ed. Giorgio Melchiori (Manchester: Manchester University Press, 1984)

———, *Jacke Drums Entertainement* (London, 1601)

———, *The Malcontent* [QA] (London, 1604)

———, *The Malcontent* [QB] (London, 1604)

———, *The Malcontent*, ed. George K. Hunter (Manchester: Manchester University Press, 1975)

———, *'The Malcontent' and Other Plays*, ed. Keith Sturgess (Oxford: Oxford University Press, 1997)

———, *The Malcontent*, ed. W. David Kay, 2nd edn (London: A & C Black, 1998)

———, *The Malcontent*, ed. George K. Hunter, Revels Student Editions (Manchester: Manchester University Press, 2000)

———, *The Metamorphosis of Pigmalions Image* (London, 1598)

———, *Parasitaster, or The Fawne* (London, 1606)

———, *Parasitaster or The Fawn*, ed. David A. Blostein (Manchester: Manchester University Press, 1978)

———, *The Plays of John Marston*, ed. H. Harvey Wood (3 vols, Edinburgh: Oliver and Boyd, 1934–1939)

———, *The Scourge of Villanie: Three Bookes of Satyres* (London, 1598)

———, *The Scourge of Villanie Corrected, with the addition of newe Satyres* (London, 1599)

———, *What You Will* (London, 1607)

———, *The Works of John Marston*, ed. A.H. Bullen (3 vols, London: J.C. Nimmo, 1887)

Marston, John and John Webster, *The Malcontent* [QC] (London, 1604)

Mason, John, *The Turke* (London, 1610)

———, *The Turke*, ed. Joseph Quincy Adams (London: David Nutt, 1913)

Middleton, Thomas, *The Blacke Booke* (London, 1604)

———, *The Collected Works*, ed. Gary Taylor, John Lavagnino, with Macdonald P. Jackson, John Jowett, Valerie Wayne and Adrian Weiss (Oxford: Oxford University Press, 2007)

———, *The Phoenix* (London, 1607)

———, *The Phoenix: A Critical, Modernized Edition*, ed. John Bradbury Brooks (New York: Garland, 1980)

———, *The Second Maiden's Tragedy 1611*, ed. W.W. Greg (Oxford: Malone Society Reprints, 1909)

———, *A Tricke to Catch the Old-one* (London, 1608)

———, *The Works of Thomas Middleton*, ed. Alexander Dyce (5 vols, London: Edward Lumley, 1840)

———, *The Works of Thomas Middleton*, ed. A.H. Bullen (8 vols, London: John C. Nimmo, 1885)

Montaigne, Michel de, *The Essayes*, trans. John Florio (London, 1603)

Nichols, John (ed.), *The Progresses, Processions, and Magnificent Festivities, of King James the First* (4 vols, London: J.B. Nichols, 1828)

Oldmixon, John, *Amintas* (London, 1698)

————, *An Essay on Criticism (1728)*, ed. R.J. Madden, The Augustan Reprint Society, 107–108 (Los Angeles: William Andrews Clark Memorial Library, University of California, 1964)

————, *The Governour of Cyprus* (London, 1703)

————, *The Grove, or Love's Paradice* (London, 1700)

————, *The History of England, during the reigns of the royal House of Stuart* (London, 1730)

Osborne, Francis, *Traditionall Memoyres on the Raigne of King Iames* (London, 1658)

Overall, H.C. and W.H. Overall (eds), *Analytical Index to the Series of Records known as the 'Remembrancia': Preserved Among the Archives of the City of London, AD 1579–1664* (London: E.J. Francis for the Corporation of London, 1878)

Palsgrave, John, *Lesclarcissement de la Langue Francoyse* (London, 1530)

Peele, George, *Dramatic Works of George Peele*, ed. Charles Tyler Prouty (3 vols, New Haven: Yale University Press, 1961)

————, *The Famous Chronicle of King Edward the first* (London, 1593)

Pepys, Samuel, *The Diary of Samuel Pepys [1660]*, ed. Henry B. Wheatley (10 vols, London and Cambridge: George Bell & Sons and Deighton Bell & Co, 1893–99)

Persons [Parsons], Robert, *An Answere to the Fifth Part of Reportes Lately Set Forth by Syr Edward Cooke* (St Omer, 1606)

Phillips, John, *The Life and Death of Sir Phillip Sidney, late the gouernour of Flushing* (London, 1587)

Plautus, Titus Maccius, *Amphitrvo*, ed. David M. Christenson (Cambridge: Cambridge University Press, 2000)

R.S., *The Phoenix Nest* (London, 1593)

Rowley, Samuel, *When You See Me You Know Me* (London, 1605)

————, *When You See Me You Know Me*, ed. F.P. Wilson (Oxford: Malone Society Reprints, 1952)

Sanderson, Sir William, *Aulicus Coquinariae: or a Vindication in Answer to a Pamphlet, entituled The Court and Character of King James* (London, 1650)

————, *A Compleat History of the Lives and Reigns of Mary Queen of Scotland, And of her Son and Successor James: The Court and Character of King James* (2 vols, London, 1656)

Shakespeare, William, *The Cronicle History of Henry the fift* [Q1] (London, 1600)

————, *The Complete Works of William Shakespeare*, ed. Charlotte Porter and Helen A. Clarke (12 vols, New York: Thomas Y. Crowell & Company, 1903–1905)

————, *The First Folio of Shakespeare*, ed. Charlton Hinman (New York: Norton, 1968)

————, *The First Quarto of 'Henry V'*, ed. Andrew Gurr (Cambridge: Cambridge University Press, 2000)

————, *Hamlet*, ed. Ann Thompson and Neil Taylor, Arden 3 (London: Thomson Learning, 2006)

————, *Hamlet: The Texts of 1603 and 1623*, ed. Ann Thompson and Neil Taylor, Arden 3 (London: Thomson Learning, 2006)

————, *Henry the Fourth, Part 1, 1599*, ed. Charlton Hinman, Shakespeare Quarto Facsimiles, 14 (Oxford: Clarendon Press, 1966)

————, *Henry V*, ed. Gary Taylor (Oxford: Oxford University Press, 1982)

————, *King Edward III*, ed. Giorgio Melchiori (Cambridge: Cambridge University Press, 1998)

————, *King Henry IV, Part 1*, ed. Arthur Humphreys, Arden 2 (London: Methuen, 1960)

————, *King Henry IV, Part 1* [Q1] (London, 1599)

————, *King Henry IV, Part 2* [Q] (London, 1600)

————, *'King Lear', 1608 (Pied Bull Quarto)*, ed. W.W. Greg, Shakespeare Quarto Facsimiles, 1 (London: The Shakespeare Association and Sidgwick & Jackson, 1939; repr. Oxford: Clarendon Press, 1964)

————, *Measure for Measure*, ed. Arthur Quiller-Couch and John Dover Wilson (Cambridge: Cambridge University Press, 1922; rev. edn 1950)

————, *Measure for Measure*, ed. J.W. Lever, Arden 2 (London: Methuen, 1965)

————, *Measure for Measure*, ed. Mark Eccles, *A New Variorum Edition of Shakespeare* (New York: Modern Language Association of America, 1980)

————, *Measure for Measure*, ed. Brian Gibbons (Cambridge: Cambridge University Press, 1991)

————, *Measure for Measure*, ed. N.W. Bawcutt (Oxford: Oxford University Press, 1991)

————, *The Norton Shakespeare*, gen. ed. Stephen Greenblatt, with Walter Cohen, Jean E. Howard and Katharine Eisaman Maus (eds), 2nd edn (New York: Norton, 2008)

————, *The Oxford Shakespeare: The Complete Works*, ed. Stanley Wells and Gary Taylor (Oxford: Clarendon Press, 1988)

————, *Pericles 1609*, ed. W.W. Greg, Shakespeare Quarto Facsimiles, 5 (London: The Shakespeare Association and Sidgwick & Jackson, 1940)

————, *Pericles, Prince of Tyre* [Q1] (London, 1609)

————, *The Plays and Poems of William Shakspeare*, ed. Edmond Malone (10 vols, London, 1790)

————, *The Plays of William Shakespeare*, ed. Samuel Johnson (8 vols, London, 1765)

————, *The Plays of William Shakspeare*, ed. George Steevens (15 vols, London, 1793)

————, *Richard the Third 1597*, ed. W.W. Greg, Shakespeare Quarto Facsimiles, 12 (Oxford: Clarendon Press, 1959)

————, *Romeo and Juliet* [Q2] (London, 1599)

————, *Romeo and Juliet, Second Quarto, 1599*, ed. W.W. Greg, Shakespeare Quarto Facsimiles, 6 (London: The Shakespeare Association and Sidgwick & Jackson, 1949)

———, *The Second Part of King Henry the Fourth*, ed. John Pitcher (Oxford: Malone Society Reprints, 1990)

———, *The Tragedie of King Richard the Third* [Q1] (London, 1597)

———, *'Troilus and Cressida', First Quarto, 1609*, ed. W.W. Greg, Shakespeare Quarto Facsimiles, 8 (London: The Shakespeare Association and Sidgwick & Jackson, 1952)

———, *The True Tragedy of Richard Duke of York (Henry the Sixth, Part III), 1595*, ed. W.W. Greg, Shakespeare Quarto Facsimiles, 11 (Oxford: Clarendon Press, 1958)

———, *William Shakespeare: The Complete Sonnets and Poems*, ed. Colin Burrow (Oxford: Oxford University Press, 2002)

———, *William Shakespeare: The Complete Works*, ed. Jonathan Bate and Eric Rasmussen, The RSC Shakespeare (Houndmills: Macmillan, 2007)

Sharpham, Edward, *A Critical Old Spelling Edition of the Works of Edward Sharpham*, ed. Christopher Gordon Petter (New York: Garland, 1986)

———, *The Fleire* (London, 1607)

Shirley, James, *The Dukes Mistris* (London, 1638)

———, *The Duke's Mistress*, ed. Kim Walker (New York: Garland, 1988)

Sidney, Sir Philip, *An Apologie for Poetrie* (London, 1595)

———, *Astrophel and Stella* (London, 1591)

———, *The Countesse of Pembrokes Arcadia*, revised Mary Herbert (London, 1593)

———, *The Defence of Poesie* (London, 1595)

———, *The Prose Works of Sir Philip Sidney*, ed. Albert Feuillerat (4 vols, Cambridge: Cambridge University Press, 1912; repr. Cambridge: Cambridge University Press, 1962)

Stow, John, *Summarie of Englyshe Chronicles* (London, 1565)

———, *Annales, or a Generale Chronicle of England from Brute until the present yeare of Christ 1580* (London, 1580)

Symonds, E.M., 'The Diary of John Greene (1635–59)', *English Historical Review*, 43 (1928): 385–94 & 598–604

———, 'The Diary of John Greene (1635–59)', *English Historical Review*, 44 (1929): 106–17

Tasso, Torquato, *Aminta*, ed. Iacopo Castelvetro (London, 1591)

Thomas, Thomas, *Dictionarium Linguae Latinae et Anglicanae* (Cambridge, 1587)

Tyrwhitt, Thomas, *Observations and Conjectures upon some Passages of Shakespeare* (Oxford: Clarendon Press, 1766)

Webster, John, *The White Devil* (London, 1612)

———, *The White Devil*, ed. John Russell Brown (Manchester: Manchester University Press, 1996)

———, *The Works of John Webster: An Old-Spelling Critical Edition*, ed. David Gunby, David Carnegie and MacDonald P. Jackson (3 vols, Cambridge: Cambridge University Press, 2007)

Weldon, Sir Anthony, *A Cat May Look Upon a King* (London, 1652)

————, *The Court and Character of King James* (London, 1650)

Whetstone, George, *A Mirour for Magestrates of Cyties* (London, 1584)

————, *The Right Excellent Historye, of Promos and Cassandra* (London, 1578)

————, *Sir Phillip Sidney, his honorable life, his valiant death* (London, 1587)

Wilbraham, Sir Roger, *The Journal of Sir Roger Wilbraham*, ed. Harold Spencer Scott, The Camden Miscellany, 10 (London: Royal Historical Society, 1902)

Williams, Alfred (ed.), *Folk-Songs of the Upper Thames* (London: Duckworth & Co, 1923)

Wilson, Sir Thomas, *'The State of England, Anno Dom. 1600' by Sir Thomas Wilson*, ed. F.J. Fisher, Camden Society Miscellany (London: Camden Society, 1936)

Winny, James (ed.), *Three Elizabethan Plays: Edward III, Mucedorus, Midas* (London: Chatto and Windus, 1959)

Secondary Sources

Albrecht, Louis, *Neue Untersuchungen zu Shakespeares Mass für Mass* (Berlin: Weidman, 1914)

Alulis, Joseph and Vickie B. Sullivan (eds), *Shakespeare's Political Pageant: Essays in Literature and Politics* (London: Rowman & Littlefield, 1996)

Arber, Edward (ed.), *A Transcript of the Registers of the Company of Stationers of London: 1554–1640 A.D.* (5 vols, London, 1875–79; Birmingham, 1894)

Ashton, Robert (ed.), *James I by his Contemporaries: An Account of His Career and Character as Seen by Some of His Contemporaries* (London: Hutchinson, 1969)

Barroll, Leeds, *Politics, Plague, and Shakespeare's Theater: The Stuart Years* (Ithaca: Cornell University Press, 1991)

Barron, Caroline M., *London in the Later Middle Ages: Government and People, 1200–1500* (Oxford: Oxford University Press, 2004)

Beaven, Alfred B. (ed.), *The Aldermen of the City of London, Temp. Henry III– 1908* (2 vols, London: Eden Fisher & Company, 1908–1913)

Bednarz, James P., *Shakespeare and the Poet's War* (New York: Columbia University Press, 2001)

Bentley, Gerald E., *The Jacobean and Caroline Stage* (7 vols, Oxford: Clarendon Press, 1941–1968)

Bergeron, David M., *King James and Letters of Homoerotic Desire* (Iowa City: University of Iowa Press, 1999)

Biberman, Matthew S., *Masculinity, Anti-Semitism, and Early Modern English Literature: From the Satanic to the Effeminate Jew* (Aldershot: Ashgate, 2004)

Blagden, Cyprian, *The Stationers' Company: A History 1403–1959* (London: George Allen & Unwin Ltd, 1960)

Blatchly, J.M., 'D'Ewes, Sir Simonds, first baronet (1602–1650)', *Oxford Dictionary of National Biography* (2004) <http://www.oxforddnb.com/ index/101007577/Simonds-DEwes> [accessed 6 May 2011]

Bly, Mary, *Queer Virgins and Virgin Queans on the Early Modern Stage* (Oxford: Oxford University Press, 2000)

Boas, Frederick S., *Shakspere and his Predecessors* (London: John Murray, 1896)

Bowden, Brett and Michael T. Davis (eds), *Terror: From Tyrannicide to Terrorism* (St Lucia: University of Queensland Press, 2008)

Bowers, Fredson, *Principles of Bibliographical Description* (Oxford: Oxford University Press, 1949)

Bradbrook, Muriel, *The Growth and Structure of Elizabethan Comedy* (London: Chatto and Windus, 1955)

Braunmuller, A.R. and J.C. Bulman (eds), *Comedy from Shakespeare to Sheridan, Change and Continuity in the English and European Dramatic Tradition: Essays in Honor of Eugene M. Waith* (Newark: University of Delaware Press, 1986)

Braunmuller, A.R. and Michael Hattaway (eds), *The Cambridge Companion to English Renaissance Drama* (Cambridge: Cambridge University Press, 1990)

Brooks, C.W., *Pettyfoggers and Vipers of the Commonwealth: The 'Lower Branch' of the Legal Profession in Early Modern England* (Cambridge: Cambridge University Press, 2004)

Brown, John Russell and Bernard Harris (eds), *Jacobean Theatre* (London: Edward Arnold, 1960)

Brown, Keith M., 'The Scottish Aristocracy, Anglicization and the Court, 1603–38', *The Historical Journal*, 36 (1993): 543–76

Brown, P. Hume, *History of Scotland* (3 vols, Cambridge: Cambridge University Press, 1900–1909)

Budra, Paul, *'A Mirror for Magistrates' and the De Casibus Tradition* (Toronto: University of Toronto Press, 2000)

Bullough, Geoffrey, *Narrative and Dramatic Sources of Shakespeare* (7 vols, London: Routledge & Kegan Paul, 1957–78)

Burt, Richard and John Michael Archer (eds), *Enclosure Acts: Sexuality, Property, and Culture in Early Modern England* (Ithaca: Cornell University Press, 1994)

Butler, Martin, 'Ben Jonson: Catholic dramatist', Conference Paper, *London Renaissance Seminar*, Birkbeck College, University of London, 12 February 2011

Butterfield, Herbert, *The Whig Interpretation of History* (London: G. Bell and Sons, 1931)

Calendar of State Papers Domestic: James I, 1603–1610 (1857): 164–82, ed. Mary Ann Everett Green, *British History Online* <http://www.british-history.ac.uk/report.aspx?compid=14995> [accessed 6 May 2011]

Caputi, Anthony, *John Marston, Satirist* (Ithaca: Cornell University Press, 1961)

Carroll, William C., *Fat King, Lean Beggar: Representations of Poverty in the Age of Shakespeare* (Ithaca: Cornell University Press, 1996)

Cartwright, Robert, *Shakspere and Jonson: Dramatic, versus Wit-Combats. Auxiliary Forces: Beaumont and Fletcher, Marston, Decker, Chapman, and Webster* (London: John Russell Smith, 1864)

Casellas, Jesús López-Peláez, 'The Neo-Stoic Revival in English Literature of the Sixteenth and Seventeenth Centuries: An Approach', *Sederi*, 14 (2004): 93–115

Cathcart, Charles, 'Authorship, Indebtedness, and the Children of the King's Revels', *Studies in English Literature 1500–1900*, 45 (2005): 357–74

———, 'John Marston, The Malcontent and the King's Men', *Review of English Studies*, 57 (2006): 43–63

———, 'Marston, Montaigne, and Lady Politic Would-be', *English Language Notes*, 36 (1999): 4–8

———, Marston, *Rivalry, Rapprochement, and Jonson* (Aldershot: Ashgate, 2008)

Chambers, E.K., *The Elizabethan Stage* (4 vols, Oxford: Clarendon Press, 1923)

———, *English Literature at the Close of the Middle Ages* (Oxford: Clarendon Press, 1945)

Clare, Janet, *'Art Made Tongue-Tied by Authority': Elizabethan and Jacobean Dramatic Censorship*, 2nd edn (Manchester: Manchester University Press, 1999)

———, 'Medley History: *The Famous Victories of Henry the Fifth* to *Henry V*', *Shakespeare Survey*, 63 (2010): 102–13

Clayton, Tom, Susan Brock and Vicente Forés (eds), *Shakespeare and the Mediterranean: The Selected Proceedings of the International Shakespeare Association World Congress Valencia, 2001* (Newark: University of Delaware Press, 2004)

Cohen, Stephen A., 'From Mistress to Master: Political Transition and Formal Conflict in *Measure for Measure*', *Criticism*, 41 (1999): 431–64

Cohen, Stephen A. (ed.), *Shakespeare and Historical Formalism* (Aldershot: Ashgate, 2007)

Colie, Rosalie L., *The Resources of Kind: Genre-Theory in the Renaissance*, ed. Barbara K. Lewalski (Berkeley: University of California Press, 1973)

Cooper, Helen, *Shakespeare and the Medieval World* (London: A & C Black, 2010)

Corrigan, Brian Jay, *Playhouse Law in Shakespeare's World* (Cranbury: Associated University Presses, 2004)

Coward, Barry, *The Stuart Age: England 1603–1714*, 2nd edn (New York: Longman, 1994)

Cox, John D. and David Scott Kastan (eds), *A New History of Early English Drama* (New York: Columbia University Press, 1997)

Croft, Pauline, 'Howard, Thomas, first earl of Suffolk (1561–1626)', *Oxford Dictionary of National Biography* (2004) <http://www.oxforddnb.com/index/101013942/Thomas-Howard> [accessed 6 May 2011]

Curtis, Mark H., 'The Hampton Court Conference and its Aftermath', *History*, 46 (1961): 1–16

De Luna, B.N., *Jonson's Romish Plot: A Study of 'Catiline' and its Historical Context* (Oxford: Clarendon Press, 1967)

Derrida, Jacques, 'The Law of Genre', trans Avital Ronell, *Critical Inquiry*, 7 (1980): 55–81

Desens, Marliss C., *The Bed-Trick in English Renaissance Drama: Explorations in Gender, Sexuality, and Power* (Newark: University of Delaware Press, 1994)

Dessen, Alan C. and Leslie Thomson (eds), *A Dictionary of Stage Directions in English Drama, 1580–1642* (Cambridge: Cambridge University Press, 1999)

Doelman, James, *King James I and the Religious Culture of England* (Woodbridge: D.S. Brewer, 2000)

Donaldson, Ian, 'Talking with Ghosts: Ben Jonson and the English Civil War', *Ben Jonson Journal*, 17 (2010): 1–18

Donno, Elizabeth Story (ed.), *Three Renaissance Pastorals: Tasso, Guarini, Daniel, Medieval and Renaissance Texts & Studies,* 102 (Binghampton: State University of New York, 1993)

Doran, Madeleine, *Endeavors of Art: A Study of Form in Elizabethan Drama* (Madison: University of Wisconsin Press, 1954)

Dubrow, Heather, *Genre* (London: Methuen, 1982)

Dutton, Richard, *Ben Jonson, 'Volpone' and the Gunpowder Plot* (Cambridge: Cambridge University Press, 2008)

———, '"Methinks the Truth Should Live from Age to Age": The Dating and Contexts of *Henry V*', *Huntingdon Quarterly*, 68 (2005): 173–204

Early English Books Online (EEBO) 1473–1700, Chadwyck-Healey Database (Proquest) <http://eebo.chadwyck.com/home> [accessed 6 May 2011)

Edwards, Francis S.J. (ed.), *The Gunpowder Plot: The Narrative of Oswald Tesimond alias Greenway* (London: Folio, 1973)

Egan, Michael (ed.), *'The Tragedy of Richard II, Part One': A Newly Authenticated Play by William Shakespeare* (Lampeter: Edwin Mellen Press, 2006)

Eliot, T.S., *Selected Essays*, 3rd edn (London: Faber and Faber, 1951)

Erne, Lukas, *Beyond the Spanish Tragedy* (Manchester: Manchester University Press, 2001)

———, *Shakespeare as Literary Dramatist* (Cambridge: Cambridge University Press, 2003)

Farley-Hills, David, *Shakespeare and the Rival Playwrights 1606–1610* (London: Routledge & Kegan Paul, 1990)

Finkelpearl, Philip J., *John Marston of the Middle Temple: An Elizabethan Dramatist in his Social Setting* (Cambridge, MA: Harvard University Press, 1969)

Fischlin, Daniel and Mark Fortier (eds), *Royal Subjects: Essays on the Writings of James VI and I* (Detroit: Wayne State University Press, 2002)

Fletcher, Anthony and Diarmaid MacCulloch, *Tudor Rebellions*, 5th edn (Harlow: Pearson Education Limited, 2004)

Foakes, R.A., Peter Beal and Grace Ioppolo, 'The Manuscript of *The Telltale*', Henslowe-Alleyn Digitisation Project (2005) <http://www.henslowe-alleyn. org.uk/essays/telltale.html> [accessed 6 May 2011]

———, 'MSS 20: The Manuscript of *The Telltale*', Henslowe-Alleyn Digitisation Project (2005) <http://www.henslowe-alleyn.org.uk/catalogue/MSS-20.html> [accessed 6 May 2011]

Foster, Verna A., *The Name and Nature of Tragicomedy* (Aldershot: Ashgate, 2004)

Foucault, Michel, *Discipline and Punish: The Birth of the Prison*, trans. Alan Sheridan (Harmondsworth: Penguin, 1977)

———, *Madness and Civilization*, ed. Richard Howard (London: Routledge, 2001)

Freeburg, Victor Oscar, *Disguise Plots in Elizabethan Drama: A Study in Stage Tradition* (New York: Columbia University Press, 1915; repr. New York: Benjamin Blom, 1965)

Garber, Daniel and Michael Ayers (eds), *The Cambridge History of Seventeenth Century Philosophy* (2 vols, Cambridge: Cambridge University Press, 1992–98)

Gazzard, Hugh, '"Those Graue Presentments of Antiquitie": Samuel Daniel's *Philotas* and the Earl of Essex', *The Review of English Studies*, 51 (2000): 423–50

Geckle, George L., *John Marston's Drama: Themes, Images, Sources* (Rutherford: Fairleigh Dickinson University Press, 1980)

Gibbons, Brian, *Jacobean City Comedy: A Study of Satiric Plays by Jonson, Marston and Middleton*, 2nd edn (London: Rupert Hart-Davis, 1968; repr. Methuen, 1980)

Goldberg, Jonathan, *James I and the Politics of Literature: Jonson, Shakespeare, Donne, and Their Contemporaries* (Baltimore: Johns Hopkins University Press, 1983)

Gray, Charles H. (ed.), *Lodowick Carliell: His Life, A Discussion of His Plays and 'The Deserving Favourite'* (Chicago: University of Chicago Press, 1905)

Greenblatt, Stephen, 'The Forms of Power and the Power of Forms in the Renaissance', *Genre*, 15 (1982): 3–6

———, *Shakespearean Negotiations: The Circulation of Social Energy in Renaissance England* (Oxford: Clarendon Press, 1988)

Greg, W.W., *A Bibliography of the English Printed Drama to the Restoration* (4 vols, London: The Bibliographical Society, 1939)

———, 'Notes on Old Books', *The Library*, 2 (1921–22): 49–57

Griffin, Benjamin, 'Moving Tales: Narrative Drift in Oral Culture and Scripted Theater', *New Literary History*, 37 (2006): 725–38

Gurr, Andrew, *Shakespeare's Opposites: The Admiral's Company 1594–1625* (Cambridge: Cambridge University Press, 2009)

Hadfield, Andrew, *Shakespeare and Renaissance Politics* (London: Thomson Publishing, 2004)

———, *Shakespeare and Republicanism* (Cambridge: Cambridge University Press, 2005)

Hadfield, Andrew (ed.), *Literature and Censorship in Renaissance England* (Basingstoke: Palgrave, 2001)

Hale, John, *England and the Italian Renaissance: The Growth of Interest in its History and Art,* 2nd edn (London: Fontana, 1996)

Happé, Peter, *English Drama Before Shakespeare* (Harlow: Longman, 1999)

Harp, Richard and Stanley Stewart (eds), *The Cambridge Companion to Ben Jonson* (Cambridge: Cambridge University Press, 2000)

Harris, Jonathan Gil and Natasha Korda (eds), *Staged Properties in Early Modern English Drama* (Cambridge: Cambridge University Press, 2002)

Hattaway, Michael (ed.), *A Companion to English Renaissance Literature and Culture* (Oxford: Blackwell, 2000)

Henke, Robert, *Pastoral Transformations: Italian Tragicomedy and Shakespeare's Late Plays* (Newark: University of Delaware Press, 1997)

Houlbrooke, Ralph (ed.), *James VI and I: Ideas, Authority, and Government* (Aldershot: Ashgate, 2006)

Houser, David J., 'Purging the Commonwealth: Marston's Disguised Dukes and *A Knack to Know a Knave*', *Publications of the Modern Language Association*, 89 (1974): 993–1006

Howard-Hill, T.H., *Ralph Crane and Some Shakespeare First Folio Comedies* (Charlottesville: University of Virginia Press, 1972)

Hume, Robert D., 'Before the Bard: "Shakespeare" in Early Eighteenth-Century London', *English Literary History*, 64 (1997): 41–75

Hunter, George K., 'The Marking of *Sententiae* in Elizabethan Printed Plays, Poems, and Romances', *The Library*, 6 (1951): 171–88

Hyland, Peter, *Disguise on the Early Modern English Stage* (Aldershot: Ashgate, 2011)

Ingram, R.W., *John Marston* (Boston: Twayne Publishers, 1978)

Jackson, MacD. P., 'The Date and Authorship of *Thomas of Woodstock*: Evidence and its Interpretation', *Research Opportunities in Medieval and Renaissance Drama*, 46 (2007): 67–100

Jeffery, David Lyle (ed.), *A Dictionary of Biblical Tradition in English Literature* (Grand Rapids: Eerdmans Publishing Co., 1992)

Johnson, Nora, *The Actor as Playwright in Early Modern Drama* (Cambridge: Cambridge University Press, 2003)

Jones, Ann Rosalind and Peter Stallybrass, 'Renaissance Clothing and the Materials of Memory', *Cambridge Studies in Renaissance Literature and Culture,* 38 (Cambridge: Cambridge University Press, 2000)

Kamps, Ivo, *Historiography and Ideology in Early Stuart Drama* (Cambridge: Cambridge University Press, 1996)

———, 'Ruling Fantasies and the Fantasies of Rule: *The Phoenix* and *Measure for Measure*', *Studies in Philology*, 92 (1995): 248–73

Kamps, Ivo and Karen Raber, *Measure for Measure: Texts and Contexts* (Boston: Bedford/St Martin's, 2004)

Kaplan, Joel, 'John Marston's *Fawn*: A Saturnalian Satire', *Studies in English Literature*, 9 (1969): 335–50

Kastan, David Scott, *Shakespeare and the Book* (Cambridge: Cambridge University Press, 2001)

Kastan, David Scott (ed.), *A Companion to Shakespeare* (Oxford: Blackwell, 2000)

King, Thomas Alan, *The Gendering of Men, 1600–1750* (Madison: University of Wisconsin Press, 2004)

Kinney, Arthur F. (ed.), *A Companion to Renaissance Drama* (Oxford: Blackwell, 2002)

Knight, Stephen T., *Robin Hood: A Mythic Biography* (Ithaca: Cornell University Press, 2003)

Knoppers, Laura Lunger, '(En)gendering Shame: *Measure for Measure* and the Spectacles of Power', *English Literary Renaissance*, 23 (1993): 450–71

Knowles, James, 'Marston, John', *Oxford Dictionary of National Biography* (2004) <http://www.oxforddnb.com/index/101018164/John-Marston> [accessed 6 May 2011]

Knutson, Roslyn L., *Playing Companies and Commerce in Shakespeare's Time* (New York: Columbia University Press, 2001)

———, *The Repertory of Shakespeare's Company: 1594–1613* (Fayetteville: University of Arkansas Press, 1991)

Lake, David J., 'Webster's Additions to *The Malcontent*: Linguistic Evidence', *Notes and Queries*, 28 (1981): 153–8

Lake, Peter, *The Anti-Christ's Lewd Hat* (New Haven: Yale University Press, 2002)

Larkum, Eleri, 'Dymoke, Tailboys [Thomas Cutwode] (*bap.* 1561, *d.* 1602/3)', *Oxford Dictionary of National Biography* (2004) <http://www.oxforddnb.com/index/101006985/Tailboys-Dymoke> [accessed 6 May 2011]

Lascelles, Mary, *Shakespeare's 'Measure for Measure'* (London: Athlone Press, 1953)

Lawrence, Jason, *"Who the devil taught thee so much Italian?" Italian Language Learning and Literary Imitation in Early Modern England* (Manchester: Manchester University Press, 2005)

Lee, Maurice, Jr, *Government by Pen: Scotland under James VI and I* (Urbana: Illinois University Press, 1980)

LEME: Lexicons of Early Modern English, ed. Ian Lancashire, University of Toronto Press (2011) <leme.library.utoronto.ca> [accessed 6 May 2011]

Levin, Richard, *New Readings vs. Old Plays: Recent Trends in the Reinterpretation of English Renaissance Drama* (Chicago: University of Chicago Press, 1979)

Lindley, Keith, 'Riot Prevention and Control in Early Stuart London', *Transactions of the Royal Historical Society, 5th Series*, 33 (1983): 109–26

Lockyer, Roger, *The Early Stuarts: A Political History of England 1603–1642*, 2nd edn (London: Longman, 1999)

Luxford, Julian M., 'An English Chronicle Entry on Robin Hood', *Journal of Medieval History*, 35 (2009): 70–76

MacIntyre, Jean, *Costumes and Scripts in the Elizabethan Theatre* (Edmonton: University of Alberta Press, 1992)

Mahon, John W. and Thomas A. Pendleton (eds), *"Fanned and Winnowed Opinions": Shakespearean Essays Presented to Harold Jenkins* (New York: Methuen, 1987)

Manning, Roger B., *Swordsmen: The Martial Ethos in the Three Kingdoms* (Oxford: Oxford University Press, 2003)

Marcus, Leah, *Puzzling Shakespeare: Local Reading and Its Discontents* (Berkeley: University of California Press, 1988)

Marrapodi, Michele (ed.), *Shakespeare and Intertextuality: The Transition of Cultures Between Italy and England in the Early Modern Period* (Rome: Bulzoni Editore, 2000)

Mayer, Jean-Christophe (ed.), *The Struggle for the Succession in Late Elizabethan England: Politics, Polemics and Cultural Representations*, Astraea Collection, 11 (Montpellier: Université Paul-Valéry, 2004)

McCabe, Richard A., 'Elizabethan Satire and the Bishops' Ban of 1599', *Yearbook of English Studies*, 11 (1981): 188–94

McCanles, Michael, 'The Authentic Discourse of the Renaissance', *Diacritics*, 10 (1980): 77–87

McCrea, Adriana, *Constant Minds: Political Virtue and the Lipsian Paradigm in England, 1584–1650, Mental and Cultural World of Tudor and Stuart England* (Toronto: University of Toronto Press, 1997)

McElwee, William, *The Wisest Fool in Christendom: The Reign of King James I and VI* (London: Faber and Faber, 1958)

McMillin, Scott and Sally-Beth MacLean, *The Queen's Men and their Plays* (Cambridge: Cambridge University Press, 1998)

McMullan, Gordon, *The Politics of Unease in the Plays of John Fletcher* (Amherst: University of Massachusetts Press, 1994)

McMullan, Gordon and Jonathan Hope (eds), *The Politics of Tragicomedy: Shakespeare and After* (London: Routledge & Kegan Paul, 1992)

McMullan, Gordon and David Matthews (eds), *Reading the Medieval in Early Modern England* (Cambridge: Cambridge University Press, 2007)

McPherson, David, 'The Origins of Overdo: A Study in Jonsonian Invention', *Modern Language Quarterly*, 37 (1976): 221–33

Miles, Rosalind, *The Problem of 'Measure for Measure': A Historical Investigation* (New York: Barnes & Noble, 1976)

Mullaney, Steven, *The Place of the Stage: License, Play, and Power in Renaissance England* (Chicago: University of Chicago Press, 1988)

Munk, William, *The Roll of the Royal College of Physicians of London: Compiled from the Annals of the College and Other Authentic Sources* (2 vols, London: Longman, Green, Longman and Roberts, 1861)

Munro, Lucy, *Children of the Queen's Revels: A Jacobean Theatre Repertory* (Cambridge: Cambridge University Press, 2005)

———, 'The Humour of Children: Performance, Gender, and the Early Modern Children's Companies', *Literature Compass*, 2 (2005): 1–26

Newton, Diana, *The Making of the Jacobean Regime: James VI and I and the Government of England, 1603–1605* (Woodbridge: The Royal Historical Society/Boydell Press, 2005)

Nicholls, Mark, 'Fawkes, Guy (*bap.* 1570, *d.* 1606)', *Oxford Dictionary of National Biography* (2009) <http://www.oxforddnb.com/index/101009230/Guy-Fawkes> [accessed 6 May 2011]

————, *Investigating Gunpowder Plot* (Manchester: Manchester University Press, 1991)

Norman, Marc and Tom Stoppard, *Shakespeare in Love* (London: Faber and Faber, 1999)

O'Neill, David G., 'The Commencement of Marston's Career as a Dramatist', *Review of English Studies*, 22 (1971): 442–5

Ostovich, Helen, Holger Schott Syme and Andrew Griffin (eds), *Locating the Queen's Men, 1583–1603: Material Practices and Conditions of Playing* (Aldershot: Ashgate, 2009)

Paster, Gail Kern, *The Body Embarrassed: Drama and the Disciplines of Shame in Early Modern England* (Ithaca: Cornell University Press, 1993)

————, *Humoring the Body: Emotions and the Shakespearean Stage* (Chicago: Chicago University Press, 2004)

Patterson, R.F. (ed.), *Ben Jonson's Conversations with William Drummond of Hawthornden* (London: Blackie and Son Limited, 1923)

Peachman, John, 'Previously Unrecorded Verbal Parallels Between Histriomastix and The Acknowledged Works of John Marston', *Notes and Queries*, 51 (2004): 304–306

Peck, Linda Levy (ed.), *The Mental World of the Jacobean Court* (Cambridge: Cambridge University Press, 1991)

Pelling, Margaret and Frances White, 'GUERSIE, Balthasar', *Physicians and Irregular Medical Practitioners in London 1550–1640: Database* (2004) <http://www.british-history.ac.uk/report.asp?compid=17492> [accessed 6 May 2011]

Perry, Curtis and John Watkins (eds), *Shakespeare and the Middle Ages* (Oxford: Oxford University Press, 2009)

Pocock, J.G.A. (ed.), *The Discovery of Islands: Essays in British History* (Cambridge: Cambridge University Press, 2005)

Pollard, A.F., 'Wilson, Sir Thomas (*d.* 1629)', rev. Sean Kelsey, *Oxford Dictionary of National Biography* (2004) <http://www.oxforddnb.com/index/101029690/Thomas-Wilson> [accessed 6 May 2011]

Pollard, Alfred W., G.R. Redgrave, revised by W.A. Jackson, F.S. Ferguson and Katharine F. Pantzer (eds), *A Short-Title Catalogue of Books Printed in England, Scotland, & Ireland and of English Books Printed Abroad 1475–1640* (3 vols, London: Bibliographical Society, 1976–91)

Poole, Kristen, *Radical Religion from Shakespeare to Milton: Figures of Nonconformity in Early Modern England* (Cambridge: Cambridge University Press, 2000)

Postlewait, Thomas, *The Cambridge Companion to Theatre Historiography* (Cambridge: Cambridge University Press, 2009)

Potter, Lois (ed.), *Playing Robin Hood: The Legend as Performance in Five Centuries* (Newark: University of Delaware Press, 1998)

Pound, John, *Poverty and Vagrancy in Tudor England*, 2nd edn (London: Longman, 1986)

Price, Joseph G. (ed.), *The Triple Bond: Plays, Mainly Shakespearean, in Performance* (University Park: Pennsylvania State University Press, 1975)

'Prince Harry on Afghan Front Line', *BBC News*, 28 February 2008 <http://news.bbc.co.uk/go/pr/fr/-/1/hi/world/7269743.stm> [accessed 15 January 2011]

Randolph, Mary Clare, 'The Medical Concept in English Renaissance Satiric Theory: Its Possible Relationships and Implications', *Studies In Philology*, 38 (1941): 125–57

Rasmussen, Mark David (ed.), *Renaissance Literature and Its Formal Engagements* (Basingstoke: Palgrave, 2002)

Records of Early English Drama (*REED*) (1979–2010) (University of Toronto Press) <http://www.archive.org/search.php?query=records%20of%20early%20english%20drama%20AND%20collection%3Atoronto> [accessed 6 May 2011]

Redmond, Michael J., '"Low Comedy" and Political Cynicism: Parodies of the Jacobean Disguised-Duke Play', *Renaissance Forum*, 7 (2004): paras 1–13 <http://www.hull.ac.uk/renforum/v7/redmond.htm> [accessed 26 April 2011]

———, *Shakespeare, Politics, and Italy: Intertextuality on the Jacobean Stage* (Aldershot: Ashgate, 2009)

Riggs, David, *Ben Jonson: A Life* (Cambridge, MA: Harvard University Press, 1989)

Rogers, Pat, 'Oldmixon, John (1672/3–1742)', *Oxford Dictionary of National Biography* (2004) <http://www.oxforddnb.com/index/101020695/John-Oldmixon> [accessed 6 May 2011]

Russell, Conrad, 'Parliamentary History in Perspective, 1604–1629', *History*, 61 (1976): 1–27

———, *Parliaments and English Politics 1621–1629* (Oxford: Clarendon Press, 1979)

Saccio, Peter, *Shakespeare's English Kings: History, Chronicle, and Drama*, 2nd edn (Oxford: Oxford University Press, 2000)

Salkeld, Duncan, 'Literary Traces in Bridewell and Bethlem, 1602–1624', *The Review of English Studies*, 56 (2005): 379–85

———, 'Making Sense of Differences: Postmodern History, Philosophy and Shakespeare's Prostitutes', *Chronicon: An Electronic History Journal*, 3 (2007): 7–35 <http://www.ucc.ie/chronicon/3/salkeld.pdf> [accessed 5 May 2011]

———, 'The Texts of *Henry V*', *Shakespeare*, 3 (2007): 161–82

Sayle, R.T.D., *Lord Mayors' Pageants of the Merchant Taylors' Company in the 15th, 16th & 17th Centuries* (London: Privately Published, 1931)

Schanzer, Ernest, *The Problem Plays of Shakespeare* (London: Routledge & Kegan Paul, 1963)

Schelling, Felix E., *Elizabethan Drama 1558–1642* (2 vols, Boston: Houghton, Mifflin & Co., 1908)

Schoenbaum, Samuel, 'The Precarious Balance of John Marston', *Publications of the Modern Language Association*, 67 (1952): 1069–78

Schwarz, Marc L., 'James I and the Historians: Towards a Reconsideration', *Journal of British Studies*, 13 (1974): 114–34

Shakespeare in Love. Dir. John Madden. Miramax Films/Universal Pictures. 1998.

Shapiro, Michael, *Children of the Revels: The Boy Companies of Shakespeare's Time and Their Plays* (New York: Columbia University Press, 1977)

Sharpe, Kevin (ed.), *Faction and Parliament: Essays on Early Stuart History* (Oxford: Clarendon Press, 1978)

Shaw, George Bernard, *Plays: Pleasant and Unpleasant* (2 vols, London: Constable and Co., 1898)

Simpson, Richard, *The School of Shakspere* (2 vols, London: Chatto and Windus, 1878)

Singman, Jeffrey L., *Robin Hood: The Shaping of the Legend* (Westport: Greenwood Press, 1998)

Skinner, Quentin, *The Foundations of Modern Political Thought* (2 vols, Cambridge: Cambridge University Press, 1978)

Slack, Paul, *The English Poor Law, 1531–1782* (Cambridge: Cambridge University Press, 1995)

———, *Poverty and Policy in Tudor and Stuart England* (London: Longman, 1988)

Slights, William W.E., *Ben Jonson and the Art of Secrecy* (Toronto: University of Toronto Press, 1994)

Smith, David L., Richard Strier and David Bevington (eds), *The Theatrical City* (Cambridge: Cambridge University Press, 1995)

Sokol, B.J. and Mary Sokol, *Shakespeare's Legal Language* (London: Athlone Press, 2000)

———, *Shakespeare, Law, and Marriage* (Cambridge: Cambridge University Press, 2003)

Stanley, Alessandra, 'Reality TV That Puts the Boss in Meek's Clothing', *The New York Times*, 10 April 2010 <http://www.nytimes.com/2010/04/11/weekinreview/11stanleywir.html?_r=1> [accessed 20 December 2010]

Steggle, Matthew, *Wars of the Theatres: The Poetics of Personation in the Age of Jonson*, ELS Monograph Series, 75 (Victoria: University of Victoria, 1998)

Stern, Tiffany, *Documents of Performance in Early Modern England* (Cambridge: Cambridge University Press, 2009)

———, *Making Shakespeare: From Stage to Page* (London: Routledge, 2004)

Stevenson, David Lloyd, *The Achievement of Shakespeare's 'Measure for Measure'* (Ithaca: Cornell University Press, 1966)

———, 'The Role of James I in Shakespeare's Measure for Measure', *English Literary History*, 26 (1959): 188–208

Strong, Roy, *The Cult of Elizabeth* (London: Thames and Hudson, 1977)

Sturgess, Keith, *Jacobean Private Theatre* (London: Routledge & Kegan Paul, 1987)

Sykes, H. Dugdale, 'The Authorship of *A Knack to Know a Knave*', *Notes and Queries*, 146 (1924): 389–91

Syme, Holger Schott, 'Unediting the Margin: Jonson, Marston, and the Theatrical Page', *English Literary Renaissance,* 38 (2008): 142–71

Taylor, Gary, 'The Fortunes of Oldcastle', *Shakespeare Survey,* 38 (1985): 85–100

Taylor, Gary and John D. Jowett, *Shakespeare Reshaped, 1606–1623* (Oxford: Clarendon Press, 1993)

Taylor, Gary and John Lavagnino (eds), *Thomas Middleton and Early Modern Textual Culture: A Companion to the Collected Works* (Oxford: Oxford University Press, 2007)

Taylor, Gary, Paul Mulholland and MacDonald P. Jackson, 'Thomas Middleton, Lording Barry, and The Family of Love', *Papers of the Bibliographical Society of America,* 93 (1999): 213–41

Teague, Frances, 'Jonson and the Gunpowder Plot', *Ben Jonson Journal,* 5 (1998): 249–52

Tennenhouse, Leonard, *Power on Display: The Politics of Shakespeare's Genres* (London: Methuen, 1986)

———, 'Representing Power: *Measure for Measure* in its Time', *Genre,* 15 (1982): 139–56

Thornberry, Richard, 'A Seventeenth-Century Revival of *Mucedorus* Before 1610', *Shakespeare Quarterly,* 28 (1977): 362–4

Tricomi, Albert H., *Anticourt Drama in England 1603–1642* (Charlottesville: University Press of Virginia, 1989)

Upton, Albert W., 'Allusions to James I and His Court in Marston's *Fawn* and Beaumont's *Woman Hater*', *Publications of the Modern Language Association,* 44 (1929): 1048–65

Vandiver, E.P., Jr, 'The Elizabethan Dramatic Parasite', *Studies in Philology,* 32 (1935): 411

Walsh, Elizabeth, 'The King in Disguise', *Folklore,* 86 (1975): 3–24

Watson, Andrew G., *The Library of Sir Simonds D'Ewes* (London: British Museum, 1966)

Weiss, Judith, Jennifer Fellows and Morgan Dickson (eds), *Medieval Insular Romance: Translation and Innovation* (Cambridge: D.S. Brewer, 2000)

Welch, Charles, 'Myddelton, Sir Thomas (1549x56–1631)', rev. Trevor Dickie, *Oxford Dictionary of National Biography* (2004) <http://www.oxforddnb.com/index/101019685/Thomas-Myddelton> [accessed 6 May 2011]

Wells, Stanley, *Shakespeare & Co.* (London: Allen Lane, 2006)

Werstine, Paul, 'A Century of "Bad" Shakespeare Quartos', *Shakespeare Quarterly,* 50 (1999): 310–33

Wharton, T.F. (ed.), *The Drama of John Marston: Critical Re-visions* (Cambridge: Cambridge University Press, 2000)

Wiggins, Martin, *Shakespeare and the Drama of his Time* (Oxford: Oxford University Press, 2000)

Wiles, David, *The Early Plays of Robin Hood* (Cambridge: Cambridge University Press, 1981)

Williams, Gordon, *A Glossary of Shakespeare's Sexual Language* (Atlantic Highlands: Athlone Press, 1997)

Williamson, Marilyn L., '*The Phoenix*: Middleton's Comedy *de Regimine Principum*', *Renaissance News*, 10 (1957): 183–7

Willson, David Harris, *King James VI & I* (London: Jonathan Cape, 1956)

Wood, Nigel (ed.), *'Measure for Measure': Theory in Practice* (Buckingham: Open University Press, 1996)

Wormald, Jenny, *Court, Kirk and Community: Scotland 1470–1625* (London: Edward Arnold, 1981)

———, 'Gunpowder, Treason, and Scots', *The Journal of British Studies*, 24 (1985): 141–68

———, 'James VI and I: Two Kings or One?' *History*, 68 (1983): 187–209

———, 'James VI and I (1566–1625)', *Oxford Dictionary of National Biography* (2004) <http://www.oxforddnb.com/index/101014592/James> [accessed 6 May 2011]

Wormald, Jenny (ed.), *The Seventeenth Century* (Oxford: Oxford University Press, 2008)

Yates, Frances A., *Astraea* (London: Routledge & Kegan Paul, 1973)

Young, Michael B., *King James and the History of Homosexuality* (New York: New York University Press, 2000)

Index